Leveson Vernon Harcourt

The Diaries and Correspondence of the Right Hon. George Rose

Vol. I

Leveson Vernon Harcourt

The Diaries and Correspondence of the Right Hon. George Rose
Vol. I

ISBN/EAN: 9783741198144

Manufactured in Europe, USA, Canada, Australia, Japa

Cover: Foto ©Andreas Hilbeck / pixelio.de

Manufactured and distributed by brebook publishing software (www.brebook.com)

Leveson Vernon Harcourt

The Diaries and Correspondence of the Right Hon. George Rose

THE

DIARIES AND CORRESPONDENCE

OF

THE RIGHT HON. GEORGE ROSE.

VOL. I.

LONDON:
R. CLAY, PRINTER, BREAD STREET HILL.

THE

DIARIES AND CORRESPONDENCE

OF THE

RIGHT HON. GEORGE ROSE:

CONTAINING

ORIGINAL LETTERS

OF THE MOST DISTINGUISHED STATESMEN OF HIS DAY.

EDITED BY THE

REV. LEVESON VERNON HARCOURT.

IN TWO VOLUMES.—VOL. I.

LONDON:
RICHARD BENTLEY, NEW BURLINGTON STREET,
Publisher in Ordinary to Her Majesty.
1860.

PREFACE.

To publish letters which are marked "private and confidential," seems at first sight to be a breach of that confidence on which the writers insisted; but, on further consideration, it must be seen that the secrecy which they desired had reference only to their contemporaries. Their object was to prevent the entanglement of parties, and the crossing of designs which were then contemplated in the transactions of the day. For that very reason, after the lapse of half a century, when all the actors have passed away from the stage on which they played their parts, those documents not only become innocuous, but have a great interest for those who agree with the poet, that "The proper study of mankind is man;" for they are revelations of the interior workings of that state machinery on the right regulation of which the welfare of millions depends. They bring to light those little traits of character which are of more value in estimating the worth of public men than volumes of official papers and debates in Parliament. The petty jealousies and the covetous ambitions which disfigure some, are like so many beacons to warn rising statesmen from risking their characters on the same rocks; and, on the contrary, the disinterested motives by which others were actuated in taking or resigning office, and the conscientious fulfilment of their duties as public servants, secure so much approbation, when exhibited in these confidential details, that they must be great encouragement to others to follow their example.

Mr. Rose, a selection from whose private papers is here submitted to the public by the desire of his grandsons, belongs to this class. It seems to have been the guiding rule of his political life, "Nil conscire sibi, nullâ pallescere culpâ:" accordingly he was an unswerving follower of Mr. Pitt, for he never saw anything culpable in the smallest degree in the policy of his leader, with two exceptions mentioned in his autobiography; and therefore, though during the life of Mr. Pitt he was anxious that his Government should be strengthened by any members of the Opposition, with the exception of Lord Sidmouth, to whom he imputed, untruly perhaps, treachery to his friend, yet, after his death, he would have nothing to do with those who pursued a different policy.

I have therefore thought it my duty, as his Editor, to take the line which he would have wished me to take if he had been alive, and to vindicate the character of the great Statesman to whom he was so much attached, from the unjust attacks of those who have never forgiven him the long exclusion of their party from office. The pens of his opponents have been dipped in gall, overflowing in ebullitions of ill-will, misrepresentations, unfounded conclusions, and false reports; and, the writers being men of mark and of talent, very erroneous impressions have been made on the public mind, which must be disabused; and to this task I have addressed myself, with no wish to provoke hostility, but with a strong desire that the truth should be known.

I have only to add my acknowledgments to the Duke of Sutherland for his kindness in sending me the only letters which are not derived from Mr. Rose's own correspondence.

L. V. H.

London, *December* 1st, 1859.

CONTENTS.

INTRODUCTION.

Preliminary observations, 1; Mr. Rose's Correspondence, 2; his intimacy with Mr. Pitt, 2; Pitt's devotion to public affairs, 3; Lord Grenville, 4; Canning, 4; letter of Lord Glastonbury to Pitt, 4; early history of Mr. Rose, 6; Miss Rose's sketch of her father, 8; Mr. Rose, a midshipman, 9; edits the Journals of Parliament, 10; Lord Marchmont's friendship for him, 11; is made Secretary for Tax Office, &c., 11; made Secretary to the Treasury, 12; the Galloway Stewarts, 13; Lord Shelburne, 14; surliness of Lord Thurlow, 14; Mr. Rose meets Mr. Pitt in Paris, 15; progress of his political career, 16.

CHAPTER I.

Mr. Rose's account of his early life, 17; sketch of the Earl of Marchmont, 18; Lord Bolingbroke, 19; his "Essay on a Patriot King," 19; Lord Marchmont's kindness to Mr. Rose, 20; Mr. Rose loses his uncle, 21; Alexander Strahan, 22; progress of my political life, 23; am appointed Secretary to the Treasury, 24; character of Lord Shelburne, 25; I obtain the reversion of the office of Clerk of the Parliaments, 26; junction of North and Fox, 27; suspicious conduct of Lord Shelburne, 28; my last visit to him, 30; go abroad, 31; Mr. Pitt's proposal to me, 32; my attachment to him, 32; few points of difference, 32; Parliamentary Reform, 33; Pitt presses me to vote with him on it, 34; my letter to Mr. Pitt on the subject, 36; the Slave Trade, 37; Paris in 1782, 41;

the French Court smile upon Lafayette, 42; my servant, Ami Ramel, 42; return to England, 42; Mr. Fox's India Bill, 43; triumphant in the Commons, 42; the King's conduct respecting it, 46; immense efforts to overthrow the bill in the Lords, 47; success of these efforts, 48; a note of the King's on the change of Ministry, 50; editorial observations, 51; Letters from Lord Percy, 52; siege of Gibraltar, 53; Lord Cornwallis, 54; Lord Percy complains of neglect, 58; promises to come up and vote against the India Bill, 59; letters from the King on the elections, 61, 62.

CHAPTER II.

Treaty with France, 64; letter from the Marquis of Stafford to Mr. Pitt on Foreign Affairs, 64; conduct of France, 65; Mr. Pitt to the Marquis of Stafford, 67; relations of Russia and France, 67; narrow escape from war with France, 68; Mr. Rose summoned by Mr. Pitt, 69; political career of Mr. Eden, 70; Commercial Treaty with France, 71; letters of Mr. Eden to Mr. Rose, dwelling on his own merits, and soliciting an Irish Peerage, 72—81; Sir George Rose, 81; Sir Hugh Rose, 82; letters of Mr. Wood, Principal of St. John's, Cambridge, 82; letter of Mr. Pitt to Marquis of Stafford, on the state of Foreign Affairs, 84; the King's illness, 86; Mr. Pitt's interview with him, 86; the Prince of Wales, 87; Pitt's interview with him, 87; state of affairs during the King's illness, 88; Mr. Fox, 89; Ministerial difficulties, 90; Mr. Pitt visits the King, 90; meeting of Parliament, 91; Mr. Pitt's consideration for the King, 91; Mr. Pitt to the Marquis of Stafford, on the King's illness, 92; Mr. Pitt to Earl Gower, 93; the King's recovery, 93; Miss Rose's recollections of the King's illness, 94; nature of the King's insanity, 94; observations of the King during his illness, 96; conduct of Lord Thurlow, 9 5; Lord Grenville, 96; letter to Mr. Pitt from the King, 97; the King's cordial approbation of Mr. Pitt's conduct, 98; Mr. Pitt to Mr. Rose, on Lord Thurlow's dismissal, 98; reckless extravagance of the Prince, 100; expenses of Carlton House, 100; the Prince's debts, 104.

CHAPTER III.

Trafficking in Church Preferment, 107; our East India trade, 109; Treaty of Gralutz between Russia and Turkey, 110; affairs of Russia, 111; prosperous state of the revenue, 111; jobbery, 112; Mr. Pitt appointed Warden of the Cinque Ports; 113; state of France, 114; Mr. Pitt to the Marquis of Stafford on prospects abroad, 115; Pitt's views on the advisability of allowing the French to settle their own affairs in 1792, 116; Lord Macartney, 117; negotiation with the Chinese, 119; Letters from Lord Macartney, previous to his leaving for China, and on his voyage there, 120; Captain Mackintosh to Mr. Ross, stating his convictions that the Chinese Embassy was a failure, and giving his views of the causes of failure, 124; surrender of Valenciennes, 127; check at Dunkirk, 128; taking of Toulon, 129; death of General O'Hara, 132; outbreak of the war with France, 133; the war justly chargeable on France, 133; French animosity to England, 134; arrest of Lord Gower in Paris, 136; impudent conduct of Chauvelin, 137; Chauvelin's labours with Mr. Fox, 138; declaration of war by France, 138; Lord Brougham's charge against Pitt, 140; defence of Mr. Pitt, 141; union projected between Pitt and Fox, 142; defeated through the pride of Fox, 143; Mr. Fox blames the Government for not going to war sooner, 144; inconsistency of Mr. Fox, 144; contrast between Whig and Tory policy, 145; anarchical state of France, 146; overtures for peace, 147; criticism of Lord John Russell, 148; Pitt's objects in the war, 149; obstinacy of the Convention, 150; the National Convention, and the London Corresponding Society, 151; conduct of Mr. Fox, 152; alienation of his party, 152; Lord Malmesbury's opinion of Fox's policy, 153; Fox's pleasure at the triumph of France over England, 153; dangerous state of public feeling, 154; Mr. Fox, 155; vindication of Mr. Pitt from the imputation of Lord John Russell, 156; M. Chauvelin, 157; war declared by France against Hungary and Bohemia, 160; French violation of treaties, 161; Count Kobentzal, 162; M. de Noailles, 162; haughty conduct of France, 164; Lord John Russell's mode of settling the war, 165; fallacy of his views, 165; Holland, 167; Jacobin negotiations for the overthrow of the British constitution, 168; Dumourier's picture of France after the 10th of August, 170; Lord John Russell's attacks upon Mr. Pitt, 175; Mr. Fox's patriotic doctrine quoted against himself, 177; French liberty, 179; Lord John Russell charges England with being the aggressor in the war, 180; the Duke of Brunswick's proclamation, 181; proposal of the Duke of Brunswick, 181; Debate on the Canada question, 182; Lord John Russell's false charge of an intention to partition France, 183; the Duke of Brunswick's declaration to the contrary, 184; conclusion of the defence of Mr. Pitt, 186; Lord John Russell at Aberdeen,—an unconscious defence of Mr. Pitt, 186-7; Lord Malmesbury sent to negotiate at Lille, 188; Lord Grenville differs with Mr. Pitt, 188; fixed determination of the French Government to continue the war with England, 188; Pitt's anxiety for peace, 189; conversation between the King and Mr. Rose, on the subject of the war, 189; proves Pitt's desire of peace, 190; the King averse to treat without knowledge of allies, 191; Mr. Pitt to Mr. Rose, 192; negotiations with the Opposition, 193; Mr. Rose's dissatisfaction regarding them, 193; details of the new cabinet, 193; the Duke of Portland, 194; Mr. Rose's confidence in Pitt, 195; unfavourable turn of affairs abroad, 196; letter from the Duke of Brunswick to the Duke of York, announcing his retirement from the command of the army, 197; dissensions amongst the allies, 198; letter of Mr. Pitt to Mr. Rose, announcing an intention to attack the Duke of Northumberland, 200; Sir R. Cotton, 201; reversion of Clerk of the Parliaments, 202; granted to Mr. Rose's son, 203; high price of corn, 203; measures to ascertain amount of corn in the country, 204; Mr. Valentine Jones, 205; enormous expenditure in the West Indies, 206; letter of Lady Chatham, Mr. Pitt's mother, to Mr. Rose, touching on Mr. Pitt's health, 208; Mr. Sheridan, 209; the Convoy Bill, 209; subscription for carrying on the war, 210; the King's subscription, 211; Miss Rose's dislike to Addington, 211; her influence over her father, 211;

extract from Miss Rose's Diary, 212; Mr. Pitt's health, cause of duel between Mr. Pitt and Tierney, Nicholas Vansittart, 212; conversation at the Speaker's dinner, insinuations of Mr. Addington, 213; Pitt's confidence in Addington, 214.

CHAPTER IV.

Battle of the Nile, 215; the French report it a victory for them, 216; Lord Nelson and Lady Hamilton; Nelson's personal vanity; Lady Hamilton compliments him, 217; alienates him from his wife; Separation from her; 218; Lord Holland's malignant insinuation; cold reception of Nelson at Court, 219; Nelson at Naples, 220; Prince Caraccioli, 221; Sir William and Lady Hamilton, 222; Lord Nelson's attachment to Lady Hamilton, not criminal; Lord St. Vincent's opinion, 223; Lady Hamilton's extravagance, 224; letter to Lord Nelson from Sir William Hamilton, 225; success of Sidney Smith at Acre, Sir Sidney Smith's pompous announcements, 225; death of Captain Wilmott, 226; approximation of Russia and Austria, 226; honesty of Cardinal Ruffo, 227; letter of the King of Naples to Cardinal Ruffo, 231; state of Naples, 232; the King's instructions, 235; letters of Sir William Hamilton to Cardinal Ruffo, 236; Mr. Rose's efforts to assist Lady Hamilton, 239; his advice to her, 240; characteristic letter of Lady Hamilton to Mr. Rose, 240; her opinions of Lord Grenville and Mr. Pitt, 241; Lady Hamilton's mother, Mrs. Cadogan, to Mr. Rose, 243; death of Nelson, 243; illness of Lady Hamilton, 343; defends herself against the charge of showing Nelson's letters, 244; accuses herself of being the cause of Nelson's death, 244; Captain Hardy, 245; last wishes of Nelson, 246; Mr. Rose promises to urge them upon Mr. Pitt, 246; efforts to assist Lady Hamilton, 248; unsuccessful, 249; her distress, imprisonment, escape, finds an asylum in France, 249; Mr. Rose to Lady Hamilton, on the state of Pitt's health, including discussion of her affairs, 250; Mr. Rose urges Lady Hamilton's claims upon Mr. Canning, 252; trusts that provision will be made for Nelson's adopted daughter,

263; the delay in doing justice to Nelson's adopted daughter, pleaded as a reason for not doing it, 254; letter to Lord Abercorn, stating Lady Hamilton's case, 254; Lady Hamilton's claims stated, 257; Mr. Lavie to Mr. Rose, 260; reply, 261; letters of Canning respecting Lady Hamilton, 263; caution of Lord Grenville, 263; inaccurate statements of Lady Hamilton, 266; Mr. Rose's letter to Lady Hamilton, 268; correspondence between Mr. Canning and Mr. Rose, on the subject of Lady Hamilton, 268; memorial to the Prince Regent, 270; Lady Hamilton's life at Calais, 272.

CHAPTER V.

Vacancy in the office of Lord Privy Seal of Scotland, 274; Lord Auckland's disappointment, 274; Mr. Rose, in forwarding Lord Auckland's claims, suggests his own, 275; Pitt's reply, 276; scarcity of the year 1800, 280; Lord Holland's sarcastic observation on Mr. Addington, 281; early meeting of Parliament, 282; high price of wheat, 282; measures devised for allaying the panic, 282; the distillers urged not to work from grain, 284; mode of selling corn, 284; middlemen, 284; Mr. Addington influences members against Catholic Emancipation; Mr. Addington at the Queen's House, 286; notes by Mr. Rose, and letters from February to May, 1801, relative to the proposal for Mr. Pitt's resigning office, 288; Pitt to the King, 288; the King's reply, 289; the King sends for Mr. Addington, 290; Mr. Rose's opinion of Mr. Addington, 292; Canning's marked manner to the Speaker, 293; apprehension in the city at Pitt's expected resignation, 293; Lord Auckland complains of ill-treatment, Mr. Pitt's rejoinder, 294. Lord Chatham, Attorney-General, Bishop of Lincoln, fall in the funds, Canning canvasses for people to go out of office, 295; constitution of the new Ministry, 296; call on the Speaker, Lord Chatham retains office, 296; Lord Loughborough retires, 297; attend the levée, the King expresses his marked approbation of Mr. Pitt's conduct, 297; Mr. Pelham, Vansittart, Mr. Yorke, the loan of 27,000,000l., 298; Lord St. Vincent accepts the Admiralty, Lord Hobart, interview with Lord Loughborough, 299; the King requests Lord Loughborough's opinion whether he (the King) could grant Catholic Emancipation consistently with his coronation oath, 299; Lord Loughborough's reply, 300; the King's dread of Catholic Emancipation, Lord Clare, Lord Castlereagh, 301; the Prince of Wales favours Catholic Emancipation, position of principal politicians with regard to it, 302; Addington's intrigues, 303; conversation between the Chancellor and Mr. Dundas, 304; Mr. Pitt supposed to be urged on by Lord Grenville, 305; conversation of Lord Loughborough with the King, 306; Sir William Grant, Mr. Perceval, 307; Mr. Vansittart goes to Denmark, 308; the budget, 308; conversation with Mr. Pitt, Pitt's agitation, regrets that he did not prepare the King's mind for Catholic Emancipation, 309; the King's illness, 310; Lord Eldon, 310; becomes Lord Chancellor, 310; the Prince of Wales sends for Mr. Pitt, Mr. Pitt consents to advise subject to conditions, derangement of the King, 311; Dr. Willis, Lord Granville Leveson, Lord Eldon, 312; Lord Eldon complains of Mr. Addington's treatment of him, 313; Lord Eldon's conversation with the King, Mr. Pitt, 314; Dr. Willis's account of the King, 315; state of the Administration, 316; Mr. Pitt and the Prince of Wales, advice of the Bishop of Lincoln, 317; Mr. Addington's intrigues, the King's health, 318; the Loan Bill, delicate position of affairs consequent on the King's illness, 319; the Regency Bill, Sir Robert Peel, want of confidence in Addington, Pitt's confidence in the fair conduct of Opposition, 320; Mr. Sheridan and Fox justify this confidence, Mr. Pitt's speech, 321; improvement in the King's health, Mr. Canning, 322; Bishop of Lincoln, Buonaparte attributes the King's changing his Ministers to derangement, 323.

CHAPTER VI.

The King's state not so favourable, Mr. Fox takes the oaths, 324; details of the King's illness, 325; details of the Regency Bill, negotiations with the Prince of Wales, 326; the King's complete recovery, 327; his conversation with Dr. Willis Lord Chatham, Lord Moira, 328; the Duke of York, the Duke of Cumberland's conduct on the occasion of the King's illness, 330; Horne Tooke, 331; Mr. Pitt, Lord St. Vincent, Lord Eldon, 331; Mr. Addington's interview with the King after the King's illness, 332; the King's opinion of Fox and Sheridan's conduct during his illness, 332; the Chancellor's interview with the King, 333; influence used with Mr. Pitt to resign, 334; martial-law in Ireland, 335; augmented allowance to the Princess Charlotte, 335; the King's kindness to Mr. Pitt, 336; pension to Lady Louisa Paget, the King and Princesses at cards, 336; the King's attack in 1788-89, and 1801 compared, 336; the King's expenses, a wish to retain Pitt as a friend if not as a Minister, 337; Mr. Pitt's fixed resolution not to accept a public grant, 338; the King speaks to Lord Grenville on Mr. Pitt's affairs, 338; Mr. Rose quits the Treasury, 339; meets the Prince of Wales at Mrs. Malenlin's, the Great Seal given to Lord Eldon, the drawing-room, 339; accounts from Copenhagen, private conversation with Lord Eldon, 340; coarse conduct of Lord Thurlow, Mr. Addington in Downing-street, 341; state of Denmark, Addington wishes to make Mr. Rose a Privy Councillor, 342; Mr. Rose declines to receive the honour through Addington's intervention, 343; the King sees the Duke of York on military matters, 344; death of the Emperor Paul at St. Petersburgh, 344; battle of Copenhagen, 345; conduct of Sir Hyde Parker discussed, 345; the King's illness threatens to return through over-fatigue, 346; line of conduct pursued by the Prince of Wales, 346; details of the battle of Copenhagen, 347; recall of Sir Hyde Parker, 348; conversation with Lord Loughborough on his recent interview with the King, 349; bill for preventing seditious meetings,

350; Mr. Rose offers his house at Cuffnells for the King's use, during his journey to Weymouth, 351; Mr. Rose writes to Mr. Addington to decline the honour of being made a Privy Councillor, 352; the King's visit to Weymouth, the King hurt that no congratulatory address has been offered to him on his recovery, 353; the King's annoyance at being separated from the Queen, 354; the King takes an aversion to Dr. Willis, 355; extraordinary conduct of Mr. Addington, 356; wavering conduct of Mr. Tierney, illness of Mr. Rose, 357.

CHAPTER VII.

Correspondence on Mr. Pitt's retirement from office, in 1801, 358; the Bishop of Lincoln on the Catholic Relief Bill, 359; letters on the retirement of Mr. Pitt, 360; letter from Mrs. Stapleton, a friend of Pitt's mother, to Mr. Rose, expressing Lady Chatham's anxiety to be furnished with all particulars touching her son's resignation, 363; letter from Lord Auckland, in which he states that he is "stunned, grieved, and aggrieved," 365; Mr. Rose's reply, 365; letters on the offer of Privy Councillor to Mr. Rose, 367; Mr. Rose wavers, 369; desires an appointment for his son, 370; the King's visit to Weymouth, 370; letter from Dr. Willis to Mr. Rose on the subject of the King's visit to Cuffnells, 371; characteristic letter of Lord Eldon to Mr. Rose, 372; Church preferment, 376; close of Pitt's first Administration, 377; Lord Malmesbury's account of the close of this Administration, 377; charges Pitt with want of respect to the King, 377; Pitt's conduct considered, 378; Lord Brougham's remarks on it, 379; his views discussed, 379; Lord Brougham's tribute to the King, 380; Perceval and his party, 380; Lord Brougham's statement that the King hated the Prince of Wales considered, 380; character of the Prince of Wales, 381; unfilial conduct of the Prince of Wales, 382; Fox and his followers, 383; the treatment of the King by the Prince of Wales and the Duke of Kent contrasted, 384; the Prince of Wales's complaint to Lord Malmesbury, 384; Lord Malmes-

bury's reply, 384; the Princess Charlotte's education, 385;
the Prince of Wales publishes the King's private correspondence, 385; insincerity of the Prince, 386; the King's reasons
for refusing Catholic Emancipation, 387; the agitation of this
question the cause of the King's illness, 389; conversations of
Sir George Rose with the King, 390; charge of pride against
Mr. Pitt considered, 391; Mr. Pitt's position with respect
to Catholic Emancipation considered, 393; Mr. Pitt relents,
394; Pitt's attachment to the King, 396; unjust surmises
of the Marquis of Buckingham, 396; conduct of the Grenvilles, 397; the King's views of his duties, 398; hostile
conduct of Lord Auckland, 400; Mr. Rose declines Lord
Auckland's further acquaintance, 400.

CHAPTER VIII.

Negotiations respecting the payment of Mr. Pitt's debts, 402;
Mr Pitt's habits and tastes, 403; princely offer of George III,
403; Difficulties of Mr. Pitt, 404; the Cambridge Commemoration, 405; Pitt's creditors become clamorous, 405; various
modes of paying his debts suggested, 406; Mr. Dundas, 407;
Lord Camden to Mr. Rose, 408; Mr. Pitt's debts, 408; efforts of
his friends, 409; plan of Lord Camden, 409; sale of Hollwood
proposed, 410; Mr. Rose to Lord Camden on the subject of
Pitt's debts, 411; some merchants of London offer to raise
100,000l. to pay Mr. Pitt's debts, 412; the Bishop of
Lincoln to Mr. Rose on the same subject, 415; Lord Camden
to Mr. Rose on the same, 418; the Bishop of Lincoln to Mr.
Rose on the same, 420; the Bishop of Lincoln sees Mr. Pitt
on the subject, 422; his conversation with Pitt, 424; Pitt's
promise not to agitate the Catholic question, 426; good
harvest, 427; the Catholic question, 428; contributors
towards the payment of Mr. Pitt's debts, 428; signature
the preliminaries of peace, 430; Mr. Pitt to Mr. Rose on the
subject of an official situation for Mr. Rose's son, 430; acts
of treachery towards Mr. Pitt, 431; anxiety of Mr. Pitt's
friends respecting them, 432; wish Mr. Pitt to withdraw his
advice from Mr. Addington, 433; Addington's desire to kick
away the ladder, 434; the Bishop of Lincoln's injunctions to

Mr. Rose to watch the debates for any symptoms of the above, 434; Mr. Rose urges upon Mr. Pitt that there is a systematic plan to injure him with the King and the public, 436; Mr. Rose acquiesces in Mr. Pitt's wish that he should become a Privy Councillor, 437; writes to him on the subject of a post for his son, 439; Mr. Addington to Mr. Pitt, announcing that the King makes Rose and Long Privy Councillors, 440; Bishop of Lincoln to Mr. Rose, 441; Mr. Pitt goes to Cambridge, to Duckden, to Hollwood, 441; the Bishop of Lincoln remonstrates with Mr. Pitt on his support of Addington, 442; the distilleries' bill, 442; the Catholic question, 442; Pitt's uneasiness about the state of affairs, 444; expectation of a fresh convulsion in Paris, 444.

CHAPTER IX.

The civil list, 445; meeting to celebrate Mr. Pitt's birth-day, 447; Mr. Pitt's health, 447; Election at Southampton, 448; the elections, 448; the Bishop of Lincoln's dissatisfaction with Pitt's line of conduct, 449; state of affairs at home, 450; the Bishop of Lincoln seconds Mr. Rose's intention to make a statement in the House of Commons hostile to the Ministry, 450; Lord Grenville, 452; Mr. Canning's desire to regulate his conduct in accordance with Mr. Pitt's wishes, 453; Mr. Pitt goes to Bath for his health, 455; his conduct on the opening of Parliament, 456; Mr. Canning on Lord Grenville's position towards Mr. Pitt, 456; the navy estimates, 457; Mr. Canning wishes Pitt's opinion, 458; Fox's conduct towards the Addington Ministry, 459; state of our relations with France, 460; Mr. Canning to Mr. Rose on the naval estimates, and on the conduct to be pursued towards the Addington Administration, 462; Lord Hawkesbury, Mr. Fox, Mr. Canning, and others on the naval estimates' bill, 464; successful speech of Mr. Sturge's, 465; Mr. Canning to Mr. Rose, on the attitude of affairs, 485.

CHAPTER X.

Mr. Rose's Diary continued, 470; Mr. Rose's wish for the return of Mr. Pitt to office, 470; Pitt's difficult position,

471; Addington's dissatisfaction with Pitt, 471; French proceedings in Switzerland, 473; the First Consul's treatment of Switzerland, 474; French projects against the Spanish Settlements in America, 475; the Italian Republic, 476; Malta, 476; Elba, 477; French interference in Switzerland, 478; our interference against France, 481; comparative state of our navy, from 1793 to 1801, 481; our means of going to war in 1801, 482; imbecility of Ministers, 483; Pitt approves of Mr. Addington's conduct respecting Switzerland, 485; Mr. Pitt announces his intention of being present at the opening of the session, 486; changes his intention, 487; Mr. Pitt exhibits his reluctance to resume office, 488; Mr. Canning visits Mr. Pitt at Bath, 489; Lord Hawkesbury seeks Mr. Pitt's advice, 489; Mr. Pitt declines to give it, 490; plan agitated by influential persons to induce Mr. Addington to resign, 490; Lord Grenville's confidence in Mr. Pitt, 491; Pitt prepared to resume office, 492; his plan of action, 493; aggrandisement of France, 495; general desire to see Mr. Pitt resume office, 496; war expected with France, 496; Lord Bathurst, 497; indiscretion of Mr. Canning, 497; apathy of the House of Commons, 498; able speech of Lord Grenville, 499; Pitt's return to office the only safe course, 500; protection of the Government by Mr. Fox, 501; objections of Mr. Ryder, 501; Fox's contradictory sentiments, 503; Pitt's embarrassing position, 504; pointed observations in the *Courier* on Mr. Fox's conduct, 506; Fox's ardent wish to keep Pitt out of office, 508; Count Woronzoff's opinion of the Addington Ministry, 509; anecdote of Lord Chatham, 509; elaborate and virulent attack on Mr. Pitt in the *Times*, 509; debate on the vote for seamen, 510; Pitt's vexation at the attack in the *Times*, 511; regards it as sanctioned by Mr. Addington, 512; Addington departs from Pitt's policy, 513; the Prince of Wales's income, 514; Lord Castlereagh's conversation with Pitt, 515; Mr. Addington seeks an interview with Mr. Pitt, 516; Mr. Dundas's peerage, 517; another libel on Mr. Pitt, 518.

DIARIES AND CORRESPONDENCE

OF

THE RIGHT HON. GEORGE ROSE.

INTRODUCTION.

THE RIGHT HONOURABLE GEORGE ROSE has always been numbered amongst the celebrated statesmen and political writers of the conclusion of the last century and the commencement of the present.[1] From the time when he entered upon the serious business of life, he was exclusively employed in public offices of great importance, which brought him into contact with many of the most distinguished men of the age; and their letters are included in the correspondence which is now introduced as a biographical contribution to the history of that period. Much belonging to the same epoch has been already published in the shape of Memoirs, Diaries, and Correspondence, but they convey for the most part only the fleeting impressions of the hour, and are sometimes marvellously disfigured by political

[1] His portrait is included in the series of "Portraits of the most eminent persons now living, or lately deceased, in great Britain or Ireland," published by Cadell and Davies, in 1812.

passions and ignorant mistakes. If, therefore, we rely upon any of these taken alone, the truth comes to us as much distorted, as if we were looking through the multiform refractions of ill-made glass. They are indeed all useful in their way; for the history of mankind is but half written, when it is composed of State papers and Parliamentary debates; but it is only by comparing these revelations of the inner life of statesmen, by eliminating some errors and correcting others, that we can arrive at an accurate notion of the character of those who move the mechanism of nations.

From the important posts which Mr. Rose occupied, his correspondence and diaries are especially useful for this purpose. He saw so much of the secret springs which give motion to the wheels of Government, and was admitted so far into the intimacy of the great actors upon the public stage, that he could tell of much which was invisible to the outside spectators. But especially does his intimacy with Mr. Pitt, and the confidential terms on which they lived, from the commencement of that great minister's first administration to the end of his life, give an original interest to their correspondence. It is an interest, however, of a very peculiar nature; it is not that which arises from curious discoveries, large views, striking reflections, literary criticisms, piquant anecdotes, whispered slanders, or speculations even in politics; but it is an interest entirely owing to the light which it throws on the character of Mr. Pitt, and the tone of his mind throughout the long series of letters which are now first presented to the public.

Whether in office, or out of office, Mr. Pitt was so entirely devoted to public affairs, that nothing seemed to have any attraction for him, which was not in some degree connected with them. As long as he supported the Addington administration, he studied the measures which were brought forward, almost as much as if he was to bear the responsibility; and when he grew discontented with them, and ceased to be consulted, he still took the greatest pains to arrive at the facts which would either justify or condemn the conduct of the Government. His statesman-like caution in writing is very remarkable. He never expatiates upon passing events; he never reveals his intentions even to his most intimate friend; he never trusts his opinions to the perfidies of the Post-office; but is always contriving the most convenient means of personal intercourse, when any measure is to be discussed. It may be thought that this habit would detract much from the interest of these letters; but everything which furnishes an additional lineament to the picture of such a man is worthy of notice. This principle is recognised even by the unfriendly pen of the Duke of Buckingham, who, wishing to damage the character of Pitt by an inference drawn from Lord Sidmouth's destruction of all documents in his possession, remarks how strange it was "that this immense mass of letters should have been consigned to the flames, when every other correspondent of that illustrious man has preserved them with the greatest care and veneration."[1] Moreover, it is worth while to take the widest possible survey of his private correspondence, in order to bring out more fully this very amiable feature in his character, that when he is unbosoming himself in the most confidential communications with his dearest friend, not a word of ill-nature escapes him. He never abuses any one; he never depreciates his adversaries, and, though in conversation he is reported to have said of Lord Grenville, who had irritated him, "I will teach that proud man that I can do without him," yet nothing of that kind appears in his letters. Mr. Canning went so far as to regret his having so much of the milk of human kindness, that he never would punish those who had betrayed him.[2] Mr. Rose's share of the correspondence is characterised by the same good qualities which Lord Glastonbury, a cousin of Lord Grenville, and therefore in office, ascribes to a pamphlet written by him on the subject of finance in the following letter:

LORD GLASTONBURY TO MR. PITT.

"MY DEAR SIR,

"It is impossible for me not to read with the fullest attention and the most anxious curiosity any

[1] Duke of Buckingham's Memoirs, vol. iii. p. 142.
[2] Lord Malmesbury's Diary, iv. 26.

work on the trade and manufactures of the country, and much more so a publication which comes forth under the sanction of your pen. I cannot, therefore, omit troubling you with a few lines to express my warmest thanks for the perusal of the pamphlet you had the goodness to send me last week. It is a work which, in sound argument, good sense, perspicuity of statement, and elegance of language, I will venture to say, is to be equalled by few, surpassed by none. Though frequently alarmed, I have at no period of this awful contest despaired of our final success. But this statement has increased my confidence; for who was sanguine enough last year to be assured that the unprecedented weight of taxes which it was judged wise and expedient to impose, would not affect the produce of the old funds?

I am persuaded that our remaining resources will suffice to carry us through this storm, in which the trade, commerce, and manufactures of the world are staked against the plunder of it. But the former have this advantage; they are better applied, and will prove more permanent than the latter. My chief anxiety arises from the depression of the landed gentleman with a small property, who resides on his estate. This useful and necessary class of men suffer most, and will be annihilated by the weight of taxes.

"I am, my dear Sir,
"With a very sincere regard and esteem,
"Your most faithful and obliged Servant,
"GLASTONBURY.
"Conduit Street, 12th March, 1700."

[Mr. Rose left behind him materials different in character for three distinct periods of his life. For the first, which reaches up to the commencement of Mr. Pitt's first administration, there is a short autobiography, but no correspondence; for the second, which ends with his own retirement from office on Mr. Pitt's resignation, there is a copious correspondence, but neither autobiography nor diary; for the third there are both diaries and correspondence. In most autobiographies the domestic life of the writer occupies a large space. They contain minute details of his parentage, his early habits, and education. Of all this, very little is said by Mr. Rose. He was pre-eminently a man of business, and he hurries forward to the period when he began to be employed in the service of the State. Thus, though he was a Tory all his life, he thinks it not worth while to tell how much his father suffered in that cause, nor how he was thrown into prison in 1745, for too much complicity with the leaders of that rebellion, which, however, accounts sufficiently for his being himself so ill provided for in early life, and for his uncle's taking charge of him; and though he travelled abroad, yet he records no adventures, no remarks, no incident, except that he met with Mr. Pitt at Paris.

With respect to his marriage, which must have been the most interesting passage in his life, not political, he makes no mention either of the fact, person, or date. Indeed we only collect the circumstance from an incidental reference to his wife. As the whole narrative consists of reminiscences penned at a late period of his life, all dates and numbers seem to have been forgotten, and the blanks were never filled up. His daughter, however, with true feminine instinct, and predilection for the interesting minutiæ of private life, has supplied many valuable particulars, which were wholly omitted in the autobiography. Unfortunately she adopted the habit of writing more with her pencil than her pen, and therefore much is now illegible which might have conveyed useful knowledge.

During the second period of his life, Mr. Rose's time and attention were too much absorbed by the manifold duties of his office to allow him sufficient leisure for writing a diary, or taking much notice of what was passing around him. Nor indeed was he at any time addicted to pleasantries, anecdotes, or gossip; but when he was out of office, or held a post of less anxious nature, he recorded in a diary, till the year 1811, every event that occurred in the political world, with the single exception of the year 1805, respecting which almost a complete silence is observed. Whether this was owing to ill health, of which he was beginning to complain, or to some slight coolness which had sprung up between him and Mr. Pitt, with reference to the formation of the administration, or the policy of the war, of which some traces are perceptible, we have not sufficient evidence to determine. He says so little about himself that it may be convenient to introduce here the dates of the principal events of his political life.

In 1772, he was keeper of the Records at Westminster; in 1776, he was Secretary to the Board of Taxes; in 1782, Secretary to the Treasury, which office he vacated in the spring of 1783, but was re-appointed by Mr. Pitt in December; in 1784, he was returned by the Duke of Northumberland as Member of Parliament for Launceston, in Cornwall; in 1788, he vacated his seat by being made Clerk of Parliaments, but was returned for Lymington, and in 1790 for Christ Church; in 1801, on the resignation of Mr. Pitt, he vacated the Secretaryship to the Treasury; in 1804, when Mr. Pitt came again into office, he was appointed Joint Paymaster-General of the Forces and Vice-President of the Board of Trade, till January, 1806, when Mr. Pitt died."

In 1807, under the Duke of Portland, he was appointed Treasurer of the Navy and Vice-President of the Board of Trade. Miss Rose's sketch of her father's life, which is here subjoined, will be the most fitting introduction to his own autobiography, and will show how much he has omitted of his early history.—ED.]

"Mr. Rose was the second son of his father by his second wife. When little more than four years of age, he was adopted by his mother's brother, at that time living at Hampstead, and educated by him. He was for a short time at Westminster School, but at an early age was sent by his uncle to sea, under the friendly care of Captain Mackenzie, of the Navy, and served for three or four years as a younker and midshipman. During this time, neither the risks nor hardships of the service disinclined him to it, though he had a considerable share of both. He always spoke of his first years in the Navy with pleasure, and continued his predilection for it through life.

"He must have entered the naval service at a very early age. His first voyage was to the West Indies; and in May, 1758, he served in the Channel as a midshipman, and steered one of the boats from which the troops commanded by Charles, Duke of Marlborough, were landed in Cancale Bay; and in 1759 he was again in the West Indies, and was twice severely wounded during the naval campaign there. From the effects of one of these wounds he continued to suffer to a late period of his life.

"It has been stated that he received the appointment of purser to the ship, but, in fact, it appears that Captain Mackenzie was his own purser. Mr. Rose kept his book, which is signed in a boy's handwriting. The pay was given by favour, probably, and the whole was under the captain's control; but his uncle was discouraged in his hope of advancing him, and on the peace of 1763, he quitted the service.

"He was then in his nineteenth year, and his own master. His uncle, his only relation in England, was dead, and the small bequest he expected to inherit from him (about 5,000*l.*), he was deprived of, under circumstances so painful, that he scarcely ever alluded to them further than to state that, when he returned, he learnt that no will of his uncle's had been found, and that no trace remained of his property. Young as he then was, he had gained the regard of his uncle's respectable friends; he also obtained an introduction into the best literary society of that day, and through private friendship was appointed a clerk in the Record Office.

"When it was determined by the House of Lords, about the year 1767, to print their Journals and the Rolls of Parliament, a person competent to the work was sought for, and Mr. Rose was found well qualified for the undertaking. An office was formed for the purpose under his direction, which, when he became Clerk of Parliaments, was absorbed into that department,—Mr. Rose having resigned the emoluments, amounting to about 500*l.* a-year for his life, for a pension of 300*l.* on Mrs. Rose.

"While this work was in progress, the active intelligence of his mind, which led him to pursue with energy every duty which he undertook, attracted the notice of the peers who composed the committee for directing it; especially of the last Earl of Marchmont; and the foundation was then laid of that confidential and affectionate friendship which led him within a very few years afterwards to name Mr. Rose his sole executor for his English property; a friendship which increased with years, and was marked at Lord Marchmont's death by a renewal of that trust, conveying to him, besides a pecuniary legacy, his books and papers.

"While directing the printing of Rolls and Journals, Mr. Rose had been appointed, on the death of Mr. Morley, joint keeper of the Records with Mr. Farrer, at whose death he became the sole principal of that office.

"About the year 1777, Mr. Rose was appointed Secretary of the Tax Office, on the resignation of Mr. Chamberlayne, and was frequently consulted, during the latter part of the administration of Lord North, on business connected with that department.

"When Lord John Cavendish became Chancellor of the Exchequer, he advised on general financial regulations with Mr. Rose, who then suggested to him the measure for the consolidation of the Customs, which he had afterwards, under Mr. Pitt's administration, the satisfaction of seeing perfected.

"During that time, Lord Shelburne requested Mr. Rose to call on him, to give him some information respecting the revenue. He did so. At the close of the conversation, Lord Shelburne asked him what were his future views. Mr. Rose replied, to obtain the reversion of the office of Clerk of Parliaments, which he had been led to look forward to, after the present possessor, in consequence of his employment in the service of the House of Lords, and as Clerk Assistant, if the Patent, which had been closed in compliance with an address to the King, ever should be opened again. Lord Shelburne replied, 'Good God, Mr. Rose, have you not more ambition?'

"When Lord Shelburne became First Lord of the Treasury, he desired Lord Thurlow, with whom Mr. Rose then lived in habits of private friendship, to offer him the situation of Secretary to the Treasury. His first impulse was to refuse it, and not to abandon a moderate but permanent office for a very precarious one, which might embark him in party politics. He was strongly urged to take the time offered him by Lord Shelburne for consideration. At the end of a week, the advice of his friends, and probably the temptation of the field being opened to him for those improvements in the management of the revenue which he had contemplated from the time he was employed in a financial department, determined him to accept the situation offered to him, on one condition only,—that he should not, while holding it, sit in Parliament.

"Lord Stafford also urged his acceptance of Lord Shelburne's offer. He was Lord Thurlow's friend; but I have strong reason to believe that Lord Stafford, then Lord Gower, took a strong interest in my father's fortunes on private considerations, apart from his knowledge of his ability in the general business

of the House of Lords. I always remember traces of
it. By Lady Gower, though she never visited my
mother (indeed, she visited very few), and by all her
family, he was treated as a familiar associate; and by
her favourite brother, Mr. Stewart, as his attached
and intimate friend. His wife told me, when I was
thirteen years old, that her husband informed her
when he married her, that she must be intimate with
Mrs. Rose, as he felt sure she would like her, for Mr.
Rose was his earliest friend. She said, when I asked
her where the early intimacy had been formed, she
could not tell, it had often puzzled her. I then
asked where my grandmother and her children were,
and who protected them when my grandfather was
imprisoned in London, in 1745? She replied, 'The
Galloway Stewarts.' She had once before told me
that the name of Stewart, borne by my uncle and
brother, was derived from the Galloway Stewarts.
This gave me light, and explained the intimacy with
Lord Galloway and his family, though it fell off from
Lord Galloway, whom my father did not like.

"In one respect, my father had no cause to regret
his compliance. Lord Shelburne fulfilled his expectations as far as the short period of his administration
and the difficulties he had to encounter permitted, in
the department he belonged to; but he resigned his
employment under him with satisfaction, though he
left it, when Lord Shelburne resigned the seals,
without any remuneration for having given up a

permanent office. At that time, in addition to the small salaries from the Record and Journal Offices, he had a moderate private fortune, vested in the precarious security of a West Indian property, and the remote prospect of succeeding to the offices of Clerk Assistant of the House of Lords, and Clerk of Parliaments, after the lives of Mr. Strutt and Mr. Ashley Cowper. The Patent had been opened, in consequence of an address to the King from the House of Lords, moved by the Earl of Marchmont, for the nomination of Mr. Strutt and Mr. Rose in succession, on the ground of Mr. Rose's former and continued services to the House.

"There was then what was called a six weeks' interregnum, during which nothing was done but what was absolutely needful, only the King's special act, as in the case of Dr. Moore's nomination to the Archbishopric of Canterbury.

"Lord Shelburne never took any concern in my father's object, nor supported his friends in the House of Lords, on the address, &c. It was done entirely by the peers, who attended to the particular business in that house, independent of politics,—Lord Stafford, Lord North, &c. This was known to the King, and approved by him. When Lord Shelburne resigned, Lord Stafford wished to give up the privy seal, but declared he would keep it to complete my father's patent, then in progress. Lord Thurlow, in one of his sulky moods, held it back, until the King asked him 'if he had not a patent for the Parliament office for *his* signature.' This, the King told himself.

"Immediately after quitting the office of Secretary to the Treasury, Mr. Rose went abroad with Lord Thurlow, and returning in the autumn of 1783, through Paris, he there met Mr. Pitt, whom he had previously known when he was Chancellor of the Exchequer in Lord Shelburne's administration, and of whom he at once formed a true estimation. At Paris they became more fully acquainted with each other. They returned to England impressed with the same views of the important occurrences of the time, too well remembered to require a more particular mention here.

"When Mr. Pitt became Prime Minister in 1784, Mr. Rose was again appointed Secretary to the Treasury, which office he held during the whole of Mr. Pitt's administration, and his objections to sitting in Parliament being removed by his knowledge of Mr. Pitt's character and his perfect reliance on him, he was, in the general election in 1784, returned member for Launceston. Mr. Pitt's sense of the sacrifice Mr. Rose had made in resigning the office of Secretary to the Treasury, was met by his appointing him, unsolicited, to the first situation for life which fell to his disposal, the Mastership of the Pleas in the Court of Exchequer; which place he afterwards allowed him to resign in favour of his youngest son. My father was brought into Parliament, in

1784, by the private friendship of the Duke of Northumberland, grandfather of the present Duke.

"In 1768 he succeeded, on the death of Mr. Ashley Cowper, to the office of Clerk of Parliaments,—Mr. Strutt having died during Mr. Cowper's life, in consequence of the effects of a fall. This succession vacated the seat for Launceston, and for the short remainder of that Parliament he sat for the borough of Lymington. At the general election in 1796 he was returned one of the members for Christ Church, which borough he continued to represent for the remainder of his life.

"When Mr. Pitt resigned the seals, in 1801, Mr. Rose quitted the office of Secretary to the Treasury, and was at Mr. Pitt's request named by the King of the Privy Council, and by his Majesty's command one of the members of the Board of Trade. When Mr. Pitt resumed office in 1804, Mr. Rose was appointed one of the Joint Paymasters of the Army and Vice-President of the Board of Trade, which offices he resigned on Mr. Pitt's death. Under the Duke of Portland's administration he was appointed Treasurer of the Navy, a post he continued to hold until his death, in 1818."

CHAPTER I.

REFLECTIONS AND OBSERVATIONS, ARISING FROM THE EXPERIENCE OF A LONG LIFE, THE GREATEST PART OF WHICH HAS BEEN SPENT IN THE ACTIVE SERVICE OF THE PUBLIC — WITH THESE PERHAPS MAY BE INTERSPERSED STATEMENTS OF, OR ALLUSIONS TO, CIRCUMSTANCES AS THEY MAY OCCUR TO MY RECOLLECTION, WITHOUT REGARD TO DATES OR TO PARTICULAR PERIODS.

Cuffnells, September 17th, 1817, in my 74th year.

As this paper is intended for the information of my son, and of those who may follow him, I begin it naturally with some account of myself, to show how I attained my present situation in the world. I was born in 1744. I am descended paternally from the family of Rose of Kilravoc, in the county of Nairn, in Scotland; maternally from the family of Rose of Westerclune.

A brother of my mother,[1] who was very respectably settled in England, took me from my parents, when four years old, and gave me as good an education as possible.

At an early age I entered in the Naval Service, under Captain Jas. Mackenzie, who treated me like a

---

[1] This brother was maternally descended from Archbishop Sharp's daughter, who was with him when he was murdered.

parent, and with whom I lived for some time at his own table. Losing, however, all prospect of promotion in the only desirable line in the Navy, I quitted it permanently in 1762.

In the beginning of 1763, I applied myself to the study of Records, and in 1767, when the House of Lords decided to print their early proceedings, all the Record officers were ordered to attend the committee appointed for that purpose; amongst whom I appeared for Mr. Morley, who was then keeper of the Records in the receipt of the Exchequer, preserved in the chapter-house at Westminster.

Of that committee the late Earl of Marchmont was in the chair, to whom I was an absolute stranger. It was upon my attendance there that my acquaintance with him commenced, which formed to a very great extent the comfort, as well as led to the advantages, of my future life. Here, therefore, I think it right to make some mention of him. He was a man of most distinguished talents and learning; he had read more deeply in the classics, history and in civil law, than any man I ever knew,—combining the three branches. He entered public life at an early age, having been chosen for the town of Berwick, and soon made a considerable figure in the House of Commons in opposition to Sir Robert Walpole; which party he led after the secession of Mr. Pulteney. When his seat became vacant on his succession to the peerage on the death of his father, Sir Robert said to Mr. Morley (who lived on terms of great private familiarity with him) that he was relieved from the most troublesome opponent he had in the house.

The Earl had lived in habits of the closest intimacy with Lord Bolingbroke, both in England and in France. This afforded opportunities, in frequently repeated conversations, for his lordship's stating to me everything interesting which passed in the reign of Queen Anne and George the First, as familiarly as if the occurrences had taken place in his own time; some of these will probably be stated hereafter.

I will here, however, in justice to the memory of my invaluable friend, say that on religious points there was no union of sentiments between these two men. On the other hand, it appears by a letter of Lord Bolingbroke's, dated in 1740, from Angeville, that he had actually written some essays dedicated to the Earl of Marchmont, of a very different tendency from his former works. These essays, on his death, fell into the hands of Mr. Mallet, his executor, who had at the latter end of his life acquired a decided influence over him,[1] and they did not appear among

[1] This influence was acquired by constant attention, and principally by exposing to his lordship the breach of engagement of Mr. Pope, in allowing Lord B.'s Essay on a Patriot King to be printed. His lordship had printed six copies of it himself, which he gave to Lord Chesterfield, Sir Wm. Wyndham, Mr. Littleton, Mr. Pope, Lord Marchmont, and to Lord Cornbury, at whose instance he wrote it. Mr. Pope lent his copy to Mr. Allen, of Bath; who was so delighted with it that he had an impression of 500 taken off, but locked them up securely in a warehouse, not to see the light till Lord Bolingbroke's permission should be obtained. On the discovery, Lord Marchmont (then living in Lord Bolingbroke's house at Battersea) sent Mr. Gravenkop for the whole cargo, who carried

his lordship's works published by Mallet; nor have they been seen or heard of since. From whence it must naturally be conjectured that they were destroyed by the latter, for what reason cannot now be known; possibly, to conceal from the world the change, such as it was, in his lordship's sentiments in the latter end of his life, and to avoid the discredit to his former works. In which respect he might have been influenced either by regard for the noble Viscount's consistency, or by a desire not to impair the pecuniary advantage he expected from the publication of his lordship's works.[1]

Besides Lord Bolingbroke, Lord Marchmont lived in the most intimate habits with Lord Chesterfield, Lord Cobham, Lord Stair, Sarah Duchess of Marlborough, Mr. Littleton, Lord Cornbury, Mr. Pope, and other eminent persons. And his memory being perfect, to his death, made his society most interesting,

them out in a waggon, and the books were burnt on the lawn in the presence of Lord Bolingbroke.

[1] The letter to Lord Marchmont, here referred to, has a note appended to it by Sir George Rose, the editor of the "Marchmont Papers," who takes a very different view of its contents from his father. He justly remarks, that "as the posthumous disclosure of Lord Bolingbroke's inveterate hostility to Christianity lays open to the view as well the bitterness as the extent of it, so the manner of that disclosure precludes any doubt of the earnestness of his desire to give the utmost efficiency and publicity to that hostility, as soon as it could safely be done; that is, as soon as death should shield him against responsibility to man." Sir George saw plainly enough that, when he promises, in those essays, to "vindicate religion against divinity and God against man," he was retracting all that he had occasionally said in favour of Christianity; he was upholding the religion of Theism against the doctrines of the Bible, and the God of nature against the revelation of God to man.—Ed.

as he was in the habit, with me, of constantly narrating anecdotes, and mentioning what had passed in the former parts of his time.

It was to this highly distinguished nobleman I owe my introduction into life, and consequently to everything that has since followed. It was to him entirely (then an absolute stranger, as already observed) I was indebted for my being employed in the publication of the Lords' Records, in April, 1707.

In the year 1772, Mr. Morley died, at a very advanced age; and a recommendation in my favour to succeed him was sent by the Committee of Lords, to Lord North, who put aside an appointment he had intended, and gave the office to me. At my own request, however, Mr. Farley, who had been for a very long time chief clerk in it, was joined with me, but he dying a few years afterwards, I became sole keeper of the Records, in which situation I still remain.

In the interval between my quitting the navy and my employment by the House of Lords, I lost my uncle, who died without a will, in a fit of apoplexy. He had been my great stay in affection as well as in pecuniary support. By his death, under these circumstances (the particulars not worth detailing here), I was left in a most unprotected state. With a good education, however, and living in the best society, the advantages of which I have largely experienced, I was nearly domesticated in the house of one friend, whose name I mention on account of the very peculiar benefits I derived from his kindness. This was Mr.

Alexander Strahan, who entered into the world with a large fortune, which he greatly impaired by the South Sea scheme in the year 1720. The remains of it he principally sunk in annuities, from whence he derived a considerable income, and was enabled to live well. When I was introduced to him, he was at a very advanced age, and was never out of his house, except when he changed his residence from one house for another he had at Knightsbridge, during the summer. At his table (a regular one every day, and which I frequented whenever I had no other engagement) I met almost every man and woman of letters of the time: Mr. Hume, Dr. Johnson, Mr. Mallet, Dr. Armstrong, Mr. Scott, who had been preceptor to the King, Mr. Richmond Webb, Mrs. Macaulay, Mrs. Lennox, praised by Dr. Johnson, and others.

The life of Mr. Strahan closed almost immediately after my being employed by the House of Lords; to which duty I devoted myself so entirely, that it would in any event have taken me much from that society by which I had greatly profited.

I continued in the execution of the duty entrusted to me so completely to the satisfaction of the Lords, that the House presented an address to the King, laying before him a report of their Committee, recommending me in strong terms to his Majesty. When that report was presented by the Chancellor, Lord Bathurst, his Majesty expressed himself very graciously respecting me, so as to lead to a hope of my being considered when the patent of the Clerk of the

Parliaments being opened, should afford an opportunity for it.

In the year 1777, on Mr. George Chamberlayne's resignation of the Secretaryship of the Tax-Office, upon his becoming a Roman Catholic, Lord North appointed me his successor, without any solicitation whatever on my part. The offer was made in the most gratifying manner, through the brother, Mr. Edward Chamberlayne, then a clerk in the Treasury. In that situation I remained till July, 1782.

In April, 1782, Lord North was removed from the head of the Treasury, and was succeeded by Lord Rockingham,—Lord Shelburne, and Mr. Fox being Secretaries of State. In the July following, Lord Rockingham died. During his short administration, Lord John Cavendish, the Chancellor of the Exchequer, consulted me on everything. He had been advised (as he told me) by various friends to apply to me for assistance.

On the death of Lord Rockingham, there was a struggle for the Treasury between the Duke of Portland and Lord Shelburne, the former eagerly supported by Mr. Fox; but the latter prevailed; on which Mr. Fox and his political friends resigned, amongst whom was Lord John Cavendish. I was one of the very first to whom his Lordship made the communication, lamenting earnestly that I would not permit Lord Rockingham and himself to propose anything for me while it was in their power.

After leaving Lord John, I went to Lord Thurlow, the Chancellor, on a pressing message desiring to see me; when he at once asked me abruptly if I would be

Secretary of the Treasury; which was followed by a question from me, 'Are you to be First Lord?' to which he replied with an oath, 'No; but Shelburne is.' A conversation followed, in which I expressed great surprise at the proposal, and at its being made through him. He accounted for it, by Lord Shelburne thinking if it had been made by himself I should have refused it, and that probably his lordship (Thurlow) might prevail with me to accept it. I, however, stated a strong objection to it, and under that impression left the Chancellor. On my reaching home, I learnt from Mrs. Rose that Mrs. Strachey had been with her, and mentioned that she was looking out in Westminster for a house, as her husband, a very old friend of mine, understood he was to continue one of the Secretaries of the Treasury, in which office he was placed by Lord Rockingham.

After several days' deliberation, I was prevailed upon to accept the offer, with a considerable disinclination on my part. I made no bargain or condition of any sort for the event of retiring, though I gave up the valuable situation, a permanent one, of Secretary of Taxes, worth then more than £000 a year, with a certain prospect of improving, besides a small office in the Exchequer that required only a few days' attendance in the year, to take the very precarious one, under an unsettled Government, of Secretary to the Treasury.

A stranger to Lord Shelburne, and in utter ignorance of the line of politics he meant to pursue, I made it an express condition that I would not come into Parliament.

On the opening of the session, however, it was found that Mr. Orde (my colleague, afterwards Lord Bolton) was under great difficulty in getting in; and Lord Shelburne, without any communication with me, prevailed on Sir Richard Worsley to vacate his seat for Newport, in the Isle of Wight, that I might be chosen for that place. In the course of the summer and autumn I had experienced very uncomfortable feelings from the temper and disposition of Lord Shelburne; sometimes passionate or unreasonable, occasionally betraying suspicions of others entirely groundless, and at other times offensively flattering. I have frequently been puzzled to decide which part of his conduct was least to be tolerated.

This proceeding to force me into Parliament occasioned much heat on both sides; but I maintained my resolution, and Mr. Pepper Arden, the Solicitor-General, was chosen for Newport.

Having made no conditions whatever on giving up my former employments, I thought it an act of justice to myself to secure what was evidently intended for me by the House of Lords and the King. Till now I had been contented to wait for events respecting the Parliament office, as I had not before a political or private enemy to impede my access to it. Sure however, although not in the House of Commons, of now becoming an object of resentment, I was naturally desirous of protecting myself against suffering by that; and I was indeed urged most strongly by Lord Marchmont, who expressed his determination to bring the matter under the consideration of the House. The first step was to open the means of granting the office in reversion. In a subsequent year there was a very long and strict investigation by a Committee of Lords, respecting the whole conduct of matters in the Parliament office, when it was proved that great abuses had been committed by the Clerk of the Parliaments, in the sale of employments under him, and in diverting allowances made by the public to private objects. This induced an address to the King, to request his Majesty would not in future grant the office in reversion. This obstruction was removed by Lord Marchmont moving an address, which was carried unanimously, praying the King would grant the office in the manner heretofore accustomed, not doubting that his Majesty would consent.

Within two days after, the patent granting the office of Clerk of the Parliaments was made out in favour of Mr. Samuel Strutt, the Clerk Assistant of the House of Lords, and to myself in reversion, after the death of Mr. Ashley Cowper, then more than eighty years of age. Thus was secured to me the succession to the office on the death of Mr. Strutt, and the situation of Clerk Assistant (if I should choose to take it) on Mr. Strutt becoming Clerk of the Parliaments. In the proceeding for opening the patent Lord Shelburne had no share; he was not even in the House when Lord Marchmont moved the address; Lord Thurlow, the Chancellor, had given it all the countenance in his power, and Lord Shelburne consented.

In the interval between the appointment of Lord Shelburne to the Treasury in July, and the meeting

of Parliament in the winter, his Lordship made every
exertion in his power to gain strength in the House of
Commons; the King, at his instance, having written
earnestly to Lord North and to some others, who it
was thought might be influenced thereby, to support
the administration. It was, however, found soon after
the commencement of the session, how ineffectual those
exertions were. Lord Shelburne had entered upon
office without previously ascertaining what support
he could rely on, or might have reasonable prospect
of receiving; and it soon appeared how formidable
an opposition he had to encounter. A coalition was
formed between Lord North and Mr. Fox, uniting
the two great parties who had long acted under these
eminent leaders:—the principal agent in which was
Mr. Eden, afterwards Lord Auckland, who made
much use of Mr. North, the eldest son of his father, in
bringing the two principals together.

This junction was made manifest by the vote on the
Peace, which was carried by a majority of seventeen.
The numbers being 190 to 207. The person who
moved the censure upon it was the Earl of Surrey, who,
during the short administration of Lord Shelburne,
had obtained everything he asked; professing the
most determined attachment to his lordship, and living
much at his table. During that period, very little interesting to myself occurred, except the alternate
violence and flattery of Lord Shelburne, before alluded
to; which made my situation so thoroughly unpleasant
to me, that I felt the certain removal from office as a
relief. There were other qualities in his lordship that

were uncomfortable to me; a suspicion of almost every
one he had intercourse with, a want of sincerity, and
a habit of listening to every tale-bearer who would
give him intelligence or news of any sort.

Under these circumstances, I parted from him with
feelings of no pleasant nature, and I believe he had no
regret at the separation. He took not the least notice
of the unprovided state in which I was left, from having
made no conditions for myself when I came to the
Treasury. It was the first instance of a gentleman
giving up an income to take the Secretaryship of the
Treasury, without something being secured to him on
his retiring or being removed, or being given to him
previous to his removal. It is true I had the reversion
of the place of Clerk of the Parliaments, but there was
a life in it before me very nearly as good as my own,
for Mr. Strutt was only two years older than myself,
and the grant had no relation whatever to my acceptance of the Secretaryship of the Treasury. So far,
therefore, as Lord Shelburne was concerned, I was
left completely upon the pavement; of which, however, I made no complaint to any one, nor remonstrance
to his lordship, though my case was strengthened by
my having reduced the income of the Secretary greatly.

The income had arisen from fees on every instrument that was issued from, or passed through, the
office; an unpleasant and objectionable source, which
induced me to propose that all the fees received in
the department should be carried to a fund, from
which the secretaries and clerks should be paid.
I settled the income of the Secretaries, with the
approbation of the Board, at £3,000 a year in peace

and war, at which it remained till the year 17 , when Mr. Pitt, thinking that too low for the increased expense of living, and utterly insufficient for maintaining the appearance necessary to the situation, and the unavoidable charges of it, added £1,000 a year. When the minute was made for that addition, I wrote under it, that being in possession of a valuable sinecure office, I would not avail myself of the increased salary ; and I never took a shilling of it.

Previously to the removal of Lord Shelburne from the Treasury, an arrangement was made in the office which occasioned five vacancies. Two of these he filled himself, by Mr. Alcock and Mr. Cipriani ; one he gave to Mr. Pitt, who appointed a gentleman who soon exchanged the place for another situation; the fourth he conferred on Mr. Orde (my colleague), who appointed Mr. Joseph Smith, afterwards Mr. Pitt's private secretary. The fifth he gave to me, and I appointed Mr. Chinnery, a sort of secretary to Lord Thurlow, the Chancellor, who was likely to be turned adrift on his lordship going out of office, with little hope of receiving support from his father, who was a writing-master.

An intimation was conveyed to me by Mr. James Grenville that I might remain in the Treasury if I wished it, which he was authorized to suggest by Mr. Frederic Montague, one of the new lords: but I declined it, although I felt that I was at full liberty, not having been in Parliament, nor having mixed in Lord Shelburne's politics in any manner; having certainly no obligations of any kind whatever to his lordship.

I went out of office with Lord Shelburne on terms of civility and good correspondence, though not with cordiality; but an incident occurred a week or two afterwards which occasioned a final and determined separation. Before the Island of St. Christopher was taken in the war, Mr. Gammin (brother-in-law to the Duke of Grafton by having married the Duke's sister, and to the Duke of Chandos by the Duke having married Mr. Gammin's sister) was Collector of the Customs there. After the capture of the island Mr. Gammin was made Secretary of Excise. On the peace Mr. Gammin had the option of the two employments; he chose the latter; on which I requested Lord Shelburne to give the Collectorship of St. Christopher's to Mr. Diver, a brother of Mrs. Rose's, who was Collector of Dominica, not quite so good in point of income, and the society inferior. In this Lord Shelburne acquiesced; but on the coming in of the new government, Mr. Gammin had influence enough to obtain his former office at St. Christopher's with the consent of Lord Shelburne, retaining also the secretaryship of excise, and Mr. Diver was not restored to Dominica, which his lordship had given to Mr. Grove, the brother of one of his agents in the city.

On this transaction I had an interview with his lordship, in which I stated to him in very plain and intelligible expressions the sense I had of his conduct, and my determination never to be in a room with him again while in existence. From Lord Shelburne's in Berkeley Square I went to Mr. Pitt, then staying with his brother, Lord Chatham, in Savile Row, and explained to him all that had passed on this private subject, telling him at the same time the determination I had taken to separate for ever from Lord Shelburne; adding that it would be most painful to me if that should be the occasion of a separation from him also, but, distressing as such an alternative would be, I must encounter that rather than have any intercourse whatever in future with Lord Shelburne. Mr. Pitt expressed great regret at the communication, but entered on nothing confidential.

During the nine months of the administration I had not much intercourse with Mr. Pitt except at the Board, and sometimes at dinner at Lord Shelburne's; but such as I had was remarkably pleasant and satisfactory.

Finding myself quite at liberty, after the change of administration, I made a tour on the Continent with Lord Thurlow, from whom the Great Seal was taken. We started in the month of July, 1782, and went by Calais, through Lisle, to Spa; whence after some stay, to Aix-la-Chapelle, crossed the Rhine to Dusseldorff, and up the banks to all the places on the side of that river to Frankfort, from thence to Strasburgh, and followed the river to Basle. From Basle through Switzerland to Geneva, and from thence through Lyons to Paris. About ten days after my arrival at the latter place I received a letter from Mr. Pitt at Rheims, desiring I would stay at Paris till he could get to me, which he said he would do as soon as possible.

On our meeting, the conversation was quite confidential. In the course of it I found he was as little disposed to future connexion with Lord Shelburne as myself, and he manifested an earnest desire for a permanent and close intimacy with me. I explained to him, that, out of Parliament, I could be but little useful to him in politics. He, however, expressed so much anxiety on the subject as to induce me to a most cheerful and cordial assent; having hesitated only from a consciousness of my own insignificance as to any essential service I could render him, and I gave him my hand with a warm and consenting heart. From that moment I considered myself as inalienable from Mr. Pitt, and on that feeling I acted most sacredly to the last hour of his invaluable life; never for a single moment entertaining even a thought of separating from him, except in one instance. Nor do I recollect differing from him on more than two points. I may as well mention them here, though out of the order of time, because they are immediately connected with the ground on which I professed and maintained my attachment to him.

The first was on his plan for Parliamentary Reform. When that question was first agitated, I sat for Launceston, a seat of the Duke of Northumberland's, who told me he was sure I should vote with Mr. Pitt, and that I could not do otherwise. If, therefore, I had any delicacy towards his grace (which might have been embarrassing), this conduct of his set me perfectly free. I naturally gave such an important matter the fullest and most deliberate consideration, having before often weighed it in my mind as a speculative point on which I was not likely to be called upon to act. The result of my deepest reflection was that, if the question of Reform should be carried, it could not fail to be attended with the most direful consequences. It is not necessary here to enter on all that occurred to me on the subject.

Mr. Pitt's plan was for a limited alteration, to suppress what were called the rotten boroughs, allowing compensation to those who had the influence in them; adding to the county members, and giving members to all towns in which there were three hundred taxable houses. In that, the reformers of all descriptions concurred, notwithstanding the avowed dislike of many of them to the insufficiency of the measure; but who concurred in it under a persuasion that if any change could be effected, it would not stop at the first inroad, but that the door being once opened, the Reform might be carried to the extremest length.

[Mr. Pitt had proposed another kind of Reform, in the interval between Lord Shelburne's Administration and his own in 1783, in favour of which he brought forward certain resolutions which were designed to secure purity of election, and gave the first impetus to the question which is still agitating Parliament.

1. That it was the opinion of the House, that it was highly necessary to take measures for the future prevention of bribery and expense at elections.

2. That for the future, when the majority of voters

for any borough should be convicted of gross and notorious corruption, before a select committee of that House, appointed to try the merits of any election, such borough should be disfranchised; and the minority of votes not so convicted, should be entitled to vote for the county in which such borough is situated.

3. That an addition of Knights of the Shire and of representatives of the Metropolis, should be added to the state of the representation.

He also proposed Reform in the system of fees and patronage out of perquisites, the abuse of which had arisen to an almost incredible height. Lord North, it is said, cost the country £1,300 in one year for stationery; one item being £340 for whip-cord.

In pursuance of the same principle, two years afterwards Mr. Pitt introduced the bill to which Mr. Rose objected. It transferred the franchise of thirty-six boroughs to counties and unrepresented towns; but a clause for giving pecuniary compensation to the disfranchised boroughs, was the cause of its rejection.—ED.]

Mr. Rose's Diary resumed.

This great question had been discussed out of doors for a long time, particularly in Middlesex and Yorkshire. The general topic was, that taxation and representation should be inseparable, on which ground Mr. Pitt's plan was altogether unsatisfactory. In truth, nothing could come up to the principle short of the Duke of Richmond's suggestion of an universal right of voting, because the lowest and meanest inhabitants of the country paid taxes in some shape or other, if they burnt a rush-light and used soap for washing their linen.

Under the strongest conviction that if a breach should once be made in the representation, all the talents and weight of Mr. Pitt and other moderate reformers would not be able to prevent, in a short time, its being widened to a ruinous extent, I determined against an acquiescence in Mr. Pitt's plan, which he pressed with enthusiasm, not only in the House of Commons but in private, with such friends as he thought he could influence. It was quite natural that he should urge me in a very particular manner; not from any importance that could be attached to my vote individually, but that a person in my confidential post, taking a different line from him on a question of such infinite magnitude, might lead to a doubt of his sincerity.

Mr. Pitt could not be insensible to that, and he pressed the question upon me with great earnestness, frequently when alone, during some weeks, never referring to the effect that might be produced personally to himself. I felt that most forcibly, however, and in the last conversation on the subject, I told him he ought to be aware that from my conduct his zeal at least would be questioned; that the only remedy for which would be my retiring, assuring him at the same time that my attachment to him would not be abated thereby; to which he would not listen. On my going home after that conversation, I urged him earnestly to allow me to retire, which he answered very positively in the negative, and there ended our personal discussions on that distressing question.

I subjoin my letter to Mr. Pitt, on my declining, after repeated solicitations, to vote with him, on his motion for Parliamentary Reform.

"MY DEAR SIR,

"I find it so painful, as well as difficult, to explain myself to you in conversation on the subject of Wednesday's question, that I incline rather to attempt it in this manner. In doing so I avoid all professions of sincerity and attachment, because I am sure if your observation of my conduct does not impress you favourably on these points, nothing I can say will. Having never, however had a political connexion but with you, and looking to no other possible one, I shall be the more readily believed in declaring that in the line I am about to take on the present occasion, I act upon the advice of no man living, nor do I follow any one's opinion. In so nice a matter I must be governed by my own feelings, were I even at liberty to consult others upon it.

"I will not trouble you with a repetition of the pain I have felt in differing with you in this only instance, which has been increased in proportion as I have observed your exertions to prevail with your friends to agree with you in supporting the measure. Every proof of your uncommon anxiety on the subject, has added to my mortification; and I do lament, from the bottom of my heart, that I cannot endeavour to promote the success of it as cordially as I am persuaded I shall wish to do every other attempt of yours to do good to the country. I have considered the heads of the bill very attentively, and I do assure you most solemnly that I could not give my consent for leave to bring one in upon the ground of them, without doing a violence to my feelings, which I know you too well to believe you would wish me to do. At the same time, however averse I am from neutrality, I feel so anxious a concern that your sincerity should not be questioned, from the circumstance of one in my situation taking an opposite part to you, that I have determined not to vote against the question, although I think I could state reasons for my conduct in such a case, incapable as I am of expressing myself in public, as would prevent malignity itself, from imputing insincerity to you on my account."

I need hardly add that at the distance of no very long period, as his judgment ripened and he derived advantage from experience, he came over decidedly to my opinion, and acted upon it.

The other point I have alluded to was the Slave Trade,—more painful in respect to feeling than the first. This trade, most highly objectionable as it was when considered as it ought to be with reference to general principles of humanity, had been carried on and encouraged by Parliament for more than a century. So lately as during the ministry of the late Mr. Pitt (afterwards Earl of Chatham) an Act of

Parliament was passed, the preamble of which ran thus: "Whereas the trade to and from Africa is very advantageous to Great Britain, and necessary for the supplying the plantations and colonies thereunto belonging, with a sufficient number of negroes, at reasonable prices."

This consideration for the West India colonists and others who were deeply interested in the question; who had expended large fortunes in the cultivation of lands there, or who had made heavy advances to the proprietors, could not be allowed to preponderate against the feelings of humanity; but it entitled those persons to expect that their interest would be attended to as far as might be found consistent with the principles which it was pretty generally intended should be acted upon.

It was with that view that I suggested to Mr. Wilberforce, on his first bringing forward the subject, the means of obtaining the abolition in a manner the least likely to be resisted by the African traders and the powerful body of the West India planters and merchants, and at the same time the most beneficial to the poor negroes. My proposal was, to impose a duty on the importation of slaves into the islands, increasing annually till it should reach such an amount as would be prohibitory; and in any event that the importations should finally be closed at the end of a period to be fixed, perhaps ten or twelve years. During that period a considerable revenue would be raised, which might be applied in bounties to the mothers, in proportion to the number of children they should rear to the age of five years. This would operate as an inducement to the care of infants, to the almost universal neglect of which was justly attributed the decrease of slaves on the plantations. At the end of a term to be fixed, I suggested that freedom should be given to the good nursing mothers, and some provision for the remainder of their lives, out of the fund to be raised in the manner alluded to; and if that should be insufficient, then by grants from the public.

I argued that a sudden and immediate abolition would probably be the occasion of much blood being spilt on the African coast, as the slaves are brought there from very remote countries, sometimes twelve, eighteen, and twenty months on their journey; and if on their arrival no market should be found for them, they must inevitably be put to death, as the owners would not be at the trouble and expense of carrying them home again. The event proved that I was right as to the continuance of the trade by this country for many years, while the discussion was going on from session to session, at the end of which time the abolition was incomplete even in England; and much more so with other nations, who, profiting by our competition having ceased, supplied their own colonies plentifully, and cheaper than before.

Laws of the utmost severity have hitherto not produced the complete effect, and the public has been put to an enormous charge in purchasing captured cargoes of negroes on their passage to the West Indies, infinitely to a greater amount than the sum that would have been necessary for premiums to the mothers for taking care of their children. Spain and Portugal are still carrying on the trade to a great extent (in 1817) and France to a limited one.

It is not my intention to pursue the subject further. I have introduced it solely for the purpose of showing the ground on which I acted. I thought we had no right to interpose in the manner we were doing, and that we had no means of enforcing the assumption we attempted. I had not the satisfaction in this instance, which I had in the other in reference to Parliamentary Reform, of Mr. Pitt coming round to my opinion; he persevered in the course adopted by Mr. Wilberforce of immediate suppression of the trade in slaves. This drew from me the subjoined letter:—

" My dear Sir,

" I have had more than a common degree of anxiety to continue to make the same sacrifice to you in the Bill respecting the Slave Trade that I did on another occasion by persevering in my resolution of not saying a word or giving a vote on the subject; but the provisions of the Bill, as it came from the Committee, render it, according to the best judgment that I can form, so severely mischievous, that I should do a violence to myself, you would not, I am persuaded, desire to have inflicted on me, if I were not to attempt to state my reasons very shortly against the measure.

" It is not possible for me to have a clearer opinion on any point than on this, independently of any private interest whatever. But it would be uncandid if I were to pretend that the immediate hazard or certain gradual destruction, according to the strong impression on my mind, of the property of myself and all my nearest connexions is a matter of indifference to me.

"I remain, with the truest attachment," &c.

I return now to the narrative from which I have digressed.

During my stay at Paris very little occurred worthy of notice; but I was struck with surprise at the freedom of the conversation, on general liberty, even within the walls of the King's palace. On a Sunday morning, while we were waiting in an outer room to see the King pass in state to the chapel at Versailles, where several of the great officers were, there was a discussion almost as free as I have heard in the House of Commons, in which Monsieur Chauvelin[1] was the loudest, who was in some employment about the person of the King, for he dropped on his knee and gave his majesty a cambric handkerchief, as he went through the room.

My surprise, however, abated, on a little reflection as to the conduct of the Court. When France took part with the United States of America to weaken the power of Great Britain, the King was prevailed with to issue a proclamation, in which he stated, in substance, that the people in British America were not in possession of that degree of freedom which all mankind were entitled to by nature. Weak man! To suppose his own subjects would not apply the sentiment to themselves! The young men of rank who were sent to America to assist in the Revolution there, returned with enthusiastic notions of general freedom, very dif-

[1] He was first Valet de Chambre.

ferent from those formerly prevailing; and the Queen actually went to meet the greatest of all mischievous and conceited coxcombs, Monsr. de la Fayette, on his approach to Paris, and took him into her carriage.

A few days before I quitted Paris, I discovered, by the information of Mr. Walpole's servant, that the man I had taken to travel with me was under a very strong suspicion of having robbed and murdered his former master. The character I had with him from Mr. Woodly, through his sister, Mrs. Bankes, was an unexceptionable one, and as he had acquitted himself in a remarkably useful manner through the whole tour, which was so near the close, I determined to take no notice of the information. I brought him home, and then discharged him. It had been my intention to have kept him in my service; he was a Frenchman, of the name of Ami Ramel, and I believe he afterwards figured in the Revolution.

On my return to England, in October, 1783, I found Mrs. Rose in a furnished house at Portswood, near Southampton, rented of Mr. Lintot. I went there in a day or two after my arrival in England. I travelled post to Winchester, where my phaeton met me. It was on a Sunday, and as the horses did not get there till after me, I set off on foot, with orders to the coachman to follow me when the horses should have had their bait and sufficient rest. At Compton, a little village two miles on the road, I was overtaken by a shower, which made me seek shelter in a small public-house, the extreme neatness of which I could not help contrasting with the dirt and inconvenience of the houses by the roads on the Continent. The parlour, in which the family were going to sit down to dinner, was as clean and neat as possible; and on the table were a nice piece of roasted beef and a plum pudding,—articles I had not seen for a long time.

I found Mrs. Rose quite well; the two boys were at school; George, at the College at Winchester; William, at Mr. Richards's, a private seminary there. I remained quietly with them till the meeting of Parliament, soon after the opening of which I repaired to town at the pressing instance of Mr. Pitt, but not till after the second reading of the celebrated India Bill. The history of this measure, of such infinite importance in its consequences, I had, till I received the summons, learnt only from newspapers.

Mr. Fox having, by his union with Lord North, formed, as was generally believed, an exceedingly strong government, was desirous of making it a permanent one. In order to that he resorted to the measure above-mentioned. There had been for a long time well-founded complaints of abuses and incapacity in the management of the affairs of the East India Company. For the avowed purpose of finding a remedy for these, but for the real object of establishing his own power permanently, he framed this famous Bill. Under the provisions of it, a supreme Board was instituted, at the head of which Lord Fitzwilliam was named, and in the members of this Board, the whole patronage of India was placed. Not only the appointments, civil and military of every description, governors, commanders-in-chief, councillors at the several inferior Boards, judges, collectors of the revenues, and all the immensely valuable employments in the different settlements at Bengal, Madras, and Bombay; but also the writerships at home which were to lead to those employments. In the military line these Commissioners were invested with as extensive an authority, from the nomination of officers of the highest rank to the appointment of cadets who were to go out for the junior commissions. So far for direct patronage; but, in addition to that, the Commissioners were to control and direct the whole commerce of the country; and, of course, to bestow on their mercantile friends, with whom they might connect many of their political and private adherents, the profitable purchases and sales of the Company.

In this patronage, divided amongst four-and-twenty private individuals, not nearly so extensive as intended, now to be concentrated in one person, the President (for he would, as in other political Boards, have had the influence exclusively), no danger had been apprehended; but these Commissioners were not to be removable by the Crown; they were to be established for a term of years. The King might change his ministers, but he could not shake the Commissioners; they were unalterably fixed for five years, within which period there would be a general election; on which occasion the exercise of their widely-extended influence would have enabled them to exert themselves with great effect. It was quite evident to the most common observers that this patronage, taking in the whole scope of it, would operate much more powerfully than the patronage of the Crown could possibly do, curtailed and cut down as the latter was by various recent laws and proceedings of the Treasury. It might fairly, therefore, be considered, without exaggeration, that Mr. Fox was by this measure taking to himself a much larger share of power than the King possessed or the Minister could exercise. It was a bold one, and the produce of a daring spirit. He was encouraged in it by the opinions of some of his devoted followers, but warned by others of the risk he was about to incur. Amongst the latter was the Chief Justice, Lord Mansfield. Relying upon a strong support, he determined to proceed, and the Bill went through the House of Commons with triumphant majorities.

I had thought, from the first formation of the coalition, that Mr. Pitt was extinguished nearly for life as a politician, and wished to see him at the bar again, under a conviction that his transcendent abilities would soon raise him to great eminence in his profession. In this opinion I was strongly confirmed by what occurred on the Indian Bill; I mean as to the exclusion of Mr. Pitt from high office.

The bill had not, however, been in the House of Lords more than a day or two before matters assumed a different appearance. The King felt how deeply his authority would be wounded, and how entirely he should be placed in the hands and under the dominion of Mr. Fox, from which he had suffered severely during the recess, principally in matters respecting the Prince of Wales. The whole correspondence on that point, his

Majesty put into the hands of Mr. Pitt, who showed it to me, consisting of letters from the King, the Duke of Portland, Lord North, and Mr. Fox. Those from his Majesty to the Duke and Mr. Fox were eloquent, dignified, and admirably well-reasoned; to Lord North, they were equal to the others in those respects, while they were also deeply affecting. The King remonstrated with his Lordship on his putting him, bound, into the hands of Mr. Fox, after all that had passed. He reminded him of the steady support he had given him for twelve years, through the whole of his administration, till his lordship had himself desired to retire, from the impossibility he found of carrying on the Government; and, in a very gentleman-like way, called to his recollection the protection and reward he secured to him on his going out of office; alluding to the circumstance of the Duke of Richmond and Lord Shelburne pressing urgently for some punishment on Lord North when he went out of office; instead of which the King insisted peremptorily on a reward for his Lordship's long services, by a grant of the Cinque Ports for his life, with an income of 4,000*l.* a-year; which he held before during pleasure, with the military salary of 1,200*l.*, or something thereabout.

The feeling which led to that correspondence was awakened and very naturally greatly strengthened by the certain consequences which could not fail to attend his Majesty being put, completely fettered, into the hands of Mr. Fox. This induced him to adopt any course that could afford a chance of his being extricated from the perilous situation in which, unhappily, he was placed. The King, therefore, certainly conveyed to some peers about his person, and to others over whom he had or was supposed to have some influence, that he wished the Bill might not be passed. How far his Majesty, in this, acted upon his own judgment, or was encouraged to it by the advice of Lord Temple, who had access to the Closet, and spoke the opinions of others, could not, I think, be ascertained by any one; but it can hardly be doubted that there was a mixture of both.

The effect produced by this intimation from the King soon became manifest; and on some inquiries made by myself, chiefly through Lord Stafford, with whom I had long been in habits of intimacy, it appeared to me to be very well worth while to try what could be done by active exertions. Lord Stafford encouraged this with animation, at his advanced time of life. He had no acquaintance with Mr. Pitt, never having been in a room with him, but he was impressed with a belief that the country could be saved from the impending danger only by him. He applied himself, therefore, with uncommon zeal to the undertaking, keeping an open table for the purpose; and the Duke of Bridgewater, who never before went across a room for the attainment of any political object, exerted himself in a most extraordinary manner, by seeing every one he thought he could influence or make sensible of the threatened mischief. At night we used, at Lord Stafford's house, or at dinner, to talk over the occurrences of the day.

The effect of these very earnest endeavours was the loss of the Indian Bill in the House of Lords, on the 15th of December, by a majority of eight; the numbers were 79 to 87.

The debate lasted to a late hour. Now long before the conclusion of it I went into Waghorn's coffee-house for some refreshment, and met Mr. Adam and Mr. St. John coming out. In the dark they did not observe me, and I heard the former say to the latter, " I wish I were as sure of the kingdom of heaven as I am of our carrying the Bill this evening." I returned into the house, and on the steps of the throne I witnessed the effect of the division on the countenances of those gentlemen. The Earl of Marchmont was the first peer who went below the bar; on seeing which Mr. Adam made an audible exclamation.

The resignation of the Ministers followed the rejection of the bill; and a loud cry was instantly raised by them against the means that had been resorted to for obtaining the rejection, as unconstitutional on the part of the King to interfere in a measure depending in either House of Parliament. It was urged with great violence that his Majesty had done this with the Lords of his Bedchamber, and others, by which the question was carried; and it was imputed in particular to Earl Temple, that he had been very instrumental in this proceeding; which he and his friends defended as perfectly constitutional, even if the King had acted on such advice as was alleged; because a peer, as an hereditary councillor of the crown, had a right to approach the throne to suggest opinions on extraordinary occasions.

Measures of attack and defence were resorted to with great vehemence on both sides; the one charging the Ministers with a deliberate plan to destroy the very essence of the Constitution, by transferring to a party the power and influence which belonged only to the sovereign, by which they would be enabled to maintain themselves in office, however offensive their conduct might be to the King, to Parliament, or to the people. This ground, as before stated, was well founded. If the Bill had been carried Mr. Fox's power would have been established. He boasted, indeed, during the debates on the India bill, that he owed the consequence he had to the support of a number of great families and interests, and not to the crown.

On the other hand, the Ministers alleged that Mr. Pitt and his friends availed themselves of the dislike the King had to them, for their conduct during their short administration, (principally respecting the Prince of Wales,) to persuade his Majesty, by secret advice, to take steps for their removal, which they worked up with great industry.

The resignation of the Ministers having taken place, the formation of a new Administration became, of course, indispensibly necessary: in that there was great difficulty. All those who held office under the late Government were unavoidably excluded; so were Lord Shelburne and his immediate friends, with whom there had been no direct communication from the time of his Lordship's retirement.

These difficulties led Mr. Pitt, who was struggling under them, almost to despair. Lord Stafford, personally almost a stranger to him, had told me he thought Mr. Pitt was the only man who could extricate the country from its perilous situation; and he would therefore take office, if it should be thought his doing so would give strength to a Government to be formed; or he would give his best support to it without taking office,—much preferring the latter, for his own convenience. While these endeavours by Mr. Pitt and his friends were going on, the King remained in a state of the utmost anxiety. While the success of forming the new administration continued somewhat doubtful, his Majesty wrote the following note to Mr. Pitt:—

"On the edge of a precipice, every ray of hope affords some comfort. I have the utmost confidence that Lord Gower,[1] Lord Thurlow, the Duke of Richmond, and Mr. Pitt, will be able to fill up the several

[1] As Lord Gower here stands first on the list of the King's friends on whom he relied for the construction of a new cabinet, and as some of his letters will be introduced, it may be necessary to state a few circumstances which marked his accession to office. He was very much opposed to Fox's East India Bill, and when it was rejected, and the Whigs resigned, he offered his services to Mr. Pitt, with whom he had no personal acquaintance before, in any situation in which he could be useful. From his character and position he was appointed President of the Council; but he was so much above the ordinary meanness of pride, that in the following year he willingly descended from that high office to the inferior post of Lord Privy Seal, in order to accommodate Lord Camden, who having been Lord Chancellor, thought it derogatory to accept any but the highest office in the Council. Two years afterwards he was made a Marquis, and was much consulted by Mr. Pitt. His intimacy with Mr. Rose has been already shown.—ED.

offices; if that however fails, you know my determination. One o'clock will be quite agreeable to me."

[In the brief sketch of Mr. Rose's life, by his daughter, it may be observed that he is said to have owed his seat in the House of Commons, for the borough of Launceston, to the private friendship of the Duke of Northumberland, the grandfather of the present duke, and of his successor also. Of the first Duke's friendship there is no other evidence; but with the second he seems to have been on terms of great intimacy as long as he remained Lord Percy.

His letters to Mr. Rose were very numerous, and some extracts from the earliest of them are here given, which describe a season of remarkable severity and very unfavourable to health. A few of the others show his dissatisfaction with the Government, on account of the neglect with which he had been treated, and which certainly seems inexplicable, in the absence of all evidence as to the motives. His admiration of Mr. Pitt was great, and his determination to support him in the general election of 1784, was probably influenced by this feeling. In return for which, he seems to have thought himself at liberty to ask for various favours, some of which, it will be seen, were instantly granted, but not all; and hence arose the quarrel between him and Mr. Rose, which ended in the latter declining to be his nominee for Launceston. As it is of some importance to correct the mistakes of preceding historians, and to shew what erroneous conclusions may be drawn by those who are not admitted behind the curtain, to view the working of the machinery, it is worth while to notice, that Mr. Grenville writes thus to the Marquis of Buckingham:—

"Our cousin of Northumberland, has, I think, decidedly joined the independent party."—ED.]

LORD PERCY TO MR. ROSE.

"Stanwick, June 15th, 1792.

"DEAR SIR,

"I wish I had any information to send you from hence that could amuse you; but, except that our grounds are drowned with rain and chilled with cold, and that within this fortnight the hills to the west of us were covered with snow, I think we have nothing extraordinary. The season is more unhealthy in this neighbourhood than ever was known, owing to the unseasonable weather. No family is exempt from illness, whether rich or poor. A great number of the lower people here have died. Two clergymen, with whom I conversed the other day, assure me that they have buried more persons within this last fortnight than they have done for three years before. My family amongst the rest has not been free from sickness.

"Your's sincerely,
"PERCY."

LORD PERCY TO MR. ROSE.

"MY DEAR SIR,   "Stanwick, Sept. 26th, 1782.

"You will easily conceive my astonishment at that part of your letter, which mentions the intention of appointing Lord Faulconberg our *Custos Rotulorum*. What encouragement is there for any man of rank to exert himself in the service of his King and country, when the only reward he is likely to meet with is total neglect and inattention, and constantly to have the mortification of seeing every person, without either weight, consequence, or merit, preferred before him in every instance, both civil and military? I may without vanity assert, that there is not an officer in the army who has done his duty, in the line of his profession, with more zeal and attention than myself; and, in consequence of that, it is now fourteen years since I have received the smallest mark of approbation from his Majesty or his Ministers. You may depend upon it I shall mention nothing of this matter till I hear from you again. I beg you will be assured that I ever am, with the greatest truth,

"Yours most sincerely,
"PERCY."

LORD PERCY TO MR. ROSE.

"DEAR SIR,   "Stanwick, Oct. 6th, 1782.

"Many thanks to you for your kind attention in sending me any news which occurs; and particularly for your last good accounts from Gibraltar. I do trust that something will be done by Government for its gallant governor. The army want a spur; and now is the time for Lord S. to ingratiate himself effectually with his old profession. I protest I have neither private views nor private friendship to gratify, in urging some mark of approbation for General Elliot, for I have not the happiness to have any particular intimacy with him; but I wish well to my profession, and, after the shameful prostitution we have seen of military honours, I want merit for once to be rewarded; that the army may recover the spirit which they have almost quite lost; and may hope, for the future, that their services will meet with some encouragement and reward. As for myself, the event of every day confirms me still more and more in my idea of quitting the public service. With respect to the appointment of Lord F. the affair is now over, and I shall not give myself the trouble to think any more about it. I am very willing to believe Lord S. could not prevent it; indeed, I am sure of it, as you say so. Adieu, dear Sir, and be assured I ever am, with the greatest truth,

"Your most sincere friend,
"Percy."

LORD PERCY TO MR. ROSE.

*Stanwick, Oct. 31st, 1782.

"By the by, I see the papers announce an intention of sending Lord Cornwallis out to Command-in-Chief in India. I believe I have often told you my opinion of his Lordship. He is a worthy, honest, brave man; but more than all that is necessary to make a good general. I know him well; and I thought, since his last business in America, everybody else had known him also. One thing I will venture to foretell (and I beg you will remember it), that if this step is determined upon, he will lose his reputation—and we, our territories in that part of the world. He is as fit to Command-in-Chief as I am to be Prime Minister.

"I ever am, with the greatest truth,
"Yours most sincerely,
"PERCY."

LORD PERCY TO MR. ROSE.

"DEAR SIR, "Stanwick, Dec. 9th, 1782.

"I never thought that the pleasure of your acquaintance could ever have been of any disadvantage to me, but really the millions of applications I have, under the idea that you, or I, or both of us, are omnipotent, make me almost think the contrary. In short, it is ridiculous to conceive the number of letters, containing the most extravagant requests, which I receive by every post, founded on my intimacy with you, and the certainty that if I would solicit, and you would only speak, even the most absurd and preposterous demands would be complied with. Amongst this variety, I endeavour to select only such, to trouble you with, as I really think deserve to be noticed; and am ashamed of the continual trouble I give you on this head.

The occasion of my writing to you at present, is in consequence of a letter which I have received from the Rev. Mr. Nicholls, at Leicester. He is one of the unfortunate American sufferers, who have lost everything for their loyalty and attachment to this country. He is the child of misfortunes; having begun life with the prospect of an ample inheritance, in the island of Barbadoes, which was totally destroyed by the great fire at Bridgetown. Since this time he has been struggling with adversity."

[In the conclusion of the next letter Lord Percy renews his complaints of neglect; but at this time was so far from being discontented with the political state of the country that he was very much opposed to the schemes of the Reformers. Though Mr. Pitt was the person who had been propounding an extensive measure of Parliamentary Reform, the sentiments of both afterwards diverged in opposite directions.—ED.]

LORD PERCY TO MR. ROSE.

"Stanwick, Dec. 21st, 1789.

"DEAR SIR,

"With regard to my resignation, I can only say that fourteen years' unnoticed services have almost wearied me out. Especially as during that time, except for the three last years, I have paid an attention to my duty unequalled by any officer of the same rank in the army. And, to add still to my mortification, I am the only officer, who served in my rank from the commencement of the American war, to whom some particular mark of approbation has not been given. This, you must own, is not exactly the light in which a military man likes to be held out to his brother officers. Not feeling conscious that I deserve less than others who have served with me, some of whom are even my juniors, I confess I am not quite satisfied with such treatment. However, as I shall soon be in town, I shall at present take no immediate steps. Our Yorkshire meeting have drawn up a moderate petition to Parliament, in order, if possible, to take in the moderate men. I wish their resolutions had been as decent. As for myself, not wishing any alteration in our most excellent Constitution, I cannot approve of their proceedings, even though I am convinced that if they are carried into execution it will be the means of flinging the greatest weight into the aristocratical scale that ever was yet done. However, I hope I am too good a patriot ever to wish my own advantage to the prejudice of the public in general.

"I ever am, dear Sir,
"Your most sincere and much obliged friend,
"PERCY."

LORD PERCY TO MR. ROSE.

"Stanwick, Jan. 25th, 1783.

"DEAR SIR,

"You know I never had much hopes of success with respect to Johnston's business. The event will prove whether I judged right or not. To tell you the truth I have been so long used to the unmeaning professions of Ministers, that I am rather become a sceptic as to their sincerity. The great comfort, however, is that I do not want them; for, being always determined to live within my income, I trust I shall be ever independent. It is true, indeed, in the younger part of my life I was foolish enough to pant after military fame and reputation; but having lived to see the first honours of the profession prostituted to party purposes, and that whilst abilities and faithful services lay neglected, the loss of armies and empires met with the greatest rewards, I am, thank God, now most perfectly cured of my folly, and only wonder at my former blindness. I have, however, the comfort to reflect that I have acted my part in my profession like a good citizen and zealous servant.

"Yours, most sincerely,
"PERCY."

LORD PERCY TO MR. ROSE.

"Stanwick, Nov. 20th, 1783.
"DEAR SIR,

"The last post brought me your letter of the 22d, for which I return many thanks. I see with horror for this country the fatal effects that Mr. Fox's Bill will produce if it is carried; but surely you yourself must own that neither any party, nor my country itself, has any right again to expect exertions from me. When I went to America in 1774, I sacrificed for its sake every domestic ease and comfort that a mortal could enjoy; I devoted my poor abilities and my life to its service, and the only return I have ever met, is the most perfect indifference and neglect. Nay, you yourself know many instances in which I may almost any I have been treated with insult. All this surely ought to have taught me philosophy enough, to look with the most perfect indifference on every occurrence that may happen.

"I lament the blindness of the public, who prefer the tinselled show of oratory to the more substantial good qualities of the head and heart; but as it is out of my power to correct that blindness, I can only lament and despise their ignorance. I will, however, make one effort more (as far as lies in my power) to save them from destruction; thoroughly convinced, at the same time, that I shall meet with no thanks for any inconvenience I may put myself to on the occasion. If, therefore, the Bill should pass the House of Commons—and you will be kind enough to give me timely notice when it is expected to be debated in the House of Lords, I will set out for London to attend it, notwithstanding the inconvenience of travelling 500 miles at this time of the year (for I shall return the moment the business is decided). You will please to remember that the post is three days in coming down here, and that it comes to Stanwick only on the general post days, and that I shall be three days in going up. Adieu, dear Sir, and be assured I ever am,

"Yours most sincerely,
"Percy."

LORD PERCY TO MR. ROSE.

"Dear Sir,   "Stanwick, Dec. 25th, 1783.

"I have this instant received your letter, and cannot say I am grieved at the contents of it, for I am really angry. You knew what my opinion was from the beginning of this business:—that it should not be undertaken at all unless they were certain of being able to go through with it; and, in that case, that it should have been done directly, and a dissolution take place immediately. I am sure no House of Commons can be more against them than the present one, with which I can easily foresee that it will be impossible for them to go on. The only thing that can now be done is to form something like the following arrangement:—Mr. Pitt should be Minister and Secretary of State, Lord Gower first Lord of the Treasury, Thomas Pitt Chancellor of the Exchequer, Lord Stormont President of the Council, and Sir Joseph Yorke Secretary for the Foreign Affairs.— Depend upon it the high opinion in which he is held abroad, added to the perfect knowledge he must have of the political interests of the different powers in Europe, will greatly outbalance any slowness in negotiation which he may have acquired by his long residence in Holland. It is absolutely necessary to widen the bottom as much as possible; and, after all, if there is not energy enough in Government to put an effectual stop to illegal and improper violence, wherever it is found, and at all risks, no administration will be able to go on long. One hint I must give you in case of a dissolution; that is, that Mr. Drummond, the late Archbishop's son, is the most popular man in York; and if he is with you, and will stand, nobody can possibly oppose him to effect in that city. I am not at all sorry for the long journey

I have taken. The Bill was of such a nature that it
became every man, who wished well to this country,
to stand forward in opposition to it, exclusive of every
party motive whatever.

"I shall be much obliged to you if you will write
now and then, for I cannot help, I own, being very
anxious about the final issue of all this bustle.

"Yours, most sincerely,
"Percy."

[The great interest which the King felt in the election, on the issue of which the existence of Mr. Pitt's newly-formed administration depended, is shown by the minute information he collected about the politics of the candidates, and the care he took to have the most exact intelligence concerning the returns and the probabilities of success. In supplying him with this information, Mr. Rose seems to have been most assiduous.—ED.]

THE KING TO MR. ROSE.

"Queen's House, April 5, 1784,
"52 min. past 7, A.M.

"The comparative statement Mr. Rose has sent is very satisfactory. I desire he will continue it, as also the sending the list of returns as they arrive. I can correct his list, and make it still more favourable. Mr. Pultney, brought in by the D. of Rutland for Bramber, certainly should have stood amongst the Pros., and also Mr. Richard Howard, brother to Lord

Effingham, the new member for Steyning (by mistake called Pultney, by the post-master). I have reason to believe Mr. Penton, the member for Winchester, may at least be called hopeful; and, by his declaration at Cirencester, Mr. Blackwell.

"G. R."

THE KING TO MR. ROSE.

"Queen's House, April 4, 1784,
"20 min. past 9, A.M.

"I am much much pleased with the punctuality and expedition shown by Mr. Rose in transmitting the list of members returned, which seem on the whole more favourable than even the most zealous expected. I am sorry to hear Sir Richard Simmonds will probably be defeated at Hereford.

"The reason of my writing this morning is from a desire of knowing how the election at Cambridge has terminated, though I trust, Mr. Pitt must prove successful. "G. R."

CHAPTER II.

1786—1780.

CORRESPONDENCE WITH MR. EDEN, AFTERWARDS LORD AUCKLAND, RELATIVE TO HIS EXPECTED PEERAGE—THE KING'S ILLNESS—THE PRINCE OF WALES'S DEBTS.

[THE subject of Mr. Pitt's next letter is the commercial treaty with France, which Mr. Eden, afterwards Lord Auckland, was authorised to conclude. It was the first service he had rendered to Mr. Pitt, and laid the foundation for his employment in other missions, which enabled him to display his diplomatic skill, and contributed to build up his fortunes, the progress of which the ensuing correspondence explains.—ED.]

MR. PITT TO THE MARQUIS OF STAFFORD.

"Hollwood, Sunday, Aug. 27th, 1786.

"MY DEAR LORD,

"The papers which accompany this letter will show your Lordship the state of the French negotiation; and, as it seems drawing to a point, I am anxious to know your Lordship's sentiments upon it. On the different occasions in which this has been under consideration, I think we have been all agreed that the concessions in favour of France were such as we might very safely make; and we

certainly shall procure a most ample equivalent by
the admission of our manufactures on the terms
proposed. I flatter myself, therefore, that there
will be no objection to empowering Mr. Eden to
sign, if he and the French Ministers agree in the
manner we may expect from his last dispatch. Indeed
the advantage to be gained by this country seems to
me so great that I cannot help feeling impatient to
secure it.

"Colonel Cathcart has arrived from the Mauritius,
to which place he had been deputed by the Government
of Bengal, and has brought with him a provisional
treaty concluded with the French Governor-General
on the point of dispute which had arisen in India.
It seems to be a subject which will still require much
discussion, but, in the mean time, everything bears
the appearance of its being amicably settled.

"I am, with the greatest respect and esteem,
"My dear Lord,
"Your Lordship's most obedient and faithful servant,
"W. PITT."

THE MARQUIS OF STAFFORD TO MR. PITT.

"MY DEAR SIR,

"I have despatched the messenger back as
soon as it was possible, considering the voluminous
papers that were to be read by the Chancellor and
me, especially as a public day here took place the day
after the messenger's arrival on the night preceding.
I am extremely sorry to find that though the affairs

of Holland are now more likely to come to a point than when I quitted London, yet that point is not of the most eligible sort—an amicable adjustment of the business. France seems to me to drive her friends in that country to an unaccountable extremity, unless she foresees at a distance some additional aid to her efforts there. I am sorry to find that we are at last forced to take that disagreeable step of hiring troops upon the Continent, which will eventually embark us further than we at first intended, and will, I am afraid, be an unpopular measure in this country. France could certainly have prevailed upon Holland to have made submission to Prussia for the insult offered to that monarch's sister, which would probably have been sufficient in the outset of that business. She must, therefore, have had some reasons for not advising that measure. May it not be to draw off the Prussian forces from the side of Silesia to favour the Emperor, if he chooses the opportunity; or to use the Emperor's forces that are drawn to the Netherlands, if the Brabantine troubles should subside?

"These may be foolish conjectures at a distance, and I must own that having thought originally that it would have been unpardonable in this country to allow France to avail herself of the powers and faculties of that Republic against England in a future war, and stand by indifferent spectators, so I at present see *vestigia nulla retrorsum;* and if 1. W. F. must go, he must go, though I wish our assistance to the Republic could have been restrained to pecuniary aids."

[The uneasiness occasioned by the information sent by Mr. Eden (our Minister at the Hague), in August, 1787, though not so alarming as that which arrived in the following month, was sufficient to call for some demonstration in favour of the established order of things at the Hague; and Mr. Pitt having determined to make it, sought for the approbation of his colleagues. It was a constant feature of his policy to preserve or restore the balance of power in Europe, to hire foreign mercenaries to be placed under our own command, or to subsidize one power against another. The germ of this policy was developed in both ways on this occasion, when the fermentation of revolutionary principles threatened the subversion of all constituted authorities, and even the republic of Holland was not republican enough. A timely demonstration of resistance, it was hoped, might deter France from lending her aid to the malcontents. It will be seen that the event justified the calculation, and the danger was staved off for a time by the interposition of a Prussian army. But Lord Stafford was doubtless right in his anticipation, that the employment of foreign levies would be unpopular in this country. The measure has always been viewed with considerable jealousy, however great might be the necessity and the advantage.—Ed.]

Mr. Pitt to the Marquis of Stafford.

"My dear Lord,   "Downing Street, Aug. 24th, 1787.

"I have postponed troubling you on the subject of what is passing on the Continent, because it seemed each day likely that the situation would draw more to a point. The last communications from Prussia, and what is now going on in Holland, seem to have that effect. The despatches sent herewith will explain fully to your Lordship the actual situation. The object which you long ago wished for, of Prussia being completely embarked, appears now to be fully attained. We seem, therefore, to have no choice left but to encourage that power to proceed, by showing a readiness to give our support, if necessary. At the same time I have little doubt that by making our conduct towards France temperate as well as firm, we may avoid extremities and bring the business to a better issue than could have been expected.

"As the King of Prussia's marching will probably be followed by the assembly of a French army, it seems impossible for us to do less than to endeavour to secure German troops, though I hope we shall have no occasion to use them. The measures taken in Holland seem also to require farther pecuniary assistance to enable our friends to meet them; and what is spent in this way, for the purpose of prevention, will in the end, I hope, be good economy. I regret much the distance of your Lordship and the Chancellor; but I trust you will approve of the steps we have recommended under circumstances which would not well admit of delay.

  " Believe me, My dear Lord,
   " Most sincerely and faithfully yours,
           " W. PITT."
" Marquis of Stafford."

[The following letter was written in consequence of some information received from Paris, which prepared Mr. Pitt for a notification made to the English Court, at a later hour on the same day, by the Court of France, threatening to take part with the Dutch democrats against the Stadtholder. Mr. Pitt replied that, in that case, England would take part with the Stadtholder. Warlike preparations were made on both sides, and hostilities seemed to be imminent, when the danger was averted by the King of Prussia throwing his sword into the scale of his brother-in-law. The Duke of Brunswick was sent with an army to his assistance, and soon overran the United Provinces, and brought them back to their allegiance. France was glad enough to back out of such a hopeless quarrel; and in November disavowed the intentions which in September she had announced. The only light which this letter throws upon the transaction is the perfect confidence in the soundness of Mr. Rose's judgment, which Pitt must have felt when he summoned him instantly to his aid on a political subject of great importance, with which, as Secretary to the Treasury, he had nothing whatever to do.—ED.]

Mr. PITT TO Mr. ROSE.

"DEAR ROSE, [*Secret.*]

"Despatches came late last night from Eden, which look very serious. As much will have to be done in a short time, I do not scruple to beg you to come up as soon as possible, but occasioning as little observation as you can.

"Ever yours,

"W. P."

"Hollwood, Sept. 10th, 1787. 9 A.M."

[The early information which Mr. Eden seems to have communicated to the Government on this occasion was, no doubt, one of those services for which, in the two next letters, he claims a reward which most persons in these days will think more than commensurate with the duties performed. He was a shrewd, ambitious politician, with a very inflated opinion, not only of his importance to the Government, but of his merits in the eyes of the world at large. A remarkable confirmation of Walpole's satirical axiom, that every man in the British Legislature had his price; for Pitt thought him worth purchasing. And, though he had previously been engaged in active opposition to him up to the session of 1785, when he censured the Minister's plans, and denied the accuracy of his statements, yet he evinced so much insight into matters of finance and trade, that no pains were spared to secure his co-operation. He endeavoured to bargain for the office of Speaker, but to that Pitt could not consent. It was then proposed to create a new place for him, as Superintendent of the collection of the Revenue; but that scheme was also abandoned. At last it was resolved to send him to Paris, in January, 1786, not as an ambassador, though he seems in his argument to assume that dignity (for the Duke of Dorset was the ambassador), but as an envoy to negotiate a commercial treaty with France, which he accomplished very satisfactorily in September 1786, and more completely in January 1787. It was in that capacity he was remaining at Paris, and being more expert than the ambassador in diplomacy, supplied Mr. Pitt with useful information. He did not succeed immediately in the object which he had so much at heart, but probably strengthened his claims by similar services, first at Madrid, and afterwards at the Hague; for in the following year he obtained an Irish peerage, and, in 1793, the reward which he most of all coveted, and for which he argued with so much dexterity,—an English peerage. But the third letter shows the truth of the proverb, that "Hope deferred maketh the heart sick." When he entered on the scene of his labours in Spain, he could no longer contain his ill-humour at the delay, and it was necessary to pacify him with the Irish peerage, though it was only like throwing a tub to the whale.

The Duke of Buckingham gives some additional particulars of his claims upon Pitt, in chronicling these transactions. The commercial treaty with France, curiously enough, was negotiated by Mr. Eden, who had held the office of Vice-Treasurer of Ireland, under the coalition, and who was the first person to break away from that heterogeneous confederacy, and ally himself with Mr. Pitt. His defection was the more memorable from the fact that the coalition is said to have originated with him. At all events he divides the credit of the project with Mr. Burke. Distinguished by his zeal and activity, he was soon afterwards raised to the peerage under the title of Baron Auckland.—Ed.]

Mr. Eden to Mr. Rose.

"Paris, January 27th, 1788.

"My dear Sir,

"I am deeply and cordially sensible of the kindness with which you invite me to tell you freely what mark of approbation of my public service I alluded to in my late letter to Mr. Pitt. I will profit by it to unbosom myself in confidence upon the subject. If I had had any settled and specific ideas respecting it, I would have expressed them long ago; but I have only general or confused notions.

"There is not, I believe, any party or description of political observers in Europe, who do not think and say that my situation here has eventually been instrumental in obtaining great and brilliant advantages for England. I fairly and honestly give the principal merit to Mr. Pitt's government, and in truth to his personal communications and exertions; but I fairly and justly feel at the same time, that the predicament in which it places me, however subordinate in point of deserts, is at the moment not inconsiderable in the eyes of Europe. I feel also that his credit will receive no diminution by my being ostensibly distinguished as the instrument selected by him (such was the wise and just policy of his father with regard to those whom he employed); and I at least have the merit of having exerted a most indefatigable zeal and integrity in his service, with an activity and perseverance which those only can conceive who have been witnesses of it, and to whose despatches and testimony to every court in Europe I am willing to refer.

"Lastly, I feel that if the moment is lost, it may be irrecoverably lost. Still, however, you will reply, 'What is it you seek?' and there is my embarrassment. Perhaps I ought to answer, I can only regret that the pretension is not seen by Government in the same light as it is seen by me; and even by some who profess political enmity to me, but who tell me, generously and without scruple, to make the best use of the crisis in which I find myself. If government had the same sentiment respecting me, instead of my being sent to be buried (perhaps in all senses), in a distant part of the globe, ideas would have occurred which I am unable to form, because I have not sufficient information. Still you ask me, ' What are my own ideas?' and I am unable to answer you. Shall I say an English peerage? I feel that I have no chance of obtaining it, if I were to look towards it, and if I were sure that I ought to look towards it. At the same time I must assert that my pretensions in point of services are at least equal to any of the professional pretensions which in my experience have led to peerages. In point of family I have no difficulty; for mine has been opulent and respectable upon the same spot above three hundred years, and is intermarried also into all the first families. But I am sensible that it is bad policy for the country to multiply peers who have not fortunes, nor the prospect of fortunes, to maintain the dignity. Shall I say an Irish peerage?—Certainly, if I thought it expedient to accept it, I should not think it too much to ask. I have pretensions in Ireland, exclusive of all other claims. I framed and established their National Bank; I moved the Habeas Corpus, &c. &c. &c. &c.; and I have the friendship and almost the attachment of all the leading people of that country.

"The ancient seat of my family, and still in their possession, is Auckland; and Lord Auckland, of Ireland, would sound better as ambassador to his Catholic Majesty, than plain Monsieur. But this would give all the inconveniences of the peerage to my son, without any of the advantages; and the only benefit of it would be that it affords me some security for provision against events, instead of leaving me without any. Shall I say the Red Ribbon? To tell you the truth,—though I am in a career where every minister, even in the second and third order, even poor Saxony, Denmark, Wirtemberg, &c., except the Duke of Dorset and myself, is covered with stars and decorations, and still more in Spain than here,— I look forwards to passing fifteen or twenty years of my life at Beckenham, and such gew-gaws will make a laughable appearance in my shrubbery. Nor could this commonest of all the orders, ever have been an object to me unless it had come in some particular mode and moment calculated to give credit to it. By the by, in constituting the Irish order, it would in many points of view have been useful if two had been appropriated to the foreign ambassadors, and would have given to Ireland an ostensible as well as a real connexion with foreign politics.

"Last of all, there remained merely the finding and grabbing some respectable office for life; and I discovered long ago, that such a speculation was not to be encouraged. Here then we come to the point from which we set out. I feel that I am losing a moment most important to me, and I should have hoped, not unacceptable to Mr. Pitt; but I can only say so, and I can say nothing further; 'si quid novisti rectius istis candidus imperti.'

"There is nothing new here. I inclose an impudent piece of sedition, as an *échantillon* of the liberty of the French press.

"I happened yesterday at dinner to meet a Comte de Châteauvieux, a most respectable Swiss, who talked of your son with all the affection and cordiality that you could have done, and told us many little anecdotes respecting the young man's character and conduct at Geneva, which do great credit to him.

"I am, my dear Sir,
"Ever most sincerely yours,
"WILLIAM EDEN."

MR. EDEN TO MR. ROSE.

[*Private.*]

"Paris, Feb. 21st, 1788.

"MY DEAR SIR,—

"I will not abuse your friendship and indulgence by writing more than seems necessary in reply to your last. It must be unpleasant to you, and troublesome to Mr. Pitt, and I need not add that it is painful to me to prolong our present discussion. You tell me, however, 'that I ought to communicate freely as the only chance of enabling those who wish well to me to do good.' I feel the force of this, and in truth I have no reserves as to any part of the subject in question. It is fair, and reasonable, and honourable, (in every sense of the word) that I should seek to elevate myself and my family upon the ground of public services, as far as all candid observers may think those services entitled to recompense from the King and from the public; and I certainly am at the crisis where, if I receive no mark of approbation, I must never expect to receive any. For I am now quitting the French mission, and am entering into a distinct and distant career, in the course of which the impression of what has passed will gradually be superseded by new events, and will be weakened, obliterated, and in effect forgotten.

"It is not an answer to this to tell me that at the close of my embassies I shall be entitled to the usual retirement. If I live to that day I feel that such a retirement would be a just expectation, even if I had no other pretensions than other ambassadors have had (and have), who have gone through the same career inoffensively and inefficiently. In short, I consider it as the prospect of a retreat at which I may possibly never arrive; but which the justice of my sovereign and the general sense of mankind would of course open to any person who had filled offices of such responsibility as I have done and shall have done. Turning, therefore, from that prospect as a distant and unconnected speculation, I consider myself as having two years ago undertaken a public enterprise of great importance, risk, and difficulty. It is known that under Mr. Pitt's instructions I accomplished it most successfully. It is also known to have been followed by several other services equally signal and successful, and of essential consequence; and though I was only the fortunate instrument in able hands, Mr. Pitt is too classical in his sentiments to throw aside with disregard the weapon which he used in the field of his victories, and to let it rust and waste forgotten in a corner.

"Here then I place my pretensions; and I consider the present moment as the properest, and indeed the only one, for urging them. Under this impression I 'communicate freely' the hope entertained by me, that my arrival at the Court of Madrid may be preceded or accompanied by some ostensible testimony that my conduct and exertions in the French mission have been honoured with approbation. I rest that hope on the reasonings which I have stated. Yet I might add, that such a testimony, exclusive of its importance to me personally, would be ministerially useful at the high-minded Court to which I am going; that it would become farther useful if I am to pursue this line of foreign service, and that it is an underrating of the foreign politics of the last two years if the epoch is to pass undistinguished by any mark of favour.

"Your letter has fairly discussed all the modes which occur. You state, and I cannot dispute it, that at present Mr. Pitt has no means of giving an office for life. Ought I to seek for my son the second reversion of a Tellership? Would it be worth seeking (subject, of course, to the resignation of the pension)—would it be attainable? Upon the chapter of ribbons, I am sure you feel with me, that a mere red ribbon is not what I ought to have or accept. It was honourable to the late Sir Thos. Wroughton, at the Court of Stockholm, and to Sir Horace Mann, at Florence. It was even a decoration to my friend and predecessor, Lord Grantham, because he supported it with his peerage, and such exterior circumstances are not indifferent in a foreign Court. But if I were to take it without any

other distinction, it certainly would be considered as
a pendant or companion to the Duke of Dorset's blue
ribbon, and would not add credit.

"Next, you remark (and I feel the justice of it), that
as none of the ribbons of the order of St. Patrick were
originally reserved for Englishmen, it would not easily
be practicable now to give one, and, at all events, not
without the peerage. Thus we seem to be reduced to
the single consideration of the peerage, and I acknowledge, on the first view of it, that if I should not live to
see my son established in life, it might become an
incumbrance to him. But the question is whether,
subject to that objection, this pursuit of the peerage is
not preferable to relinquishing all pursuits whatever;
for we agree that there are no other opened to me.
Reduced to this point, and I feel that I am reduced to
it, I incline to think that I ought to seek the English
peerage; or even, in the supposition of its not being
given, the Irish one. I have thought much and coolly
upon the subject. After a residence of two years in a
Court so constituted as that of France, it is possible
that my English ideas on such a point may be
erroneous. But proceeding as I am from this Court
to a considerable embassy, I feel it better to have
even the Irish peerage (under the presumption of not
obtaining the other), than to go without any mark of
the King's favour. Though in some respects it might
prove inconvenient to my family, in others it would
be advantageous, and at all events honourable.

"Having now stated explicitly and unreservedly all
that occurs, I leave it in your hands. I have not yet

mentioned the subject to any other person, not even
to the Archbishop of Canterbury, because, whatever
may be the result, I should be sorry to give a colour to
the surmise that I shall feel myself treated by Mr.
Pitt otherwise than with justice, friendship, and even
favour. Such a surmise would be grating and injurious
to me, whatever may be the event. I shall now, however, in consequence of your suggestion, write in
confidence to the Archbishop, and state to him the
substance of what has passed between us; and if anything should arise respecting me, on which Mr. Pitt
might have the goodness, either through you or personally, to confer with the Archbishop, his affection and
judgment will furnish the best aid that I can have.

"As I take leave on Tuesday next, and shall go
from Paris in about three weeks, you will allow me to
conclude by recommending this letter to an early
attention.

"I am, dear Sir,
Most sincerely yours,
WM. EDEN."

MR. EDEN TO MR. ROSE.

"St. Ildefonso, Sept. 25th, 1788.

"MY DEAR SIR,

"I wrote fully to you a few days ago, by a servant whom I had occasion to dispatch to England, and
who will probably arrive about the first of October.
I have already requested that what was there said
may be considered as addressed to the owner of Hollwood; and this saves the pain of writing to him, in

consequence of the friendly letter which arrived this day from you at the same time with the news of certain promotions.

"In writing thus by the post, though on matters merely private, some obscurity of expression must be adopted. Certainly the person who feels himself so sincerely sensible of your kindness would have reason to complain, not only of a want of friendship in the owner of Hollwood, but he might carry his complaints beyond that want. It is not easy to forget by what authority he was informed in September, 1786, of its 'being the first object of anxiety to communicate some distinguishing mark of royal approbation' for services which, in point both of brilliancy and solidity, were afterwards multiplied tenfold, and which remain not only unacknowledged, but effectively depreciated in the eyes of the world, by ostensible marks of attention to all who acted subordinate parts in the several businesses. Neither is it easy to forget by what authority 'those services were formally and repeatedly acknowledged as essential, both politically and commercially.' Nor, lastly, let it escape recollection, that when the English peerage (for the Irish is utterly out of the question) was talked of, it was answered, 'that whatever might be the wish, there were insurmountable objections which prevented any from being given to any person.'

"In short, it is not possible for your friend to suppose that those for whom he continues to feel both respect and affection, and to whose fair conduct he committed his whole public existence, implicitly and unreservedly, are capable of acting towards him unkindly, unjustly, and ungenerously. He must, however, presume that there is elsewhere an ill-will of a superior influence which prevails against him; and under that construction, all that is left for him to request is, that he may be withdrawn to privacy as speedily and with as little éclat as possible. When it is asked whether in the meantime, and even before that termination, it would be agreeable to him to have the security fixed, though upon the 4½ per cents.; there can be no doubt that that security should have been fixed long ago in some shape or other, and for life; nor is it easy to persuade one who knows something of the nature and resources of Government, that means were wanting, even without having recourse to pensions. But that point your friend never urged; it was superseded by higher pretensions, which have now been treated as 'the baseless fabric of a vision.'

"His amusement for some weeks to come will be to receive from those who foretold, near three years ago, what now happens to him, such paragraphs as the inclosed.

"Believe me, my dear Sir,
"Ever most sincerely yours."

[Mr. Eden's praise of young Rose (afterwards Sir George Rose, and for many years representative of our Court at Berlin), on the Report of the Count de Châteauvieux, in the first of his letters, may very fitly be accompanied by an earlier testimony in his favour from the principal of St. John's, while he was an undergraduate at Cambridge, not only on account of the services which he himself performed for his country, but still more because he was the father of one who has attained so much distinction both at Constantinople and in Central India, Sir Hugh Rose. The parentage of an eminent man is not a matter of indifference to his countrymen — *Nec imbellem feroces progenerant aquilæ columbam.*—ED.]

MR. WOOD, PRINCIPAL OF ST. JOHN'S, CAMBRIDGE, TO MR. ROSE.

"St. John's, June, 20th, 1791.

"DEAR SIR,

"I will give you my opinion of Mr. G. Rose with great pleasure, and from the plainness with which I give it, judge of my sincerity. I think his abilities very considerable; at our examinations he has always been ranked in the first class, though I am convinced he has never given his mind fully to mathematics, or paid that attention to them he will to any subject which accords more with his inclination. I am in doubt whether he will make a good speaker. He does not want quickness of conception, but he seems not to have the art of arranging his ideas to the greatest advantage. I think I can perceive that in any sudden emergency he will judge at once what line of conduct he ought to pursue, and act with firmness upon that judgment. In his conduct, he has been much more manly than young men of his age usually are, and I have never heard him spoken of in this respect but with approbation. His goodness of heart (in that I cannot be deceived) is such as I should wish in my most intimate friend. At present he intends to read those subjects which will prepare him for the Senate House Examination, and I trust he will persevere in this resolution.

"I am, dear Sir,
"Your most obedient humble servant,
"JAMES WOOD."

"DEAR SIR, "St. John's, Dec. 4th, 1791.

"From every account I have heard of your son's Act, it appears that he has exceeded not only his own modest expectations, but the expectations of all his friends. I have just called upon the Moderator who presided at the disputation. I am happy to add his testimony in your son's favour. You will easily conceive that I am greatly pleased with the credit he has gained on this occasion, but I am much more so to be convinced that, so far from wanting abilities, he is possessed of great powers of mind. The preparation for this exercise was short. He had a Latin dissertation to write upon one of the subjects, and I know he had not taken the least trouble or thought about the questions he had to defend, before he received the exercise from the Moderator. Your worthy friend, the Bishop of Lincoln, will be able to tell you pretty exactly how he kept this act, if you inform him that the mark in the Moderator's book is (A).

left in suspense. The conclusion, however, of the provisional treaty at Loo, on which the alliance since concluded was founded, has considerably strengthened his former claim to distinction, and so many circumstances have concurred to make him extremely anxious for its not being deferred, that notwithstanding the awkwardness of having Sir Joseph Yorke the companion of his honours, I have been induced to renew the request, even with that condition coupled with it, and both are to be gratified.

"Our accounts from India of the Chev^r de Conway's return from Trincomalé, without having done anything, and of all being quiet in that quarter, are very satisfactory. The state of France, whatever else it may produce, seems to promise us more than ever a considerable respite from any dangerous projects, and there seems scarce any thing for us to regret on our own account in the condition of foreign countries, except the danger that the King of Sweden may suffer too severely for his kindness. I conclude you are returned by this time to Trentham. I hope Lady Stafford has found benefit by Scarborough, and that both she and your Lordship are perfectly well. My holidays have not yet commenced, so I am obliged to give up the prospect of my northern excursion, and with it the pleasure of accepting your obliging invitation.

"I am, my dear Lord,
"With the greatest regard and esteem,
"Faithfully and sincerely yours,
"W. Pitt."

[In the years 1788 and 1789 two events occurred of great domestic importance (of which, however, no great notice is taken in this correspondence), the King's illness, and the payment of the Prince of Wales's debts by a grant of Parliament. With respect to the former, Mr. Rose has preserved a few curious particulars of the conduct of some of the great actors on the political stage at that crisis, in which Mr. Pitt's straightforward character shows to great advantage. In Gifford's "Life of Pitt" it is stated, that the first symptoms of the King's illness appeared on the 12th of June, and, on the 24th of that month, the derangement of his mind was very visible at the levee.—ED.]

MR. ROSE'S DIARY RESUMED.

Early in October, the King was taken suddenly ill with spasms in his stomach, and suffered much for a few days.

On the 10th, his Majesty was at the levee, in order to discountenance the reports, which were circulated industriously, of his being in danger; particularly as there were speculations on the circumstance of Sir G. Baker's attendance. After which he continued unwell, and incapable of reading papers of business. No dispatches were sent to Windsor, nor even warrants to sign, for several days, when five or six warrants were sent, which were the last. Mr. Pitt saw him at Kew, and was with him three hours and forty minutes, both on their legs the whole time.

His Majesty went to Windsor on Saturday the 25th of October, and on the 5th of November he showed strong symptoms of a disordered understanding. The first decided manifestations were at dinner, on addressing himself to the Duke of York, relative to a murder. Between the 5th and the 9th, the King was thought in great danger of dying, the fever very high; but on James's powders being administered, that was got under, leaving the delirium, which continued with little alteration during the remainder of the month. He was never violent or outrageous; wandering in his discourse exceedingly, but talking coherently on the subjects to which he wandered, with intervals quite rational though of short duration.

On the 6th, the Chancellor went to Windsor, and dined and supped with the Prince of Wales. The avowed purpose of their meeting was to consider the mode of treating his Majesty, as he had been somewhat ungovernable during the night.

On the 12th, Mr. Pitt saw his Royal Highness, and had much conversation with him, chiefly on general subjects; but Mr. Pitt stated that on the meeting of the two Houses at the time to which they were prorogued, in the week following, he meant to propose an adjournment for a fortnight, to which his Royal Highness replied, 'No objection could arise to that from any one.' He expressed a wish to have further conversation with Mr. Pitt before the Houses should meet.

Mr. Pitt went again to Windsor on the 15th, with the Duke of Richmond, and saw the Prince of Wales, but the conversation was quite general.

On the 17th, Mr. Pitt went again to Windsor for the purpose of stating exactly to his Royal Highness what he intended doing on the meeting of the House of Commons; but his Royal Highness declined seeing him.

During this time there had been much conversation between his Royal Highness and Mr. Sheridan, chiefly through third persons; but one evening Mr. Sheridan, Mr. Payne,[1] and Mrs. Fitzherbert went to the Prince at Bagshot.

On the 23d Mr. Pitt went to Windsor for the purpose of effecting Dr. Addington's[2] seeing the King, and, on the 24th, received a letter from Lady Courtoun,[3] acquainting him that the Queen would take measures first, if the Duke of Montagu, Lord Aylesbury and himself would make it their joint request, which was done accordingly;[4] and, on the 25th, Mr. Pitt went to Windsor to arrange the matter, and it was settled that Dr. Addington should see the King the next day. On the same day (the 25th) the Prince of Wales sent to know if Mr. Pitt had anything to propose to him, which was answered respectfully in the negative. On the 25th, the Chancellor also was at Windsor, and kept late there, in company most of the time with the physicians, without coming to any precise point. On his return to town at night,

[1] Captain, afterwards Admiral Payne.
[2] Lord Sidmouth's father, who had been the late great Earl of Chatham's physician.
[3] Wife of Lord Courtoun, the Queen's chamberlain, and also her private friend.
[4] Mr. Fox arrived on the 24th, in nine days, from Bologna.

he came to Mr. Pitt's, in Downing-Street, where I was.

On the 26th, at night, or rather at half-past one in the morning of the 27th, Mr. Pitt was waked with a letter from the Chancellor, summoning the Cabinet to meet at Windsor, by command of the Prince, on that day (the 26th). The servant who ought to have carried the letter at nine in the evening, neglected it, and the one who came with it at the before-mentioned late hour, being asked whether the Chancellor was then up, replied, Yes, and that Mr. Fox was with him; a fact which his Lordship had not noticed. The next day when the Cabinet met at Windsor,[1] the members were long in deliberation, principally about moving the King to Kew. Previous to their meeting, the Chancellor had been with the Prince of Wales; and when all the rest of the confidential servants of the Crown went to Salt Hill to dinner, his Lordship returned to the Prince's apartments, where he had refreshments provided for him, the Prince sitting with him, having previously dined. Most of the Cabinet slept at Salt Hill. Mr. Pitt returned to town late on the 29th. He did not dine with the Master of the Rolls, but was at a Cabinet again at Lord Carmarthen's office at eight in the evening.

In the course of that meeting many inquiries were made by the Lords as to whether any one knew if Mr. Fox had seen the Prince of Wales, or held any

---

[1] Mr. Fox came straight from Saint Anne's Hill to the Chancellor's, and found that the Prince of Wales and Mr. Sheridan had been a long while with him.

communication with him, or if any one present knew anything about him;—of all which the Chancellor, amongst others, professed perfect ignorance. He even asked if anybody knew the colour of Mr. Fox's chaise, in order to form a guess from them whether it had been seen on the road to Windsor. Mr. Pitt desired to ascertain the opinions of the members of the Cabinet respecting the propriety or expediency of joining the opposition, if it should be in their choice, under any circumstances whatever. He put the question directly to the Chancellor, who said he considered it an abstract question, and could not answer it distinctly. Mr. Pitt said it was a plain question,—Would his Lordship join with the opposite party under any circumstances? to which he would give no answer. Other members, by their silence, more than anything else, left an impression on Mr. Pitt's mind that they were impressed with an idea that a junction of some sort might be expedient for the country, but his own determination was fixed beyond all possibility of being shaken—not to entertain the idea of a junction at all. No determination taken yet, though the subject was much discussed, whether on the meeting of the Houses on the 4th of next month, any proposition should be made for seating a Government.

On the 28th and 29th, Mr. Pitt saw the King at Windsor. His Majesty uncommonly kind in his manner; had great pleasure in seeing him; talked of matters which he had discussed with him in their last meeting before his Majesty was ill, but wandered incessantly from one subject to another.

On the 20th, his Majesty came from Windsor to Kew in his coach with three equerries.

On the 30th, the Chancellor saw his Majesty, by his Lordship's own desire, but left him very suddenly.

December 1st.—The Cabinet dined at the Marquis of Stafford's, for the purpose of further deliberating whether to proceed to the consideration of settling a temporary Government or not on the 4th,—when the Houses met, pursuant to their adjournment.

[During all this time, and the next three months, Mr. Pitt kept steadily in view the personal interests of the King. For this purpose all the restrictions on the exercise of the Regent's authority were introduced into the Bill proposed to Parliament, so that, in the event of the King recovering, he might not find the whole system of his Government overthrown by the rashness of unprincipled men. And for the same reason Mr. Pitt resisted the proposal to form a junction with the Whig party. For though it might have ensured him a longer continuance in office, and he knew, if he rejected it, the first exercise of the Regent's power would be to turn him out, yet he would not expose his sovereign to the pain, on his recovery, of seeing a coalition between his friends and enemies, so contrary to all his feelings.

Notwithstanding the slight symptoms which heralded the approaching disease, the King appeared in public and moved about till the month of November; and it was not till the fifth, that it assumed an alarming appearance. As soon as Mr. Pitt received the intelligence, he immediately imparted it to Lord Stafford in the following letter, and in another, four months afterwards, addressed to his son Lord Gower, requested him to move the address of congratulation in the House of Commons, on the King's recovery.—Ed.]

MR. PITT TO THE MARQUIS OF STAFFORD.

[*Secret.*]

"Grosvenor Square, Nov. 6th, 1788, 6 P.M.

" MY DEAR LORD,

" I write from Lord Carmarthen's, having just had an account from Windsor, by which I learn that the King's disorder, which has for some days given us much uneasiness, has within a few hours taken so serious a turn, that I think myself obliged to lose no time in apprising your Lordship of it.

" The accounts are sent under considerable alarm, and therefore do not state the symptoms very precisely; but, from what I learn, there is too much reason to fear that they proceed from a fever which has settled on the brain, and which may produce immediate danger to His Majesty's life. You will easily conceive the pain I suffer, in being obliged to send your Lordship this intelligence; but as you may probably think it right, under such circumstances, to be on the spot as soon as possible, I thought no time should be lost in letting you know the situation.

"I am, with great regard, my dear Lord,
"Your obedient and faithful Servant,
"W. PITT."

"Marquis of Stafford."

MR. PITT TO EARL GOWER.

"Downing Street, Friday, March 6th, 1789.

"MY DEAR LORD,

"Under the peculiar circumstances of the speech that is to be made on Tuesday by the Commissioners appointed to hold the Parliament, which will announce the happy event of his Majesty's recovery, I cannot help expressing a wish, that your Lordship would undertake to move the Address to be proposed in the House of Commons. The nature of the occasion will, I hope, justify my troubling you with this request, and it will afford me on every account particular satisfaction, that the first step previous to our entering again on public business should be brought forward with so much advantage. I shall be extremely happy if your Lordship will permit me to take an early opportunity of communicating to you the particulars of the Speech. I have the honour to be,
"My dear Lord,
"Your Lordship's most obedient and faithful Servant,
"W. PITT."

"Earl Gower."

[Miss Rose has preserved the following particulars of the occurrences of that interesting period not mentioned by her father.—ED.]

1788. The King stopped at Kew on his way from Windsor to London; ate a pear, got his shoes and stockings wet, and did not change them . . . . Sometimes he talked rationally, which continued through every return of his illnesses. Dr. Baillie told us, that in the last, there was no sign of failure of intellect; that he always thought and reasoned correctly, though on certain points under erroneous impressions; and that if once the diseased impression was removed, the mind would act with its former power.

Sir William Grant, the Master of the Rolls, repeated the same thing, giving two instances. He said, the King's insanity was on two points; one that all marriages would soon be dissolved by Act of Parliament; the other that his Hanoverian dominion was restored, and that he was shortly to go there.

The physicians attended in rotation. Dr. Halifax had been some time absent, and returned to his attendance, when the Commissioners made their usual visit. To engage the King in conversation, some one said, "Dr. Halifax is returned; he has lately been in Dorsetshire." The King inquired for many residents there, remembering the members of their families as agreeing or not agreeing with Dr. Halifax's report. At last he mentioned the family of the Deputy Judge Advocate. The King said, "When I go to Hanover, Mr. —— must go with me." "Why so, Sir?"

"Because the Deputy Judge Advocate must be with me to correspond with the Judge Advocate, who cannot leave England, and he must have a direct official correspondence with me."

No one present was aware of that but himself. If Hanover had been restored during his life and insanity, his reasoning would have been erroneously true. The other instance was, on being asked if he would like to hear news, he replied, "any common occurrences, marriages, deaths, &c. &c." (he always avoided the subject of politics or official concerns, except as to Hanover). Amongst the news of the day was the almost sudden death of the Marchioness of Buckingham. He said, "He was very sorry for it, she was a very good woman, though a Roman Catholic." He expressed great regret for the Marquis, saying, "that he believed if she had lived till the marriages were dissolved, he would have desired to renew his. By-the-by," he added, "I do not think many of my friends would do so."

Lord Eldon, in his "Recollections," states that he did not believe Lord Thurlow had any communication with the opposition at the time of the Regency !!! He must have known it from those he afterwards lived with. He subsequently states that he did not know the cause of his dismissal from office; though he proves at least the expediency of it, stating that Lord Thurlow said that he could not blame Mr. Pitt, as he would have done the same by Mr. Pitt if he could. Assuredly Lord Thurlow, whatever was his motive, provoked it, but worked less on Mr. Pitt's temper than on Lord Grenville's, who was then leader on the

side of Government, in the House of Lords. Lord
Thurlow continually impeded, and at last treated him
with insolence. Lord Grenville was speaking; Lord
Thurlow rose from the Woolsack, and addressed the
House, "Is it your Lordships' pleasure to adjourn?"
Lord Grenville continued to speak, merely waving
his hand. Lord Thurlow repeated the question,
and Lord Grenville his sign of hearing and disregard-
ing it, without noticing it in words. My brother
William, then reading Clerk, came to us as soon as
the House adjourned, and described the scene. We
learned from my father that Lord Grenville went from
the House of Lords to Mr. Pitt, and told him, that if
Lord Thurlow continued Chancellor, he must resign
his office. Mr. Pitt acquainted the King with the
whole, and he at once acceded to the dismissal. Next
day the King came in from Windsor full of the surrender of Seringapatam, and rode gaily through the
Park.

Mr. Pitt, quite convinced that if Fox had carried
the India Bill, he would have the Government entirely in his own hands, and the King be a cypher,
had resolved to make no sacrifice of principle to
obtain a share of power, but, to use the phrase
I then heard, "to take his blue bag, and return to
the bar."

[After the Regency Bill had passed through the
Commons, and was still under debate in the House of
Lords, the arduous contest was terminated by the

King's recovery, and Mr. Pitt was rewarded for his fidelity by receiving the following letter from his Majesty.—Ed.]

The King to Mr. Pitt.

"Kew, Feb. 23d, 1789.

"It is with infinite satisfaction I renew my correspondence with Mr. Pitt by acquainting him with my having seen the Prince of Wales, and my second son; care was taken that the conversation should be general and cordial; they seemed perfectly satisfied. I chose the meeting should be in the Queen's apartment, that all parties might have that caution which, at the present hour, could but be judicious. I desire Mr. Pitt will confer with the Lord Chancellor, that any steps which may be necessary for raising the annual supplies, or any measures that the interests of the nation may require, should not be unnecessarily delayed, for I feel the warmest gratitude for the support and anxiety shewn by the nation at large during my tedious illness, which I should ill requite if I did not wish to prevent any further delay in those public measures which it may be necessary to bring forward this year, though I must decline entering into a pressure of business, and indeed for the rest of my life, shall expect others to fulfil the duties of their employments, and only keep that superintending eye which can be effected without labour or fatigue. I am anxious to see Mr. Pitt any hour that may suit him to-morrow morning, as his constant attachment to my interest and that of the public, which are inseparable, must ever place him in the most advantageous light.

"G. R."

[The reader will doubtless have observed that the Chancellor had reduced himself to a very unfavourable predicament, by the trimming policy which he desired to adopt. It is not surprising, therefore, that Mr. Pitt's friends should have jumped to a conclusion adverse to him, with the precipitancy of partisans, who are apt to overrun the intentions of their leaders. It is impossible not to admire the considerate and judicious tone of this remonstrance, showing, as it does, the great forbearance with which Mr. Pitt endured the weaknesses of his adherents.—Ed.]

MR. PITT TO MR. ROSE.

[*Private.*]

"DEAR ROSE,

"Priory, Sunday, 1 p.m., Nov. 8th, 1789.

You will stare a good deal at the circumstance which makes me write this letter, and which you will perceive must not be taken notice of to any one else, but which I think it as well to mention to you without delay. A person, on whom I can entirely rely, told me yesterday that the Chancellor had said to him very lately, that he understood he should probably soon receive a letter from Mr. Grenville to give up the seals, for that Mr. Rose had said before a person, who he must have known would repeat it, that we had made up our minds to it and would go on very well without him. You will easily imagine what degree of credit I give to this absurd story; but strange as it is, it is very capable of making an impression on his mind. The chief thing I wish is, that you would recollect whether in any company, where you thought yourself safe, you have used any warm expression about him, as might very naturally happen, which could afterwards be exaggerated or perverted into something that may have laid the foundation for this suggestion. As to your having said anything like what is represented, I do not entertain a moment's idea of it; and my object is to trace, if possible, where so mischievous a suggestion has originated, and to consider whether it may be worth while to convey some contradiction of it to the Chancellor. This I can easily do if the circumstances make it prudent; but if you recollect any expression on which this idea can have been engrafted, and which any one can have been base enough to repeat and to give such a colour to, it will be best to say nothing at all about it.

"Yours most sincerely,
"W. Pitt."

"P. S.—For a reason, which I will explain to you when we meet, I wish you could let me know pretty nearly what are the profits which Cowper has from his office of Clerk Assistant, compared with yours, and on what the profits depend."

[Under the Duke of Portland's administration in 1797, Mr. Fox being one of the Secretaries of State, the Prince of Wales came of age, and it was proposed to apply to Parliament for an allowance of 100,000*l.* a-year; but we learn from a letter of Mr. Fitzpatrick, that the King disapproved of it, and said, that he could not think of burthening the public, but was ready to give 50,000*l.* a-year from the Civil List, which he thought sufficient (the Prince had 12,000*l.* a-year besides from the Duchy of Cornwall, and Parliament was asked to grant 30,000*l.* to pay his debts); and that he found, that notwithstanding all the professions of the ministers for economy, they were ready to sacrifice the public interests to the wishes of an ill-advised young man. These Whigs had certainly a right to be called a *liberal* administration.

During the next three years this prodigal son so wasted his substance in riotous living, that he contracted debts beyond his income to the amount of more than 100,000*l.*, besides 50,000*l.* laid out on Carlton House. The following document is introduced only to show that Mr. Pitt's government resisted the reckless extravagance of the Prince.—ED.]

[1789.] The Chancellor of the Exchequer acquaints the Board that he had received a letter from Lord Southampton, enclosing, by the command of his Royal Highness the Prince of Wales, several papers and estimates respecting the expenses at Carlton House. That not being certain, from the nature and terms of the communication, whether it was intended to be laid officially before the Board, or to be submitted in the first instance to his Majesty, he had requested Lord Southampton to signify to him his Royal Highness's commands on this point. That in consequence of Lord Southampton's answer, he thinks it his duty to lay these papers before the Board.

The Chancellor of the Exchequer also communicates the estimates received from his Royal Highness's officers on the 14th May, 1787; the copy of the report made to Mr. Lyte by Sir Wm. Chambers, Mr. Couse, and Mr. Craig, on the 20th July, 1787, and a memorandum delivered by Mr. Holland, 14th March, 1789.

Read these several papers, and also the resolutions of the House of Commons of the 24th May, 1787, 10th of December, 1787, and the 15th of June, 1789.

The Board observes that the Resolution of the House of Commons of the 24th of May, 1787, humbly desires His Majesty to be graciously pleased to direct the sum of 20,000*l.* to be issued on account of the works at Carlton House, as soon as an estimate should be formed, with suficient accuracy, of the whole expense for completing the same in a proper manner.

That previous to this resolution an estimate of the works at Carlton House appears to have been delivered by his Royal Highness's officers on the 14th of May, 1787, stating the sum of 49,700*l.* for the expense of those works; and at the same time an estimate for the furniture, stating that as several of the apartments and rooms are not built, formed, or finished, and as a great part of the furniture is in an unfinished state, it is impossible to ascertain or describe exactly what will be wanted; but from as exact an account as can be ascertained, the sum of 5,500l. will be necessary.

The estimate of 49,700l. for the works at Carlton House, appears to have been referred to the examination of Sir William Chambers, Mr. Couse and Mr. Craig, and to have been reported upon by them on the 20th July, 1787.

That, on the 17th August, 1787, the sum of 10,000l. was issued for the works at Carlton House, under the King's warrant; and a farther sum of 10,000l. for the same purpose, and in the same manner, on the 23rd of November following.

That a further sum of 10,000l. was issued for the same purpose, and in the same manner, on the 5th September, 1788.

On the 10th December, 1787, the House resolved that a sum not exceeding 20,000l. be granted to his Majesty, to make good the like sum which has been issued by his Majesty's order, in pursuance of the address of this House for carrying on and completing the works at Carlton House.

That on the 14th March, 1789, an application was made to the Treasury by Mr. Holland, referring to both the estimates above mentioned, but observing that the estimate for the furniture was not likely to prove sufficient, referring also to the resolution of the

House of Commons of the 24th May, 1787, and stating that Mr. Holland was informed that payments had been made since that time to the amount of 30,000*l.*

That in consequence of this application, the further sum of 15,000*l.* was issued under the King's warrant, on the 1st May, 1789; and on the 29th May, 1789, a further sum of 10,200*l.*, being the remainder to complete the sum of 55,200*l.*

That an account of these several sums issued in 1788, and 1789, was laid before the House of Commons; and on the 15th June, 1789, it was resolved, that a sum not exceeding 35,200*l.* should be granted to his Majesty, to make good the like sum which had been issued by his Majesty's orders, in pursuance of an address of the House of Commons, for carrying on and completing the works at Carlton House.

The Board observes that the account, No. 2, transmitted by Lord Southampton to the Chancellor of the Exchequer, states a sum of 50,950*l.* as the estimated expense "of furniture and decorations "ordered for the state apartments, to replace some of "that which was intended at the time of the appli- "cation to Parliament in 1787, and to furnish other "apartments not then projected, together with an "estimate of the expense thereof."

Under these circumstances it does not appear to the Board that this additional estimate of 50,950*l.* comes within the intention of the resolution of the House of Commons of the 24th May, 1787, and the

Board does not think itself authorised to direct a warrant to be prepared for the issue of any further sum out of the Civil List in pursuance of the said resolution. The Chancellor of the Exchequer is desired humbly to submit the foregoing minute to his Majesty.

[It must be admitted, that the leaders of both the great political parties were very indulgent to the royal spendthrift; for the House of Commons offered no opposition to grants which amounted in the course of three years to 101,000*l.* for the payment of his debts, and 55,200*l.* for Carlton House, although, the King had, in the meantime, added 10,000*l.* a-year to his income, out of the Civil List, and exacted from him a promise that for the future his expenditure should not exceed his income. But it must be remembered that the finances of the country, under the management of Mr. Pitt, were then in a very flourishing condition, and that both the leaders were men who could not be very sensitive on such subjects, since both of them afterwards incurred a large amount of debts, which were discharged either by their friends, or by the nation; but there was this difference between them—Mr. Fox's debts were contracted by gambling; Mr. Pitt's by inattention to his pecuniary concerns; all his thought being occupied not only with great schemes of policy, but by attention to the minutest details of administration. In

the management of these, he depended very much
upon the assistance of his friend, Mr. Rose; and
his letters show that the least things appertaining
to the conduct of affairs were not exempted from
his care. The following concerns the payment of the
Prince's debts :—ED.]

MR. PITT TO MR. ROSE.

"Hollwood, Sunday, July 14th, 1789.
"Half-past 4 P.M.

"DEAR ROSE,

"I do not think there would be much objection
to authorising Mr. Coutts to issue the money to any
persons whom the Prince shall direct, provided it is
once arranged beforehand amongst his officers, in what
proportions it is to be applied to his debts. The
only person with whom I have had communication is
Mr. Anstruther. He has, I believe, seen the principal
creditors, and formed a plan, according to which the
sum of 40,000*l*. would answer the present purpose.
Most likely as large a sum as 3,000*l*. would have to be
allotted to the Brighthelmstone creditors, and Captain
Payne may be as good a channel as any other. But
it might lead to great confusion to settle anything with
Captain Payne, except in concert with Mr. Anstruther.
The only thing, therefore, which occurs to me in the
first place, is, that you should see Mr. Anstruther first,
and afterwards Captain Payne with him. If you find
from them that it is arranged to Mr. Anstruther's
satisfaction, I should see no objection to making any
alteration in the letter to Coutts which may be neces-

sary. I have, to save time, written to Mr. Anstruther to desire him to call upon you before eleven to-morrow. If it prove necessary to alter the authority given to Coutts, the best mode will be to withdraw your original letter and send him a new one.

"I have marked words which I imagine would answer the purpose, but I shall like any others as well. You will, of course, mention to Mr. Anstruther all that I have here said.

"Yours sincerely,
"W. PITT."

CHAPTER III.

1790—1798.

COMMENCEMENT OF THE WAR WITH FRANCE IN 1793—WHIG CALUMNIES AGAINST MR. PITT'S GOVERNMENT, ETC.

[THE trafficking in Church preferment, and the exercise of patronage from interested motives, merely for the sake of obtaining some return for it from those who sought the favour, without the smallest reference to the worthiness or fitness of the persons recommended, several instances of which occur in the following correspondence, painfully remind us that we are engaged in the history of the eighteenth century. —ED.]

MR. PITT TO MR. ROSE.

"Downing Street,
"Monday Evening, April 5th, 1790.

"DEAR ROSE.

"I have made up my mind to offer the Deanery of Canterbury to Dean Butler; and you will be so good as to inform him of it, contriving at the same time to make sure of the *return* we wish, as far as you can with *propriety*.

"I have got your's respecting Southampton; and am very glad the point is likely to be settled by a

meeting, the result of which will at all events, I think,
set us quite at ease. I found everything at Cambridge very favourable both for Euston and myself.

"Yours sincerely,
"W. Pitt."

[The next series of letters, in the years 1790, 1791,
and 1792, are on matters of business, the allusions in
which it is not worth while to disentangle from their
obscurity, and therefore most of them are omitted;
they have little or no other interest, except as they serve
to show the character of the communications which
passed between the two friends. It is a remarkable
feature in this correspondence, that while the revolutionary mania in Paris was disclosing its horrors and
crimes more and more, we look in vain to these letters
for any intimation of what was going on. There is
not a symptom of alarm or indignation, or even
astonishment; both writers seem to be wholly intent
upon the interior administration of the country, in a
calm and undisturbed atmosphere. A few, however,
of these letters of business are given, because they
illustrate the nature of Mr. Pitt's administration,
which was not a government by departments, except
so far as those who presided in them attended to the
ordinary routine: but it is evident that Mr. Pitt himself transacted much of the business of the Foreign,
Colonial, and War Offices, and of the Commissariat
also; not only as to the appointment of the inferior

commissaries, but even as to the contracts for provisioning the army.—Ed.]

Mr. Pitt to Mr. Rose.

"Stowe, Sunday, June 10th, 1700.

"Dear Rose.

"I forgot before I left town to mention to you that I wish much to employ Scott, the East India Director, to converse confidentially with a certain Mr. Vander Meulen, who has been sent over from Holland for the purpose of trying whether any plan can be formed for a commercial arrangement of mutual benefit, between our Company and the Dutch. Vander Meulen has no ostensible commission, and the matter would at present be considered as entirely private. I think Scott, from his being so conversant with the details of Indian commerce, is fitter than any one else for such a discussion, and I imagine he would have no objection to being so employed; but I understand he is at Bath, or at least was very lately. If you find he is still there, I wish you would write to him, stating the business, and desiring to know when he will be in town. It is material that, if possible, it should be within a week from this day. I mean to stay here to-morrow, but shall certainly be in town by five on Tuesday, and shall be very glad if you can dine with me.

"Yours sincerely,
"W. Pitt."

[In order to explain the latter part of the following letter, it is necessary to remark, that peace between

Russia and the Porte was concluded at Gralutz, on 11th of August, by the mediation of Prussia and the threats of England, whose forces were augmented to enforce her remonstrance. By this treaty Russia acquired the fortress of Oczakow, and all the country between the Bog and the Dniester, with the only condition that the navigation of the last named river should be left free. Better terms for Turkey might have been obtained, had not Mr. Pitt been thwarted by Mr. Adair, who was sent to St. Petersburg by Mr. Fox, for that very purpose.—ED.]

MR. PITT TO MR. ROSE.

"*Downing Street, August 10th, 1701.*

"DEAR ROSE,

"I have an application to present to a living, on the ground of the right coming to the Crown, in consequence of its having been disposed of simonically by the patron. I recollect an application of the same sort, which you brought me some months ago, respecting another living, which I think I complied with; but some previous inquiry was made to ascertain that there was sufficient ground to proceed upon. If you recollect in what manner the inquiry was made, pray let me know that I may put this in the same train.

[*Secret.*]

"We have an account from St. Petersburg of the Empress's answer, which contains assurances of not obstructing the navigation of the Dniester, and which modification (slender as it is, our ministers will have accepted, and there the business will end; not very creditably, but better so than worse.

"The Gralutz Congress is resumed, and in a fair way of terminating very well. The consequence is, that I hope we shall very soon begin to disarm, and shall be able so to manage it as to have no additional bill to pay. In the mean time our revenue still continues to rise; and, including the present week, we are already 178,000*l.* gainers in this quarter. So much for news.

"I know of nothing that need disturb your holidays at present, and I rather hope in about a fortnight or three weeks to call on you in my way westward, if you continue at Cuffnels.

"Yours sincerely,
"W. P."

Mr. Pitt to Mr. Rose.

"Downing Street, Tuesday, Aug. 30th, 1791.

"Dear Rose,

"I shall leave town the end of this week, in my way westward; and mean to have the pleasure of calling on you in the course of my journey. If I find the Speaker is at liberty, I must stop at Woodley for a couple of days, and in that case shall not be with you till Monday; otherwise I perhaps may by Saturday, supposing you have no engagement to interfere with it. If you have pray let me know, and I will take my chance as I return. I enclose you a letter from a Captain Smyth, concerning whom you may perhaps be able to give some information, and whose style is rather suspicious. Return his letter that I may order some answer to be given him. Do you know of any person who has strong pretensions, and would be fit for collector in the province of Upper Canada, and any other who would make a good consul at Tripoli? I have an application for the former from a Mr. Antrobus, a Cambridge constituent, which I am rather inclined to attend to.

" Yours sincerely,
" W. Pitt."

[The following letter is given as a specimen of the spirit of jobbing by which ministers were formerly pestered in the administration of civil as well as of ecclesiastical patronage, and the ridiculous length to which it was sometimes carried. Happily, in these days of severe responsibility and competitive examination, such things are no longer possible.—Ed.]

" Burton Pynsent, Sept. 10th, 1791.
" Dear Rose,
" Since I wrote to Long yesterday I have seen a Mr. Metcalfe, whom, I know not why, Sir J. Honywood chose to employ instead of a messenger, to bring a letter applying for the Receivership of Kent, either for himself (I mean Sir John) or his son, a child of five years old.

" The latter request is ridiculous. I told Mr. Metcalfe I could say nothing at present to the first. I gave much the same answer, though rather more discouraging, to a Mr. Retford, the present deputy, who came with a recommendation to Sir Charles Farnaby. Gipps, of Canterbury, has also written to me for himself, and the Duke of Dorset, with a different suggestion. I enclose the Duke's letter, and my answer both to him and Gipps, that you may see how the business stands. Be so good to forward the two last letters. I think the whole must stand over for consideration, and it will be material to know what Sir E. Knatchbull says, from whom I have hitherto heard nothing. Is Bamber Gascoigne at last dead or alive? My last account from Long prevented my writing to the Duke of Beaufort and the Duchess of Rutland. I shall go from hence on Wednesday, and probably to Weymouth Thursday or Friday.

"Yours sincerely,
"W. PITT."

[Mr. Pitt was appointed Warden of the Cinque Ports in 1791. The King insisted upon his taking it; declared he would receive no other recommendation to the office, and signified his resolution to that effect to the other chief ministers. He was anxious to make provision for a man who, during the seven years of his premiership, had not only not asked, but had refused to take anything for himself. The simplicity with which he relates the fact to his friend is very observable, and how immediately he passes from it to a matter of business. The reduction of taxes shows the increasing prosperity of the country.—ED.]

Mr. Pitt to Mr. Rose.

"Dear Rose,   "Burton Pynsent, Aug. 7th, 1792.

"I have had a letter from the King making the offer in the handsomest way possible, and have accepted. The advertisement is very right except that, with a view to effect, it would be better to enumerate the taxes repealed.

"Ever yours,

"W. P."

[The next is an important letter, because it shows so clearly what Mr. Pitt's political views were at a time when the crimes of France had alarmed all sane politicians. Bound as we were by treaties to protect Holland, not revolutionized Holland, but Holland under her old established form of government, some demonstration was necessary to produce the desired effect; but, if that should prove successful, Mr. Pitt's next object was to produce a general pacification of the European powers by persuading them to abstain from meddling with France; to leave her to arrange her domestic concerns, and to work out her social system in any way she liked. Lord Stafford seems to have been more in favour of stronger measures.—Ed.]

Mr. Pitt to the Marquis of Stafford.

"My dear Lord,   "Downing Street, Nov. 13th, 1792.

"The strange and unfortunate events which have followed one another so rapidly on the Continent, are in many views matter of serious and anxious consideration.

"That which presses the most relates to the situation of Holland, as your Lordship will find from the enclosed despatch from Lord Auckland, and as must indeed be the case in consequence of the events in Flanders. However unfortunate it would be to find this country in any shape committed, it seems absolutely impossible to hesitate as to supporting our ally in case of necessity, and the explicit declaration of our sentiments is the most likely way to prevent the case occurring. We have therefore thought it best to send without delay instructions to Lord Auckland to present a memorial to the States, of which I enclose a copy. I likewise enclose a copy of instructions to Sir Morton Eden, at Berlin, and those to Vienna are nearly to the same effect. These are necessarily in very general terms, as, in the ignorance of the designs of Austria and Prussia, and in the uncertainty as to what events every day may produce, it seems impossible to decide definitively at present on the line which we ought to pursue, except as far as relates to Holland.

"Perhaps some opening may arise which may enable us to contribute to the termination of the war between different powers in Europe, leaving France (which I believe is the best way) to arrange its own internal affairs as it can. The whole situation, however, becomes so delicate and critical, that I have thought it right to request the presence of all the members of the Cabinet who can, without too much inconvenience, give their attendance. It will certainly be a great satisfaction if your Lordship should be of that number. At all events, I wish to apprise you as well as I can of what is passing, and shall be happy to receive your sentiments upon it either personally or by letter.

"I am, with the greatest regard,
"My dear Lord,
"Faithfully and sincerely yours,
"W. Pitt.
"Marquis of Stafford."

THE MARQUIS OF STAFFORD TO MR. PITT.

"MY DEAR SIR,

"It is difficult, I believe, for the best informed of his Majesty's servants to give a decided opinion as to what this country ought to do in this alarming crisis of Europe. Such mystery has accompanied the negotiations and transactions of the Austrian and Prussian cabinets, that I wonder not that you have dealt in general language; at the same time procrastination (unless the adverse armies were in winter quarters) may give opportunities to embarrass the present untoward situation of affairs still more.

"Uninformed as I have been for these four months respecting the connexions, the jealousies, &c. of the Courts of Europe during this unprecedented state, it is impossible for me to enter *en détail*. I wish our interference respecting Holland, and our adhering to the faith of treaties, may produce the desired effect; and France indeed can have no just reason to attack Holland, even upon her own avowed system of politics, if she has any system.

" These times require such attention and circumspection at home, that every political question must be now doubly embarrassing. I wish you may not find it necessary at the meeting of Parliament, by some means to strengthen the hands of the executive government, for the seditious are going great lengths; and, if possible, the *principiis obsta* is the wisest doctrine.

"I trust and believe that the King's Ministers have done the best that could be done in the present posture of affairs. I know how very desirous you gentlemen of finance are to avoid giving the least alarm to the funds; otherwise not being unprepared for events might give confidence, and have some effect on our allies the French, who, more cautious I understand, are equipping a fleet to recover their West India Islands. I mean to be in town the middle of December; you will scarce have got your answers from the respective Courts to whom you have written, before that time.

"I am, my dear Sir,
"&c. &c.
" STAFFORD."

[The subjoined letter from Captain Mackintosh, who accompanied the expedition when Mr. Pitt sent an embassy to Pekin, throws all the blame of its failure upon Lord Macartney. It would be unjust, therefore, to that nobleman to withhold two letters of his which point to a very different conclusion; not that they contain anything relative to the embassy itself, for they are both of an earlier date; but, from the evidence they give of the character of the man, the truth of the charge appears to be utterly improbable. They are the letters of a man without foolish pride, self-conceit, or any diposition to domineer, or to give needless provocation. The spirit of self-sacrifice and the humble-minded anxiety which he showed to do his duty to his country, and to those who appointed him, are wholly inconsistent with the frame of mind which would offer unwarrantable insults to the Emperor or his mandarins. Captain Mackintosh took too mercantile a view of the case; he expected great advantages to accrue to this country from facilitating commerce with China—advantages which still are doubtful, though the road to them has since been opened by coercion—and to obtain them he would have sacrificed the honour and character of Great Britain. It is evident that he did not understand the Chinese Government—that Government of which the proverb is eminently true, that if you give it an inch of concession, it will take an ell. There would have been no end to the oppressions and humiliations to which the English would have been forced to submit, if Lord Macartney had consented to perform the degrading ceremonies required of him; and the French missionary, Huc, has shown how much may be done by invariably asserting the dignity of his nation, and not swerving a hair's breadth to the right hand or to the left from the strict line of equity by which European dealings should be guided. If Lord Elgin has been more successful than Lord Macartney was, it is not because he was more flexible, but because he was armed with sufficient power to administer a wholesome correction to the vanity of the Celestial Empire, and to assert international rights with a determination not to be trifled with.—ED.][1]

LORD MACARTNEY TO MR. ROSE.

" DEAR SIR,   " LION, Spithead, Sunday, Sept. 23rd, 1792.

" I AM to acknowledge the honour of your letter, covering Mr. Pitt's speech, which you were so good as to send me by Sir Andrew Douglas. I have been highly gratified by both. The speech I had already seen, but I have perused it again more at leisure, and together with your tract, which had particularly engaged my attention in the winter, it has given to my mind a degree of information and satisfaction which I do not recollect to have experienced before, on any political subject; independently of the composition, which, however masterly, is, I know, with the authors of those writings, only a secondary consideration. The view of the present, and the prospect of the future afforded by them, are so clear and pleasing, that merely as a well-wisher to the public prosperity, I ought to hope for its continuing to be long entrusted to the same hands which have brought it to the pitch at which we now see it. My private feelings of the very handsome and liberal proceeding of Mr. Pitt in

---

[1] Recent events fully confirm this view of the subject. Mr. Bruce's mission failed because he was not accompanied by a sufficient force to make himself respected by the most perfidious of mankind.—ED.

the whole course of the business of the embassy, lead me likewise to form the same ardent wishes; and the assurances you are pleased to give me of his cordiality towards me, and of the entire confidence he is so good as to place in me, are not only peculiarly grateful to my mind, but give fresh alacrity to all my undertakings in the public service; and he may firmly depend both upon my personal attachment to him, and upon my most zealous and honest exertions in whatever station he may think fit to place me. Accept, at the same time, my dear Sir, my best thanks for the kind disposition you have testified in my favour, and for the opportunity you have lately afforded me of cordial and confidential conversation at your own house; and since I wish to consider it as fixing an intimacy and friendship which I shall, at all times and from all places, endeavour to cultivate, equally from public motives and private regard, I beg you to believe me, with every sentiment of respect and esteem,

"Dear Sir,
"Very sincerely yours,
"MACARTNEY.

"P.S. Sir Erasmus Gower says he thinks we shall sail to-morrow. We have been settled on board these three days."

LORD MACARTNEY TO MR. ROSE.

"DEAR SIR, "Lion, at Sea, April 14th, 1793

"As my despatches to Mr. Dundas, which no doubt you have seen, contained everything worth mentioning that has occurred since our leaving England, I did not mean to trouble you with a letter before my arrival at Pekin; but having some days since met a French ship in her way from Manilla to the Isle of France, I thought you might not dislike to hear from me the latest news of that part of the world. Though the Spaniards there are a good deal discontented with their own Government, yet they entertain a strong abhorrence to the late subversion in France, and have manifested it on every occasion to the people of that country, wherever they come among them. The ship we spoke with, which is called the 'La Fayette,' but is immediately to have another name (Petion, Marat, or Robespierre, I suppose), sailed with two others, a few months since, from the Isles of France and Bourbon to Manilla, where they sold their cargoes, amounting to the value of 60,000 to 80,000 dollars, through the medium of a French agent, resident there, and had agreed to take sugars in return, which are now equally excellent and plentiful at that place; but their countryman, having got their affairs entirely into his hands, it seems, played the rogue with them, and refused either to supply the sugars, or to refund the money. The Government connived at his conduct, and denied them justice, so that the three ships have been obliged to come away empty; the consequence of which is a very serious loss to the navigators and owners. They talked very loudly on the subject, and of complaining at home, and returning to redress themselves. 'The place,' said the captain, 'we could easily take; or I wish,' addressing himself to one of our people, 'I wish you would take it again from them, which would be the same thing for us.' They represented the island of Luconia as a most valuable possession, and which, in any other than Spanish hands, would in a short time become one of the most opulent and important settlements in the East, abundantly producing sugar, cotton, rice, indigo, wheat, and cattle of every kind. Nevertheless, from ill policy, prejudice, or ignorance, all foreign trade was, till lately, prohibited to this island; an island possessing, as above mentioned, such ample materials for being enriched by it. The port of Manilla is at present only open for a limited time, which expires in September next. The people, indeed, have written home in the strongest manner for a prolongation of the term, but they complain much of being neglected, not having had any ship direct from old Spain these three years past, nor any letters or news from thence, but through the channel of the Acapulco galleons.

"I understand that the Isles of France and Bourbon are in a state of considerable improvement, and that their attempts to cultivate the clove, nutmeg, and cinnamon, have been attended with success, and promise great advantage. Most of the French whom we have met in our passage are strong partisans of the late subversion at home. This happens to be the passion uppermost at present; but with regard to England, there is little doubt of their entertaining at bottom as much envy and animosity as ever.

"I know not how your affairs are likely to turn out with Spain, nor what order of things may arise from the present anarchy in France, but I am disposed to flatter myself that the connexion between those two nations (which, in truth, was only a connexion between their two Courts) is now almost entirely at an end, and that the advantages which Spain might derive by renewing her ancient friendship with England, she might repay us with large interest, and, at the same time, suffer no real prejudice herself. But I fear you will think me travelling very fast at this distance from the source of proper information; I shall, however, beg leave to add to you what I hinted to Mr. Dundas, in a private letter, that if, after we have executed our present instructions, it should then be found, from the circumstances of things, that either my services, or those of the ship and people who are with me, could be employed with any prospect of utility to the public, either on the North-west coast of America, or in the South Seas, in giving assistance, making observations, or obtaining intelligence, I should readily obey any commands that might be laid on me. This I mentioned without the smallest idea of offering new projects, or proposing new undertakings, and merely to show my attachment to Government and my zeal for its success. In this light I trust it will be understood, and that you will do justice to my public sentiments, as well as to those private ones of esteem and regard with which

"I have the honour to be, dear Sir,
"Your most faithful
"And affectionate humble servant,
"MACARTNEY.

"P.S. I flatter myself you will excuse my using Colonel Benson's hand on this occasion, as I am at present disabled by the gout, which, for the first time, has very unseasonably and very painfully attacked my right wrist."

CAPTAIN MACKINTOSH TO MR. ROSE.

"April, 1795.

"DEAR SIR,

"Motives of prudence, as well as a conviction that the failure of the Chinese Embassy was beyond any present remedy, have induced me hitherto to be silent respecting the causes of its not succeeding. But, weighty as these considerations have been in my mind, I really feel myself now compelled, by a strong sense of duty to my country, my employers, and the Ministers, to state, for the information of the latter, what fell immediately under my own observation in the course of that business. How reluctantly I do this, you, Sir, will easily believe, from the readiness with which I undertook to be the bearer of Mr. Pitt's wishes to Lord Macartney, respecting his going on the mission, and the partial opinion I entertained of his lordship, whose kindness to me was almost uninterrupted, and who even offered unequivocal and considerable proofs of his liberality.

"I premise this, to impress on you my real inducement for this communication, which are, most sincerely, no other than a love of truth and an anxious wish that the mistakes committed on the late occasion may, if possible, be prevented in a future one. I am led to make it now, from understanding that another mission to China is proposed, and, in a certain degree, acceded to; which, however it may answer the purposes of individuals, I cannot think is the best adapted to obtain any important national benefit. I therefore send you, herewith, a plain narrative, by attending to which, it will be seen that, instead of giving readily in to the sober and orderly manners of the Chinese, we did nothing but tease, irritate, and provoke the Ministers and Mandarins, and that at two different times the Emperor was actually insulted in person. If we had conducted ourselves properly, we might have remained at Pekin till this time; and I have no hesitation in declaring my most sincere and firm belief that all the principal objects we had in view might have been obtained, which may fairly be inferred from the following circumstance.

"The favourite Calao, and Minister of the Emperor, was afflicted with a disorder that the medical men of China had not been able to cure, and our physician was requested to attend and prescribe for him. On that very evening, several persons came to our apartments, and repeatedly said to the interpreter, *Cure him*, (meaning the Minister) and get into his good graces, and, (with strong asseverations) if you want *a Province, you will get it.*

"I have further to observe, that in the arrangements now thought of, I am recommended to a flattering and a very lucrative appointment; but if it be adopted in its present form I certainly shall withdraw my claim, determined not to be an instrument in the hands of any men, to carry on a measure of which I disapprove. My principles would prevent me, in any situation, from embarking in the business as concerted; and my circumstances lead me to no temptation to act contrary to these, if my feelings did not restrain me. Having premised so much, I have only to add, that I am particularly anxious that this disclosure, made under the strong impression of private friendship and of public trust, be communicated only to those more materially interested,—I mean Mr. Pitt and Mr. Dundas,—and to them, under a solemn pledge of secrecy; for to speak in the language of a seaman, Lord Macartney carries too much weight of metal for me; and unpleasant consequences might arise from my being rendered an object of resentment, not only to all those who composed the Embassy, but to every other adherent and dependent on his Lordship and Sir George Staunton.

"Whenever you may think it a proper time to communicate this information, I should wish to be present to give further explanation, or answer any questions that may occur.

"I have the honour to be, dear Sir,

"Your obliged and very obedient servant,

"W. MACKINTOSH.

"George Rose, Esq."

Mr. Pitt to Mr. Rose.

"*Downing Street, July 31st, 1793.*

"Dear Rose,

"I enclose you two letters from Brook Watson, which accompanied the account of the surrender of Valenciennes. The terms are still more satisfactory than those at Mayence, as the French deliver up their arms. Our loss is very slight; but I am afraid from what I hear, the Lord D——, who is mentioned to be wounded, is a relation of Mrs. Rose. I ventured to open Brook's letters, thinking they might contain something material to be attended to, and I will take care that he shall have directions about the bât and forage money.

"The account of the supplies of forage is, on the whole, satisfactory, as I take for granted, after October we shall have no great difficulty in procuring further quantities of oats; but I mean to see the comptroller and Scott on the subject to-morrow. The banks seem likely to give us some time in discharging the Exchequer Bills.

"Yours sincerely,
"W. Pitt.

"I have kept Watson's official letters."

Mr. Pitt to Mr. Rose.

"*Downing Street, Sept. 13th, 1793.*

"Dear Ross,

"Before I received your letter respecting the Southampton livings, I had had one from Sir H. Martin, recommending the schoolmaster, which I forwarded to the Chancellor, and he told me yesterday that he would give him the living applied for. He did not return me Sir H. Martin's letter, but I take it for granted the person and the living in question are the same you mention.

"I hardly think it worth making a second application for the other living; but, under the circumstances you mention, the recommendation of the Corporation seems likely to succeed. You will have seen the accounts of our disappointment before Dunkirk. It is certainly a severe check, but I trust only a temporary one; and it ought only to have the effect of increasing, if possible, our exertions. By the last accounts the Prince of Cobourg was on the point of making the attack on the covered way at Quesnoy. After that event is decided his army will probably draw towards the Duke of York's. In the meantime, General Beaulieu's success is a great circumstance.

"Yours ever,
"W. PITT."

MR. PITT TO MR. ROSE.

"DEAR ROSE,   "Downing Street, Sept. 16th, 1793.

"The enclosed letter to you came last night, and was brought to me. It would be hardly worth forwarding, but for what it mentions about *the bread*, which puzzles me, as I never heard of his applying for anything but biscuit; and, on the most diligent search, no trace of any application for *bread* can be found, nor would such a supply answer any purpose. I rather imagine he uses the term bread, as synonymous with biscuit; if so, part is sent, and the rest going as quick as possible. I shall write to Mr. Watson on the subject to-night. The Dutch have been driven from Menin with, I am afraid, a good deal of confusion, and our army obliged, in consequence, to fall back to Thurout; but I am in hopes will make a stand there, and be joined by Beaulieu. The enclosed *Gazette* confirms in the most satisfactory manner all the particulars from Toulon.

"Yours ever,
" W. PITT."

MR. PITT TO MR. ROSE.

"DEAR ROSE, "Downing Street, Sept. 23rd, 1793.

"IF any thing should arise to make you wish to stay beyond to-morrow se'nnight, you need have no scruple in doing so, as I must be here, and no inconvenience will arise from a short interval between Long's going and your arrival. I have fixed, at Sir C. Grey's recommendation, on a Mr. Jeffray as Commissary General for the West Indies; we want besides, a Commissary of accounts, two assistant Commissaries at 20s. per day, and three more at 10s. I have consulted with the comptrollers, and do not find much prospect of filling their places from the half-pay list, which consists of but few, and those chiefly superannuated. Does any body occur to you?

"I believe the Chancellor has determined to give Mr. Meares the living.

"The accounts from the interior of France are

excellent, and we are preparing very fast to make a good use of Toulon.

"Yours ever,
"W. Pitt."

[With all this multifarious business occupying Mr. Pitt's time and thoughts, it is no wonder that the trivial impertinencies of some of his correspondents, and the importunities of others, did not meet sometimes with that attention which in their self-complacency they thought their due. But as most people resent the appearance of being slighted or neglected, this was the source of much dissatisfaction and unpopularity, as the following letter from Lord Bulkely to the Marquis of Buckingham, shows.

"I left Percy in town, and I set Rose and Steele to coax him a little; for the old grievance sticks by him, and he wants much persuasion to efface the memory of it. Sir Hugh is here, and complains much of never having had one letter answered since Pitt has been in power. I am afraid more rats will run in consequence of Pitt's inattention to these trifles, than on any other account whatsoever. Indeed, I heard as much in town. Rose and Steele may laugh at such details, but they are necessary, and the constituent will not believe the member's assiduity, unless he sees real or ostensible evidence. I gave my 100*l.* to the Westminster election in consequence of a letter from Rose. I could ill spare it; but finding others were dosed in the same manner, I gulped in the grievance."[1]

If a private Secretary had been invented then, this inconvenience might have been avoided.[2]

The unfortunate event alluded to in the following letter, was a gallant, but ill-managed exploit at Toulon. When it was in our possession the French had opened a battery to cannonade the town, and it was necessary to destroy it. Our troops got possession of this battery and the height on which it was placed, but, flushed with victory, they rushed on the flying enemy with disordered impetuosity. The French general rallied and reinforced his troops, and drove back the broken ranks of his assailants. The English commander, O'Hara, arrived at the redoubt too late to remedy the disaster, and while he was endeavouring to organize the retreat, received a wound from a bullet which disabled him, and he was taken prisoner.—ED.]

MR. PITT TO MR. ROSE.

"Wimbledon, Wednesday, Dec. 25th, 1793.

"DEAR ROSE,

"Your account of what you have written to Chamberlayne is perfectly satisfactory, and also the enclosure from Mr. Reid respecting the Scotch remit-

[1] Duke of Buckingham's Memoirs, vol. ii. p. 110.
[2] In a letter which Lord Grenville sent to Lord Wellesley, in 1804, he speaks of the bad habit which Pitt had contracted, of never writing to any one.

tance. You will see that we have already gained considerably in this week's revenue. The letter from Mr. Halyburton seems to be a sensible one. I am sorry to say that the account of General O'Hara has proved true. You will see the particulars in a Gazette Extraordinary, which we thought it best to publish immediately, that the public might know exactly what has passed.

"On the whole, the event, though unfortunate, is far from uncreditable, and I think there is still a very good chance of all proving right in that quarter.

"I have not yet had time to look at your notes, having had a good deal of different sorts of business on my hands, but I hope to accomplish it to-morrow. I have not, however, received any fresh papers from Chinnery.

"It will be necessary to make some inquiry as to the deputy recommended by the Duchess of Manchester, as I suspect the Duke thinks he has a right to recommend; and another Duchess will then have something to say upon it.

"Ever yours most sincerely,
"W. Pitt.

"I missed Mr. Gurton every time he called. Where can I send to him?"

[Mr. Rose collected together a great number of remarkable facts, bearing upon the relations between England and France before the breaking out of the war in 1793, showing that Mr. Pitt wished to avoid going to war until it was forced upon him by the progress of events. These facts seem to have been designed for the heads of an argument, which may have formed the substance of a speech in the House of Commons, though not embodied in any written form; but since a great deal of undeserved obloquy has been heaped upon the Minister of that day, by his Whig opponents, it is worth while to notice the succession of events, which are indicated rather than detailed by Mr. Rose. Nobody could doubt Mr. Pitt's pacific views in 1792, when he repealed taxes, and reduced the naval establishment, especially the number of seamen, to 10,000, although France had 80,000; and although the year before, a French frigate had violated the treaty of commerce by a positive aggression. When, in April, France declared war against Austria, measures were taken to ensure the neutrality of Great Britain; and Mr. Pitt made a formal avowal to a deputation from the city, that she would not meddle with the affairs of France. The proclamation against seditious writing was made a grievance; but it was only aimed at those who were in correspondence with the French Revolutionists, who proclaimed open war against all the higher ranks of society. On December 15th, the National Convention avowed itself faithful to the principles of the sovereignty of the people, which does not permit them to acknowledge any institution that militates against it, and

instructs the French generals, into whatever country they may go, to proclaim this same sovereignty, and the abolition of all constituted authorities: and also declares that the French will treat as an enemy that nation, which, refusing liberty and equality, should choose to preserve its Prince and privileged orders. The executive council in commenting upon this, strengthened the language, and concluded thus:—
"The general interest of restoring peace to Europe, can be obtained only by the annihilation of the despots and their satellites. All conspires in inducing us to treat such a people according to the rigour of war and conquest." This is applied particularly to England, and Holland, and especially to the church of the former. In like manner, during the previous month, the National Convention had declared that France was ready to assist every state, which was willing to rebel against its own Government. That we were enumerated amongst the threatened nations was decisively proved by the rejection of Barrillon's proposal to exclude Great Britain, and confine the decree to countries in actual hostility with France.

On the 31st of December, the very day on which Lord Grenville signed his note stating the terms on which a rupture might be avoided, Monge, the Minister of War, in a circular letter to the seaport towns, said:—"We will make a descent on that island; we will hurl thither 50,000 caps of liberty; we will plant there the sacred tree, and stretch out our arms to our brother republicans. The tyranny of their Government shall soon be destroyed." Equally violent and hostile language was used by other members of the Convention; but if such a dispatch had been issued by Count Walewski or any other Minister of Napoleon III., at the present time, the most factious radical in the House of Commons would have been clamorous for war. Chaussard, who was sent by the Council to execute their decrees in the Austrian Netherlands, about the same time announced their object in these unequivocal terms:—"A war *ad internecionem* is declared between the Republic and all monarchies."

On January 3rd, in the following year, instructions were dispatched to Genet for forming, with America, an offensive alliance against England; and on the 13th, the very day on which an evasive answer was given by the Executive Council to the conciliatory offers of Lord Grenville, orders were issued to commission thirty ships of the line and twenty frigates, in addition to the twenty-two of the line and thirty-two frigates already employed, and forty-five more of both were to be built; while the armament on our side, at which they took so much offence, only raised the total amount of British seamen to 25,000, which is not more than sufficient to man eighteen sail of the line, with frigates.

Another subject of complaint, in singular contrast with the existing state of things, was the Alien Bill, which applied to all foreigners, though it was only taken up by France. The objection was principally founded on the 4th article of the Treaty of Commerce. But the French had violated that article much more, by a very rigorous decree, inflicting fine and imprisonment on all strangers resident in France, who neglected to make a certain declaration within eight days: and Lord Gower, our ambassador, had been arrested on his way from Paris till orders arrived for his liberation. Yet no complaint was made by us, because the step was declared to be necessary for internal tranquillity. But the rule which they pleaded in their own favour, they were not willing to allow to others. It was necessary to the tranquillity of England to prohibit the circulation of assignats, not only to save her inhabitants from the ruin of an inconvertible currency, but to preserve them also from the corruption which the bullion purchased by French Agents was employed to effect. It was a measure of domestic self-defence, which the French Government had no right to meddle with at all; but they seemed bent upon quarrelling with our internal legislation. They complained of the bills which forbade the exportation of arms and of wheat, although they themselves had previously forbidden the exportation of both the one and the other from France. The singular fact, that they had been buying up all the wheat they could get in England, at a much higher price than they had to pay for it elsewhere, produced a strong conviction, that, knowing how much a scarcity of corn had contributed to their own revolution, they were desirous that a similar discontent should effect similar commotions in England. Certain it is, that they neglected no means in their power to stir up rebellion in this country. Chauvelin, an impudent republican who had been the ambassador from Louis the 16th, was now the agent of the Executive Council to foment disturbances, by sowing disloyalty throughout the land with the aid of English Jacobins and revolutionists. But so great was Mr. Pitt's love of peace, which was quite necessary to the success of his most cherished plans, that he held conferences with this man, and with another unacknowledged agent, Maret, in the hope that war might yet be averted; for our ambassador was withdrawn from Paris after the death of the King, to whom he was accredited, and the Secretary of Legation also, in consequence of the murder of some Englishmen in the massacres of September, and there was then no settled Government to which credentials could be addressed. The changes of rulers were like the changes in a kaleidoscope; at least the variety was as great, though all the symmetry was wanting.

But all negotiation was useless. It was evident, that while Mr. Pitt was extremely anxious to preserve peace, France was determined on war, which was definitively shown by Le Brun's paper, considered as an ultimatum, and delivered to Lord Grenville on the 13th of January; and, indeed, the Convention had solemnly decreed that they would acknowledge no kingly government.

Chauvelin, who had persuaded the Convention to let him stay in London without credentials, because it would not be prudent for France to lose the fruit of his labours with Mr. Fox, and some of the opposition, and their *subsequent services*—had now proved himself, with their assistance, so dangerous an incendiary that it was necessary to check the mischief he was doing by sending him away; with a notification, however, that the Government would still listen to terms of accommodation. This step, his friend Mr. Fox chose to consider an act of aggression upon France. Unfortunately however for his argument, it appears that Lord Grenville's order to Chauvelin to leave the kingdom was dated January 24th; while, in a letter written by Dumouriez from Paris on January 23d, it is stated, that orders had been already given for his return. Now, it will be observed, that up to this time, not the smallest inclination to go to war can be discovered on the part of Great Britain; the object kept uniformly in view was an honourable peace. But what was the next event in this great drama?

In the beginning of February,[1] France formally declared war; which was announced by the King in the speech from the throne, and preparations were then made accordingly. It was, however, no more than might be reasonably expected from the doctrines propounded by one of the leaders in that revolutionary delirium. Brissot said, "War is now become neces-

[1] Gifford says the first; Alison, the third.

sary. France is bound to undertake it, to maintain her honour,—it is to be regarded as a public blessing; the only evil you have to apprehend is, that it should not arrive:—it is no longer with governments that we must treat, but with their subjects." He proposes, therefore, to get the start of those nations who are hostilely disposed, because "he who is anticipated is already half vanquished."

In the face of all this mass of evidence, which after all is far short of what might be adduced, is it not most lamentable, that the three Whig historians of that time should be so blinded by party prejudices, as to lose the perception of truth in their narrative of the facts? Of these, Lord Holland leads the way with a mild misrepresentation, which looks more like ignorance than malice. He says, "that it was neither wise nor just to involve Europe in a war, from feelings of commiseration for Louis the 16th, who was not under the protection of our laws. But it was a moment of passion, and England has paid severely for indulging it." Compassion doubtless was felt from one end of the kingdom to the other; but to suppose that it influenced Mr. Pitt's conduct, is to betray great ignorance of his character. No one could more regret the want of wisdom and justice that ruled the hour; but folly and injustice held their throne on the other side of the channel.

The next assailant was that venerable statesman, in whose matured wisdom the lees of his Whig educa-

tion have not so wholly subsided as to leave it calm
and pure; and, therefore, the fermenting spirit will
sometimes explode in vehement vituperation without
sufficient regard to truth: and so he pours forth these
groundless calumnies against the object of Whig antipathy. " The very worst offence of which a Minister
can be guilty, is the abandonment of his own principles
for place, and counselling his sovereign and his country,
not according to his conscience, but according to what
being most palatable to them, is most beneficial to
the man himself. Mr. Pitt joining the war party in
1793 is the most striking and most fatal instance of
this offence. His thoughts were all turned to peace,
but he preferred flinging his country into a contest,
which he and his great antagonist, by uniting their
forces, must have prevented; but then he must also
have shared with Mr. Fox the power which he was
determined to enjoy alone and supreme."[1] This
Lord Brougham calls "a flagrant political crime."
Even if this accusation had been true, such a coalition
was plainly impossible. It could not have outlived
the ridicule of being represented like the two Kings
of Brentford smelling at the same nosegay. The
constitution of our Government required that one
should be premier, and the other subordinate.

Superior talent has sometimes submitted to own
another head of the Cabinet, on the condition of being

[1] Historical Sketches of Statesmen in the Time of George III.
By Lord Brougham.—p. 62.

THE RIGHT HON. GEORGE ROSE.   141

leader in his own house; but it is ridiculous to suppose
that the leaders of two rival parties could ever work
together long in the same chamber of Parliament. It
is true, that Mr. Pitt had refused to submit to this in-
feriority when office was offered to him in the Coalition
Administration. What does Lord Brougham himself
say upon that subject? " Mr. Pitt, though a man of
vast talents as well as spotless reputation, was not
permitted, without a sacrifice of personal honour, to be
the ally of Mr. Fox in serving their common country."[1]
If then Mr. Fox was wrong in imposing this condition
when the Minister was young in office, and scarcely
the leader of a party, how could any man in his senses
expect that Mr. Pitt would voluntarily descend from
his throne of power and popularity, to lay himself
at the feet of Mr. Fox, especially when there was no
rational prospect, that, even by this self sacrifice, he
could purchase the success of his favourite policy?
For this is the acknowledgment of the same high
authority when, spurning the trammels of party, he
paid homage only to truth. "There is not," he says,
" much reason to suppose that, had the parties changed
positions in 1792, the Whigs would, as a matter of
course, have been against the war. How little disposed
they showed themselves after Mr. Pitt's death to make
sacrifices for the great object of pacification!"[2]

But the accusation is not true in any part. It is not
true that Mr. Pitt joined the war party from selfish

[1] Historical Sketches, p. 189.   [2] Ibid. 306.

motives, for it has been shown that he had no option; that he was dragged into the vortex, not only against his will, but in spite of repeated struggles to avoid it; and that he actually went to the extremest limits of forbearance that prudence could tolerate, for national amity with France in that crisis of which Lord Holland dreamed, would have been "concord with Belial;" and to shew good feelings towards her new institutions would have been to encourage instability, bloodthirstiness, impiety, and the subversion of all social order. It is not true, therefore, that any union between Mr. Pitt and Mr. Fox could have prevented the war; and it is wonderful how a statesman so well versed in public affairs as Lord Brougham, could have entertained such an opinion for a single moment. Lastly, it is not true, that Mr. Pitt would not share power with Mr. Fox, because he wanted to enjoy it alone. Lord Holland shews the contrary. He says, "Mr. Fox about this time had a very secret interview with Mr. Pitt, in which the latter proposed a coalition of parties with many conditions, somewhat unpalatable, though NOT *utterly inadmissible*, or in the least dishonourable, except the exclusion of men, and particularly of Sheridan, to which Mr. Fox would not listen. He would not sacrifice him to the popular clamour founded on the immorality of Sheridan's private character."[1]

Nothing can be more strangely improbable than

[1] Memoirs of the Whig Party, p. 31.

that Sheridan's private character should have prevented an alliance to which Mr. Fox was admitted as a principal; for if the former was more than "a gnat," the latter was not less than "a camel" of immorality. But, in point of fact, we know from a different quarter what the real obstacle was. In Lord Malmesbury's diary this statement occurs :— "June, 1792. Dined at Lord Loughborough's with Fox; he doubted Pitt's sincerity, and suspected he had no other view than to weaken their party and strengthen his own. He contended that it was impossible ever to suppose Pitt would admit him to an equal share of power, and that whatever might be his own feeling, or readiness to give way, he could not, for the sake of the honour and pride of the party, come in on any other terms. Pitt *must* have the Treasury; and he on his part had friends in the House of Commons he must attend to. He spoke with acrimony of Pitt, and repeatedly said, that the pride of the party must be saved. He held out on the *impossibility of his acting under Pitt.*"

It is now tolerably clear which of the two great antagonists was guilty of "the flagrant political crime" of sacrificing his country to the interests of his party, and refused to share power, when it was offered to him, because he "was determined to enjoy it alone and supreme."[1] Lord Brougham justly observes, that "he (Mr. Fox) constantly modified his principles

[1] Historical Sketches, p. 62.

according to his own situation and circumstances as a party chief, making the ambition of the man and the interests of his followers the governing rule of his conduct."[1] It only remains to show, from Mr. Fox's own confession, how much the noble lord was right when he surmised that, if the Whigs had been in power, their policy would have been the same. Mr. Fox declared in Parliament, that "the Decree of the 19th of November he considered as an insult, and the explanation of the Executive Council as no adequate satisfaction. It was said, we must have security; and he was ready to admit that neither a disavowal by the Executive Council of France, nor a tacit repeal by the Convention, on the intimation of an unacknowledged agent, of a decree which they might renew the day after they had repealed it, would be a sufficient security, if the invasion of the Netherlands was what now alarmed us; and that it ought to alarm us, if the result was to make that country an appendage to France. There could be no doubt, we ought to have interposed to prevent it in the very first instance."

So that our fault was not in going to war, but in not having gone to war sooner. Having thus routed the enemies of Mr. Pitt with their own weapons, so far as his two principal opponents are concerned, we may well smile at the warlike aspirations of Lord John Russell, who sounds the alarm after this fashion:

[1] Historical Sketches, pp. 179—199.

"It will be my business, if I should be able to continue this work, to point out the utter want of foresight by which the conduct of Mr. Pitt was marked, when he led the people of England into a crusade against the people of France." It might, perhaps, without injustice, be denominated a crusade against anarchy, and there was certainly a dash of chivalrous feeling in the hearts of the war party. This is a fault which was never charged upon the Whigs, and therefore Mr. Burke abandoned them. Mr. Fox might be pardoned for not foresceing the events, which by his own admission would have altered his opinion, and which Mr. Pitt did foresee; but how any man, looking at the facts of history, can impute want of foresight to that Minister, would be quite incomprehensible, were there not proofs enough that writers who are afflicted with Whiggery labour under an incapability of discerning truth. As in physics, there is a condition of the sight called colour blindness, which disables individuals from distinguishing certain colours, so that red appears blue, or *vice versâ*,—so party blindness falsifies the aspect of truth, and incapacitates some persons from discerning its real hue. Herein lies the cause of the inconsistencies and fallacies which disfigure their writings. Thus Lord John Russell, in his anxiety to censure Mr. Pitt, states that at the commencement of the Revolution, "the fear of French principles, horror at French crimes, and disgust at French excesses, were constantly put forth as *incentives* to war." If he had said in justification of the war, he would have spoken the truth. But why that term, "incentives?" It is plainly an insinuation that Mr. Pitt was pugnacious, and wanted to stir up a reluctant people to engage in the war. He might have learned better from his great ally, who, though equally bent upon assaulting the leader of the Tories, had yet the candour to allow that all Mr. Pitt's thoughts were ever turned towards peace, and that he not only professed, but undoubtedly felt an ardent love of peace;[1] and that was shown by his repeated efforts to terminate the war, as soon as a reasonable prospect of success appeared. At first negociation was impossible; for during the chaos and anarchy that reigned in France for some time after she had declared war, and insulted, as Marshal St. Cyr acknowledges, not only all kings, but every existing government, there was no ruling power there in which any confidence could be reposed; none on the stability of which, from month to month, any reliance could be placed.[2] As soon as a somewhat more settled form of government gave the

[1] Historical Sketches, &c. by Lord Brougham, vol. L book 2, § 193.

[2] "Mr. Pitt said, with great truth, At present (under Robespierre), there is no security for the continuance of peace, even if it were signed, for a single hour; every successive faction which has risen to the head of affairs in France, has perished the moment that it attempted to imprint moderation on the external or internal measures of the Revolution. It is a contest for the security, the tranquillity, and the very existence of Great Britain, connected with that of every established government, and every country in Europe."
—Alison's Hist. vol. ii. p. 449.

slightest hope that treaties might be effected and respected, several attempts were made by Mr. Pitt to bring about a negociation.

The first overtures for peace from the British Government were made through Mr. Wickham, in Switzerland, in 1796, but failed, because France insisted on keeping all the conquered territories which had been annexed to it by a decree of its own legislature—Savoy, Flanders, both Dutch and Austrian, &c. The second attempt was made by overtures from Great Britain in the same year, through the Danish Ambassador; but they were flatly refused by France, on the ground of their not being made by a direct communication to the Directory; although Lord Grenville's note requested a passport for an ambassador, to go to Paris to negociate. A third attempt was made in September of the same year, by a direct application, and at the end of October Lord Malmesbury went to Paris; but the terms were refused by France, without any counterproject being offered, and he was ordered to quit Paris. The terms were, that Great Britain should resign all her conquests; France to restore the Netherlands, to evacuate Italy, and to make peace with Germany. Lastly, another attempt at negociation was made in June, 1797, in consequence of the preliminaries being signed at Leoben between France and the Emperor, and the plenipotentiaries met at Lisle. The terms offered on our side were most liberal;—to surrender all our conquests from France, and to claim nothing in return; but France required the cession of all that we had conquered from Spain and Holland besides; and, by insisting upon this as a preliminary, the treaty was broken off. And who was it in England that opposed this peace? Who was it that put forth arguments as incentives to war? It was Mr. Fox, who objected to the Ministers getting out of a contest, which, at the same time, he styles most unjust and most impolitic, by a peace *quelconque;* and would not acquiesce in their making such a peace as could be justified only upon consideration of the condition in which they had brought us.[1]

But as Fox was thus blind to the fact, which has been incontestably proved, that the war was not unjust, and that the Ministers did not bring us into it, and that it was not their own policy, but a policy to which they were reluctantly obliged to submit,—so Lord John Russell is equally unable to see the natural consequences of the war; and the sagacity of Mr. Pitt's foresight is favourably contrasted with the retrospective blindness of his critic. He asks with the most *naïve* simplicity, how war could extirpate French principles, or arrest French crimes? As if Mr. Pitt or any one else ever contemplated the possibility of extirpating the one, or arresting the other in France. And yet, if they had really wished it, it would not have been unreasonable to expect that war, by diminishing the power of the criminals, who were a

[1] Mr. Fox to Lord Holland, Hist. Sket. vol. iii. p. 133.

small minority of the nation, might have encouraged the more sober-minded majority to resist their detestable proceedings. In all probability, if the abuse of power by the higher classes had not deprived them of sympathy, and left the bulk of the people in a profound indifference to political changes, the offer of foreign aid might have roused them from their apathy, and the successive factions that waded through blood to power might have been checked in their career; their principles might have been repudiated, and their crimes arrested.

But Mr. Pitt had no such object in view, which, indeed, his incautious censor himself elsewhere confesses. By his own acknowledgment, "Mr. Pitt was ready to admit that we had nothing to do with the internal government of France, provided its rulers were disposed and able to maintain friendly relations with foreign governments. He sought to confine France within her ancient limits, to oblige her to respect established treaties, and to renounce her conquests; he treated Robespierre and Carnot as he would have treated any other French rulers, whose ambition was to be resisted, and whose interference in the affairs of other nations was to be checked and prevented."[1] This statement is fully borne out by the historian of those times: "The basis of the alliance with Russia was, that the French should be left entirely at liberty to arrange their government and their internal concerns for themselves,

[1] Page 33.

and that the efforts of the allies should be limited to prevent their interfering with other states, or extending their conquests or propagandism beyond their own frontier."[1] But they did interfere with other states, and extended not only their conquests, but their propagandism beyond their own frontiers. The Convention infringed the treaty of Munster by opening the navigation of the Scheldt, and violated the rights of nations by a decree, that the Austrians should be pursued into the Dutch territories; and with what fatal effects the spirit of propagandism stalked abroad beyond the frontiers, the same historian thus describes:—"Addressing herself to the discontented multitude in every state, paralyzing the national strength by a division of its population, and taking advantage of that division to overthrow its independence, France succeeded in establishing her dominion over more than one half of Europe. Experience proved that the freedom which the Jacobin agents insidiously offered to the deluded population of other states, was neither more nor less than an entire subjection to the agents of France, and the peril incurred was even greater in peace than in war. The continuance of amicable relations was favourable to the secret propagation of the revolutionary mania, and she made more rapid strides towards universal dominion during one year of pacific encroachment, than in six years of hostilities."[2]

These were the consequences which Mr. Pitt *foresaw*,

[1] Alison's Hist., vol. iii. p. 88.   [2] Ibid. vol. iii. p. 619.

and from which he wisely determined to save his
own country, when he accepted the challenge to battle
thrown out by France. War was the *cordon sanitaire*
by which he saved it from the contagion of her Jacobinical principles, and from participation in her destructive crimes. That the danger which reconciled
Mr. Pitt to the abandonment of his pacific policy was
real and alarming, is abundantly proved by the language used in the National Convention, when compli-
mentary addresses were sent to them by the London
Corresponding Society, and forty others of the same
stamp. In November, 1792, they were convinced that
England was labouring in the throes of a similar
revolution to their own; and the President, Gregoric, is
reported to have said, that " the respectable islanders,
who were once their masters in the social arts, had
become their disciples; and, treading in their steps,
would soon strike a blow that should resound to the
extremity of Asia." What then but that party prejudice, which clouds the clearest understanding, could
induce Lord John Russell to assert, that " there never
was a more unfounded fear than that which induced
the great majority of the nation to dread the overthrow of their constitution by a small minority enamoured of French principles;" an assertion practically
refuted by the example of France itself, where the
horrors of the revolution were perpetrated by a
minority of the population; and contradicted, according to his own confession, not only by the great

majority of the nation, who were certainly better judges of their own danger than one who has had no opportunity of feeling the fevered pulse of those times, but also by the great majority of his own party. It is a singularly startling confession, and one for which his friends will not thank him. "'Thus,'" says he, "while Mr. Fox gave to his friends the most PATRIOTIC (which means republican and revolutionary) counsels, the great Whig party, which he led, broke off into two divisions; he was left almost alone, his popularity was gone, and his name held up to detestation: he was purely and simply a Whig." What a severe satire upon his party! He then, who is purely and simply a Whig, is a person whose name is held up to detestation for his principles; who is renounced and denounced by his dearest friends.

The Duke of Portland, at the head of forty peers and a hundred and seven commoners, yielded to this necessity at last,[1] though he was long restrained from adopting such a course by personal partiality for the man. Sir Gilbert Elliot stated to him, in the strongest manner, the conduct of Fox; that it was founded on the worst of principles—on those on which the French Revolution was founded; that it went to overthrow the country; that it was essential, for the honour of the party, to separate from him; and that it was impossible for them not to express publicly their entire disapprobation of Fox's conduct and principles. And

[1] Lord Malmesbury's Diary, vol. ii. p. 488.

Lord Malmesbury says,[1] "It grieves me to separate from him; it grieves me still more to see how completely he has set the whole country against him. If he is sincere, he is dangerous, acting upon principle; if insincere, he is dangerous, acting without principle."[2] And he was very anxious to save his party from partaking of all the odium and disgrace which Fox had brought upon himself by his conduct.[3] These partisans were evidently not of the right sort to please Lord John; they had not learned sufficiently from Fox's patriotic counsels, to hate the government of their country, and to rejoice in the successes of the Republic.

This is no prejudiced picture of that type and model of a pure and simple Whig; it is his own description of his feelings, for thus he writes to Mr. Grey: "'The truth is, I am gone something farther in hate to the English Government than perhaps you and the rest of my friends are, and certainly farther than can with prudence be avowed. The triumph of the French Government over the English does, in fact, afford me a degree of *pleasure* which it is very difficult to disguise."[4] The isolation of Mr. Fox may be thought to favour the assertion, that the fear of the Constitution being overthrown by the small minority of those who were enamoured of French Jacobinism,

---

[1] Lord Malmesbury's Diary, vol. II. p. 416.   [2] *Ibid.* p. 600.
[3] *Ibid.* p. 486.   [4] Memoirs and Correspondence of C. J. Fox, vol. iii. p. 349.

was quite unfounded. But it is to be remembered, that those who deserted him were only the sensible, well-educated men in Parliament. But, again, no other confutation is needed than Lord John's own confession; for he admits that, at a later period, some violent men appear to have meditated a revolution, but "the conspiracies were abortive" (why?), "because their designs were shallow, and their plans immature." But what if their designs had been deeper laid, and their plans more matured? "the insignificance of the party" would not have prevented them from deluging the land with blood. The fact is, the party was not insignificant. How could it be so when the King was fired at in the park, and the mob had almost succeeded in dragging him from his carriage? when the cry of "No king—no nobles" was heard in the streets? when 2,000 people, at the Crown and Anchor tavern, drank the toast, for which the Duke of Norfolk was most justly deprived of his Lord Lieutenancy, "The people—the sovereign"? when conventions were formed in various parts of the country to coerce the Parliament, and demagogues were agitating the principal manufacturing towns, to organise a National Convention, in imitation of that in France? And what if Mr. Fox himself contradicted this rash assertion of unfounded fear?

In 1706 he thus writes to his nephew: "At present I think that we ought to go further towards agreeing with the democratic or popular party than at any former period .... we as a party can do nothing; and the contest must be between the Court and the democrats. These last, without our assistance, will be too weak to resist the Court; or, if they are strong enough, will go probably to greater excesses, and bring on the only state of things which can make a man doubt whether the despotism of monarchy is the worst of all evils."[1] Thus, with his eyes open to the probable consequences, he proposed to assist the democrats to do what he deprecated, rather than submit to a constitutional monarchy. And such were the patriotic counsels which he gave to his friends. But this is not all. In another letter he says, "The country seems divided between the majority who are subdued by fears, or corrupted by hopes; and the minority, who are waiting sulkily for opportunities for violent remedies." And again, "It is a duty to brave all calumny that will be thrown upon us, on account of the countenance which we shall be represented as giving to the Corresponding Society, and others who are supposed to wish the overthrow of the monarchy. My view of things is, I own, very gloomy, and I am convinced that in a very few years this Government will become completely absolute; or that confusion will arise of a nature almost as much to be deprecated as despotism itself..... I cannot disguise from myself that there are but too many who wish for this."[2]

In the face of this evidence—unexceptionable evi-

[1] Vol. iii, p. 135.   [2] P. 164, and 70.

dence, since it is furnished by Mr. Fox himself—Lord John Russell will do well to abstain from raking up the almost forgotten embers of Whig incendiarism, which only serves to throw a stronger light upon the superior wisdom of Mr. Pitt.

Since this vindication of Mr. Pitt from the imputations of Lord John Russell was penned, he, with the usual recklessness of his dauntless spirit, has actually attempted to redeem his pledge by repeating the same charges nearly in the same words, and with as little success. Still, as it occupies a considerable portion of his second volume of the "Life of Fox," it is a duty to expose once more the weakness of the attack. Some apology is due to the reader for repeating several passages which have been already given; but when a man in the high position of Lord John Russell, deliberately endeavours to deceive mankind by repeating the old fallacies more insidiously and elaborately dressed up, apparently on the principle that water indents the stone,—not by any native force, but by the incessant repetition of its drops;—and when his settled purpose is to damage the character of a more exalted statesman than himself; to drag him before the bar of his country, and to impeach him of high crimes and misdemeanours;—the interests of justice require us to meet the enemy with the same weapons which have foiled him before, and, without expecting the reader to bear in mind all that has been already adduced, to lay before him again the strongest points of evidence,—whether they have been used before or not,—in order to exhibit the light of truth in more striking contrast with the haziness of Whig sophistry.

Well, then; Lord John now renews his impotent attempt to prove Mr. Pitt guilty of needlessly involving his country in war at the time of the French Revolution; and in this second attack we may fairly conclude that he has exhausted his armoury, and used every argument which party zeal could suggest to favour his attempt.

It will be my business to show that he had much better have let it alone. Being, however, a cunning fencer, he makes many desperate lunges at his adversary whenever he thinks he can wound him. They are easily parried, but being constantly almost the same, the defence must partake of the monotony of the assault; and as there is little diversity in the arguments except in outward form, there must necessarily be much repetition in the confutation of them. After first explaining the position of Mr. Pitt and his government at that period, with remarkable impartiality and perspicuity, he seems to bethink himself that it is time to disparage him, in order to magnify his rival, Mr. Fox; for which purpose he proceeds to weave a web of sophistry, some of the salient points of which it is necessary to disentangle. He makes common cause with M. Chauvelin, the French Emissary, who had the assurance to ask our Government to recognise the justice and necessity of the war which

France had declared against Austria, after various outrages for which no reparation had been made, on the plea that she had sheltered the emigrants, and that England had not suffered other powers to lend the smallest assistance to rebellious subjects.

Had, then, France so soon forgotten the no small assistance which she had lent to British rebels in America? But he also pointed out the marks of a conspiracy against free states which threatened universal war, and England was called upon to stop the progress of that confederacy, which threatened the peace and happiness of Europe. Who could believe that this proposition came from a Government that had recently promised its assistance to all nations who wished to overthrow monarchy? Lord Grenville was not moved by these impudent suggestions to depart from the pacific policy of Mr. Pitt—the policy of non-intervention;—that policy on which Lord John now so strenuously insists. Nevertheless, in Lord Grenville, he imputes it to a secret wish for the success of a design to conquer and despoil France. And from this imputation he could only have escaped by making war upon the allies.

On this principle England has had a narrow escape from a declaration of war against Austria in the late Italian campaign; for the distinction which he proceeds to draw would have exactly reduced us to that dilemma. "It is one thing," says he, "to decline to interfere in the internal affairs of another country; it is a totally different thing not to interfere with an external war which is intended to effect the conquest and share the spoils of one of the great members of the European confederacy. The first is a due homage to the independence of another nation; the second is a culpable indifference to the peace of Europe, and the treaties upon which that peace was founded."[1] But Austria intended to effect the conquest of Piedmont, and actually invaded that member of the European Confederacy, and had set at nought the Treaty of 1815. Therefore, on his own showing, our Minister at War displayed a culpable indifference to the peace of Europe, and the treaties upon which that peace was founded, by not interfering against Austria. But in the war of the Revolution the truth is exactly the reverse of the representation of it by Lord John: for which nation was it that not only intended to conquer and despoil her neighbours, but had actually commenced that conquest and spoliation by a war wholly unprovoked? It was France. True it is that, in 1701, Russia and Sweden had proposed an invasion of France to the German Powers in favour of the King; but, at the interview which took place at Pilnitz, the King of Prussia betrayed violent signs of disapprobation, and the views of Leopold were too pacific to adopt so bold and hostile a measure.[1]

Nevertheless, France declared war against the King

[1] Life of Fox, vol. ii. p. 298.
[2] Annual Register for 1792, p. 389.

of Hungary and Bohemia in the following year; and since it would have been "culpable indifference" in Prussia to take no part in resisting that unjust aggression, she joined the Emperor in his attempt to liberate France from the dangerous turbulence of anarchy. The allies had sufficient causes of complaint, as most people will think, in the confiscation of the feudal property of the German Princes, the opening of the Scheldt, the seizure of Avignon, and the conquest of Savoy. But Lord J. Russell is so determined to see everything from a French point of view, that although Mr. Fox had laid down this rule, that the justifiable grounds of war are injury, insult, and danger,[1] all of which were combined in these measures, and others which he overlooks; yet, he sets them down as mere pretexts,[2]—nay, even the declaration that the allies intended to restore the King of France to liberty, that he might confer a constitution upon his subjects, is asserted to have been only a pretext;[3]—the real motive being the conquest and spoliation of France,—a wild assertion, which will be noticed again before I have done with him. At present, it is enough to say that, so far from wishing to share in the spoils of France, the allies declared, in their proclamation, that in the just war which they had undertaken they entertained no views of personal aggrandisement, which they expressly renounced. And what nation was it that threatened the peace of Europe, and violated the

[1] Life of Fox, vol. ii. p. 336. [2] Ibid. p. 231. [3] Ibid. p. 230.

treaties upon which that peace was founded? It was France, which had alarmed Europe by seizing upon her neighbours' territories without the smallest pretence of right: Savoy and Avignon, and Basle on the south, and Belgium on the north; for Belgium was invaded some time before the Austrian declaration of war. It was France that had violated the treaty by which the navigation of the Scheldt was closed against foreign nations,—a treaty, made with the sanction of England, between the two Governments of the countries through which that river flows.

Nor was this all. She had violated the treaty of Westphalia, which, with several subsequent treaties, guaranteed to the German Princes in Alsace and Franche Compté many political rights and ecclesiastical privileges which the Constituent Assembly had annulled. Surely, then, the best friends of Lord John will scarcely refrain from a smile when, from these premises, he infers that a fair and honest neutrality was not the policy of the Cabinet of England, and taunts the Government with looking on with complacency on the invasion of France, and being restless and menacing when Flanders was conquered. He may imploringly stretch out his hands to them, and say, " Risum teneatis, amici;" but it would be all in vain. There is something too ludicrous in his unhappy attempt to shift upon the policy of Mr. Pitt the blame which sits so heavily on the shoulders of France. It is not that he is enamoured with the French Revolution, like his hero,

Mr. Fox; he does not, like that statesman, admire it as "the most stupendous and glorious edifice of liberty which had been erected on the foundation of human integrity in any time or country." On the contrary, he goes so far as to admit that the French were the aggressors against the institutions of Europe, and that the panic in England was increased by the insane provocations of the Convention. But, unfortunately, he had given a pledge to bring in Mr. Pitt guilty of the war, and he could not redeem it without plunging into various absurdities, and building up his indictment upon the quicksands of sophistry. Thus, for instance, he says: "In the preceding spring, Austria and Prussia had maintained a large body of armed Frenchmen on the frontiers of France with the avowed intention of overthrowing the Constitution to which the King of the French had pledged his faith."[1]

Nothing can be further from the truth than this assertion. In March, Count Kobentzel assured M. Noailles, that his Court was far from wishing to intermeddle in the interior concerns of France, and that it by no means intended to support the interests of the Emigrants.[2] A short time before, the Emperor had insisted that the Emigrants should make no attempt to disturb the public tranquillity.[3] Notwithstanding these pacific explanations, France declared war on April 20th; and it happens that we know, from the best authority, what

[1] Life of Fox, vol. ii. p. 300.
[2] Annual Register for 1792, p. 281.   [3] Ibid. p. 277.

was the real motive; not the flimsy pretext advanced by M. Noailles, but " it was the abolition of royalty," said Brissot, in a pamphlet,[1] " which I had in view in causing war to be declared." No wonder, then, when they were thus compelled to stand on their defence, and felt the imminent danger of their positions, if the German powers resolved to unite, not against the King of France, nor against any constitution of which he approved, but against the wild beasts who were thirsting for their blood, the enemies of society, whose cry was, " Havoc, and let slip the dogs of war." These were the principles of self-defence which the Allies declared on entering France. But how could that justify the principles of universal aggression proclaimed by the bandits opposed to them, and the premium which they offered to rebellion in every nation they could reach? What then could induce Lord John to ask so strange a question as this : " Who could wonder that the French should proclaim their principles as loudly as the Allies had proclaimed theirs, and should offer the assistance of their arms to all nations which should accept their principles?"[2] The same remarkable ignorance of the true posture of the respective parties is shown in " the real cure of the evil " which he, with singular infelicity, suggests. He says, " If Austria and Prussia had been called upon to renounce all interference in the internal affairs of France, the Convention might, on such a pledge being given, be called upon to repeal its decree of November. The hostility

[1] Annual Register for 1792, p. 273. [2] Life of Fox, vol. ii. p. 300.

of England might well have been proclaimed the penalty of that power which should refuse to comply with such an impartial decision."

This passage must have been penned in utter ignorance or forgetfulness of the events which preceded the war. Germany had distinctly explained that if France would not interfere with her neighbours, they would not interfere with her. Nothing could be more impartial than the terms proposed; and since France rejected them, England was, by Solomon's own decision, justified in inflicting the penalty of joining the Allies. But even if Solomon's cure had been attempted, and Mr. Pitt had offered his mediation, the result would have very much resembled that of the cures proposed by other quacks; we have reason to know, that it must have failed. M. Thersaint, a zealous supporter of Brissot, stated in a semi-official report, January 1st, 1793, that one of Mr. Pitt's plans was to bring the Republic to a peace with its enemies by his mediation. He was, however, haughtily told, that "he deceived himself, for that France would receive laws only from herself. It is fit he should know you are not afraid of kings, and that if you allow them still to exist, as such, you will at least have no treaties with them, or only those which are ratified by their nations. The first cannon fired at sea would impose upon them the duty of emancipating Holland, Spain, and America."[1]

Let us next examine another specimen of states-

[1] Annual Register for 1793, p. 182.

manship. "There can be little doubt that if instead of waiting till the end of December, Mr. Pitt had by that time obtained the co-operation of Russia; if this concert had been notified at Paris, and if part of the Low Countries had been ceded to France, or the whole of Belgium erected into an independent state, as was done forty years afterwards, peace might have been restored to Europe. Possibly the life of Louis XVI. might have been spared."[1] What a strange hallucination does this writer labour under! he assumes what is directly contrary to the truth; that France was then under the government of reasonable and moderate men, who would be contented with equitable terms. But let us look into the particulars upon which this "little doubt" reposes. Mr. Pitt knew perfectly well from what had occurred at Pilnitz, that he would not have the co-operation of Russia; the Czar and he entertained the most opposite views upon the subject: the one was for interference, the other was against it. The communication of December 27th, conveying Mr. Pitt's views, was only the reply to an inquiry without any hope of consent; and there were two other Courts to be consulted, one of which had only just lost the Netherlands, the cession of which is so coolly proposed. But this had occurred only three or four weeks before; for the citadel of Antwerp surrendered on the 8th, and Lord John must be sufficiently acquainted with diplomatic delays, and Austrian impracticability, to be quite sure how impossible it was

[1] Life of Fox, vol. ii. p. 309.

to bring things to such a conclusion in so short a time before the invention of electric telegraphs.

But why was Austria to surrender the Netherlands so easily without any compensation? On the principle of *uti possidetis?* But it was so recent an acquisition by France that it could scarcely be looked upon as a possession; nay, the French themselves did not look upon it in that light; they declared that it was only a temporary occupation till peace was restored, and that they did not covet Belgium; they only desired that its liberty and independence might be secured. Might then the Belgians have chosen to live under the Emperor again? No. They could not have become an independent state, as they became forty years afterwards, by accepting a monarchy. That was not French liberty. They who were so jealous of interference with their own Government, insisted upon dictating to others what theirs should be. But were all the four Courts to crouch under the heel of France, and sanction all her usurpations? Was she to be allowed to oust the German Princes from Lorraine and Alsace, and to retain Avignon and Nice, and Basle, and Savoy on the same principle of *uti possidetis?* of all which, according to the policy professed by Lord John, " no one would have any right to complain. There is " little doubt," therefore, that peace would not then have been restored to Europe; and any interference to save the life of Louis would have been treated with the same scorn as the remonstrances of the King of Spain.

Lord John's statement with regard to Holland is equally destitute of truth. He says, she was dragged by England most reluctantly into the war.[1] She desired, indeed, most earnestly, to be neutral; but her neutrality was most unscrupulously violated by France, who forced the passage of the river Scheldt in defiance of her protest, and ordered her generals to pursue the routed Austrians into the Dutch territory, if they retired there.[2] And though the French Government gave the most positive assurance that its conquest should not be attempted, so long as that country should confine itself within the bounds of a strict neutrality, yet, three weeks antecedent to that promise being given, it had resolved upon an invasion of the United Provinces, which was solely delayed for a time, that it might afterwards be undertaken with the greater safety; and accordingly it was included in the declaration of war made against England in the following year. In his anxiety to make out how much more folly there was on this side of the Channel than on the other, Lord John proceeds to say, that "a fear crept upon persons of property, that the democratic principles of France might take root in England; and it was thought, that by turning the thoughts of the people to foreign war this danger might be averted. . . . This view of the question shows very little trust in the attachment of the people of England to their own

---

[1] Life of Fox, vol. ii. p. 304.
[2] Annual Register for 1793, p. 165.

institutions, and very little disposition to do justice to the French nation.... Yet that the war was a war of panic I do not mean to deny."[1] That is to say, the war was an unjust war, and the panic was irrational fear. But when there were about thirty clubs in London, the object of which was to disseminate seditious principles, besides twenty-two towns in which one or more corresponding societies were established for the same purpose; when it was shown in Parliament that in every town, and in almost every village in the kingdom their emissaries had found means to distribute gratuitously among the lower classes publications of a very dangerous tendency; that, under the specious mask of Reform, they had propagated the most destructive doctrines, sparing no pains to excite discontent in the minds of the populace; that they recommended to imitation the revolutionary example of France, for attaining their objects; that the time had now arrived for the people to redress themselves; and had held out to the lower classes the strong temptation of an agrarian law; that they had secretly negotiated with the Jacobins of France for the subversion of the British constitution; when to their machinations were imputed the most alarming of the riots which had broken out under various false pretences;—was it not unavoidable, was it not reasonable, that the public mind should feel a considerable degree of agitation, oppressed with anxious forebodings, and dreadful apprehensions

[1] Life of Fox, vol. iv. p. 304.

of some political convulsion already in preparation
and ready to explode?[1]

Mr. Pitt stated, that when the Convention received
the addresses sent to them by several English societies,
too contemptible in the opinion of some even for
notice, they always considered such addresses declara-
tory of the sentiments of the English nation, and he
quoted the letter of Monge, the minister of the French
Marine, in which he said, "The King of England and
his Parliament mean to make war upon us:" will the
English republicans suffer it? Already their freemen
show their discontent, and their repugnance to bear
arms against their brethren in France. Well, we will
fly to their succour; we will make a descent upon
their island ... then will the tyranny of their government be soon destroyed."[2] Was there not a cause
then, not for a panic, which is a foolish fear, but for
rational alarm, not only amongst the landed gentry,
but amongst all owners of property, and lovers of
order? And what could have averted some dreadful
catastrophe if they had not combined to show those
traitors, who scrupled not to say, that the attainment

[1] Annual Register for 1792, p. 247.
[2] He inferred this from the increase of our forces by sea and land,
which was only a prudent precaution of self-defence against the
known and avowed hostility of the Convention, who gladly made
use of the inference as one of the pretexts for declaring war. It is
to be feared there are those now in France, who, if they were at the
head of affairs, would pursue the same line of conduct; but happily
for the peace of Europe, the destinies of that country are not now
under the sway of a tyrannical and dishonest republic.
[3] State Papers, Annual Register, p. 204.

of their objects would be worth the expense of blood, that there was a large majority against them, determined to frustrate their designs? Whenever a fatal epidemic breaks out, wise men will not sit down with folded arms to await their destiny; they will hasten to adopt remedies, to organize sanitary precautions, and to remove, as far as they can, all predisposing causes; but if they succeed, and because they succeed in arresting its progress, will any sane man argue that, therefore, there was no danger? It was because the majority of Englishmen were attached to their institutions, that it was necessary to use strong measures to prevent a turbulent and unscrupulous minority from disturbing the peace of the country. Yes, —it was well for England that her gentry were at last "thoroughly frightened," and roused to stand upon their defence. Lord John would have had them resemble the lamb described by Pope,—

"Pleas'd to the last he crops the flow'ry food,
And licks the hand just rais'd to shed his blood."

With respect to doing justice to the French nation, he will scarcely deny, that if any one is likely to do justice to them, it would be a countryman of their own, a general employed by the Convention—the general who won the battle of Jemappes, and conquered the Netherlands for them. What then is the picture which Dumouriez gives of them at that time, after the 10th of August? He says, "All the departments (but more especially the wretched city of Paris) were delivered up to pillage, to denunciations, proscriptions, and massacres. No Frenchman, the assassins and their accomplices excepted, had either his life or his property in security. Bands of pretended federates ran through, and laid waste, the departments; and of the seven hundred individuals who composed this despotical and anarchical body, four or five hundred groaned and decreed, and decreed and groaned, exposed to the exterminating sword of the Marats and Robespierres ... The decree of the 19th of November has provoked all nations, by holding out to them our aid, provided they will consent to disorganize themselves .... During the last month all the decrees have been marked by the most insatiable avarice, by the blindest pride, and more especially by the desire of maintaining power by calling to the most important posts of the state no other than daring, incapable, and criminal men, by driving away or murdering men of enlightened and high character; and by supporting a phantom of a republic which their errors in administration and in policy, as well as their crimes, had rendered impracticable. .... We see throughout the tyranny which flatters the wicked, because the wicked alone can support the tyranny; and in its pride and its ignorance this Convention orders the conquest and disorganization of the whole universe. ... And what has it done to maintain the war which it has provoked against all the powers of Europe?[1]

[1] State Papers, Annual Register, p. 306.

The only way of "showing a disposition to do justice" to these persons, would be by sentencing them to be hanged; and the proclamation of the Duke of Brunswick was, after all, not so much to be blamed, in making them responsible for the safety of the King under the penalty of losing their own heads. And here another gross misrepresentation has to be noticed. Lord John says, "If the Allies had reached Paris, if they had liberated Louis, if they had hung the majority of the Convention" (as they deserved), "and shot thousands of mayors, magistrates and peasantry, according to their own declared intentions, how would such proceedings have tranquillized France?" If they had liberated Louis and enabled him to take up his residence in some frontier town, which was their declared wish, where he could negotiate in safety with his subjects, France would have been tranquillized, as far as the Allies were concerned; for they would have gained their object. Their proclamations had distinctly stated that this was the only object of the invasion, and they disavowed, as already observed, all desire to intermeddle with the interior concerns of France. The imputation of sanguinary intentions is wholly incorrect: it was only in case of open resistance that punishment was to be inflicted, which is entirely suppressed in the accusation.

War without giving quarter is very shocking, but by no means unusual; and that was the whole amount of the threatened severities, threatened for the sake of intimidation, but not carried into execution; and even the Convention would have kept their heads, richly as they deserved to lose them, if Louis had been left uninjured. They, as well as the mayors, and magistrates, in the provincial towns, were made responsible for any crimes which they might and ought to have prevented; so that a great deal of virtuous indignation has been thrown away upon imaginary crimes. But all this misrepresentation was not without an object. Lord John wanted it to assist him in his vituperation of Mr. Pitt, and give some colour to his next assault upon that minister. "The tacit consent and secret favour given to this invasion of France was a serious mistake" on Pitt's part. As long as the favour was secret, it is difficult to see how any statesmanship was concerned in it. Lord John probably concurs with Mr. Fox in condemning it as "a horrid and profligate scheme to ruin the liberty of the world." But most Englishmen, no doubt, viewed it with secret favour, in which I presume to think there was no harm at all. I should much wonder if it were otherwise: but why is "the tacit consent" of the Government to be reprobated? What would he have had them do? Go to war with Austria and Prussia if they persisted in the invasion, and so find themselves in the ridiculous position of being engaged in war with both the opposed parties at once? With the Allies because they would not take our advice; and with France, because we withdrew our ambassador from Paris after the 10th of August, and would not accredit another to a government so unstable, that Brissot, who in the height of his popularity was the author of the war, was guillotined with twenty of his adherents before that year was closed.

As our connexion with the Allies had nothing to do with the war which Mr. Pitt declared; so our separation from them would not have prevented it. Even Mr. Fox with all his democratical sympathies, if he had been in office, would not have gone the length of entering into an alliance with France, and yielding everything that she demanded. Lord John Russell says, that "his course would evidently have been an armed negotiation!" A strange oversight for any one to make who has read the history of those times. Why it was the very fact of our having assumed the attitude of armed negotiation, which was one of the pretences for the declaration of war. Unarmed negotiation, if it means anything, implies a menace that if the negotiation fails the negotiator is ready to have recourse to arms. This course therefore Mr. Fox could not take, unless he had made up his mind to go to war in case of failure; for he had said in the debate on the peace with Russia, "I cannot conceive any case in which a great and wise nation having committed itself by a menace, can withdraw that menace without disgrace; . . . without seriously meaning to enforce it.' Again, "he would

¹ Life of Fox, vol. ii. p. 208.

have taken ample security for the independence of
Holland."—What security could he have had when
dealing with persons of such bad faith, that at the
very time when they were promising to respect its
neutrality, they had issued orders to invade its territory?—And " he would have guaranteed France
against another invasion." As if Austria and Prussia
were provinces of England, bound to make war or
peace at her dictation. This is a specimen of that
spirit, which in other persons would be called pre-
sumptuousness, but which is a well-known characteristic of the noble Lord; and what glory may
we not expect to accrue to this country in her foreign
relations under the conduct of a minister who has
so much confidence in her political omnipotence, that
he fully relies upon it as a means by which that
success might have been achieved which Mr. Pitt failed
to obtain.

Again, Mr. Pitt declined to expose England to the
humiliation which Spain experienced, of preferring a
request which was sure to be scornfully rejected; but
that too was another " serious error." Mr. Fox would
have succeeded; and so would Lord John Russell; but
how? He would have advised our King to say to the
French Ambassador, in May, 1792, that " he would
not allow any interference in the internal government
of France, nor any conquest by France under whatever
pretext it might be covered. He would probably have
saved the King of France's life, and prevented a war in

Europe."[1] Can Lord John be really serious in making this statement, or is it a secret satire upon diplomacy to show with how little wisdom he thinks mankind may be governed? Of course, the Allies would have answered; "We have not the slightest intention or thought of interfering with the internal government of France;" nor had they till two months afterwards, and then only for the personal safety and liberation of Louis, who though not yet in prison, was not at liberty to go where he pleased. But they would have added; "We entirely object to your offensive language. You talk of not allowing us to do this or that! We cannot allow you to speak to us in that peremptory way." On the other hand, the French would have equally objected to such dictatorial style, and might say as the Hebrew said to Moses, when he interposed, and asked, "Why smitest thou thy brother? Who made thee a prince and a judge over us?" As to their conquests, they would easily have contrived to delude our credulous Minister, and to pacify him with smooth words till interference would be useless, all the while laughing at him in their sleeves, from the knowledge that they had actually then 130,000 men ready to pounce upon the Netherlands, which were only guarded by 10,000 Austrians, and which they had already poisoned with discontent. After this, the conquest being once accomplished, according to Lord John's own doctrine, and that of

[1] Life of Fox, vol. ii. p. 348.

Mr. Fox, "the only wise course that remained would be to make peace with events which had been completed, and accept a state of affairs, against which no providence had guarded."[1]

And again, the enemy "stands upon the ground of conquest, and we must agree to treat with him with regard to his present posture."[2] It is true that the first attempt was not successful, but the second was, and France extended her frontiers on every side. She was obtaining that preponderance in Europe by appropriating to herself the territories of her neighbours on every side, by which the balance of power was destroyed; and therefore, on the authority of Mr. Fox himself, when he was in a patriotic mood, there was no alternative for the British Government but war: for even he did not counsel the indignity of submission, when there had been danger of a rupture with France, from her designing to assist the malcontents in Holland, to subvert their government. He maintained the soundness of " the political maxim, that Great Britain ought to look to the situation of affairs on the Continent, and take such measures as should tend best to preserve the balance of power in Europe: upon that maxim he had founded all his political conduct .... there are but few and short steps between the maintenance of that balance, and the insecurity of our national independence; the balance of power can only be overthrown by the prepon-

[1] Life of Fox, vol. ii. p. 299.   [2] Ibid. p. 303.

derance of one great state . . . a great preponderant state would threaten the independence of all its neighbours, and Great Britain would only have a choice between submission and war."¹ *Oh si sic omnia!*

Happily for us, our foreign minister acts better than he writes. He acts upon the political maxim of Mr. Fox, though he condemns it in Mr. Pitt. But it would have been better for his reputation as a statesman, if he had abstained from a sentimental lamentation about "the blood that flowed, and the treasures that were expended in the two wars; and about kings and nations engaging in a contest which the event proved to be unnecessary."² Surely if Mr. Fox was right, nothing could more strongly demonstrate the wisdom of his maxim, than the event of those two wars. The preponderance of one great state was taken away, and that balance of power was restored which it has been the constant aim of the European nations in general, whether in peace or war, to maintain unimpaired. The event proved them to be necessary. After all, however, it appears that this lofty arbitration to be imposed upon the contending parties, by which the life of Louis might have been saved and war prevented, was not the right mode of proceeding; for Mr. Pitt "committed the mistake of thinking that England could remain an unconcerned spectator of a war against all liberty on one side, and all monarchy on the other."³

¹ Life of Fox, vol. ii. p. 202. ² *Ibid.* p. 231. ³ *Ibid.* p. 340.

What! after labouring so much to prove that Mr. Pitt was guilty of involving his country in war, is he now to be condemned for his neutrality? If it was a mistake to suppose that England could be an unconcerned spectator of the war, it was necessary to side with one party or the other. For the futility of any other interference was manifest enough; and Lord Grenville stated with good reason, that though England was ready to concur in the re-establishment of peace, amongst the powers of Europe, by such means as were proper to produce that effect, yet the intervention of her counsels or good offices would be of no use unless they were desired by all parties "interested."[1] Since then to remain unconcerned spectators of the war, was either a great mistake or an impossibility, nothing remained for us to do, but to side with one party or the other; and we may conclude that if it had been our good fortune to have had Lord John Russell at the head of our councils instead of Mr. Pitt, he as a Whig would, Brennus-like, have thrown his sword into the scale of liberty and France.

But the dilemma is most inaccurately stated. It is true that on one side the war was against all monarchy,—for so it had been proclaimed in the Convention—but it is not true, that on the other side it was against all liberty. Here truth is sacrificed to antithesis. The Allies made no war against British liberty, or Swiss liberty, or American liberty; or even

[1] State Papers. Annual Register, 1792, p. 264.

against liberty in France to reconstruct any government they liked, under a monarch. They might have adopted the English model without one word of remonstrance from the Allies.

It was only a war against the French interpretation of liberty—liberty to commit crimes—to molest others — to impose their own laws and opinions upon their neighbours—to unhinge society, and to subvert governments by promoting rebellion and encouraging insurrection. No Englishman, except a disciple of Mr. Fox, could hesitate as to which side should be supported by those who could not be unconcerned spectators of the war. But Mr. Fox had said that it was a horrid league to effect the ruin of the liberty of man; and that was enough for Lord John Russell. It is not worth while to expose all the extravagant misrepresentations and sophisms of the great Whig orator, who might assert many things in the House of Commons, which he would not have committed to writing, although Lord John usually adopts his sentiments as the oracles of the idol which he worships. Nor indeed is it desirable to pursue the wearisome work of laying bare the fallacies of his disciple much farther. But there is one more floundering accusation of Mr. Pitt, which must not pass unnoticed ;—" He made his country clearly the aggressor in the war."[1] Now, how does Lord John attempt to prove this? The argument upon which he seems

[1] Life of Fox, vol. II. p. 347.

most to rely is, that our government had not committed the folly of offering to guarantee France against a renewal of the Duke of Brunswick's march, and the execution of the majority of the Convention as traitors and murderers.

It is scarcely necessary to remind the reader again, that the Duke's threat of vengeance was only intended to make the Republicans responsible for the life of the King, as long as such interference could save him; but when it was too late, nothing was ever said about punishing his murderers. Indeed, the Convention themselves took very good care in the course of the following year to save him that trouble. During the truce in September, before the retreat of the Prussians from the French territory, the Duke of Brunswick had thus expressed his objects to General Thouvenot: "We know that we have no right to prevent a nation from giving itself laws, and from tracing out its internal government: we do not wish it. We are only interested for the fate of the King. Assure us that a place will be assigned him in the new order of things, under any denomination whatever, and his Majesty the King of Prussia will return to his own states and become your ally."[1] Could any arbitration have proposed more moderate terms than these? But it was useless to negotiate with the men who then misgoverned France. At the time, however, when the probability of war was discussed in Parliament, the Allies

[1] Annual Register for 1793, p. 61.

were no longer on French ground; the French army had invaded Germany, and the Allies had much more reason to ask for a guarantee against another invasion. But one of the most extraordinary assumptions of this strange expositor of statesmanship is, that we could have demanded in favour of the Allies the evacuation of the conquered territories without their being parties to the treaty, and consenting to the counter stipulations to which France would be entitled. The only other argument, if argument it can be called, by which he tries to bolster up his false reasoning, is derived from "the temper in which the Government viewed the failure of the attempt to divide France and to crush democracy." Mr. Pitt certainly could not wish well to those principles which he described as breaking all the bonds of legislation that connected civil society, established in opposition to every law human or divine, and presumptuously relying on the authority of wild and delusive theories.[1] It is no wonder, therefore, that Lord Grenville expressed his disappointment that the attempt to make head against those democratical principles which threatened to desolate all Europe had failed; but on this subject we may say to Lord John, in the language of Cicero: "Habes quod accusatori est maxime optandum, confitentem sereum, sed tamen ita confitentem, se in eâ parte fuisse, quâ tc," Mr. Fox;[2] for he also had a share in it.

In the debate on the Canada question that gentle-

[1] Annual Register for 1703, p. 262.   [2] Orat. pro Ligurio.

man had complained of the unkindness of Mr. Burke
in imputing to him democratical or republican sentiments. In fact, however much Lord John may take it
under his protection, Mr. Fox had no affection for the
democracy then reigning in France. But with respect
to dividing France, nothing can be more unfortunate
than his blind attachment to that charge. He reiterates
it in every form of words; he harps upon that string
for ever, without perceiving the falseness of the note
which it utters. He talks perpetually about "sharing
in the spoils of France," the "division of France," the
"partition of France," the "dismemberment of
France,"[1] till one is almost disposed to exclaim with
the Latin orator, "Quousque tandem, Catilina, abutere
patientiâ nostrâ"[2] (Catiline was a Whig); for there is
not a shadow of foundation for the charge, in any
speech, in any document, in any state paper, from first
to last. Lord Grenville had said in a private letter,
not meant for the public ear, not in his public capacity, but confidentially to his brother, that he was
glad "we were not tempted to join in the glorious
enterprise of the Allies by the hope of sharing the
spoils in the division of France;" alluding, of course,
to the prospect of gaining possession of some of the
French Colonies. From this vague and careless expression the whole accusation is inferred; imput-

[1] Life of Fox, vol. ii. p. 272.
[2] "How long, O Catiline, will you continue to exhaust our patience?"

ing views to the Allies which they distinctly denied. Both Courts declared in their manifesto, on August 4, that they entertained no views of personal aggrandizement, which they expressly renounced.

The Duke of Brunswick declared before he invaded France, that they had no intention to enrich themselves by making conquests; and the Prince of Cobourg proclaimed that he did not come upon the French territory to make conquests, but to give to France her constitutional King, and the constitution which she had formed for herself, and might rectify as she pleased, if it was imperfect. In the prosecution of the war, it may be said that Valenciennes was taken, and that the Emperor claimed it as his own. But what was this compared with the number of large territories which the French had previously taken possession of—the Duchies of Deux Ponts, and Luxembourg, Trèves, and the Netherlands? Will any one contend that the right of invasion was all on one side; that it was innocent in the Democracy of France, and criminal in the German Empire? That the one might exercise the severest tyranny (for at Deux Ponts, the clergy, the nobles, and the judges were banished), while the other was quietly to submit and be precluded from the most moderate retaliation, like the servant in Terence, who remonstrated with his master on the inequality of their position: "Tu verberas; Ego vapulo tantùm?"[1]

[1] "You are the beater, I am only the beatee."

So far were the Allies in the first instance from wishing to appropriate anything to themselves, that after their first successes, they issued a proclamation on the 20th July, not banishing the magistrates, as the French had done at Deux Ponts, but reinstating their predecessors in the offices which they held before the Revolution, and re-establishing the ancient laws.[1] They disclaimed conquest as long as they had reason to hope that the largest part of the population favoured their views; but after the death of Louis, when they encountered unmixed hostility, they naturally took the course which all nations adopt in war. The object of each party is to cripple the other as much as possible, by making conquests, which, according to their importance, and the relative position of the combatants, may either be retained at the conclusion of the war, like Malta and Gibraltar, and the Cape, or surrendered for equivalent advantages. Thus, the peace of Amiens was purchased, by the surrender of many conquests by England. We may well, therefore, "be lost in amazement at the effrontery" which could, in the first place, indite such maudlin sentiment as this, of which a schoolboy would be ashamed: "When we find an Emperor of Germany appropriating a fortress, and a King of Great Britain conquering an island, we are lost in amazement at the effrontery which could cover a scheme of plunder with the cloak of religion and

[1] State Papers, Annual Register for 1793, p. 310.

humanity;"[1] and in the next place, could any one on such flimsy pretences accuse Mr. Pitt of being the aggressor in this war? In 1814, the nations of Europe, taught by bitter experience, and "the insane provocations" of Napoleon I., entered with heart and soul into that coalition which "the wisdom and foresight of Mr. Pitt" had projected long before, and effected the objects which he had in view. They marched upon Paris, and restored the constitutional King, and took from France her plunder and the dominions which she had unjustly usurped. But there was no partition, no division, no dismemberment, no sharing in the spoils of her proper territory, and the kingdom was preserved in its original integrity, as one of the first-rate powers of Europe. And now, *causa finita est*,—the pleadings are over; and to the shade of Pitt, if he could be supposed to care for the opinion of posterity, we may safely predict that this will be the verdict of mankind, "Solventur risu tabulæ, tu missus abibis." That is to say, the lawyers will laugh as they fold up their briefs, and you may depart unharmed by this impeachment.

Lord John Russell, however, is a much more reasonable person when he throws off the shackles of party, and allows himself to take a common sense view of international law. In his speech at Aberdeen, on the state of Italy, he is reported to have made these just

[1] Life of Fox, vol. ii. p. 378.

remarks: "I think with regard to this matter of state and nations regulating their own government, it is not very different from that of a man regulating his own house. But at the same time it is possible, that a man may manage his house in such a way as to be a great nuisance to his neighbours: for instance, he may start a pyrotechnic manufactory in his house, and amuse himself with sending up sky-rockets into the air every evening, in order to see the effect. This would not seem to be agreeable, because other householders might conceive that their houses might be set on fire. Instead of wishing to encourage the gentleman to do whatever he pleases in his own house, the Lord Provost might be called on to interfere with that gentleman, because he was likely to set fire to the houses of his neighbours. But has anything of that sort occurred in Italy?" Of course not, and therefore it is difficult to see why it was introduced, unless it is to be looked at as a palinodia which his conscience compelled him to offer as an atonement to the manes of Mr. Pitt; for it is a full justification of that minister's interference with France, even if he had been the aggressor, only the argument is much stronger in this case;—because France had not only been indulging in pyrotechnic displays, but had set fire to her own house, and had declared her intention of involving those of her neighbours in the same conflagration. And they might well be startled by the truth of that saying, "Tua res agitur paries cum proximus ardet." In the spirit of good sense he quite agrees with Mr. Pitt, in thinking all nations should be allowed to have the sort of government which they prefer, *provided they do not interfere with their neighbours,* as the French undoubtedly did.

If further proof be required of Mr. Pitt's devotion to pacific policy, as soon as a diminution of danger appeared to warrant a hope of success, we have it in the despatch of Lord Grenville, declaring the minister's anxiety to make it evident to the world that the negotiation in 1796 failed from the hostile determination of those who governed France, and from their resolution to admit of no terms of peace which were consistent with the safety, interests, and honour of the other powers of Europe.[1] And again, in the following year, when Lord Malmesbury was sent to Lisle to renew the negotiation, "Lord Grenville was decidedly opposed to this step," and long argued it with Pitt; but the latter remained firm, repeatedly declaring, that it was his duty, as an English Minister and a *Christian*, to use every effort to stop so bloody and wasting a war. He said he would stifle every feeling of pride to the utmost to produce the desired result.[2] Why, then, was this result not obtained? Because, as we learn from the negotiator, "there was a fixed determination on the part of the French Government to continue the war with England."[3] Of the five Directors then

---

[1] Lord Malmesbury's Diaries, &c., vol. iii. p. 301.
[2] *Ibid.* p. 369.   [3] *Ibid.* p. 518.

ruling in France, two, Barthelemi and Carnot, were moderate men, who would probably have listened to reason, and on that account were obnoxious to the other three, who were violent haters of England, and who succeeded in turning their colleagues out of office. The just conclusion, from all the correspondence is, that Pitt was not only sincere in his overtures for peace, but anxiously eager to obtain it on almost any conditions, short of dishonour.[1] Even this exception seems scarcely to have had due weight with the minister in the estimate of his royal master; as appears from a conversation between the King and Mr. George Rose, mentioned by the latter in a letter to his father. He says:—

"I hunted yesterday with the harriers, and had an hour and a half's conversation with the owner of them. Nothing can exceed his eagerness for the result of Lord Malmesbury's mission, respecting which, and a variety of subjects, his conversation was as unreserved as possible. We were nearly all the time *tête-à-tête*. I went out again to-day, in hopes of renewing the conversation, on account of the news of Lord Malmesbury's arrival. After having told me the circumstances you mention, and that nothing could be inferred from what had passed, he seemed inclined to think the negotiation would fail; as, if the French were really desirous of peace, they would have made some opening, and not observed such extreme circum-

[1] Lord Malmesbury's Diaries, vol. iii. p. 598.

spection, and waited to catch from Lord M. what he may have to offer. He stated that the hitch to be apprehended, perhaps foreseen, is respecting our allies; and, going into the question, considered it precisely in the same point of view in which it struck us, and dwelt forcibly, though temperately, on the precipitation which forced on the negotiation without a previous concert with the Emperor, when nothing rendered haste more necessary than it was some weeks back; and added, that though we felt strongly the necessity of pleasing Parliament, foreigners were not obliged to feel it equally with us, or be expected to understand it. All this rendered a perfect understanding the more indispensable. He doubted, extremely, whether the Emperor would agree to send any one to treat for him; and said, we must expect a good scolding from the Empress of Russia, to whom the Emperor has complained of us. He added that in one respect they gave us a right to insist upon bringing our allies into the negotiation, as they said they must consult theirs. He is extremely glad the business is in Lord M.'s hands, and not in those of a friend of ours (meaning Mr. Pitt), who, he says, would have begun by yielding up everything."

In an undated letter from the King, which, however, must plainly be referred to this same year, 1796, he expresses the same feeling on this subject more strongly in a postscript:—

"'The paper received this morning from Mr. P. would require much more time for inspection, before any opinion was given on its purport, than the press of the moment will admit. As it seems to allude to a decision of Council being made on the question in the course of this day, and I am desirous Mr. P. should communicate to them my view of the subject, previous to their forming any formal opinion, I therefore request that my suggestions may be canvassed, without attending to the irregular mode in which they are stated, as it was impossible to arrange them properly when placed so rapidly on paper.

"I think this country has taken every humiliating step for seeking peace that the warmest advocates for this object could suggest."

It will be seen that this is a very sufficient refutation of the injurious and unjust suspicion, entertained by Lord Holland, that Mr. Pitt "would have sacrificed his opinion (with regard to the Roman Catholics) rather than his power, if he had not foreseen the necessity of making a peace humiliating to his pride."[1] The former part of the King's letter may possibly have referred to a proposition for strengthening the administration, by admitting into it some of the opposition; for Mr. Fox himself seems to have had a lucid interval at that period, though not indeed quite free from his usual obliquity of political vision. He told the House of Commons that the Directory was composed of very reasonable men, who would be quite ready to make peace upon any reasonable terms. We

[1] Memoirs of the Whig Party, vol. I. p. 171.

have seen, that in this, as well as in most of his other opinions, he was entirely mistaken. However, he seemed to rejoice in the design of offering peace, and anticipated, in the event of its rejection, a unanimous support of the war. Mr. Pitt, therefore, not calculating upon the brittleness of his loyalty, seems, in the following letter, to have had hopes of his support; though, like a prudent general, he mustered all his forces, in case he should have to encounter war within the House, as well as on the Continent.—ED.]

MR. PITT TO MR. ROSE.

"*Downing Street, Dec. 26th, 1794.*

"DEAR ROSE,

"It seems indispensably necessary that we should, in our address on Thursday, renew in the strongest manner the assurances of support, and express a decided opinion on the merits of the case. The enemy has given us, in all respects, such unanswerable ground that one hardly knows where there can be a difference of opinion: but the moment is so important, that I am more than usually anxious for as full an attendance as possible. I hope you will be able to muster some recruits, both from Hampshire, and on the road; and whoever comes, will, I am sure, pass his holidays more pleasantly afterwards in consequence. No news from our fleets. I am submitting to the confinement of a London fireside, in order to get rid by Thursday of a cold, which, if it continued, would place me rather *hors de combat*.

"Ever yours, W. P."

[That some advances were made to the opposition at this time, may be inferred from an expression in one of Fox's letters: "There is a great unwillingness in our friends to have anything like a junction with the Pitts and Grenvilles."[1] There might be an unwillingness to change sides altogether, but there was no reluctance to disavow Fox's policy, for in the Commons he was left in a minority of 37 to 212, and in the Peers of 6 to 86. Two years previously, as has been already mentioned, a large body of his party deserted him, on account of his sympathy with the Jacobins of France, and the dangerous state of the country; and their leaders were admitted into the Cabinet. This, however, gave much dissatisfaction to Mr. Rose, who unburthened his mind upon the subject to the Bishop of Lincoln, in the subjoined letter.—Ed.]

Mr. Rose to the Bishop of Lincoln.

"I directed a letter to you on the subject of the new arrangement of the Government one day last week to Buckden. Since writing, I learn that Lord Spencer is to be the Privy Seal. The Cabinet therefore will stand thus:—

Mr. Pitt.	Duke of Portland.
Lord Grenville.	Earl Fitzwilliam.
Mr. Dundas.	Lord Chancellor.
Lord Chatham.	Lord Spencer.
Lord Amherst.	Lord Mansfield.
Duke of Richmond.	Mr. Wyndham.
Lord Hawkesbury.	

[1] Vol. iii. p. 222.

This is not what I think ought to have been proposed by the one or submitted to by the other. It has not now the appearance of taking in two or three men of considerable weight or talents who were acting with Mr. Pitt, and by whose means he wished to give additional efficiency to his administration; but of a junction of parties on a footing of mutual interest, or of sharing power to preserve a continuance of it.

"I have my fears that this measure will convert an effectual support into a weak assistance, or what is worse, into embarrassments in the deliberations of the Cabinet. The only considerable talents gained are Wyndham's, and I conceive him to be an impracticable man. These are the considerations which disturb me most. There are others from which much future inconvenience may arise. Numbers of Mr. Pitt's friends, who would have liked marks of favour or of honour, remained perfectly contented and satisfied without them, aware of the difficulties in the way of their obtaining them; almost every one of whom will feel mortification and grow uneasy when they see the Duke of Portland's adherents carrying their point. His Grace, and those who come in with him, may be honourable, fair men, but he is an atrocious jobber. My next apprehension is, that Mr. Wyndham, who will lead that set, will induce Mr. Pitt, or strengthen him in his determination, to pursue the war in Flanders and on the Northern Frontier *offensively*, by sending farther numerous and powerful reinforcements from this country, when the Emperor and the King of Prussia are relaxing in their co-operation. The number of lives, and the amount of finance expended in expeditions must render the Government unpopular, and disincline the nation to a war, the continuance of which I still think is indispensably necessary to our existence, and the tranquillity of all civil society.

"We cannot carry on operations on such an extended scale as I allude to, without increasing the capital of our debt next year four or five-and-twenty millions, if we borrow in the Three Per Cents. Such an enormous expense, and consequent taxes to the amount of a million, without a hope of attaining anything effectual, except in sanguine minds, is to me extremely uncomfortable.

"I have great confidence in Mr. Pitt. His full information on points which I know only superficially, and, above all, his superior judgment, sometimes encourage me even under the most unpromising appearances; but on this occasion I cannot raise my hopes much. I stated to him in conversation a few days ago what occurred to me respecting the carrying on the war *offensively* on the Continent; but on the Cabinet arrangements it would have been useless, as they were settled. From the very bottom of my heart I hope I may be mistaken as to the consequences of both; I wish for that, and pray for it on the strongest of all possible grounds—strong personal attachment and affection, and a conviction that his continuing to direct the councils of this country is absolutely necessary to our existence. There is not a personal motive which can influence my mind on the subject. I feel some relief in thus opening it to you, to whom alone

I can express myself with the freedom I have herein done.

"Mr. Pitt will learn from Lord Cornwallis the true state of matters in Flanders and on the Rhine; and we must trust he will decide for the best now. Respecting the next campaign, there will be time and opportunities for deliberation.

"You will, I am very certain, consider this communication as sacredly secret; part of it may be useful.

"I am,

G. R.

"Old Palace Yard, July 14th, 1794."

[While these changes were going on in the administration of affairs in Great Britain, the fortune of war was turning against our arms. The allies, on whose assistance we had relied, preferred their own private quarrels to the public good. The jealousies that have always disunited the Courts of Berlin and Vienna, rendered all concerted plans of the campaign abortive; and the best and honestest general amongst them, the Duke of Brunswick, retired in disgust from the command of the Prussian army. But he thought it necessary to explain his conduct to the Duke of York in the following letter; and it is much to the credit of that prince, that the Duke of Brunswick seems to have held him in such high estimation.—Ed.]

From the Duke of Brunswick to the Duke of York.[1]

"Sir,

Your Royal Highness inspires me with the most lively gratitude for deigning to interest yourself in my withdrawal from the army of the King. Nothing but circumstances as harassing as they are uncommon, such as those in which I find myself involved, could have induced me to take a step so afflicting to myself.

"It has been infinitely flattering to me to have sometimes found occasion to approach your Royal Highness and to admire the talents which place you in the rank of the great men of the age. Europe has need of such, in a struggle where near 400,000 armed men and eighty vessels of the line, assisted by an intestine war, have not yet been able to check the confederation of crime which tyrannizes over France. I consider myself very happy that you have deigned to remark my zeal for the public good. What a misfortune it is that internal and external dissensions have often paralysed

---

[1] "Monsieur,

"Votre Altesse Royale m'inspire la plus vive reconnoissance en daignant prendre part à ma retraite de l'armée du Roi. Il n'y a que des circonstances aussi fâcheuses que peu communes, comme celles dans lesquelles je me suis trouvé enveloppé, qui ayant pu me conseiller une démarche aussi affligeante pour moi.

"Il m'a été infiniment flatteur d'avoir trouvé quelquefois l'occasion d'approcher Votre Altesse Royale et d'admirer en Elle les talens qui vont la mettre au rang des grands hommes du Siècle. L'Europe en a besoin dans une lutte où près de quatre cent mille hommes armés, et quatre vingt Vaisseaux de Ligne, secourus par une guerre intestine, n'ont pas encore pu mettre un frein à cette fédération de crimes qui tyrannise la France. Je m'estime très heureux de ce

the movements of armies at periods when the greatest activity was required. If after the surrender of Mayence we could have fallen upon Houchard and beaten him, we might have prevented the march of the reinforcement towards the army of the north, and consequently the check before Dunkirk.

"Saar-Louis ill-provisioned, and at that time almost without protection from bombs, would probably have fallen in a fortnight. Then Alsace would have found itself turned by the Saar; the taking of the lines of the Lautre would have been followed by solid advantages, and if the enemy's army of the Rhine had by all these means been separated from that of the Moselle, and we could have gained the bridge of Boucquenom, Pfalzbourg would have been threatened, and Landau would probably have fallen. Pardon me for imparting to you my regrets: I feel all the uselessness of complaints, but they give me a momentary comfort. Permit me here to add, once more, that if you have any power over my successor, conjure him to employ all his credit to prevent the too great subdivision of the army into separate detachments. Every

qu'Elle a daigné remarquer mon zèle pour le bien. Quel malheur que des dissentions internes, et externes, ont souvent paralysé les mouvemens des armées, dans des époques où la plus grande activité auroit été nécessaire.

"Si après la reddition de Mayence l'on fut tombé sur Houchard, qu'on l'eut poussé et battu, l'on prévenoit la marche du renfort vers l'armée du Nord, et par conséquent l'échec de Dunkerque.

"Saar-Louis mal approvisionné et alors presque sans abri contre les bombes, auroit tombé vraisemblablement dans quinze jours. Dès lors l'Alsace se trouveroit tournée par la Saar; la prise des lignes de la Lautre auroit eu des suites solides, et si l'armée ennemie du Rhin eut été par tous ces moyens séparée de celle de la Moselle, et que

where feeble, it is thus reduced to act upon the defensive; a species of warfare which it is necessary to avoid with the enemy opposed to us. I reckon upon departing hence on the 27th or 28th, according to the date of M. de Möellendorf's arrival, and when I shall have had time to put him in possession of all the details. I cannot say how much it costs me to separate from your Royal Highness, and to quit an army which has inspired me with the highest degree of esteem, admiration, and attachment. Nothing equals, nor ever will equal, the very sincere attachment and high consideration with which I have the honour to be,

"Sir,
"Your Royal Highness's
"Most humble and most obedient servant,
"CHARLES DUKE OF BRUNSWICK.

"Mayence, 24th January, 1794."

L'on eut gagné le pont de Boucquenom, Phalsbourg étoit menacé et Landau seroit tombé vraisemblablement.—Pardonnez que je vous communique mes regrets. Je sens toute l'inutilité des plaintes, elles soulagent cependant un moment. Permettez que j'ajoute encore ici que si Elle a quelque pouvoir sur mon successeur, qu' Elle le conjure d'employer tout son crédit pour prévenir la trop grande subdivision de l'armée en divers Détachemens. Faible partout, l'on est réduit à la défensive, ce qui est un genre de guerre qu'il est nécessaire d'éviter avec l'ennemi qui nous est opposé. Je compte partir d'ici le 27 ou le 28, selon le jour que M. de Moellendorf arrivera, et que j'aurai eu le tems de lui remettre tout ce qui regarde nos détails. Il m'en coute infiniment de m'éloigner de votre altesse Royale, et de quitter une armée qui m'a inspiré le plus haut degré d'estime, d'admiration et d'attachement.

"Rien n'égale et n'égalera jamais l'attachement très sincère et la haute considération avec laquelle j'ai l'honneur d'être,
"Monsieur,
"De votre Altesse Royale
"Le très humble et très obéissant Serviteur,
"CHARLES DUC DE BRUNSWIC."

"à Mayence, ce 24 Janvier, 1794."

[Mr. Pitt's attempts to conciliate the Duke of Northumberland, by acceding to his demands, totally failed, and his dissatisfaction continued to increase, till at last, notwithstanding his previously expressed contentedness with the constitution of the Government, he joined the revolutionary party, and open hostilities broke out between him and the minister, who shortly afterwards insisted upon his joining the militia or resigning his command.—ED.]

MR. PITT TO MR. ROSE.

"Downing Street, Sept. 10th, 1795.

"DEAR ROSE,

"I have no scruple about attacking the Duke of Northumberland at Launceston, or anywhere else where there is a chance of doing it with effect; and I think Cull's good intentions should be encouraged as much as possible. Saltash, I believe, must now wait till we meet. It is suggested to me that on the new right the Butler interest is far from decisive, and that government might with proper management do a great deal.

"The Duke of Leeds has written to his agent to do everything in favour of Gregor. I have just now written to Lord Hawkesbury to see what can be done respecting Lady Bute. You once mentioned an arrangement respecting the office in Bahama, which would open one here for Mr. Sturges, of Windsor. I wish you would send me the name. If this will answer, it must supersede Mr. Chrystie's application.

I shall stay in this neighbourhood another week at least, and probably a little longer if the King returns as is expected.

"Before that time I hope you will be perfectly recovered from your accident, and be able to return to town, as I should be glad of a day or two with you before I set out. I am very sorry for the awkwardness respecting Rolle, which is certainly unpleasant, though he seems to make it more serious than he need.

"Yours sincerely,
"W. Pitt.

"I forgot to return Sir R. Cotton's letter sooner. I had, before it came, engaged myself in favour of Mr. Seabright, who I believe has much the best interest, and is more to be depended upon than Sir Corbett, whom I do not take to be as steady as his relation, Sir R. Cotton."

[Careless as Mr. Pitt was about his own affairs, his anxiety to make some provision for his friend, or at least for his family, is evinced in the two following letters; the conclusion of the second is, as usual, full of matters of business; but in the first we see him intent on recreation, which is very unusual.—Ed.]

Mr. Pitt to Mr. Rose.

"Downing Street, Friday, Sept. 11th, 1795.
"Dear Rose,

"I have had an opportunity of conversing with the Chancellor respecting the reversion of Clerk of

Parliaments, and, as far as he is personally concerned I have the satisfaction of finding that he has no wish or object whatever respecting it; but he seemed desirous of ascertaining, more fully than he could then by recollection, the state of what had passed at different times in the House of Lords, which might affect the propriety or the mode of granting the office. He will probably himself trace it in the Journals, but it may perhaps be useful if you can furnish me with a note of reference to any passages that are material. Our intended party for Southampton is now fixed for Monday se'nnight, the 21st. As it is not impossible that there may be some difficulty at such a time in procuring lodgings, I should be much obliged to you if you could, without inconvenience, contrive to ensure that point for me, either at the hotel, or, if that is full, anywhere in the town; and I undertook to make the same request for Dundas, who will bring Lady Jane and his daughter with him. We have accounts from Paris, that most of the sections there have accepted the Constitution, but rejected the proposal for re-electing two-thirds of the present Convention, which is a very fortunate event.

" Yours ever,
" W. P."

Mr. Pitt to Mr. Rose.

" Walmer Castle,
" Sunday, Oct. 10th, 1795, 1 p.m.

" Dear Rose,

" The Chancellor is perfectly satisfied with the reversion being granted to your son in the usual form, and without any new limitation; and I have just written to the King, to propose it in the manner you suggest; and so as I think to avoid any chance of difficulty. I wish you would send me, with the papers about the register, a copy of your notes on the other taxes in question, to which I hope you will have been enabled to add an account of the value of different articles of manufactured cotton goods, and some estimate of the amount of funds on the Receipt Tax.

"I shall also wish much to know the produce of the Consolidated Fund. Mornington has signed the warrants, which I have given to be forwarded to Townshend.

"Yours ever,
"W. Pitt."

[The observations alluded to in the following letter do not appear, but they are noticed in Mr. Pitt's answer. They seem to have contemplated a measure which has recently been the subject of much discussion,—the expediency of obtaining some agricultural statistics, either by compulsion or otherwise.—Ed.]

THE MARQUIS OF STAFFORD TO MR. PITT.

"MY DEAR SIR,

"I have received, as *Custos rotulorum* for the County of Stafford, a letter from the Duke of Portland, conveying his Majesty's commands to convene the Magistrates, to take into consideration subjects of inquiry concerning the present high price of corn.

I shall not fail to carry these commands into execution, but I hope you will excuse my enclosing some observations on this measure. If they prove useless, you will have the trouble of throwing them into the fire; but I shall have the satisfaction that this gives me an opportunity of assuring you, with how much regard, I am,

"Your faithful and obedient servant,

"STAFFORD."

MR. PITT TO THE MARQUIS OF STAFFORD.

"Downing Street, Nov. 6th, 1795.
"MY DEAR LORD,
"I think myself very much obliged to you for the suggestions which you have had the goodness to send me, relative to measures for ascertaining the stock of corn in the country. I feel very strongly the difficulty of obtaining accurate information without some compulsory power, but I have at the same time great doubts whether the alarm and dissatisfaction which would be produced by having recourse to those means would not outweigh the advantage to be obtained by them; and, as far as I have hitherto had any opportunity of judging, I am inclined to think this would be the general impression. We must, therefore, I believe, be contented with such general information as magistrates can furnish from their observation and inquiry, which, though far from precise, may lead to some tolerable ground of comparison with the ordinary produce.

"We are still without any direct accounts of a recent date from France, or any particulars of the late operations in Germany.

"Believe me to be, with sincere regard and esteem,
"My dear Lord,
"Your Lordship's most faithful
"And obedient servant,
"W. PITT.

"Marquis of Stafford, &c."

[The following letter, addressed to Mr. Valentine Jones (in the year 1797), then in the West Indies, shows what severe but well-merited rebukes Mr. Rose inflicted upon persons in the service of Government who were guilty of too great profusion in the expenditure of which they had the charge.—ED.]

MR. ROSE TO MR. VALENTINE JONES.

"SIR,

"In my public letter to the Commander-in-Chief and yourself of this date, I have communicated the opinion of the Board respecting your bills, which have lately appeared, and those of which there are threatening symptoms; for not having even the common advice of them, we can only conjecture what are to come, but I cannot let the packet sail without expressing my deep and sincere regret at your conduct, as well as the disappointment of what I thought well-founded expectations, arising from the experience we had of you in the situations of Commissary at Barbadoes, and Commissary of Accounts on the Staff. I am not disposed to doubt but that the enormous sums for which you have drawn have been laid out, or that you will be able to produce probably regular vouchers for them hereafter to the auditors; but that such expenditure can have been necessary appears to me impossible. I should entertain that opinion strongly if no services had been carried on in the West Indies previously to your present appointment; but when the expenses during Mr. Jeffrey's time, when the most active operations were in progress, are compared with yours, it puts your want of economy in the strongest possible point of view. The situations you have held gave you a full opportunity of knowing how the services were carried on. We are so entirely in the dark relative to the expenditure under you that I cannot even guess from what source the great outgoings have arisen. The amount may be larger than in the period before alluded to. There were then, I think, about 20,000 men victualled; but there can be no increased numbers to account for the immense difference. Mr. Jeffrey, too, was supposed to have left with you a considerable store of provisions, rum, and other articles necessary for the use of the troops. Serious as the immediate mischief is, attendant on the almost insurmountable difficulties you have involved us in at present, we have still some formidable ones to apprehend, as it will not be easy to get rid of the system of extravagance; *but it must be done*, otherwise we shall be subject in times of peace to hearing demands from the islands altogether unheard of in former times.

"As far as I am enabled to judge at present, the whole charge of the department of the Commissary-General, the Quartermaster-General, the Barrack-master-General, and the Hospital, did not amount to 1,000,000*l.* sterling, for the period preceding your arrival in the West Indies. Compare this with yours! I had heard nothing of the circumstances you allude to in your private letter to me, except from the correspondent to whom you communicated them. If you had performed your duty in the way I hoped and trusted you would have done, no one could have hurt you; but, in any event, the parties you alluded to cannot benefit by your suspension or removal.

[The following letter from Lady Chatham is here introduced, not only because it brings us into some acquaintance with the mother of so eminent a man as Mr. Pitt, to whose early training it is probable he was under considerable obligations; but also because, being written at the end of 1798, it gives a distinct contradiction, in the happy account which she had received of his health, to a report which Mr. Addington seems to have joined in circulating with respect to some derangement of his mind. It would indeed have been a very singular coincidence, if the minister and the monarch had been subject to that calamity at the same time.—ED.

LADY CHATHAM TO MR. ROSE.

"Burton Pynsent, Dec. 8th, 1798.

"SIR,

"I am most sincerely obliged to you for the great pleasure I received from the perfectly happy account of my dear son's health, after so long an exertion of his strength. I flatter myself he felt much satisfaction in the success that has attended his speech.

"Now, sir, I must desire you will accept my best thanks for the kind trouble which you have been so good as to take in giving me the true state of the wild and indecent behaviour of Croft. There certainly can be no excuse for him, and he has undone himself. What extravagance provoked him to such conduct there is no guessing. He has children by his *first* wife, who was a servant of mine, and a very honest, good woman. What power he has to take care of his family I know not; but I am inclined to imagine it very little. The only thing that he can be allowed to have must be of a totally private sort. If there should be any chance, so far, I should be glad for the sake of those belonging to him. However, I have no wish, if there is the smallest objection to what I have named.

"The weather is so horridly bad, in consequence of the continued fog, that one can neither see, nor feel at all comfortable. I hope in God the effects will be escaped by those I am interested for.

"I am really ashamed of having troubled you so

long, and will therefore add only that I beg you to believe me, Sir,

"Your obliged and most humble servant,
"H. CHATHAM."

[Mr. Sheridan had stated in the House of Commons, that the Ministers were unpopular in America; and, with the violent democrats of that country, it is probable enough that they were; but the following letter from their Ambassador shows that it was not the feeling of her statesmen.—ED.]

MR. RUFUS KING TO MR. ROSE.

[*Private.*]

"Great Cumberland Place, 23d June, 1798.

"DEAR SIR,

"Accept my acknowledgments for your letter of yesterday. I am very glad that it has been thought advisable to introduce the alterations which have been made in the Convoy Bill; the effect, I am persuaded, must be alike advantageous to both countries. It will be my duty, which I shall experience great satisfaction in performing, to represent this subject in its true light to the American Government, which must see therein the same sincere desire on the part of Great Britain that itself feels, to increase and confirm the friendship and intercourse that at present so happily subsists between the two countries.

"You will not doubt the pleasure it has given me to be assured of the friendly sentiments that I have always flattered myself you entertained for my country, whose origin, language, laws, and manners are so many titles to the friendship of England.

"With perfect esteem and respect, I have the honour to be,

"Dear Sir,
"Your obedient and faithful servant,
"RUFUS KING.

"George Rose, Esq. &c. &c."

[The two next letters relate to the King's subscription for carrying on the war. Lords Romney, Eldon, and Kenyon, Messrs. Pitt, Dundas, and Addington, subscribed on that occasion 2,000*l.* each, in lieu of their legal assessments; Lord Bridport and Admiral Colpoys, 1,000*l.* each. The King subscribed one-third of his privy purse, or 20,000*l.* annually.—ED.]

MR. PITT TO MR. ROSE.

"Wimbledon,
"Thursday, half-past 8 P.M., Jan. 25th, 1798.

"DEAR ROSE,

"The mode of payment certainly ought to be by instalments. I have just now received a letter from the King, authorizing me to take all the steps necessary, and as I think a minute of the Board is the only way of stating the case publicly, I will return to town to-morrow morning, and wish you to fix a Board at half-past twelve. You will of course be enabled to say all you wish to Mr. Kemble.

"Yours ever,
"W. P."

Mr. Pitt to Mr. Rose.

"Wimbledon,
"Friday, 10 a.m., Jan. 26th, 1798.

" Dear Rose,

"On consideration, I have thought it best simply to write a letter to the Bank, announcing the King's subscription, and to give up the idea of a minute of the Treasury, which could not, I think, be so framed as not to appear a studied and laboured apology. You will probably have time to countermand the Board, and if not can explain to them the circumstances. Give my letter to Carthew to be entered before it is sent to the Bank. Pray bring Abbott's paper with you to-morrow.

"Yours ever,
"W. P.

"Bring also the abstract of the payment in the different classes of the civil list, compared with the amount some years back, and with the estimate given in to Parliament under Burke's bill.

"Some business will keep me here to-day, but you will be sure to find me at Hollwood to-morrow."

[Miss Rose, who was a clever and strong-minded woman, took a great dislike to Mr. Addington, and no doubt exercised a considerable influence over her father's mind, already predisposed to dislike any successor to Mr. Pitt, and to institute disadvantageous comparisons between them. Notwithstanding, however, the accusations so strongly urged against him, it will be seen in the end that the alienation produced by them was only temporary.—Ed.]

EXTRACT FROM MISS ROSE'S DIARY.

In the autumn of 1799, my father was ill, and I went to London with my aunt Frances, to stay with him. Mr. Pitt, whose health had for some time been failing, was persuaded by Mr. Addington, then Speaker, to go to his house in the country rather than to Hollwood, under the plea that he would have more rest from intrusion of guests and from business. I had no liking for Mr. Addington. I thought him shallow, and mistrusted him from his conduct when Speaker; which, in fact, was the cause of the duel between Mr. Pitt and Mr. Tierney. Not only by his conduct in the House of Commons, for which the opposition blamed him (Hendon saying he had said stronger things, and had taken stronger things, and would do so again), but from his knowledge of what was passing afterwards, and not taking any means of preventing the duel. During the time I was in London I found that a new set of people were about my father. Nicholas Vansittart, and Dr. Beck, who afterwards was his assistant financier, dined with him. I thought them shallow; very important about trifles and little matters, and very assiduous in getting information from my father. I remember when I returned to Cuffnells I told my mother that there were strange birds getting about my father, and pecking his brains; that I did not understand what was going on, and did not like it.

The spring before, Mr. Pitt, whose health was then failing, was suffering great depression of spirits, arising, as I afterwards believed, from suppressed gout. He was advised to rest his mind as much as possible, and did not go for some time to the House of Commons.

For a time, except when the Bishop of Lincoln was in London, he saw only my father and Lord Melville. In the spring of 1800, we dined at the Speaker's. My father had that morning returned from Hollwood; and at dinner, Lord Bathurst, and other friends of Mr. Pitt's, talked of the place, and of the changes Mr. Pitt was making. He was always amusing himself with some work there. My father spoke of his having removed a plantation of willows, which his friends then present had disapproved of when made. I sat next to the Speaker, at the *side* of the table, he sitting at the bottom; Lord Bathurst sat on my right hand. The Speaker, in an under but distinct tone, said to Lord Bathurst, across me, "I do not think there could be a clearer proof of the aberration of Pitt's mind last year than his having made that plantation." Lord Bathurst made no reply; and I suspected at the time, from his manner, that he did not distinctly hear what Addington had said.

A few days before this diary begins, my father, who we had seen was annoyed, as he was occasionally when he could not fix Mr. Pitt's attention on business particularly under his management in the House of Commons, spoke of it at that time as particularly

inconvenient, as it related to some matters that must
be brought into the House of Commons soon, and he
said, "I will go to the Speaker to-morrow, and get
him to remind Mr. Pitt that it must soon come before
the House." I believed he had a false confidence in
the man, and said hastily, "And do you think the
Speaker is really attached to Mr. Pitt?"—"Yes, certainly."—"*I do not,*" I replied. Then, on his question-
ing my reason for this opinion, I told him of the speech
I heard Mr. Addington make to Lord Bathurst. My
father was the more astonished, as he said, as he had
before done to us, when such reports were afloat the
preceding year, that there was not the slightest mental
failure in Mr. Pitt, nothing but depression of spirits—
overwork on a slight constitution. Before this conversation, my father had said to the Speaker that he
would call on him. Going to his house, he overtook
Mr. Hatsell, the Clerk of the House of Commons, who
said if he was going in, he should not be able to see
the Speaker before he went out, and that it would prevent his going out of town, as he wished to do, next
day. My father then gave way to him, desiring him
to tell the Speaker he would call on him on Monday.
In the meantime the change took place, and my father
wrote to Addington, that the matter on which he
wished to speak to him no longer existed.

CHAPTER IV.

1798-9.

FIRST INTELLIGENCE OF THE VICTORY OF THE NILE—LORD NELSON'S PROCEEDINGS IN THE BAY OF NAPLES IN 1799—GROUNDS OF LADY HAMILTON'S CLAIMS—MR. ROSE'S EFFORTS TO OBTAIN COMPENSATION FOR HER, FROM 1804 to 1813.

[THE following letter from Mr. Pitt, amidst many matters of ordinary business, contains the first intimation that reached this country of the glorious victory achieved by Lord Nelson at Aboukir, on the 1st of August, 1798, over the fleet which conveyed General Buonaparte to the shores of Egypt; and it gives us a curious specimen of the system of averting discontent from the people of France by falsifying the events of the war.—ED.]

MR. PITT TO MR. ROSE.

"Walmer Castle, Friday, Aug. 10th, 1798.

"DEAR ROSE,

"I return the draft of the warrant appointing the Commissioners for the sale of the Land-tax, and think it in general perfectly right, but have put two queries in the margin, which you can easily answer. In the meantime, send the warrant to the King, without waiting to hear from me again. I think I shall probably be in town for a few days about the 20th, but shall hardly meet you on the 23d, as I have a scheme (which I mean to say nothing of) of running down for a week at that time to Somersetshire. On my return from thence, I hope we shall be able finally to arrange both the bills for the contribution and the warehousing. I am at present strongly prejudiced against a total repeal of the act of last year, and I know that Lowndes has always a rage for putting everything into one act of Parliament; whereas, nine times out of ten, and particularly I should think in the present case, the provision would be made much better by reference. I have received French newspapers of the 7th and 8th, containing vague reports of an action between Nelson and Buonaparte, and some pretending that the latter had been victorious. They serve only to confirm the belief that something has happened, but it may still be some time before we have any authentic account, though they probably will not be long able to disguise entirely the result, even in France.

"Yours ever,

"W. P.

"I enclose an application from Mr. Dornford to be a Commissioner, which, however, ought not to be attended to, unless approved by the Tax Office. Pray inquire, and let me know whether any thing has been done respecting the late Lord Montagu's estate. I have an application on behalf of Lady Mostyn, desiring that no grant may be made of it till she has time to present a memorial to the Treasury, stating her claim, and I want to return some answer."

[But the glory of the victory of the Nile was dearly purchased by the loss of honour which flowed indirectly from circumstances connected with it, and which sadly tarnished the lustre of Lord Nelson's name. The facts are thus briefly stated by Lord Holland: "When, distracted at having missed the French fleet, he came to Palermo, he obtained, chiefly through the influence of Lady Hamilton (the wife of the ambassador), whom he had not seen since 1795, the stores and provisions which enabled him to put to sea again, and to overtake the enemy in the Bay of Aboukir. He returned therefore to Naples overflowing with gratitude for the service which she had rendered him."[1] Unfortunately, Lord Nelson's personal vanity came powerfully in aid of his gratitude, and completed a most infatuated attachment to Lady Hamilton; for he is said to have pressed her to sing the most fulsome couplets to his honour, and to have acknowledged with the utmost naïveté that his preference of her society to Lady Nelson's arose from the warm praises she bestowed upon him; after which the congratula-

[1] Redding, in his "Fifty Years' Recollections," says that Nelson was Lady Hamilton's dupe; she persuaded him that *she* had obtained the victualling of his fleet. It was her husband, who made her his agent with the Queen (vol iii, p 103).

tions of his wife were, he said, cold, flat, and insipid. She thus alienated his affections entirely from his wife, ill estrangement led to a total separation when he returned to England, although he acknowledged that his wife had committed no fault. His biographer says, "Further than this there is no reason to believe that this most unfortunate attachment was criminal; but this was criminality enough, and it brought with it its punishment." Dishonour was the punishment of both, and the remark of the Roman moralist was signally verified:—

> "Raro antecedentem scelestum
> Deseruit pede poena claudo."

It was not, however, at a slow pace that retribution overtook these offenders. On his return to Naples, Nelson dishonoured his character and sullied his glory by listening to the violent counsels of a woman whose passionate zeal for her friends overleaped all the boundaries not only of discretion, but of justice. He became her accomplice in perfidy and murder. These seem to be hard terms to use of a man of whom in other respects England is so justly proud. But they are the terms used by Lord Holland, and not unwarranted by impartial history, as we shall presently see, on describing George the Third's reception of Nelson at Court, after his return from the Mediterranean; a reception which must have been peculiarly galling to Nelson, to whom worldly distinction was all in all. He had yet to learn that England expects every man to do his duty in morals as well as in battle. The passage in which the charge is made is curious, because it brings before us in so broad a light the character of the writer, sneering at a morality with which he had no sympathy, and blinded to the most obvious truth by a Jacobinical hatred of royalty.

"It is certain," says Lord Holland, "that her (Lady Hamilton's) baneful ascendancy over Nelson's mind was the chief cause of his indefensible conduct at Naples, and that neither he nor she was ever disavowed or discountenanced by our Court for that conduct. He never was a favourite at St. James's; his amour with Lady Hamilton, if amour it was, shocked the King's morality, and though the perfidies and murders to which it led were perpetrated in the cause of royalty, they could not wash away the original sin of indecorum in the eye of his Majesty Nelson's reception at Court after the victory of Aboukir was singularly cold and repulsive."[1]

The malignity of the insinuation that perfidy and murder in the cause of royalty would have been a recommendation to the monarch's favour if they had not been more than counterbalanced by the scandal of a doubtful intrigue, can only be ascribed to the blindest hatred. But that Lord Holland should be equally blind to the inconsistency of his own statements is more extraordinary. He first asserts that

[1] Memoirs of the Whig Party, vol. II. p. 30.

neither Nelson nor Lady Hamilton were discountenanced by the Court for their conduct, and then proceeds to show, that though the King could not disavow acts which were not disavowed by his Ministers, yet that he did in the most marked way discountenance the doer of them. And there can be no doubt in the mind of any reasonable man, that it was "for that conduct" Nelson was so discountenanced; though the adultery, to which appearances attributed it, could not fail to increase the feeling of disgust in one who understood the value of Christian morality even to public men, so much better than Lord Holland did. This sad episode in Nelson's life cannot be more fitly related than in the words of his impartial biographer.

"The castles of Uovo and Nuovo were chiefly defended by Neapolitan revolutionists, the powerful men amongst them having sought shelter there. They were strong places, and, if they were taken, the reduction of Fort St. Elmo, which commands Naples, would be greatly expedited. Cardinal Ruffo proposed to the garrison to capitulate, on condition that their persons and properties should be guaranteed. This capitulation was accepted. It was signed by the Cardinal, by the Prussian and Turkish commanders, and by Captain Foote, commander of the British forces. Thirty-six hours afterwards, Nelson arrived, and annulled the treaty, declaring that he would grant rebels no other terms than those of unconditional submission. The Cardinal objected to this; nor could all the arguments of Nelson, Sir William Hamilton, and Lady Hamilton, who took an active part in the conference, convince him that a treaty of such a nature, solemnly concluded, could honourably be set aside. He retired at last, silenced by Nelson's authority, but not convinced. Captain Foote was sent out of the bay, and the garrisons, taken from the castles under the pretence of carrying the treaty into effect, were delivered over as rebels to the vengeance of the Sicilian Court."[1]

Prince Caraccioli, at the head of the Marine, after a service of forty years, had escaped before the capitulation, and went to Sicily, but was permitted to return to Naples to save his estates from confiscation. For a few days he was *compelled* by the French to serve on board their fleet,[2] for which he was hanged by Nelson, after a two hours' trial by a court of Neapolitan officers, presided over by a personal enemy; and Lady Hamilton not only was on board the ship, but present at the execution.

In that part of the correspondence which bears upon these transactions, there is, first, a copy of a proclamation issued to the army by the Neapolitan Government, not very well or clearly written, but probably forwarded to Mr. Rose in justification of

[1] Southey's "Life of Nelson," vol. ii. p. 18.
[2] Captain Troubridge says in one of his letters to Lord Nelson, "I am assured by all the sailors that Caraccioli is not a Jacobin, but has been forced to act as he does."—*Clarke and McArthur's "Life of Lord Nelson,"* p. 543.

Nelson's conduct. It need not be added, that in this respect, too, it entirely fails; for whatever authority that Government might have given to him, it could not authorize him to break the laws of honour and rectitude. It ordered that he should be consulted, and that regard should be paid to his opinion in those military arrangements which would secure a victory over the rebels; but the Commander-in-chief of the Neapolitans was the Prince Royal, who seems to have delegated his entire power to Cardinal Ruffo, for he does not appear at all in the correspondence. To him there might have been an appeal from Cardinal Ruffo's decision, but none to Nelson.

Secondly, there are some letters written by Sir William Hamilton, who had been thirty-five years ambassador at that court, but written, no doubt, at the instigation of his wife, whose eager friendship for the Queen would suffer no obstacles to stand in her way, no considerations of right or wrong, in serving the interests of the royal cause.

Thirdly, there is a series of letters written by that strong-minded woman after her return to England, in 1800, in which her utter inability to appreciate the delicacy of her position in the eyes of the world, her fervid admiration of the Admiral, her perseverance in urging a suit which everybody combined to reject, her persistence in making inadmissible statements, and at last, her indignation and brokenheartedness, stand out in strong relief.

This correspondence is extended, at wide intervals of time, from 1802 till near the close of her life, when her setting sun was clouded by imprisonment, exile, and dependence on the charity of her friends; one of whom, no doubt, was Mr. Rose, who was at all times her steadfast advocate. Previous, however, to entering upon this subject, a letter from Sir W. Hamilton to Lord Nelson of an earlier date may here be fitly introduced; partly because it notices a similar foible in the character of another eminent officer, after another great success against Buonaparte, which finally defeated his project of conquest in Syria; and partly because it furnishes evidence that attachment to Nelson was claimed by Sir W. as the common property of both,—of the husband and the wife.

In the " Recollections of the Life of Dr. Scott, Lord Nelson's Chaplain," it is said, with regard to his unfortunate admiration of Lady Hamilton, that neither Dr. Scott, nor any of his most intimate friends, believed in its criminality. Lord St. Vincent used to call them a pair of sentimental fools; and it is a fact that Lady Hamilton never was a mother. It has been thought by some who witnessed Nelson's intimacy with royalty at Naples, that Horatia Nelson might lay claim to a far more illustrious origin than has been supposed. This solution, if a true one, accounts equally well for the miserable state of mind which Lord Nelson's letters written from Naples betray. It may be feared that this misery was the consequence of guilt; but if so, such uneasiness was the conscientious compunction of an habitually upright mind.'

Lady Hamilton, writing to Dr. Scott, September 7th, 1806, speaks of "our virtuous Nelson," and "we have innocency on our side," and, "you know the great and virtuous affection he had for me." He might be virtuous towards *her*, but if she could apply that term to one whom she knew to be guilty of adultery with another, she could not have much principle for her own defence. At Lord Nelson's death, Lady Hamilton had at least 1,400*l.* a year, besides the little estate at Merton; but her vanity and extravagance found this no competence. Her affairs were put into the hands of a financier, who advised her to go into retirement for two or three years; but she soon returned, and committed wilder extravagances than ever, and was again a suppliant for relief to the friends whose advice she had disregarded. The financier declared that all attempts to serve a person of her character must be in vain. She died abroad in great poverty.

Mr. Rose, who considered that every one belonging to Lord Nelson was a legacy to himself, did everything in his power to fix the attention of Government

---

' Whoever the mother might be, there seems to be no doubt that Mrs. Horatia Nelson Ward was Lord Nelson's daughter, from the letters which he wrote as a father to his child, and his sending her in one of them his parental blessing. Those letters were published by Sir Nicholas Harris Nicolas.

upon Dr. Scott as a man closely connected with Lord
Nelson's memory; but all his representations were
attended with no more effect than the petitions which
he drew up for Lady Hamilton, to be presented to
successive Ministers.—ED.]

LETTER TO LORD NELSON FROM SIR WILLIAM HAMILTON, AMBASSADOR AT THE COURT OF NAPLES.

"Palermo, 12 o'clock,
"Monday, 27th May, 1799.

"MY DEAR LORD,

"I hope the felucca that sailed from hence
yesterday at noon has brought your Lordship Ball's
despatches that were sent to me by express from
Messina. Your letters of the 25th, to Emma and me,
arrived this morning at eight o'clock, and the Queen
and Acton are informed of their contents. I think
there can be little doubt but that the French fleet
have got into Toulon, and we rejoice in the hope of
seeing you here again very soon.

"Yesterday afternoon I received a letter by the post
from Signor Raymondi, our Vice-consul at Syracuse,
with an account in Italian, signed Sidney Smith, of
his success against Buonaparte at Acre, brought by
a Russian polacca, with a copy of the instructions
given to Mr. Geo. Nicholson, one of his midshipmen,
to carry 250 French prisoners from Acre to Toulon,
with liberty to touch in any friendly island or port for
refreshments. I send your Lordship a copy of those
instructions, in Sir Sidney's usual pompous style—

'Great Cross of the Military Order of the Sword, Minister Plenipotentiary of his Majesty to the Ottoman Porte, and Commander of the Royal Fleet in the Levant Seas.' We grieve for the loss of poor Captain Wilmot, of the *Alliance*, who was killed, as your Lordship will see, the 5th of April, by a musket shot,—for I send you an English translation of Sir Sidney Smith's account, which was sent to me in Italian from Syracuse. Upon the whole, this is very good news, and Buonaparte seems to be in a bad way; but your Lordship will comprehend the good and bad of Sir Sidney's operations much better than I can.

"I enclose two letters from Graham to Sir Chas. Stuart, as your Lordship talks of sending soon to Minorca, a letter from Mr. Wyndham for Captain Lewis, and one from Lamb to Captain Hardy. Lamb is very attentive, and comes daily for orders from my lady.

"We have had here three days' gala and illuminations, the Empress of Germany having been brought to bed of an Arch-duke. I see that Constantine, the Grand Duke of Russia, is at Vienna, so that the Courts of Vienna and St. Petersburg draw well together. Adieu, my very dear Lord; take care of your health above all. Captain Ball must surely have joined you before this letter can reach you.

" Ever your Lordship's
" Most attached and obliged humble servant,
" (Signed)   Wm. Hamilton.

" P. S.—I can assure you that neither Emma nor I knew how much we loved you until this separation, and we are convinced that your Lordship feels the same as we do.

"The boatman that brings your Lordship this packet says he has no passport from your Lordship, and the three passports your Lordship left have been sent for by the King or Queen, so pray send us two or three more in blank."

[The translations from the Italian correspondence which follow, and the instructions given by the King to his troops, are indispensable to the judgment that ought to be formed of Nelson's conduct. It is quite clear that, before the arrival of the British Admiral, Cardinal Ruffo wielded all the authority of the King, for the Prince Royal, who was joined with him in the command, never appears in these transactions; and though the King reserved to himself the power of extending his clemency to the rebel leaders, yet he specially excepts the case of those who should surrender by capitulation. But he was a weak man, and Nelson, who could not bear the idea of those whom he called Jacobins escaping condign punishment, easily persuaded him to retract this equitable provision, and to annul all that his own Commander-in-chief had done; but the Cardinal was found to be so intractable that it was judged expedient to send him back to Sicily, without venturing however to disgrace him for his honesty.—ED.]

GENERAL ACTON TO CARDINAL RUFFO.

"YOUR EMINENCE,

"The King, finding it indispensable for his royal service that your Excellency should repair instantly to this capital, that his Majesty may be minutely informed by you of every event that has happened, to enable his Majesty to make important provisions for the good government of the affairs of this city and kingdom;—has therefore resolved and commanded, that you should immediately embark on board one of the men-of-war that shall be selected for this purpose by the Admiral of the British Squadron, Lord Nelson; and be conveyed immediately here for the above-mentioned object; His Majesty having already given to the aforesaid English Admiral his royal commands concerning the persons who, during your Eminence's absence, will assume the military command and regulate all civil affairs.

[1] "Em⁰ Signor,

"Il Re trovando essere indispensibile pel suo Real Servigio che V. E. si porti subito in questa Capitale per far che Sua Maestà rimanga minutamente informata dalla stessa voce del V. E. di alcuni fatti che sono avvenuti e che possa quindi la Maestà sua dare alcune importantissime provedenze relative al buon Governo degli affari di cotesta Città e Regno, ha perciò risoluto e commanda che Ella immediatemente s'embarchi sopra uno de' Legni da Guerra che sarà a tal uopo destinata dal Ammiraglio della Squadra Brittanica, Lord Nelson; e si trasferisca subito qui all accennato oggetto; avendo già S. M. dato le sovrane disposizioni all stesso Ammiraglio Inglese circa le persone che durante il tempo che l'E. V. ne starà lontana, debbono assumere il Commando Militare, ed interiormènte regolar gli Affari Civili.

"In the royal name I command speedy obedience, the corresponding orders being already given to the above-mentioned Admiral.

"Your Eminence,
"JOHN ACTON.

"Palermo, June 27th, 1799.
"To the Cardinal Ruffo."

GENERAL ACTON TO THE DUKE OF SOLANDRA.[1]

"YOUR EXCELLENCY,

"The King, having decided that Cardinal Ruffo should be conducted here by one of the men-of-war to be chosen for this purpose by the Admiral of the British Squadron, Lord Nelson, has deigned to command, that your Excellency, in concert with General Gamba, if this latter be not occupied or prevented, and Col. Baron Tschudy, be charged to execute the said removal, with all the caution that the

"Nel Real nome Io partieipo a V. E. nel pronto adempimento, provedendola di esserne già dati gli avisi corrispondenti al mentovato Ammiraglio.
"Palermo, 27 Giugno, 1799.
"Em° Signor,
"GIOVANNI ACTON.
"Signor Cardinale Ruffo."

[1] *Signor Duca della Solandra.*

"ECCELLENTISSIMO SIGNOR,

"Il Re avendo Sovramente risoluto che il Cardinale Ruffo sia arrestato e condotto qui sopra uno dei Legni di Guerra chè a tal uopo sara destinata dal Ammiraglio della Squadra Brittanica, Lord Nelson; si e degnata commandare che V. E. di concerto col Generale Gamba si costui non si trovi arrestato ni empidito, e col Col. Barone Tschudy, sia charichi di eseguire un tal arresto con tutti quelli cautell

circumstances demand, and to consign the aforesaid Cardinal to the above-mentioned Admiral, to whom his Majesty has already given the corresponding orders, that the same should be embarked and removed here. In the royal name, I urge upon your Excellency the prompt and exact accomplishment of this desire.

"JOHN ACTON.

"Palermo, 27th June, 1799."

[General Acton's letters to Generals Gamba and Tschudy were in the same words as in those to the Duke of Solandra.—ED.]

COPY OF A LETTER FROM HIS MAJESTY THE KING TO CARDINAL RUFFO.

"Palermo, June 27th, 1799.

"I have heard with inexpressible consolation of the arrival, after dinner, of my frigate from Naples, and also, of the happy arrival there of the very worthy and faithful Admiral, Lord Nelson. I have read

che le circonstanze richiedono, e che quindi consegni il referito Cardinale al mentorato Ammiraglio, al quale ha già S. M. dato gli avvisi corrispondenti, perche il medesimo sia imbarcarto e qui trasportato. Io partecipo nel Real nome a V. S. pel pronto e esatto adempimento di sua parte.

"GIOVANNI ACTON."

"Palermo, 27 Giugno, 1799."

Copia d'una lettera di S. M. il Re al Cardinale Ruffo.

"Palermo, 27 Giugno, 1799.

"Ho inteso con inesprimabile consolazione, l'arrivo della mia frigata da Napoli, e dalla medesima che vi è felicimente arrivato colla sua squadra il ben degno e fedele Ammiraglio Lord Nelson. Ho letto

the declaration which he, in form of observations, has despatched to you, which could not be more wise, reasonable, and adapted to the end, and truly evangelical.

"I do not doubt that you immediately conformed to it, and acted in consequence on his advice. Otherwise that would be which is impossible, after the many proofs of fidelity and attachment given me in the past.

"May the Lord preserve you, as with all my heart I desire.

"FERDINANDO B.

"To the Vicar-General, Cardinal Ruffo."

[The original in the King's own handwriting.—ED.]

EXTRACTS FROM THE INSTRUCTIONS TO THE TROOPS OF HIS MAJESTY, ORDERED TO REPAIR TO THE BAY OF NAPLES.[1]

"The circumstances of Naples requiring the prompt expedition to that place of a force of infantry, with

la Dichiarazione che egli in forma di osservazioni vi ha spedito, che non può essere piu savia, ragionata, ed adatta all' effetto, e veramente evangelica.

"Non dubito che immediatemente vi ci sarete conformato ed avete agito in consequenza all' istante. Altremente sarebbe ciò che non è possibile mai dopo tante riprnove per lo passato datemi di fidelta ed attaccamento.

"Il Signor vi conservi come di tutto cuore io ve lo desidero.
"FERDINANDO B.
"Al Vicario Generale, Cardinale Ruffo."

[1] *Istruzioni per le Truppe di S. M. destinate a portarsi nel Cratere di Napoli.*

"Richiedendo le circonstanze di Napoli la pronta spedizione a quella volta di una Forza di Linea all effetto di secondare gli sforzi

the design of aiding the inhabitants of that capital, devoted to the defence of religion and the crown, and to assist the operations of the Vicar-General, Cardinal Ruffo,—Admiral Lord Nelson has thought proper, on mutual advice, and in concert, to make arrangements to act, conjointly and efficiently, with the renowned British force under his command, to re-establish peace in this kingdom by the recovery of the capital, and to liberate this people from the yoke of anarchy and rebellion.

"1st. The declarations and memorials of numerous subjects in Naples and its environs, who pant to break the yoke imposed on them by the most infamous treachery, have caused in reply permission to be given to the true royalists, on the appearance of the Squadron in the Gulf of Naples, to be ready all to take arms, and then make use of them at the signal that shall be given by Admiral Lord Nelson, either contemporaneously with, or immediately after the intimation that will be made by a flag of truce, for

degli abitanti in quella capitale dediti alla difesa della religione e corona, ed a coadjuvare le operazioni del Vicario Generale Cardinale-Ruffo; Ha stimato l'Ammiraglio Lord Nelson, sull' avviso passatogliene, e con concerto, di disporre l'occorrente per concorrere efficacemente con le rispettabili forzi Brittaniche sotto il suo comando, a ripristinare la quiete in quel regno, mercè il riaquisto della capitale, ed a liberare quei popoli dal giogo dell'anarchia e rebellione.

"1º Le dichiarazioni e suppliche di numerosi sudditi che anelano in Napoli e sue adjacenze, di scuotere il giogo imposto loro dal più infame tradimento, hanno prodotto in replica la prevenzione ai buoni Realisti di dover essi al comparire della squadra nel Golfo di Napoli, trovarsi disposti a prendere tutti le armi, e farne poi uso al segno che verrà loro dato dall' Ammiraglio Lord Nelson, o contemporaneamente o in seguito delle intimazione che si farà fare da un

the surrender and submission of that capital to the royal army. For this reason several boats will convey trusty persons to meet the Squadron, as it approaches the islands.

"2d. Advices are in consequence despatched to Cardinal Ruffo, of the determination taken by the aforesaid Squadron to present itself before Naples, and to procure the possession of it to the royal arms, in order to accelerate his advance to the capital, with all the force that he thinks proper to lead there.

"3d. The forces of the Cardinal will alone be permitted to enter the capital, in the number and selection which he may think fit to make from the appointed corps, in addition to the troops of the line.

"4th. All the military and political operations shall be agreed upon by the Prince Royal and Admiral Lord Nelson. The opinion of this latter always to have a preponderance, on account of the respect due to his experience, as well as to the forces under his command,

Parlamentario per la resa e sottomissione alle reali armi di quella capitale. Si porteranno a questo effetto varj battelli con persone fidate all' incontro della squadra, nell' avvicinarsi di questa alle isole.

"2º Si sono spediti in conseguenza avvisi al Cardinale Ruffo della determinazione presa di presentarsi la squadra predetta avanti Napoli, e di procurarne il possesso alle reali armi, affinche acceleri esso il suo avvicinamento alla capitale con tutte le forze che credera di doversi portare.

"3º Le sole forze del Cardinale potranno introdursi nella capitale in quel numero, e con la scelta che egli stimerà di fare dei corpi destinati, in supplemento delle truppe de linea.

"4º Tutte le operazioni militari e politiche, saranno concertate tra il Principe Reale, e l'Ammiraglio Lord Nelson. Il parere di quest' ultimo sarà sempre di preponderanza per li riguardi dovuti alla di lui esperienza come alle forze da esso dipendenti, e che

which will determine the operations; and also because we are so deeply indebted to him for the zeal and attachment of which he has given so many proofs. Therefore, should the attack take place, the employment of the royal forces, and all other means tending to obtain the surrender of Naples, shall be thus decided.

"5th. The summons to the rebels to surrender, and any invitation or declaration to the people, and to the erring or misled, shall, for the base and rule of the expression or promises, agree with whatever has been specified in the law given by his Majesty to Cardinal Ruffo on the 29th of April last, as well with respect to the principal criminals generally, as with regard to the clemency to be shown them, the which is and always shall be the right of his Majesty. The spirit of these new declarations shall therefore approximate as much as possible to the sense of the aforesaid general law.

"6th. Therefore, in the military capitulation which

---

decidono dell' operazione; e per quanto altresi devesi al medesimo per lo zelo, ed attaccamento, de quei ha dato tante riprouve. Onde se avranno luogo gli attacchi, si decidera con questo metodo l'impiego delle reali forze, ed ogni altro mezzo tendente ad ottenere la resa di Napoli.

"5ª Le intimazioni ai ribelli per arrendersi, e ogni qualunque invito, o dichiarazione ai popoli, ed ai traviati o sedotti, dovranno per la base e norma nelle espressioni o promesse, riferrissi a quanto viene fissato per legge data da S. M. al Cardinale Ruffo nel 29 Aprile p°.; tanto per i rei principali in generale, che per la clemenza da usarsi, la quale è, e sarà sempre propria di S. M. Si dovrà pertanto approssimare il piu che sarà praticabile, lo spirito di queste nuove dichiarazione al senso della citata legge generale.

"6° Nella capitolazione militare però, che occorresse farsi con i

may take place with the enemy that occupy St. Elmo, the power of stipulating for their departure may be extended to several rebels, even the leaders, according to circumstances, if the general good, the promptitude of the operation, and reasons of weight make it advisable. The same measures will serve also for Capua and Gaeta, if it shall happen that this same operation embraces the question of the surrender of those places.

" 7th. When Naples shall be entirely surrendered and subdued, the Vicar-General shall at once take possession of the entire government of the kingdom; and to this intent will receive from the Prince Royal the King's new ratification of this his commission and charge, with all the particular determinations that the circumstance requires, and any rules that the importance of the time and special considerations indispensably demand.

" 9th. As it is the desire of his Majesty that the forts of Naples shall be speedily evacuated by the

nemici che occupano S. Elmo, potrà ostendersi secondo le circonstanze la facoltà di stipulare la partenza e varj ribelli anche capi, so il bene pubblico, la prontezza dell' operazione, e ragioni di peso così facessero opinare. Tale misura potrà servire benanche per Capua, e Gaeta, se accaderà di intimarsene la resa nel complesso di questa stessa operazione.

"7^ Quando Napoli sarà resa totalmente, e sommessa, il Vicario Generale prenderà per ora il possesso dell' intiero governo del regno, ed a quell' effetto receverà dal Real Principe il nuovo confermo dal Re di questa sua commissione, ed incarico, con tutte le particolari determinazioni che la circonstanza esige, e con alcune norme che il momento, e speciali considerazioni richiedono indispensabilmente.

"0° Siccome è mente di S. M. che con prontezza siano evacuati i castelli di Napoli dal nemico e ribelli di adoprare oltre la forza, altre

enemy and rebels, the Prince Royal is authorized to pursue this design at any cost, and, should it be necessary, to employ any other means besides force.

"10th. The acts of clemency concerning the noted offenders, and the pardoning of the same, are reserved for the King, excepting those stipulated in the articles of capitulation.

"Palermo, June 10th, 1799."

SIR WILLIAM HAMILTON TO CARDINAL RUFFO.

"On board the *Foudroyant*, in the Gulf of Naples,
"June 24th, 1799.

"My Lord Nelson begs me to inform your Eminence that he has received from Captain Foote, commander of the frigate *Sea-horse*, a copy of the capitulation which your Eminence has judged it expedient to make with the officers in command of the castles of St. Elmo, Castello Nuovo, and Castello del Uovo; that he disapproves entirely of these, and that he is quite resolved not to remain neuter with the respectable force which he has the honour to command; 'that he has detached to meet your Eminence the Captains Troubridge and Ball, commanding his Majesty's vessels *Culloden* and *Alexander*. These Captains are fully informed of Lord Nelson's sentiments, and will have the honour to explain them to your Emi-

qualunque mezzo, che sià necessario, viene autorizzato il Real Principe, a conseguire quell' intento ad ogni costo.

"10° Gli atti di clemenza che possono riguardare i rei conosciuti, e l'aggraziare i medesimi, sono riservati al Re, eccettuandosi quanto si è detto all' articolo della capitolazione."

nence. My Lord hopes that the Cardinal Ruffo will agree with him, and that to-morrow at the break of day he will be able to act in concert with your Eminence. The object of each cannot but be the same; that is to say, to reduce the common enemy, and to make the rebellious subjects of his Sicilian Majesty submit to his clemency."

Sir William Hamilton to Cardinal Ruffo.

"June 25th, 1799.

"My Lord Nelson begs me to take up my pen again, and to acquaint your Eminence, whom he understands to speak of the Chev^{r.} Micheroux, in the present negotiations of your Eminence for the service of his Sicilian Majesty, that he is quite determined to have nothing to do with any one, be he who he may, except your Eminence, with whom alone he wishes to consult and act. My Lord Nelson also begs me to assure your Eminence, that with respect to the Russian troops, he will always keep in view the honour of his Majesty the Emperor of all the Russias, as well as that of the King his own sovereign."

The Same to the Same.

"June 27th, 1799.

"My Lord Nelson begs me to say to your Eminence, that he has no doubt you will agree with him, that, for the service of his Sicilian Majesty, it is necessary that the Castle of St Elmo should be reduced as soon as possible. My Lord proposes, then, with the approbation of your Eminence, to send the body of marines, about 1,200 men, together with the Russian corps attached to the army of your Eminence, to attack the said castle. My Lord would desire that during this attack, your Eminence would place two or three hundred men in the castles of Uovo and Nuovo, and to keep the gates of these forts closed during the operations. My Lord would also desire your Eminence to order a body of troops, with the requisite artillery, to hold themselves in readiness to aid in the attack confided to the English and Russian troops. My Lord submits to the judgment of your Eminence, whether it would not be expedient to publish an edict to prevent the French garrison of St. Elmo being provided daily with victuals and refreshments, as it is said they are at present. My Lord begs me to add, that if your Eminence judges it expedient to send Caracciolo and the rest of the other rebels to him, according to his proposal yesterday, he will dispose of them."

THE SAME TO THE SAME.

"June 26th, 1799.

"My Lord Nelson desires me to inform your Eminence, that, in consequence of an order which he has just received from his Sicilian Majesty, who entirely disapproves of the capitulation made with his rebellious subjects in the castles of Uovo and Nuovo, he is about to seize and make sure of those who have left them, and are on board the vessels in this port, submitting it to the opinion of your Eminence whether it would not be advisable to publish at first in Naples the reason of this transaction, and at the same time to warn the rebels who have escaped to Naples from the said castles, that they must submit to the clemency of his Sicilian Majesty within the space of twenty-four hours, under pain of death."

[The first subjoined letter from Mr. Rose to Lady Hamilton shows that he had not only suggested the application to Mr. Addington, but had supplied her with the form of it. But it is remarkable throughout this correspondence how constantly his own consciousness of the impropriety of her position struggles against his earnest desire to assist her; not for her own sake, but solely on account of his friend Lord Nelson, to whom he considered it an act of justice to comply with his requests. While, therefore, he endeavours to aid her views, he never fails to throw cold water upon her hopes, and to predict failure. After Lord Nelson's death he took up her cause more warmly, but with the same conviction that there was still no chance of success.—ED.]

MR. ROSE TO LADY HAMILTON.

"MADAM, "March 9th, 1804.

"In proposing to you to write the enclosed letter to Mr. Addington, I entreat I may not raise a hope in your mind that your doing so will be likely to produce any good to you. I have, in conformity with the principle I have invariably adhered to, been anxious from the first mention of your case to me, to prevent your forming an expectation of success from any application you might make to the Minister, lest I should in the remotest possible degree contribute to add disappointment to misfortune. But I think in your situation the attempt is worth making. You will at least arrive at a certainty, for I am persuaded if it does not succeed now, it never can; and this sort of application will, I think, afford you as good a chance of success as you can have. I sincerely and heartily wish you had a better than I can venture to hope for.

"If you can prevail with either the peer or the knight you mentioned to me to put your letter into Mr. Addington's hands, or to enclose it to him, I should strongly recommend your doing so. But on no account mention my name, or allude to me, as I am quite sure that would not be useful to you; and when you have copied the letter to Mr. A., I must beg you will put it in the fire.

"If anything requires explanation, I will have the honour of waiting on you any morning you please, between eleven and twelve o'clock."

LADY HAMILTON TO MR. ROSE.[1]

"MY DEAR SIR, "Clarges Street, Nov. 4th.

"You will excuse me for writing to you on the subject that I do, but my wish that Lord Nelson

[1] It is difficult to fix the date of the following letter. Welbore Ellis, if Lord Mendip is meant, died in 1802; but Mr. Pitt was

may be made happy, and his brother-in-law, Mr. Bolton, placed in a situation that he would do justice to, makes me take the liberty of asking, could you not put in a good word for the place vacant now by Welbore Ellis's death? I know your power, and inclination, and your wish to oblige Lord Nelson; and really it would be only justice in Mr. Pitt to do something for the family of a man who is doing all he can for his country. But this I know: Lord Nelson has the greatest reliance on your friendship for him, which makes me take the liberty of now writing to you. I hope you will call on me when you come to town, and I promise you not to bore you with my own claims; for if those that have power will not do me justice, I must be quiet; and, in revenge to them, I can say,—if ever I am a minister's wife again, with the power I had then, why I will again do the same for my country as I did before; and I did more than any *ambassador* ever did, though their pockets were filled with secret-service money, and poor Sir William and myself never got even a pat on the back. But, indeed, the *cold-hearted* Grenville was in then. I

at that time out of office, and could not give away places under Government. Lady Hamilton alludes to the death of Sir W. Hamilton, which took place in 1803. It was not till the following year that Mr. Pitt returned to office; and since Nelson—who died in 1805—was still living, the date cannot be sooner or later than 1804. But who then is the Welbore Ellis mentioned? There was a Welbore Ellis Agar, who was a commissioner of customs. If he died in 1804, he was the person named, and his the office wanted for Mr. Bolton. It would seem, from a subsequent letter, that Lady Hamilton had already urged her claims upon Mr. Addington during his administration, to no purpose. Her "sad story" made no impression upon him.

know if I could tell my story to Mr. Pitt he would
do me justice; but I never am to be so happy as to
be in company with that great man:—I call him the
Nelson of ministers. But I will not tire you with my
sad story. I shall be content to see Mr. Bolton
placed; for that will make a worthy family happy,
and render Nelson Mr. Pitt's and your grateful friend
for ever. Believe me, with more than I can express
of gratitude,

"EMMA HAMILTON."

[It is something in favour of Lady Hamilton, that
her first anxiety after the intelligence of Nelson's
death was not for herself, but for the family of his
sister. But the utter prostration of body and mind
which it brought on was more what might be expected from a deeply affectionate wife than from a
"*confidante* and friend." It appears that she was
obliged to get her mother to write for her; and three
weeks afterwards was still confined to her bed. From
the letter which she then wrote it seems that the
accusation was already current against her, which, at a
later period, became a more serious charge, of publishing Lord Nelson's confidential communications.—ED.]

MRS. CADOGAN, LADY HAMILTON'S MOTHER, TO
MR. ROSE.

"9th November, 1805.

"Lady Hamilton's most wretched state of mind
prevents her imploring her dear good Mr. Rose to

solicit Mr. Pitt to consider the family of our great and glorious Nelson, who so gallantly died for his country, leaving behind his favourite sister, with a large family unprovided for. Her Ladyship is confident you will exert every nerve for these good people as a mark of your true and real attachment to our lamented hero. Mr. Bolton was ever much esteemed by his brother-in-law; and, had it pleased the Almighty to have spared Lord Nelson to his family, he meant to have made them independent. They at this moment surround her ladyship's bed, bewailing their sad loss and miserable state. Lady Hamilton, whose situation is beyond description, only prays that you, good sir, will do all you can for this worthy family; it will be the greatest relief to her mind. This is written by the mother of the most to be pitied Lady Hamilton, who begs leave to subscribe herself Mr. Rose's

"Most obedient and very humble servant,
"MARY CADOGAN.

"P.S.—If Mr. Rose would condescend to acknowledge this it would be a comfort to her just now."

LADY HAMILTON TO MR. ROSE.

* Clarges Street, Nov. 29th, 1806.

"I write from my bed, where I have been ever since the fatal sixth of this month, and only rose to be removed from Merton here. I could not write to you, my dear sir, before, but your note requires that I should justify myself.

"Believe me, then, when I assure you I do not see any one but the family of my dear Nelson. His letters are in the bed with me; and only to the *present Earl* did I ever read one, and then only a part. It is true he is leaky, but I believe would not willingly tell anything; but I have been told something like some of my letters have been printed in some paper. I never now read a paper, and my health and spirits are so bad I cannot enter into a war with vile editors. Of this be assured, no one shall ever see a letter of my glorious and dear departed Nelson. It is true I have a journal from him ever since he came up to Naples to get provisions for our troops in Toulon, when he was in the *Agamemnon;* but his letters are sacred, and shall remain so. My dear sir, my heart is broken. Life to me now is not worth having; I lived but for him. His glory I gloried in; it was my pride that he should go forth; and this fatal and last time he went I persuaded him to it. But I cannot go on;—my heart and head are gone;—only, believe me, what you write to me shall ever be attended to. Could you know me you would not think I had such bad policy as to publish any thing at this moment. My mind is not a common one; and having lived as a *confidante* and friend with such men as Sir William Hamilton, and dearest, glorious Nelson, I feel myself superior to vain tattling woman. Excuse me, but I am ill and nervous, and *hurt* that those I value should think meanly of me.

"When you come to town, pray call on me. I do not know if I shall live in England, as I promised the Queen of Naples to go back to her in case of accidents. You will not be able to read this scrawl, but I am very, very ill. Mr. Bolton feels all your kindness to him, and firmly relies on you. All the family are with me, and very kind. The *Earl you know;* but a man must have great courage to *accept* the honour of——calling himself by *that* name.

"Write me a line to say you have got this, and that you believe

"Your grateful

"EMMA HAMILTON.

"You shall see what pictures I have got, and have any copied."

[After the battle of Trafalgar and the return of the fleet, Captain Hardy lost no time, as soon as he could leave his ship, in repairing to Mr. Rose, as the person in office most attached to his friend Lord Nelson, and most likely to carry into execution his dying bequest as to Lady Hamilton's interests. And he judged rightly; for he took up her cause with an ardour of zeal which made him almost overlook all other considerations, as if it were a sacred duty to give effect to his friend's testamentary desires. This, however, was not his first communication to her; for it appears from her preceding letter that he had reason to suspect

her of having availed herself of private letters to
serve her own purposes. The letter in which that
charge was intimated is missing. Mr. Rose's view of
the subject is the same which he maintained throughout the correspondence.—ED.]

MR. ROSE TO LADY HAMILTON.

"Cuffnells, Dec. 9th, 1805.

" MADAM,

" Captain Hardy had the goodness to take the
trouble (at much inconvenience to himself) to come
over here immediately after the *Victory* anchored at
Spithead, to tell me what passed in the last moments
of the life of my late most invaluable friend ; respecting whom I shall at no time attempt to express my
feelings. I learn from him that Lord Nelson, almost
with his latest breath, manifested a confidence that I
would do all in my power to make effectual the wish
he had more than once stated to me respecting you ;
the Captain, at the same time, communicating to me
the entry made in his lordship's pocket-book, just
before he went into the action in which he immor-
talized his name, recommending a remuneration to
you for the actual and important services rendered by
you to the country when the fleet under his command was in Sicily on his first return from Egypt.
I cannot, therefore, delay telling you I shall take the
very earliest opportunity of a personal communication
with Mr. Pitt to enforce that solemn request upon
him ; and, I am sure, his respect for the memory of

one of the greatest men that ever lived, and his sense of what is right to be done in such a case, will incline him to listen attentively, and I hope favourably, to the claim made for you; of which, however, I never heard anything till after he went out of office in 1801. When I last had the honour of seeing you, somewhat more than two years ago, in Mr. Addington's administration, I suggested the length of time that had elapsed subsequent to the performance of the service as an obstacle. That difficulty is certainly not lessened; but, considering when the solemn and earnest recommendation was made, and the strong attestation of the importance of your interposition, I am not without a hope of success. I am anxious, however, to guard you against entertaining a sanguine expectation on the subject, that I may not have the self-reproach of occasioning a disappointment to you. My application must be to Mr. Pitt, but the reward (to which I think you entitled both on principle and policy) must, I conceive, be from the foreign Secretary of State, on account of the nature of the service. I can promise nothing but zeal; how far that, acting on the conviction of my mind of the justice of your pretensions, is likely to be effectual, you shall know in a few days, at the latest, after I shall see Mr. Pitt, either at Bath or in London.

"I trouble you with no particulars about Mr. Bolton, as I have written to himself. The earnest manner in which Mr. Pitt wrote and spoke to me about him repeatedly, will insure to him my best

attention. He knows from me Mr. Pitt's positive
engagement to provide for him.

"I am, Madam,
"&c. &c. &c.
"G. Rose."

[After the death of Mr. Pitt, in 1806, Mr. Rose
wrote to Lady Hamilton, to apologize for not having
obtained from him any decision upon her case, and
signified his intention to resign, and consequently his
loss of power to assist her, but encouraged her to rely
on Lord Nelson's will. In another letter, a few months
afterwards, he cautioned her not to be sanguine. In
the following year, after two applications to Mr.
Canning in her favour, the language of discouragement is still stronger. Out of tenderness to her
feelings, the only objection which he represents to her
to be insurmountable is, the length of time which
had elapsed since the service to be rewarded was
performed; the application was too late; but it was
not too late for something to be done for the child
Horatia, whom Nelson had *adopted*. And so, in
writing to Lord Abercorn on the same subject in 1808,
he acknowledged the utter fruitlessness of his efforts
in behalf of Lady Hamilton, but still hoped for his
assistance in getting a pension for the child. He must
have seen from the first the impossibility of obtaining
any public grant of money for the lady; but he relied
on the Foreign Minister consenting to give something

out of the secret-service money, to reward her services; and therefore, when Mr. Lavie, one of Lady Hamilton's trustees, to whom she had sent the memorial of her claims drawn up by Mr. Rose, consulted him as to the best mode of proceeding with it, he suggested as a last resource, the possibility of obtaining from the person who was Foreign Minister at that time a certificate that it was a service which he would have rewarded if application had been then made to him. A drowning man will catch at a straw; but the hope of obtaining any assistance from the lofty principles of Lord Grenville, who was then in office,—the cold-hearted Grenville, as Lady H. called him, because he had no sympathy with her impassioned warmth of feeling,—was a straw beyond her reach. He did not share in Mr. Rose's veneration and attachment to Lord Nelson. At length, in the year 1813, she lost even Mr. Rose's support, as well as Mr. Canning's, by some false statements which she introduced into a memorial prepared by herself for the Prince Regent; and having escaped from prison for debt by the assistance of Lord Ellenborough, she hastened to find an asylum from her creditors in France, before new writs could be issued against her, and there still invoked the assistance of Nelson's friends in behalf of the little Horatia.—Ed.]

Mr. Rose to Lady Hamilton.

"Madam,

"Deeply as I am affected by the recent loss I have sustained in the death of Mr. Pitt, I cannot omit to express to you my sincere and deep regret that I had not a possible opportunity of fulfilling the engagement which the veneration I have for the memory of Lord Nelson induced me to make to you, in my letter from Cuffnells, after I had seen Captain Hardy.

"I had no alarm about Mr. Pitt's health till it was decided he should leave Bath; but on my seeing him at Putney Heath, I found him so ill as to preclude my talking to him on any business whatever; Sir Walter Farquhar had indeed positively prohibited any one from doing so.

"I shall certainly not remain in office; and respecting the arrangements that may take place in consequence of Mr. Pitt's death I am utterly ignorant; but if it shall happen that any representation of mine to those who may fill the departments of Government can have the remotest chance of being useful to you, it shall not be wanting. I am persuaded, however, that Lord Nelson's last and solemn appeal to his country for justice to be done to your claim, will be the best possible support to it.

"I will have the honour of waiting on you some morning in the course of the next week.

"I have the honour to be, Madam,
"Your faithful, and most obedient, humble servant,
"George Rose.
"Old Palace Yard, Jan. 27th, 1806."

MR. ROSE TO LADY HAMILTON.

"July 3d, 1806.

"DEAR MADAM,

"I have made arrangements for to-morrow that would render it really inconvenient to me to wait on you while you are in town. I would, however, break in upon these to call in Clarges Street, if I could have a chance of being useful to you; but I am certain I cannot. What I have repeatedly suggested I am more and more confirmed in, that the difficulty in affording you relief is increased to a great extent by the length of time that has elapsed since your claim arose, in which period there have been three administrations. If you cannot obtain attention to it now, I am sure you had better think no more of it. I do not say this from indifference in the subject, but from an anxiety that you should not continue to entertain a hope that must (if you do not immediately obtain relief) end in disappointment. Lord Nelson's codicil, I think, affords a ground for making a last attempt."

MR. ROSE TO LADY HAMILTON.

"Old Palace Yard, June 4th, 1807.

"DEAR MADAM,

"I have had a full conversation with Mr. Canning on the subject of your application. After reading your papers, he listened to my statement very patiently. The result was his promising to consider all the circumstances attentively; and that, if upon full consideration of them, he should think anything can be done, he would talk with the Duke of Portland on the subject, both as to the amount and the mode.

"Let me again caution you most earnestly against raising your expectations; that if I cannot do you good, at least that I may not be the occasion of a disappointment to you. I am the more anxious about that, because the difficulty (from delay) is, I am afraid, almost insurmountable.

Mr. Rose to Lady Hamilton.

"Dear Madam,

"It has not been owing to any want of attention on my part that you have not heard from me much earlier; the real truth is, that Mr. Canning has been so entirely occupied with urgent business, that although I put your paper into his hand on his first coming into office, I could not think myself justified in pressing him to any determination upon them; nor could I have done so on any private concern whatever, while matters of the highest importance to the public were depending. I availed myself, however, of an interval, which I was very glad to do before I left London, to talk with him fully a few days ago on the whole subject of your memorial; and I must in justice to him say, that I am persuaded the respect he has for the memory of the incomparable man who recommended you and the child to the justice and liberality of his country, would induce him to make that recommendation available to you both if he could do so; but, on the fullest and most attentive consideration of all circumstances, he thinks he cannot do that. I have so invariably endeavoured to prepare you not to expect success in your application, that I trust you will not feel much disappointment at this communication, however you may regret it. There are always people, who have no responsibility upon themselves, ready enough to say to persons who consult them, there should be no difficulty in points of a mere embarrassing nature; but I should not act fairly if I did not say that (feeling, as I do, so warm and strong an attachment to the memory of Lord Nelson), I think Mr. Canning could not now do what I thought might very properly have been done eighteen months or still much longer ago. I make this communication with deep and sincere regret; but it is better to state the whole plainly to you, than to mislead you, or to throw blame on another, taking credit for favourable intentions on my own part.

"The reward recommended by Lord Nelson for yourself, on the score of public services, seems to be now quite desperate. The only hope I can venture to hold out the remotest prospect of to you is, that Mr. Canning may possibly on some favourable opportunity propose to the Duke of Portland to recommend to the King a small pension to the child. He wishes, I verily believe sincerely, to do that; but the carrying this into execution must depend on contingencies he cannot control, and if it should never be done, you must not reproach him or me even in your own mind for a moment; for I am not authorized by him to give you the slightest encouragement. My anxiety, how-

ever, to show how eagerly I wish to fulfil the dying
request of the man I most sincerely loved, and to
whom the country is most deeply indebted, has not, I
hope, induced me to say too much.

"I send herewith the papers you put into my
hands, by a careful servant, as I know they are of
value to you.

"I am, dear Madam,

"Your most obedient and very humble servant,

"G. R.

"Old Palace Yard, August 21st, 1807."

MR. ROSE TO LORD ABERCORN.

"Old Palace Yard, April 9th, 1808.

"MY LORD,

"I am afraid two or three weeks have elapsed
since I promised Lady Hamilton to state to your
Lordship what has passed, within my knowledge,
respecting any remuneration or provision for her in
consequence of her claims on the public, from a compliance with which I have been prevented only by an
uncommon pressure of business, in which I have lately
been unceasingly occupied.

"The first mention of those claims was made to me
by Lord Nelson on his return from the West Indies,
in the summer of 1805, when he requested me with
great earnestness to submit the consideration of them
to Mr. Pitt, accompanied by strong assurances that it
was through her interposition exclusively he obtained
provisions and water for the English ships at Syracuse,
in the summer of 1798; by which he was enabled to

return to Egypt in quest of the enemy's fleet;—to which, therefore, the success of his brilliant action of the Nile was owing, as he must otherwise have gone down to Gibraltar to refit, and the enemy would have escaped.

"A few weeks subsequent to that interview with his Lordship, in London, he was again appointed to the Mediterranean command; and, previous to his sailing for that station, I met him at Portsmouth at his earnest request,—Mr. Canning, who was then in my neighbourhood, in Hampstead, accompanying me,—when his Lordship repeated his entreaties that I would recommend Lady Hamilton's case to Mr. Pitt's early consideration; an opportunity for which occurred a few days afterwards, on Mr. Pitt coming to me at Cuffnells. He listened favourably to my representation, without making any sort of engagement, but finished the conversation by saying he would discuss the subject conclusively with me when we met in London.

"The next circumstance that I recollect was Sir Thomas Hardy, Lord Nelson's captain, arriving at Spithead in the *Victory*, in November or December, with the corpse of the incomparable hero. He left the ship as soon as she anchored at Spithead, in an open boat, and came to Lymington, nearly thirty miles, and from thence to me at Cuffnells, to communicate to me Lord Nelson's dying sentiments in support of Lady Hamilton's claims. His Lordship's recommendation of them, on his going into the action, is, I believe, proved as a part of his will. I am sure it has been printed.

"Strongly impressed by these circumstances, I wrote immediately to her Ladyship, assuring her of my best exertions to obtain from Mr. Pitt an early decision on her case; under a persuasion I did not venture to convey to her, that it would have been a favourable one; but, unhappily, his last illness had made too rapid a progress before I saw him to permit me to mention any subject of business to him when we met.

"From the time of Mr. Pitt's death to the formation of the present Government, I know only of one application, and that in Mr. Addington's time; but on the appointment of Mr. Canning to be Foreign Secretary, I stated to him fully all that had passed within my knowledge from the first mention of the subject to me, accompanied with as earnest entreaties as I could use, that he would give a sum of 6,000*l.* or 7,000*l.*, out of foreign secret-service, to her Ladyship; conceiving that to be a much more proper mode of rewarding her, and likely to be attended with considerably less difficulty; but with a perfectly good disposition on his part, that effort failed: a very faint hope, however, having been afforded that a moderate pension might at some time possibly be procured for the child who lives with her, and who was recommended also by Lord Nelson in his last moments.

"These are the circumstances of Lady Hamilton's case according to my knowledge. Whenever it has been mentioned, I have uniformly expressed as strong an opinion in favour of it as I have invariably felt; but I have cautiously avoided raising an expectation in her mind on the subject, that I might not have the self-reproach of adding disappointment to misfortune. If I ever gave her the faintest hope, it must have been when I wrote to her after Captain Hardy's arrival in December, 1805; but I wish her to communicate to you any letters of mine, if she has kept them.

"My anxiety to contribute to fulfilling the dying wish of Lord Nelson is unabated; and if your Lordship shall think my calling on you can afford the remotest chance of that, I shall cheerfully obey your commands on the subject."

Memorial of Lady Hamilton's claims, drawn up by Mr. Rose in his own hand-writing, and forwarded to Mr. Lavie, one of her Trustees. Referred to in Mr. Lavie's letter which follows.

"The ground on which I found my claim for some remuneration from Government is a positive and most important service I rendered to my country in obtaining orders from the Court of Naples for the British fleet to be victualled and watered at Syracuse, in the summer of 1798, contrary to direct instructions which had been before given to furnish them with nothing. If I had not prevailed in that respect, which was attended with very great difficulty, and could have been effected only by the influence I had with the Queen, the British fleet must have gone down to Gibraltar for provisions and water, in which case the

French fleet, that was destroyed at Aboukir, must inevitably have escaped.

"This is a plain statement, most incontrovertibly true. It has been attested by Lord Nelson repeatedly under his hand and in frequent conversations; confirmed by a solemn declaration almost in the hour of death. He requested to see Mr. Rose on the subject previous to his leaving Portsmouth the last time, and urged him strongly to recommend my case to the favourable consideration of Mr. Pitt. Mr. Rose has indeed admitted to me that his Lordship's expressions of anxiety for some remuneration to me were amongst the last words he uttered when he was taking leave of him on board the *Victory*. Mr. Pitt's death having happened before Mr. Rose could have any personal communication with him, in consequence of Lord Nelson's request, I have derived no benefit from that; and I have been unsuccessful in every exertion I have used since with subsequent Governments.

"This want of success has been more unfortunate for me, as I have incurred very heavy expenses in completing what Lord Nelson had left unfinished at Merton, and have found it impossible to sell the place. From these circumstances I have been reduced to a situation the most painful and distressing that can be conceived; and should have been actually confined in prison, if a few friends, from attachment to the memory of Lord Nelson, had not interfered to prevent it, under whose kind protection alone I am enabled now to exist.

"My case is plain and simple. I rendered a

service of the utmost importance to my country, attested in the clearest and most undeniable manner possible; and I have received no reward, although justice was claimed for me by the hero who lost his life in the performance of his duty to that country, in one of the most brilliant victories that was ever accomplished, after a series of former services unexampled almost in the history of the world.

"If I had bargained for a reward beforehand, there can be no doubt but that it would have been given to me, and *liberally;* I hoped then not to want it. I do now stand in *the utmost need of it,* and surely it will not be refused to me. I accompany this paper with a copy of what Lord Nelson wrote in the solemn moments which preceded the action in which he fell; and I am still not without a hope that the dying, earnest, entreaty of such a man, in favour of a child he had adopted and was devotedly fond of, will be complied with, as well as my own application.

"The letters I have received on different occasions on this subject will show that the justness and fairness of my claims have been repeatedly admitted by those who were competent judges of the matter.

"I anxiously implore that my claims may not be rejected without consideration, and that my forbearing to urge them earlier may not be objected to me; because in the lifetime of Sir W. Hamilton I should not have thought of even mentioning them, nor, indeed, after his death, if I had been left in a less comparatively destitute state. Allow me further to add, that if any reference is necessary you will have the goodness to make it, and not leave me in my unprotected situation to press my application other than to yourself;—not entertaining, however, the slightest doubt of the justness and perfect fairness of any department to which you may refer my pretensions. If to the Naval one, where they can be well judged of, I should hope for a due attention."

Mr. Lavie to Mr. Rose.

[*Private.*]

"Sir,

"Lady Hamilton has handed me a most excellent paper, of which myself and the rest of her trustees will immediately avail ourselves; but we have some doubt whether any, and which department of Government should be applied to previous to going to Parliament. Lady H. gave me, some time ago, a copy of a memorial to the King (not in council), but I cannot learn that it was ever presented.

"I believe I could get half the City of London to sign a recommendatory paper if it would be any use.

"You may rely that any communications you may be pleased to make to me shall be held sacred. Lady Hamilton and the little Horatia are to stay at Westend till Tuesday, and I wish, if possible, to get the above matter arranged before she leaves us.

"I have the honour to be,
  "Your very obedient servant,
    "Germain Lavie.

"Frederick's Place, 1st April, 1809.

" Many years since, I had frequently the honour of meeting you at my good friend Mr. Pott's, from whom I derived all my little legal knowledge."

Mr. ROSE TO G. LAVIE, ESQ.

Old Palace Yard, April 2d, 1809.

"SIR,

" I wish I knew how to give any advice likely to be useful on the subject of your letter. I promised Lord Nelson, on my last parting from him, to endeavour to give furtherance to his recommendation of the case of Lady Hamilton; conceiving it, from his Lordship's statement, to be entitled to favourable consideration.

"I have kept that promise faithfully, and regret very sincerely my want of success. I certainly used my best endeavours in trying the ground, and seeing no prospect of doing her Ladyship any good, I avoided, carefully, raising any expectations in her mind by a fresh declaration that I could do no more. Understanding, however, that she had a hope her case, especially considering the late severe and afflicting pressure upon her, might be listened to if brought forward from another quarter,—I did not feel myself at liberty to dissuade her from the attempt, however discouraging the prospect appears to be.

" If a reward should be thought of for Lady Hamilton, for the actual service rendered to this country, as certified by Lord Nelson, it should naturally come from the foreign secret-service fund. In that event the application should be to Mr. Canning, who is not indisposed to do what would be strictly and correctly conformable to his duty; but after such a lapse of time, and different persons having filled the office he holds, he very reasonably objected to taking upon himself the responsibility of giving the reward.

"On the part of Lady Hamilton it may I believe with truth be urged, that she asked none at the time from a hope of not wanting it;—but that she now does.

"In that view of the subject, the only ray of hope (which I wish not to encourage) that could be entertained would be by prevailing with the noble lord who was Secretary of State when the service was performed, to certify, that if application had been made to him at the time he should have thought himself justified in rewarding it. Without that I do not see how even an attempt can be made; for no application can be received in Parliament without the King's consent, signified by the Chancellor of the Exchequer, for which there does not seem to be any claim in this case.

"If you should have occasion to come to town tomorrow, and will take the trouble of calling here, I will state to you anything further that may occur to me. You will be sure of finding me at home, as I am at present confined to the house, and shall be for at least a few days. From one to three I am engaged in public business. At any other hour I shall be able to see you.

" P.S.—Lord Grenville was Foreign Secretary of State, and Lord Spencer First Lord of the Admiralty, when Lord Nelson's victory of Aboukir was obtained."

MR. CANNING TO MR. ROSE.

[*Private.*]

"Claremont, July 24th, 1800.

"DEAR ROSE,

"You must have thought it very extraordinary that I did not take any notice to you, when last we met, of your letter of the 14th respecting Lady Hamilton; but I had so far misunderstood the private note which accompanied it, as to imagine that you had left me at liberty (or rather desired me) to put off reading your letter till a moment of leisure; and that moment did not arrive till yesterday, when I came here for a couple of days of rest, and brought a heap of private unanswered letters with me.

"I am sorry to find in your letter a promise to Lady H. which I shall have obliged you to break, that you would call upon her at Richmond in your way out of town, with a final answer.

"I do assure you that I should be very sincerely disposed to gratify your anxious wishes in behalf of Lady H. if I could do so. But Lord Grenville's letter, as you yourself seem aware, does not help me at all; on the contrary, it is worded with the coldest caution, and would, I think, leave it quite open to him, and is intended to leave it open to him, to say that though Lady Hamilton's services deserved reward, yet the Foreign S. S. Fund was not the proper fund out of which that reward should come.

"I confess I am myself of this opinion. I do think that a pension might be well bestowed on Lady H. But I do *not* think that, *even at the time*, the influence of a Foreign Minister's wife with the Court where her husband resides, is a fit subject for compensation by secret-service money. There is still, however, another consideration more embarrassing, particularly in the times in which we are acting. The S. S. fund is, by express designation, for *secret* services—services that *cannot be explained or avowed*. Now *here* is a service published not only in Lady H.'s memorials, and known to every person whom she has solicited, but printed in extracts of a will registered in Doctors' Commons, and accessible to all mankind. What reason upon earth is there, it will be said, that if this service is remunerated *at all*, it should be remunerated *secretly?* or how *can* it be remunerated *secretly* in fact? Would not every one whom Lady H. has solicited, and every member of opposition high and low, know that Lady H. *had* received the reward of those services, and received it from a fund not brought to account?—and why not bring to account a matter so notorious? Do you not see the multitude of inconvenient questions to which this transaction would give rise? Do you not see that by disclosing, as it does of course, the manner in which *a part* of this fund is applied, and a difference of opinion existing (as there certainly would) as to the propriety of such an application, we should risk an inference being drawn that much more was probably disposed of in a manner equally objectionable, and of which Parliament might have cognizance with quite as little inconvenience to the State?

"A *clear opinion* of Lord G.'s in *favour* of the measure would have saved *some* of these difficulties—not all; for I should then have been only paying a debt incurred and acknowledged by a predecessor, but accidentally left unsettled.

"I really feel as much pain in stating these difficulties to you as you can do in the result of them. But I wish above all things to show you that I have given a fair consideration to the subject; and rather to take your judgment upon them than to give my own.

"Believe me, dear Rose,
"Ever most sincerely yours,
"GEO. CANNING.

"I return the paper."

MR. CANNING TO MR. ROSE.

"Gloucester Lodge, Feb. 17th, 1813.

"MY DEAR SIR,

"I have received a letter from Lady Hamilton (widow of Sir William), accompanying a copy of a petition which she has presented, or intends to present, to the Prince Regent, for a compensation for her losses and services. I think her richly entitled to some such compensation, and shall be happy if any unexceptionable mode of granting it can be devised.

"But the reason of my troubling you is, that in the course of her narrative she refers to you *and me* jointly as having given assurances to Lord Nelson of Mr. Pitt's determination to take her claims into consideration, on the evening when we dined on board the *Victory*, previous to Lord N.'s sailing for Cadiz.

"Now what assurances *you* may have been then authorized to give, I of course cannot undertake to say; but very sure I am that *I* had no authority to say anything upon the subject. I very much doubt whether I at that time *knew* anything of the existence of such a claim, which, if I mistake not, was first brought under my notice by you, when I was at the Foreign Office, and when, as you know, I would gladly have done anything that I could do to show my sense of Lady H.'s services, but found (what appeared to me) insuperable difficulties in the way.

"I wrote to Lady H. (returning the copy of the petition) to point out the inaccuracy of this reference to me, in respect to the assurances given to Lord Nelson; which I do, not as meaning to disclaim the opinion that she is entitled to remuneration, but because an inaccurate statement, in point of fact, however immaterial to the merits of the case, might prejudice her application.

"Her claim is not the weaker or the stronger for any assurances which either of us may have given; but it would be very awkward for her case that I should be asked if I gave such assurances, and to be obliged to answer (as I must do to such a question) in the negative. Whether your assurances to Lord N.

were given that day in my hearing, or not, I really cannot take upon myself to say. You had much conversation with him before me, and a good deal apart from me, and I believe alone with him, while we were on board the *Victory*. Be that as it may, I have no recollection of the circumstance, and certainly could not vouch for it if appealed to.

"I very sincerely hope that the P. Rt. may be able to comply with the prayer of the petition in some shape or other.

"Yours very truly,
"Geo. Canning.

"I return your pamphlet, with many thanks for the loan of it; and very many for your criticisms, which were of use to me in more instances than one,—in one particularly.

"I trouble you in return with a small pamphlet (of no very splendid form) in which you will find some mention of Mr. Pitt, I hope not unpleasing to you. It is full of false points; but in general so obvious as to correct themselves. It is hardly worth your keeping, but you are welcome to keep it."

Mr. Rose to Lady Hamilton.

"Feb. 16th, 1813.

"Dear Madam,

"I had a letter from Mr. Canning last night, wherein he mentions your having communicated to him a petition to the Prince Regent, 'in which you refer to him and me jointly as having given assurances to Lord Nelson of Mr. Pitt's determination to take your claims into consideration,' on the evening when he and I dined on board the *Victory*, previous to Lord Nelson sailing for Cadiz. It is incumbent on me, therefore, to state to you, that Mr. Canning was not a party to the conversation between Lord Nelson and me respecting you, and could not have heard a syllable of it, as he was not near us at the time. It is not merely to state that, however, that I now trouble you, but to apprise you that your recollection is not correct as to what I told you passed between me and Lord Nelson at the time alluded to. His Lordship urged me with great earnestness to press your claim on Mr. Pitt, and I gave him strong assurances that I would do so; and, generally, that I would endeavour to be useful to you.

"Mr. Pitt's death soon after that, prevented my interposition being productive of any benefit to you; but I am persuaded you will do me the justice to admit that I endeavoured to give every support to your claim while I thought there was the remotest hope of its being entertained. I did not know you were now bringing it forward again, till I received Mr. Canning's letters."

MR. CANNING TO MR. ROSE.

"Gloucester Lodge, Feb. 20th, 1813.

"MY DEAR SIR,

"I return the papers which you were so good as to send me yesterday. They contain a very clear account of your part in Lady H.'s business, and satisfy me that my recollection was correct as to the only knowledge I ever had of it.

"I think it may be right that you should see what her impressions are upon the subject; and therefore I transmit to you a letter which I have this moment received from her in reply to that from me, the substance of which I stated to you in my former note.

"I am, dear Sir,
"Very sincerely yours,
"Geo. Canning."

Mr. Rose to Mr. Canning.

"Old Palace Yard, Feb. 21st, 1813.

"My dear Sir,

"I thank you for the perusal of Lady Hamilton's letter, which I herewith return.

"As her Ladyship certainly never saw Lord Nelson after our visit to him on board the *Victory*, the communication from him of what passed there must have been in writing, and now in her possession, to which she can refer.

"As far as she can have a chance of deriving advantage from the anxiety of Lord Nelson for attention to her claims, my acknowledgment of his urgency to me on the subject will be available to her. The hurry in which, perhaps, he wrote to her may have occasioned his expressing himself so as to have been misunderstood; but she never said anything like it to me.

"The statement of her pretensions that I sent to you was drawn by me, which, at the time I wrote it, she approved of entirely; and you will have seen that in all that passed there was not a syllable that had a tendency towards authority having been given by Mr. Pitt of any sort."

LADY HAMILTON TO MR. ROSE.

"150, Bond Street, March 4th, 1813.

"DEAR SIR,

"I have been, and am, so ill with anxiety that I have scarce strength to write. But I had written to you long since, and had enclosed you a copy of my narrative to H. R. H. the Prince Regent, and to his Ministers. I now send you one, and also a letter I sent to Lord Sidmouth; for a kind friend of mine has told me that the reason my claims have not been remunerated was owing to a most infamous falsehood raised against mine honour and that of the brave and virtuous Nelson, which is false, and it shall be made known; for I will appeal to a generous public, who will not let a woman who has served her country with the zeal I have, be left to starve and insult. You, sir, who have been ever kind, and ever will be, will, I am sure, read the letter to Lord Sidmouth, and tell me if you approve of it. I am so fatigued with anxiety, and also with my situation about my pecuniary affairs, that I can only say I am

"Your truly grateful
"E. HAMILTON.

"P.S.—Mr. Canning has a short memory, as I have Nelson's letter on the visit to the *Victory*, the 14th of

September. If you could write me a line to say when you could call for half-an-hour, Sunday excepted, I will be at home, as I wish to ask your advice. The Prince Regent is my friend, and wishes well to my cause."

MR. ROSE TO LADY HAMILTON.

"DEAR MADAM,   "Old Palace Yard, March 6th, 1813.

"I return the copies of your memorial to the Prince Regent, and of your letter to Lord Sidmouth; in doing which it is impossible for me to avoid expressing my very deep regret at your having referred to Mr. Canning and myself for assurances having been given by us to Lord Nelson, on board the *Victory*, 'that the promises made by Mr. Pitt in your favour should be fully realized,' because the accuracy of that cannot be supported by either of us.

"In a letter I wrote to you about a fortnight ago, I reminded you of what did pass in my last interview with Lord Nelson, on the eve of his sailing for Cadiz; and I must lament that your statement was not conformable to that.

"It happens that Sunday, about two o'clock, would be the most convenient time for me to wait on you; but as you exclude that day, I will endeavour to be with you on Monday, at half-past one.

LADY HAMILTON TO MR. ROSE.

"Hôtel Dessin, Calais, July 4th.

"We arrived here safe, my dear sir, after three days' sickness at sea, as for precaution we embarked at the Tower. Mr. Smith got me the discharge from Lord Ellenborough.

I then begged Mr. Smith to withdraw his bail, for I would have died in prison sooner than that good man should have suffered for me; and I managed so well with Horatia alone, that I was at Calais before any new writs could be issued out against me. I feel so much better from change of climate, food, air, large rooms, and *liberty*, that there is a chance I may live to see my dear Horatia brought up. I am looking out for a lodging. I have an excellent French woman, who is very good at everything; for Horatia and myself, and my old dame, who is coming, will be my establishment. Near me is an English lady, who has resided here for twenty-five years; who has a day school, but not for eating nor sleeping. At eight in the morning I take Horatia; fetch her at one; at three we dine; she goes till five, and then in the evening we walk. She learns everything: piano, harp, languages grammatically. She knows French and Italian well, but she will still improve. Not any girls but those of the first families go there. Last evening we walked two miles to a *fête champétre pour les bourgeois*. Everybody is pleased with Horatia. The General and his good old wife are very good to us; but our little world of happiness is in ourselves. If, my dear sir, Lord Sidmouth would do something for dear Horatia, so that I can be enabled to give her an education, and also for her dress, it would ease me, and make me very happy. Surely he owes this to Nelson. For God's sake do try for me, for you do not know how limited I am.

I have left everything to be sold for the creditors, who do not deserve anything; for I have been the victim of artful, mercenary wretches, and my too great liberality and open heart has been the dupe of villains. To you, sir, I trust, for my dearest Horatia, to exert yourself for her, and that will be an easy passport for me."

CHAPTER V.

1800 AND 1801.

CORRESPONDENCE BETWEEN MR. PITT, MR. ROSE, AND MR. ADDINGTON—MR. ROSE'S NOTES ON THE SCARCITY OF GRAIN IN 1800—HIS DIARY FROM 28TH OF JANUARY TO 28TH FEBRUARY, 1801.

[To connect the subject of Lady Hamilton's claims in an unbroken series, it has been necessary to pass over several years. We now, therefore, return to 1800. The sinecure office of Lord Privy Seal of Scotland having become vacant by the death of Mr. Stuart Mackenzie, Lord Auckland seems to have applied for it, or something else. His disappointment, when it was given to Mr. Dundas (who retained also his own office), was perhaps the grievance to which he afterwards alluded. Mr. Rose thought he had a better right to it, or at least some equivalent, after sixteen years of hard labour at the Treasury, which he began to find too much for him. But he merely suggested his claim, and bided his time. Another opportunity occurred when Lord Sidney died, a few months after. He was Chief-Justice in Eyre, and his son, on succeeding to the peerage, gave up his place at the Treasury; but Mr. Pitt had determined beforehand who should succeed them. The first office was given to Mr. Grenville, and the second to Lord Granville Leveson Gower. Mr. Rose was satisfied that what was best for Mr. Pitt was best for him, and continued to discharge his arduous duties with as much zeal as ever.—Ed.]

Mr. Rose to Mr. Pitt.

"April 8th, 1800.

"My dear Sir,

"The enclosed, from Lord Auckland, was evidently intended for you to see; under the uncertainty therefore of your being in town to-day I send it to you. I shall say nothing about myself respecting the possible openings which may occur in consequence of the event alluded to therein; meaning now, as I always have, to leave the consideration of my claims to you who alone can judge of them. My health continues better than I had a right to hope, but I feel, in more respects than one, the effect of a continuance of more than sixteen years in my present situation. I should really have not said even so much as this if I had not been desired to call to your recollection the situation of another. If I had had such an intention, I should have written to you on Tuesday. In any event, I shall always remain, what I have long very truly professed myself,

"My dear Sir,

"Most entirely yours,

"George Rose."

MR. PITT TO MR. ROSE.

"Hollwood, Tuesday, April 8th, 1800.

"DEAR ROSE,

"Till I received your letter this morning I really was not aware that you entertained at present any personal wish of the nature you refer to. I shall be very glad to have an opportunity of conversing with you upon it, with a view to such future occasions as may arise. On the present, though I am not yet able to fix precisely the particulars of the arrangement to be proposed, I had long ago settled the general outline of it, in the expectation of the event which has now taken place, of Stuart Mackenzie's death.

"With respect to Lord Auckland, I should have been truly glad (as you know) to have the means of giving him such an accession of income as he would have from the office of Treasurer of the Navy;[1] but my object must be a move in the House of Commons, and for that the Post-office would not be available.

"Ever sincerely yours,
"W. PITT."

MR. ROSE TO MR. PITT.

"April 8th, 1800

"MY DEAR SIR,

"I have felt a real anxiety to remain in my situation as long as there was a chance of my being useful in it; but the truth is I am wearing out,

[1 Mr. Dundas was Treasurer of the Navy, and continued to hold that office till the Government was broken up in the following year.—ED.]

which I have lately had symptoms of. I shall, however, most certainly not think of leaving it at a time, or in a manner, that can by the remotest possibility put you to the slightest inconvenience. I have forborne to mention to you anything respecting my views or wishes, from a most unaffected reluctance to be troublesome to you about myself, and from a persuasion that you would think of me at a proper season. If I have pretensions of any sort you know them. I never had a political connexion except with you, and I never can with any other. I was perfectly serious in saying that I should have been silent now, had I not been desired by Lord A. to bring him to your notice. And I am not less so in assuring you that I have a full confidence in your doing with respect to me what shall appear to you to be right.

"Ever entirely yours,
"George Rose."

Mr. Rose to Mr. Pitt.

"July 1st, 1800.

"I need not say that I have at no time been urgent about myself. I should be ashamed of even calling your attention to my case for a single moment, at a time like the present, for any other purpose than merely to say, that, if in the arrangement consequent on the death of Lord Sydney, an opening should occur which you might think not unfit for me, I should be perfectly satisfied to continue in my present situation, without one shilling additional income, till you can find a successor entirely to your satisfaction, for which I should cheerfully wait your utmost leisure."

Mr. Pitt to Mr. Rose.

"Downing Street, Sept. 22d, 1800.

"Dear Rose,

"I found your letter on my arrival in town this morning, and do not see any reason for your shortening your holidays before the time you propose. Our first business when we meet must be to prepare our budget, for which I hope you will have the materials collected. It is not absolutely impossible that negotiation before the end of the year may make our labours unnecessary; but that prospect is as yet very uncertain, and I think on the whole discouraging.

"Yours ever,

"W. P."

[The following letters show the intimate terms on which Mr. Pitt, Mr. Addington, and Mr. Rose lived at the close of this year, and the sort of hope which the former entertained of a peace being concluded through Lord Malmesbury's negotiation at Lisle. It appears clearly, that though Mr. Pitt was prepared for war, he desired peace.—Ed.]

Mr. Pitt to Mr. Rose.

"Dear Rose,   "Woodley,¹ Friday, Oct. 24th.

"As I should not see either Ryder or Hawkesbury, I think it would not answer my purpose to go to Hollwood. You would not perhaps think it much additional trouble, when you find yourself either on horseback or in a post-chaise, to come to me here on Sunday, instead of going to Hollwood, and it will be a great accommodation to me if you can do so. But if your coming and remaining Monday would be any inconvenience to business, let me know, and I will still go either to Hollwood or to town. The Speaker desires me to tell you that he shall be very happy to see you, and depends upon your considering this as a sufficient invitation.

"Yours ever,
"W. P."

Mr. Addington to Mr. Rose.

"My dear Sir,   "Woodley, Oct. 24th, 1800.

"I have great pleasure in hoping that you may be induced by a letter which Mr. Pitt is now writing, to come to Woodley on Sunday, and I trust you will remain here as long a time as you can spare from your business in town. If Mr. Pitt should make no further progress till you see him, I am sure you will think that his health is evidently and materially improved.

"I am ever, my dear Sir, sincerely yours,
"Henry Addington."

¹ Mr. Addington's house in Berkshire.

MR. PITT TO MR. ROSE.

"Woodley, Saturday, Oct. 25th, 1800.

"DEAR ROSE,

"You will have found by my letter of yesterday evening that I had anticipated your kind suggestion of coming here, and I am very glad to find you can do so without inconvenience. We shall expect you to-morrow, and I hope you will stay Monday. Pray bring with you (if you can get it) an account of all the corn and flour imported in each month since the beginning of the year, and all the different papers and accounts which in any way relate to corn.

"Yours ever,
"W. P.

"The market here at Reading has been very abundant to-day, and fallen 7s. per quarter, which I hope augurs well for the London market on Monday."

[The year 1800, though marked by no great political event, obtained a disastrous celebrity as a year of scarcity. At the commencement of harvest the rain descended in torrents, the lowlands were deluged with water, the crops were spoiled, the price of wheat rose to more than 120 shillings a quarter, and people resorted to all sorts of devices to economise the consumption of bread. Potatoes, potato-flour, and rice, were the ordinary substitutes, and an Act of Parliament forbade the bakers to sell any but whole meal bread. In support of that measure a fact was announced, which, though then received with ignorant incredulity, has since been admitted and confirmed. Lord Holland sarcastically observes in his Memoirs,[1] "Mr. Addington gravely informed the world, from his father's notes, that bran was more nutritive than grain." The statement is inaccurate, but the sneer might have been spared. Mr. Addington was on that subject in advance of his age. It is now well known that bran contains more of the muscle-producing ingredient of food than fine flour. This was the Brown-bread Act, repealed in the following year under peculiar circumstances, which will be noticed in their place. On the part of the Treasury, Mr. Rose was anxious to alleviate the general distress, by persuading the starch-makers and distillers to refrain from making use of grain in their respective trades, and to consent to a Bill being introduced into Parliament for their regulation. The following paper shows what steps he took for that purpose.—ED.]

MR. ROSE's *Notes on the Scarcity of Corn in* 1800.

Wednesday, October 8th.—Came to town from Cuffnells. Dined with Mr. Pitt alone; and after much conversation with him on the state of the interior, prevailed with him to incline to an early meeting of Parliament.

Thursday, 9th.—Dined with the Chancellor at

[1] Vol. I. p. 121.

Hampstead; satisfied him that it is highly desirable Parliament should meet; that if no effectual measure can be taken for relief of the country, with respect to a supply of corn, or to lessen the price, that the country may at least see the subject has not been neglected.

Friday, 10th.—Lord Grenville concurred in the expediency of the early meeting of Parliament, and the Cabinet decided on the measure.

Mr. Alderman Shaw came to me on the state of provisions; suggested the expediency of giving the bounties according to the actual prices of wheat and flour, instead of according to the average prices, as under the Act of the last session; stated the prices of wheat having been raised from 105s., as set by the Essex farmers, to 122s. by a principal factor, and alluded to Mr. C. S.

Mr. Garratt came to me, and proposed an actual survey of all the grain in the kingdom. Stated Mr. Peacock having his warehouses full of flour, and his refusing to sell a sack.

Mr. Wrench, a deputy in the city, and a dealer in corn, came to me and suggested that it would be highly expedient to compel the factors in Mark Lane to open to the market at the beginning of the day the whole quantities of grain they have to sell, as great advantage is taken by them in producing samples of small quantities to draw on buyers. He suggested also the expediency of preventing the same persons being factors and dealers. He spoke of the bounty in the same manner that Mr. Alderman Shaw had done.

Saw Mr. Suter, a starch-maker, and proposed to him to call a meeting of the trade, to propose their stopping the use of wheat in their manufactory; which he expressed himself willing to do, but was sure the others would not. Finding the wheat must be a month in steep to make starch, gave orders to the Commissioners of Excise to direct their officers to give notice to the starch-makers, that on the day of Parliament meeting (11th of November), a Bill would be moved for to prohibit their using grain, with a commencement from that day; that they would therefore steep any more wheat at their own risk: which must produce the desired effect.

Saturday, 11th.—Mr. Bonwell came at my desire, and promised to convene all the distillers, for the purpose of proposing to them to refrain from working from grain on Monday next.

Understanding there is a considerable quantity of rice in the country (especially in the capital), and that orders had been actually received for purchasing the whole for Holland, where it is selling at 40s., the price now here 35s. per quarter; wrote to the Commissioners of the Customs to direct them not to allow any of the article to be cleared out for exportation.

Sunday, 12th.—Went to Mr. Scott, at Plaistow (in my way to Eden Farm), who satisfied me he had no intent in raising the prices of the wheat last Monday, as his profit arises solely from a commission of 6d. per quarter on the wheat, as he sells only foreign; he also recommends a consideration of the alterations of the bounty.

Monday, 13th.—Mr. Bonwell returned to me to tell me two of the distillers, Mr. Bush and Messrs Smith and Co., of Brentford, positively refused to concur in not working from grain, and that therefore the rest of the trade must also work in their own defence, or they will lose their customers. On inquiry I learnt that the distillers steep their malt a fortnight before they can use it. I therefore directed the Commissioners of Excise to give notice to every distiller in and near London, before one o'clock to-morrow, that a Bill would be moved the first day of the session, to restrain them, which would narrow their working to a fortnight. Mr. Bonwell, thereupon, told me he was sure the whole, except the two before-mentioned, would concur in signing an undertaking not to work.

Monday Evening, October 13th.—Desirous of information on several points respecting the corn trade, I went up to Mr. Charles Scott's house, in Gower Street, from whom I learnt the following particulars, and obtained the opinions here stated:—Of the corn sold in Mark Lane, of English growth, nine-tenths belongs to individual farmers, from the harvest-time till the summer months; thenceforward, probably about five-sixths; the remainder to middlemen. The whole is sold by factors on commission.

The number of farmers for whom the sales are made are incalculable; many hundreds, even thousands, dispersed throughout the country, without knowledge of or intercourse with each other; sometimes the property of fifty farmers is in one vessel.

We cannot state the number of middlemen who

are dealers; in most sea-port towns there are several, and a few in inland ones, unconnected entirely with each other, and a constant jealousy amongst them.

Of persons usually selling corn in Mark Lane, there are about twenty strictly corn-factors, and about fifteen who are also dealers or jobbers; besides the haymen, about fifteen in number, who sell the Kentish wheat.

Mr. Scott himself sells about one-fourth of the foreign wheat; no English.

Another house sells about one-eighth of the English.

Mr. Scott thinks it would be highly inexpedient to compel factors to state to the purchasers in the market, in the beginning of the day, the whole quantities each has to sell; but is of opinion it may be very proper to prevent a factor being likewise a dealer.

Tuesday, Oct. 14th.—Mr. Bonwell showed me an undertaking signed by every distiller in and near London, to forbear working till the sense of Parliament shall be known.

Wrote to the Commissary-General in the Mediterranean, approving of the contract for bread in Minorca; and urging him strongly to get all the wheat and flour he can there for the supply of the troops.

Gave directions to Mr. Harrison to draw bills for the starch, distilling, and rice; the latter with an indemnity.

[Mr. Rose's Diary for 1801 contains an account of the change of the Administration when Mr. Pitt

resigned; of a brief illness of the King, produced by it; of the formation and weakness of the succeeding cabinet; of the writer's aversion to it, and other things alluded to in the letters of the same period, the most remarkable of which is Mr. Pitt's determination to receive no grant from Parliament, because he had failed to secure the prosperity of the nation.
—Ed.]

Mr. Rose's *Diary resumed.*

From 28th of January to 11th June, 1801.

On Wednesday, the 28th of January, Mr. Pitt first had distinct and clear proof of the Speaker taking an eager and anxious part in influencing persons against the measure of Catholic Emancipation.

On Friday the 30th, the Speaker was at the Queen's house for four hours!

The means taken, as above alluded to, of committing persons on the question before discussion, having been made certain, Mr. Pitt wrote his first letter to the King, on the 1st of February. The correspondence concluded on the 4th.[1]

On Thursday, the 5th of February, at 5 p.m.

---

[1] It must have been on Wednesday, the 4th, that the Speaker finally agreed to accept the propositions made to him. Mr. Pitt, however, gave him assurances the preceding day, Tuesday, the 3d, of the most cordial support throughout, on which day the Speaker was to have dined in Downing Street; but the House sitting till half-past six or seven o'clock, he did not get there till between seven and eight, when he found Mr. Pitt by himself. [Anecdote from Mr. Carthew, who went in to them at ten o'clock.]

Mr. P. sent me the letters above-named, enclosed in the one to his brother, which was the first intimation I had of the subject, or of the remotest probability of the agitation of anything that could even lead to serious consequences. I returned the whole before I went to dinner, to be forwarded by a messenger to the Earl of Chatham.

Mr. PITT TO Mr. ROSE.

"Downing Street, Thursday, Feb. 5th, 1801.
"Three quarters past four.

"DEAR ROSE,[1]

"I have been occupied till this moment, and on sending, found you were gone to the House. I should be very glad to see you any time in the evening; but as what I wish is to communicate to you some papers which I also want to send to my brother by a messenger to-day, I think the shortest way is to enclose them to you in the meantime, and beg you to return them as soon as you have read them. You will recollect what I said to you some days since on the Catholic question, though you will hardly have expected so rapid a result. As I wish you to know at once the whole of my real sentiments, I have thought it best to enclose with the other papers the

---

[1] [Mr. Rose was the first person to whom the important decision of Mr. Pitt's intended resignation was imparted, nothing having been previously known, except that some difficulty had arisen about the Roman Catholic question; for Cabinet secrets always contrive to ooze out, notwithstanding the secrecy to which the members are bound. The following letters were the first intimation of what had passed between Mr. Pitt and the King — ED.]

letter which I have but just had time to finish, and am going to send with them to my brother.

"Ever sincerely yours,
"W. P.

"Take care not to read these papers where anybody can overlook you. Dundas dines with me, but I shall be at leisure any time in the evening."

NOTES *by* MR. ROSE, *and* LETTERS, *from February to May,* 1801, *relative to the proposal for* MR. PITT's *resigning office.*

The papers sent to me by Mr. Pitt, were a long letter from him to the King, dated the 1st of February, stating his deep and sincere regret, knowing his Majesty's sentiments on the subject, to find himself under an absolute necessity of submitting to him that he felt a strong opinion, in concurrence with a majority of the Cabinet, that it would be expedient to repeal the laws which exclude Catholics from Parliament and offices, and Dissenters from the latter; that new guards were already provided by the union; that the ground of exclusion no longer exists; that the principles of the Catholics cease to be dangerous, as they disclaim the obnoxious tenets, especially by the new test in Ireland; that a denial of the power of absolution may be insisted upon, and would be as secure as the sacramental test; that it would not be difficult to have a new test against the dissenters, pointed at Jacobinical principles, which might be extended to their ministers and teachers, and would afford a new security against their active exertions; that the popish clergy would be secured by making them dependent on the State for a part of their provision, &c. &c; that these reasons operated so powerfully on his mind as to render it impossible for him to remain in office if he should be expected to give up his opinion; but that rather than disturb his Majesty on a point on which he had too much reason to fear his Majesty had a decided reluctance, he would, if his Majesty continued to desire it, endeavour, as far as could depend on him, to keep the matter from being agitated, and if agitated, he would quiet it if possible, or effect its being postponed till the country should be extricated from its present critical situation, provided his Majesty would engage to avoid expressing his opinion so as to influence others in their conduct; adding expressions of duty, gratitude, &c. &c.

Answer from the King, dated 2d February, lamenting in animated language the fixed opinion expressed by Mr. Pitt, but stating in the most explicit terms his determined resolution not to acquiesce in the alteration of the laws respecting the Catholics and the Dissenters; conceiving himself bound by his coronation oath to support them, confirmed by his having received the sacrament thereupon; and that as he had never been in the habit of concealing his sentiments on important occasions, he would enter into no engagement to act otherwise now; still trusting, however, that Mr. Pitt would not quit him while he lived.

Mr. Pitt's reply of the 3d, urged the impossibility of his continuing in his Majesty's service, knowing that his Majesty would influence the conduct of others on the Catholic question; professing at the same time a continuation of his determined attachment and gratitude to his Majesty; but requesting he would endeavour to make a new arrangement as soon as he conveniently could, assuring him of support, and his best assistance to the new Government.

To this the King, in his letter of the 4th, answered, that he deeply regretted the necessity he was reduced to, of parting with Mr. Pitt; that he would endeavour to make a new arrangement as soon as possible, and trusted that Mr. Pitt would not press him in a manner to compel him to do that too hastily.

These four letters were enclosed by Mr. Pitt in another to Lord Chatham, telling him he had not sent for him to town, as it could have answered no end; that his retiring must take place as soon as the new arrangement could be made; that the King had (as he conjectured and hoped he would) applied to the Speaker, who had accepted; that it was his determined purpose to give his best and most active support to the new administration, and earnestly entreated his brother to continue *in office*.

On the evening of February the 5th, at eleven o'clock, I received the following note from Mr. Pitt, desiring to see me before he went to rest.

"February 5th, 1801.
" DEAR ROSE.
" I have been kept till this instant. If you can come conveniently to yourself any time before twelve, I shall feel a satisfaction in seeing you to-night.
" Yours ever,
"Thursday, three quarters past ten."　　"W. P.

On going to him, he stated all that had passed, and satisfied me that the bringing the business to the point, as put in the correspondence, was, on his part, absolutely unavoidable. Mr. Pitt assured me that the Speaker taking upon him to form a new Administration, was with his concurrence and upon his advice, and that he therefore wished most anxiously all his private and personal friends to remain in office; suggesting that it could not be expected I should continue in my present situation of labour, &c.; to which I replied in the plainest and strongest terms in which I could express myself, that under such an injunction, I should not hesitate, in any other situation, to remain in office; but that after the unbounded confidence I had possessed with him, it was utterly inconsistent with my feelings to act in an official situation with another, coming in on his resignation; that it was of course my fixed and irrevocable determination to withdraw; but that I would assist him as usual in the budget, and would carry through the Tax Bills, or any other immediate business, in order to avoid the new Administration being put to any serious inconvenience, till a proper successor should be found for me; that on the best consideration I could give the subject on the sudden, however, it appeared to me the Speaker had done ill in catching eagerly at the Prime Minister's station, which he evidently must have done, by the dates of the letters of his correspondence, so early as the 4th of February, for that was communicated to Lord Chatham on the 5th; that I thought he should have thrown himself at the King's feet, with the liveliest expressions of duty, zeal, and affection, and assured him of the absolute impossibility of his undertaking the Government with the remotest chance of being able to carry it on, and conjured him therefore to find means of going on with Mr. Pitt, as the only resource against every calamity that can be dreaded by a nation.

If the Speaker was really with the King long on the afternoon of the 30th of January, it is still more unaccountable, because the first communication that could have a tendency to lead to a change in the Administration was on the 31st of January, late at night, and could not be received by the King till Sunday morning, the 1st of February.

February 13th.—I am strongly confirmed in all this on reflection, and from a variety of circumstances have a clear conviction in my mind that there was from the beginning an eagerness in Mr. A. to catch at the situation, without regard to his friend, or recollecting that he owed his political existence to him.

On Saturday, the 7th, all the Privy Counsellors in the House of Commons, and the Treasury, dined

with the Speaker, where nothing remarkable passed.
Mr. Canning's manner to the Speaker very marked,
—which the latter took notice of to me when I saw
him, on Tuesday, the 11th. In the evening, the
whole went to the Chancellor's, where also the conversation was quite general. Mr. Pitt carried me
home from the Chancellor's, and on the way I state
to him, as pointedly as I could, my opinions and
feelings respecting the Speaker's conduct in not deploring to the King any change, and declaring the
dereliction of duty he should be guilty of if he were
to take the conduct of the Government, which NO ONE
but Mr. Pitt could carry on. Late at night (half-
past eleven), Mr. Goldsmid came to tell me that on the
account of Mr. Pitt's resignation being heard in the
city, great confusion followed, a fall of 5l. per cent.
in the funds, and no market for Exchequer Bills. As
this appeared in the course of the conversation with
Mr. Goldsmid to have arisen in a great degree from
an apprehension that Mr. P. was going out of office
instantly, I thought it expedient to say to him that
there was no intention of that sort, and that Mr. Pitt
would certainly open the budget, and provide completely for the ways and means of the year, before he
quitted his situation; which Mr. G. seemed to think
would quiet people's minds sufficiently for the purpose
in view.

Mr. Wilberforce came in at the same time. The
only thing particular that passed in this conversation
was an allusion from him of the intriguing interference of a neighbour of his and mine.[1]

[1] Lord Auckland.

Sunday, February 8th.—On reflecting upon what had passed with Mr. Goldsmid last night, it occurred to me that the best mode of making the communication in the city respecting the change of Administration would be through the Governor of the Bank, both on account of his public situation and his invariable attachment and character. With Mr. Pitt's approbation, therefore, I saw him, and after explaining to him the circumstances, I sent him to Mr. Pitt to receive the proper authority for the communication he should make to-morrow.

Mr. P. this day mentioned to me his having received a letter from Lord Auckland, on Saturday, the 31st of last month, complaining of his having been treated unkindly and not with due attention, in having no communication made to him respecting the question about Catholic Emancipation,—with which he had the misfortune to differ entirely with him;—at which time no determination of the Cabinet had been taken, and of course could not be communicated to any one. Mr. Pitt therefore answered his letter the same day, and observed that however widely they might differ on the question itself, the difference of opinion would be much more wide as to which of them had the most right to complain of want of kindness and fairness. To that letter his Lordship made no reply, or took any notice whatever till this morning, remaining silent eight days under the cutting reproach before stated; during all which time he never attempted any intercourse with me. If he had been conscious of innocence in the whole transaction, he would naturally either have instantly written to Mr. Pitt, or have come to me to talk of the best mode of clearing up Mr. Pitt's misconceptions. On my coming home, I found Lord A.'s letter, No. 5, and immediately wrote the answer, No. 6.

The Attorney-General has agreed to be Speaker.

Lord Chatham's answer received; laments the result; could have done no good if he had been in town; thinks that under the unfortunate circumstance of his brother's retiring, the King could not have done better than send for the Speaker, and states his reasons; declines any answer to his brother's entreaties for his remaining in office, but says he will be in town in a *few days*. The inference I draw from that is, that he will keep his office. Lord Grenville said to the Bishop of Lincoln he thought Lord Chatham should not remain in office.

Monday, February 9th.—The communication made through Mr. Newland, by direction of Mr. Thornton, Governor of the Bank, to the city, or rather to the Stock Exchange, of the change of Administration, but that Mr. Pitt would open the budget, &c. Stocks fell one quarter per cent. only.

Mr. Canning canvassing for persons to go out of office. The two Ellis's (George and Charles) express their determination to oppose the new Government. Prevailed with Lord Granville Leveson. Lord Gower will probably go on different grounds.

Division taken that the Speaker should quit the chair immediately, and that he should send a letter for that purpose to-morrow.

Wrote to Mr. Stapleton an account of Mr. Pitt's resignation.

Tuesday, February 10th.—Mr. Pitt told me Lord Hawkesbury would be Foreign Secretary, and Lord Hobart War Secretary; the Chancellor to resign; Lord Eldon to have the Great Seal, Sir Richard Arden to be Chief-Justice of the Common Pleas, Sir W. Grant to be Master of the Rolls, Mr. Law to be Attorney-General, and Mr. Percival to be Solicitor-General.

Called on the Speaker on the subject of Sir Richard Worsley's seat offered to me; he entered into the subject of the intended arrangements, stated those above, and added that Mr. Charles Yorke is to be Secretary-at-War, and Mr. N. Vansittart to succeed me; expressed strong regret at my quitting, and said something, in a voice much agitated, that I understood to convey he was not sure whether in my situation he should do the same; which led to my writing to him, No. 7. He told me Lord Chatham had agreed to continue, in terms extremely flattering to him, the substance of which he repeated. At this time Mr. Pitt had received no answer from his brother. He expressed great resentment at Canning's conduct, and said nobody would follow his example in quitting, except Lord Granville Leveson. I told him Lord Gower would quit, whose motive probably is resentment to the King, for what passed respecting the Staffordshire Militia. On the whole, the Speaker seemed confident that he should form a strong and an efficient Government.

The Chancellor[1] sent to request to speak with me in his room; but I was prevented getting to him till within a quarter of four, my conversation with him therefore was very short,—full of kindness on his part—and in the course of it he told me his retiring was in consequence of a suggestion from the Speaker, that his doing so would enable him to make an arrangement in the law department (alluding to the one mentioned to me that morning by Mr. Pitt) that would greatly strengthen his administration. I agreed to go to him in the evening, if I could; but dining with Mr. Pitt, and talking about the budget till past ten o'clock, it was too late to go to his Lordship.

Wednesday, February 11th.—Saw Mr. Addington in the morning, at his request, when he expressed himself strongly as entering into my feelings on the ground of my retiring.

At the levee the King appeared perfectly composed and collected when speaking to Mr. Pitt; and afterwards, in a conversation of some length with me, expressed his warmest and most unqualified approbation of Mr. Pitt as to all he had done, and was now doing, particularly with regard to what has lately passed; concluding with saying, that his whole conduct was infinitely more honourable on retiring than that of *any* of his predecessors, dwelling on the word *any*, and added, beyond all comparison so, and that he possessed his highest esteem and good opinion.

Lord Chatham dined with his brother, and made

---

[1] Lord Rosslyn, then Lord Loughborough.

the first communication to him of his intention to remain.

Thursday, February 12th.—Mr. White[1] stated that the late Attorney-General complained of his having been prevailed with to take the chair without the remotest intimation of any other law arrangement, except the one in consequence of his being made Speaker; adding, that if he should be removed from the chair, he would never form another political connexion; evidently hurt beyond measure at the uncandid treatment he conceived he had met with.

Mr. Pelham, after having declined to take any employment, tells his friends he is to have an office, probably a cabinet one.

Mr. Vansittart certainly to succeed me; Mr. Long (who told me that he thought he should quit) is to remain in for some time at least.

Mr. William Elliot[2] declared his intention to Mr. Pitt to resign the Admiralty.

Mr. Yorke[3] assured me he was firmly attached to Mr. Pitt, and that no consideration could have induced him to take office, but the *imperious necessity of the times*, and being assured it would be agreeable to Mr. Pitt.

In the evening, a meeting at Mr. Pitt's, to settle the mode of bidding for the loan of 27,000,000*l.*, including Ireland; six Sets present, which again prevented my going to the Chancellor.

[1] The Solicitor to the Treasury.
[2] Afterwards Lord St. Germains, whose eldest brother married Lady Harriet Pitt.
[3] Lord Hardwicke's brother.

Friday, the Fast-day, February 13th.—Lord St. Vincent came to town in consequence of the overture to him, and professed a perfect willingness to accept the Admiralty; but suggested some embarrassment from his being committed on the question respecting the Test Act, as far as relates to Dissenters; but Mr. Pitt replied he was not bound by his acceptance of the office to any particular line in Parliament, and he left him with a determination to take the situation.

I met Lord Hobart[1] in the street after church, who told me he did not think himself at liberty to refuse the employment offered him in difficult times like the present, but that he did not accept till he was assured by Mr. Pitt it would be agreeable to him. He added, he had hoped "that Mr. Pitt would not have forced the Catholic question to a point at the present moment;" to which I did not feel myself at liberty to reply; but that impression, if not removed by a disclosure of the real state of the matter, will be prejudicial to Mr. Pitt.

In the evening I went up to the Chancellor as he had desired, and from him I had a most interesting narrative of all the circumstances bearing upon the question of admitting the Catholics to the indulgences they are in pursuit of. His Lordship began with the period of Lord Fitzwilliam's short administration in Ireland; at which time the King (without any prelude, or anything whatever having passed between his Majesty and the Chancellor on the subject) wrote a letter to him, putting three questions abruptly, and

[1] Afterwards Lord Buckinghamshire.

the Chancellor added, "rather unfairly;" meaning the taking him by surprise, and applying to him separately.

1st. Whether he could consistently with his coronation oath consent to a law freeing the Catholics and the Dissenters from the disabilities and restrictions they are under?

2d. Could he do so consistently with the Act of Union with Scotland?

3d. What would be the conduct of the Chancellor respecting his putting the Great Seal to the bill, if it should pass in Ireland?

To the *first* his Lordship answered, he did not conceive his Majesty was in any degree fettered by his coronation oath, in giving the royal assent to a measure which should have the previous approbation of both Houses of Parliament, as that could only be a *legislative* Act, in concurrence with the other branches of the Legislature; and not touching even on the words of the oath, which was devised as a security against any act of the King in his *executive* capacity, at a time too, when the Sovereign on the throne was of a religion different from the established Church of these kingdoms.

To the *second* he answered, he was clearly of opinion that the Act of Union was no bar to such legislative interference, though the words respecting the point are strong; as a proof of that he instanced the Toleration Act, and the act which put an end to the election of the clergy in Scotland, and restored the patronage to the proprietors; adding other reasons in support of that opinion.

To the *third* he answered, if any bill from Ireland should be brought to him of a tendency so mischievous in his opinion as to render it unfit for him to put the Great Seal to it, he should think it his duty to resign it into his Majesty's hands immediately.

The Chancellor told me that about this time his Majesty said to him, " he had amongst his Ministers some most valuable men, but he did not like the mixture of Scotch metaphysics;" which his Lordship applied to Mr. Dundas.

With the Chancellor's answers his Majesty appeared to be very much dissatisfied, from which his Lordship was persuaded the King had entertained a hope that he should have been supported by his opinion in his fixed aversion to the measure respecting the Catholics.

Nothing more, however, passed on the subject till the month of October last, when Lord Westmoreland showed the King a letter from Lord Clare, telling him the question was about to be agitated again, which very much disturbed his Majesty; and about that time a paper was given in to the Cabinet, by Lord Castlereagh, containing three propositions for discussion, in order that the Irish Government might be prepared to take such a line as the Cabinet should decide on.

1st. A provision for the Catholic clergy, and of course, if that should be decided in their favour, to include the Dissenting clergy also.

2d. The admission of the Catholics to Parliament, &c.

3d. Some arrangement about tithes.

On the opening of the discussion, the Chancellor asked Lord Castlereagh,[1] if any engagement had been made, or encouragement held out, to the Catholics, or to any leading men amongst them, at the time of the Union, to expect any new indulgence; to which he answered, none whatever; nor even that any suggestion of the sort would be brought under consideration.

The Prince of Wales had conveyed to Mr. Pitt, very distinctly, his opinion in favour of the measure; he had, indeed, avowed that on former occasions, and Lord Moira was known to be zealous for it.

From this time, discussions took place in the Cabinet, from time to time, but loosely, and in the most friendly manner possible, during which it appeared that the members were as under:—

For the Question.	Against it.
Mr. Pitt.	The Chancellor.
Lord Grenville—strongly.	Duke of Portland.
Mr. Dundas—strongly.	Lord Westmoreland.
Mr. Windham—strongly.	Lord Liverpool — absent, but vehement by letter.
Lord Spencer—very moderately so.	Lord Chatham—absent, but understood to be against.
Lord Camden—in no office, but decided.	

In the course of these discussions, the Chancellor asked Mr. Pitt, privately, whether he thought it would be judicious to propose a measure of this sort, to which the King was notoriously so averse, and on

[1] Afterwards Marquis of Londonderry.

which the whole bench of bishops would be against him; probably many lords from opinion, others from an inclination to follow the King; most likely, Lord Chatham, as well as others of the Cabinet, with many of his most confidential friends, such as the Speaker, the Master of the Rolls, &c.

Occasional meetings on the subject went on, or it was sometimes brought forward after other business was disposed of; Mr. Pitt from time to time proposing modifications, or a test which should secure the Church and the Constitution against any attempts of either the Catholics or Dissenters, till Wednesday, the 28th of January; on which day, at the levee, the King said to Mr. Dundas, he understood the question was agitating amongst the Ministers; that nothing could be more disagreeable or painful to him, and that he should consider the person who supported the question as his worst enemy; and repeated *that* so loud as to be heard by two or three persons standing near, which led to a cabinet being assembled the next day, when a general wish was expressed that Lord Grenville would prepare a paper, stating what would satisfy the majority of the Cabinet, as a proposition to be made to Parliament, which his Lordship positively declined; and Mr. Pitt undertook to prepare the test for the Catholics and Dissenters. He accordingly sent a draught thereof to the Chancellor, on Friday, the 30th, the day, or rather evening, on which, as before observed, Mr. Addington was seen twice with the King. On the 31st, at night, Mr. Pitt wrote his first letter to the King, the heads of which are in No. 1. This was done without any opinion of the *cabinet ministers* actually and finally expressed,—certainly without *any minute of the Cabinet*. The reference, therefore, in the letter was to a decision of the Cabinet, not formally taken, though their opinions were ascertained; and the letter was written without the knowledge of some of the members, probably of any of the minority of it. The Chancellor was himself utterly ignorant of it, and there was no further meeting on the subject; but at the levee, on Wednesday, the 4th of February, the Chancellor talked to Mr. Dundas of the foolish reports that had been in circulation for some days,—at the time utterly without foundation,—of changes in the Administration; on which Mr. Dundas replied. "What will you say if I tell you that Mr. Pitt, Lord Grenville, and myself, will be under the necessity of withdrawing?" On his repeating that seriously, the Chancellor was thunderstruck, and instead of going in to the King as he had intended, he let the Duke of Portland go in, and remained in conversation with Mr. Dundas, who explained to him the substance of the correspondence between his Majesty and Mr. Pitt, and the inevitable consequence of that. This appeared the more extraordinary to the Chancellor, because (as before observed) nothing that passed in the Cabinet led to an imagination of the consideration of the question being brought to a point suddenly, or prematurely. On the communication of the correspondence afterwards to the Chancellor by the King, his Lordship was struck with what he conceived to be the peremptory manner in which

Mr. Pitt expressed himself in his last letter, as to his resignation, when the King appeared to him to have consented not to take any steps to counteract what might be a measure of his Ministers; although he would not engage to conceal his opinions, which he had not been in the habit of doing. And his Lordship urged that as a proof of some agency acting upon Mr. Pitt between the first and second letters. He did not, indeed, hesitate to say to me, that he thought Mr. Pitt was impelled by Lord Grenville and Mr. Dundas. Lord Spencer had been extremely moderate on the point from the beginning; Mr. Windham eager upon it.

On the whole, from what passed with the Chancellor, as well as from what Mr. Pitt said to me on the 28th or 29th of January (when I showed him a note from Lord Auckland, respecting the Parliament being to meet on the 2d of February), I am very strongly inclined to believe that Mr. Pitt had not, in the first instance, an intention of pressing the Catholic question on the King immediately; and in the second, that he would have been satisfied with his Majesty's assurances of forbearance (if he had thought them distinct and clear), with perhaps some explanation. Possibly he did not act solely on his own judgment.

The Chancellor told me further, that when he went in to the King, after the levee, on Wednesday, the 11th, the King expressed himself about Mr. Pitt in the same terms I have already observed he did to me, and asked his Lordship if he did not think he might rely on Mr. Pitt continuing to act in the same honour-

able manner he was now doing, and support the new
Government strenuously; observing, at the same time,
how different the case had been with former ministers
who had retired, instancing Lord North in particular,
but imputed that to the gaming debt of George North
to Mr. Fox. To all which the Chancellor replied he
had the same confidence in Mr. Pitt's honour that
his Majesty had, and felt with perfect certainty that he
would support the new Administration to the utmost
extent of his power and talents; but how long that
might continue no one could safely predict, it not
depending upon Mr. Pitt himself; that others might
act upon him in a way he could by no caution guard
against; that he had seen repeated instances of this
in the course of his Majesty's reign; that circumstances might arise from a variety of causes which
might lead to differences of a serious nature, and important in their consequences; differences of opinion,
jealousies, &c.; and that in the particular case referred
to by his Majesty, Lord North's conduct was really
not owing to the anecdote alluded to by his Majesty
(which, however, was currently reported at the time),
but to the constant solicitation and persuasion of
friends; and that such, from disappointment, resentment, or fair opinion, might be found to practise upon
Mr. Pitt.

The Chancellor then explained to his Majesty that
his retiring from the public service was not a thing
of his seeking, but one he had no choice about; that
it was suggested to him broadly by Mr. Addington,
on Sunday, the 8th. That Mr. Addington, in the

course of conversation on that day, told the Chancellor that he thought his Government would do extremely well, and that the way would be considerably smoothed by his conciliating different parties, and that several individuals were firmly attached to him. That the Chancellor's retiring would enable an arrangement to be made in the law, which would very greatly strengthen the new Government, by securing the eminent assistance of Sir William Grant, who, by being placed at the Rolls (in the room of Sir R. Arden, to be made Chief-Justice of the Common Pleas), would have leisure to attend to the House of Commons; and by opening the Attorney-Generalship for Mr. Law, with Percival as Solicitor-General; under which statement his Lordship told the King he acquiesced, adding, that he was ready to retire to the remotest corner of Scotland if it would conduce to his Majesty's service. The King, drawing back a little, and under some apparent surprise, expressed himself with great kindness to the Chancellor, and asked him if he had any wish in which he could be gratified; to which the Chancellor answered he had not. And the King replied something must be thought of for him. The King, in this interview with the Chancellor, told him Mr. Addington had proposed Mr. Bragge as Speaker, but that he had objected to it. The Chancellor here told me he would not accept an earldom,—without dropping a hint whether he would take anything else if offered.

From this day, Friday, February 13th, nothing very interesting occurred till Wednesday, February 18th, except the intimation to me from Mr. Pitt, on Monday, the 16th, that Mr. Vansittart set off that day on a mission to Denmark (on a hope which he thought would fail), and would not return for three or four weeks, which must necessarily keep me so long in office; on which I asked what objection there would be to Mr. Riley Addington's succeeding me, instead of Mr. Long; but Mr. Pitt earnestly pressed me not to put the new Treasury to any distress.

Mr. Pitt opened the budget with a loan of 25,500,000*l.* for England, and 1,500,000*l.* for Ireland, accompanied by English taxes for 1,790,000*l.* And after a full and clear statement from him, every thing was so satisfactory that not one word was said by the Opposition; the whole passed off with unanimity, which never happened before in seventeen years of his administration. In the evening I went to him at his desire, and we were alone more than three hours, in an extremely interesting conversation; in the course of which he was, beyond all comparison, more affected than I had seen him since the change first burst upon me, but nothing particularly leading to any new disclosure occurred. The most remarkable thing that fell from him was a suggestion that on revolving in his mind all that had passed, it did not occur to him that he could have acted in any respect otherwise than he had done, or that he had anything to blame himself for, except not having earlier endeavoured to reconcile the King to the measure about the Catholics, or to prevail with his Majesty not to take an active part on the subject. I took occasion to press again as strongly as possible my opinion of Mr. Addington's conduct in catching at the Government *suddenly* and *eagerly*, instead of throwing himself at the King's feet and imploring him not to attempt to form a new Administration, and least of all to think of him, who felt himself utterly unequal to the undertaking. Mr. Pitt admitted to me that Mr. Addington had been with the King for some hours on Friday, the 30th of January, of course previous to the first of the correspondence which led in three days to the change of the Administration, but subsequent to what passed at the levee (on the 28th January) with Mr. Dundas; there was, however, no actual admission on the part of Mr. Pitt that he thought with me on the subject, but there were evident demonstrations of it, and there were painful workings in his mind, plainly discernible; most of the time tears in his eyes, and much agitated.

Lord Lewisham the head of the Board of Control.

Friday, February 20*th.*—A council at the Queen's house; at which Lord Hawkesbury, as Secretary of State, Lord St. Vincent, as first Lord of the Admiralty, and Mr. Yorke, as Secretary at War, were sworn into their offices, as Privy Councillors.

Saturday, 21*st.*—At dinner at the new Speaker's, with Mr. Pitt, Mr. Dundas, &c. &c.

Mr. Pelham, after having first refused the Secretaryship of State, and accepted the Board of Control, —having refused the latter, is now out of humour at not having the former.

The King so unwell as to induce several persons to make inquiries after his health. I did not, however, hear a syllable that led me to conjecture anything affecting his Majesty's mind; but on this day, probably, the symptoms first showed themselves. At dinner I asked Mr. John Villiers[1] whether it was right to do so, and he answered decidedly in the negative; that the complaint was nothing more than a hoarseness consequent upon a cold, and that he had played at cards with his Majesty for two hours on the preceding evening, Friday.

Sunday, February 22d.—With Mr. Pitt the greatest part of the morning, on various arrangements of no importance, previous to winding up matters, and disposing of various employments, particularly Mr. Jekyll and Mr. Carthew.[2]

No mention of the King's illness, nor did I hear a word of it during the whole day.

A long conversation with Lord Eldon respecting his acceptance of the Great Seal,[3] in the course of which he stated to me all that passed on the subject; the first proposal to him on Sunday the 8th of this month; his determination not to accept it but on Mr. Pitt's earnest entreaty, and engagement that he would be Chancellor if he (Mr. Pitt) should ever come into office again; pension to him (4,000*l.* a-year), to be secured immediately. Warmest assurances of friendship from his Lordship to myself.

In the evening at the Speaker's; nothing remarkable occurred there.

[1] Afterwards Earl of Clarendon.
[2] Mr. Pitt's private secretary.
[3] See Lord Eldon's Life, by Twiss, vol. i. pp. 367, 368.

Monday, February 23d.—On this day Mr. Pitt attended the Prince of Wales by his command. His Royal Highness said he sent for him as his father's actual Minister on the present distressing occasion. Mr. Pitt replied, that being *de facto* in the situation of Minister, he should have no hesitation in giving him the best advice and opinions in his power; but very respectfully, though firmly, stated to his Royal Highness that he would do so only on the express condition that his Royal Highness would forbear to advise with those who had for a long time acted in direct opposition to his Majesty's Government. The Prince acquiesced as to the persons immediately alluded to by Mr. Pitt; but added, he should think himself at liberty to advise occasionally with Lord Moira, which he had long been in the habit of doing.

Went with Mr. John Smyth,[1] of Heath, to make inquiry after the health of the King. Conversation with him on the way, as to my opinion of the whole of Mr. Addington's conduct throughout this unfortunate convulsion. Under the Piazza at St. James's, met Lord Essex, who told us the King was entirely deranged. Went up into the levee room, where persons were writing their names. Lord Chesterfield spoke with great apparent feeling about the situation of his Majesty, but declared he knew no particulars of the state he was in; no bulletin had

---

[1] An intimate friend of Mr. Rose's, and a very independent Member of Parliament.

then been brought from the Queen's house respecting the King's health.

On my return to Downing Street, Mr. Pitt told me there were certainly symptoms of derangement in his Majesty, and that Dr. Willis was attending him; but there were hopes that all would be right again soon; and that Mr. Addington saw his Majesty yesterday, and found him wandering on some points.

Lord Granville Leveson[1] told me he met Mr. Tierny yesterday, who dropped hints of the King's situation, and assured him there would be unequivocal proofs of it manifested beyond all doubt very soon. (A tolerable proof that some one or more of the servants have already been tampered with again.)

This day, or to-morrow at the latest, Lord Eldon having to resign the Chief Secretaryship of the Common Pleas, it occurred to me that he might be taking steps for that purpose, such as would be irrevocable, which would necessarily leave him in an unpleasant situation if the King's malady should unhappily continue upon him; I was therefore induced to convey to him by Mr. White the account of what there was too great reason to dread was the apprehensions about the King's derangement.

Tuesday, February 24th.—Lord Eldon came to me in the morning, and sat with me an hour. He told me the account conveyed to him from me through Mr. White,[2] was the only intimation he had received

---

[1] The Marquis of Stafford's second son, afterwards Lord Granville.
[2] Mr. White, Solicitor of the Treasury, an intimate private friend of Mr. Rose, and of Lord Eldon.

of the state the King is supposed to be in; on which he
expressed himself with a strong feeling of resentment
and indignation at Mr. Addington, from whom he
conceived he ought to have heard it immediately after
he knew it himself, thinking, very justly, that to him
(Lord Eldon) as the King's Chancellor, the earliest
possible communication should have been made. Mr.
Addington saw the King on Sunday, and told Mr. Pitt
he found his mind much deranged on some subjects,
but apparently collected on others; after which he was
at a cabinet where Lord Eldon was, without letting fall
a syllable to his Lordship on the subject. In consequence of this silence, Lord Eldon had written in the
morning to Mr. Addington, with an intention of remon-
strating with him on his conduct, who appointed him at
a quarter before eleven. Lord Eldon did not, however,
reach New Palace Yard till seven minutes before eleven,
when he was told Mr. Addington was gone out on
horseback! Such treatment naturally produced an
unpleasant effect. His Lordship accounted for it to a
certain extent by the language he had held to Mr.
Addington when he agreed to take the seals, viz.
that he was induced to accept them only in obedience
to the King's command, and at the advice and earnest
recommendation of Mr. Pitt, and that he would hold
them no longer than he could continue to do so in
perfect friendship with the latter. After a long discussion of the state of matters, Lord Eldon assured
me that no consideration whatever should induce him
to take the seals from the King's hand till his mind
should be as sound as his own.

Lord Eldon told me he was with the King alone for more than two hours on Friday, during the whole of which time he was as rational and collected as he had ever seen him. That he talked to his Lordship of his last malady, stating many particulars that occurred to him during the continuance of it, and especially dwelt on his feelings during some lucid intervals. The King also quoted to Lord Eldon the questions which his Lordship, as a member of the Privy Council, had asked his physicians; that he took down Blackstone's Commentaries, and showed him a passage in them respecting the point (the Catholic question) which had so long and so anxiously agitated his mind.

Mr. Pitt told me at noon, that from the accounts he had received of the King, he really entertained hopes of a tolerably speedy recovery; and that he should abstain from going to the House, to avoid questions that might be distressing or painful.

About one o'clock, went with George to the Queen's house. The news there was, in substance, that the King was not worse than yesterday.

On my return, near the parade, I met the Chancellor walking; turned back with him, and went as far as the top of the park. He told me he had heard from Dr. Willis, at eleven o'clock last night, that the symptoms were favourable; that he had left the cabinet (Lord Grenville did not attend it, but Lord Eldon and Mr. A. met at it,) to go to the Queen's house, to get the commission (which he had sent to the Queen's house last night) signed by his Majesty, for the royal assent to the Bill for repealing the Act which prohibited the use of any except brown bread.

About two o'clock the Chancellor came to me at the Treasury, and told me he had sent the commission in to the King by Dr. Willis, who brought it back signed, and told him there would be no difficulty in obtaining the royal signature to a dozen papers respecting which no detailed statements were necessary. That he (Dr. Willis) had allowed the King to see the Queen and the Duke of Cumberland, but no other of the royal family; that he should not, however, hesitate about allowing such of them to have access to his Majesty as he could see without being deeply affected at the interview. That he could not pronounce anything favourable about his Majesty's recovery with certainty; but that his hopes were very good, and thought it not improbable but that considerable amendment might appear in a week or ten days.

The Chancellor said to me, in the morning as we walked up the park, that, in the event of the King's malady lasting, it would be found useful that we are actually prepared with a measure for settling the Government and the care of his Majesty's person; as the Bill for the Regency, which passed the House of Commons, and nearly went through the House of Lords, in 1789, would be found to answer now in all its provisions, and would save much discussion and avoid serious inconvenience. [Which observation I had made to my son half-an-hour before, and nearly on the same spot.] The Chancellor, at the same time, condemned in strong terms Mr. Fox's indiscretion in committing himself on the former occasion respecting the devolving of the government on the Prince of Wales.

At this period the Administration was left in a singular situation. Of those who were to quit :—

Of the Cabinet :—

Lord Grenville, *out ;* and Lord Hawkesbury, Foreign Secretary.
Lord Spencer, *out ;* Lord St. Vincent, First Lord of the Admiralty.
Mr. Windham, *out;* Mr. Yorke, Secretary at War.
Mr. Dundas, *is,* Secretary of State ; Lord Hobart to succeed.
Lord Loughborough, *is,* Chancellor ; Lord Eldon to succeed.
Mr. Pitt, *is,* First Lord of the Treasury ; Mr. Addington to succeed.

Lords of the Treasury :—

Lord Granville Leveson, *is;* Lord George Thynne to succeed.
Mr. Hiley Addington, *is;* Mr. Nathaniel Bond to succeed.

Secretaries to the Treasury :—

Mr. Rose, *is;* Mr. N. Vansittart to succeed.
Mr. Long, *is;* Mr. Hiley Addington to succeed.

Lords of the Admiralty :—

Lord Arden, Admiral Gambier, Admiral Young, Admiral Mason, *out;* Mr. Garthstone, Sir Thomas Troubridge, Captain Markham, Mr. Adams, have succeeded.

Lord Arden appointed Master of the Mint, in room of Lord Hawkesbury.

Lord Cornwallis, Lord Lieutenant of Ireland, *is ;* was to have been succeeded by Lord Hardwick.

Lord Castlereagh, Secretary for Ireland, *is;* was to have been succeeded by Mr. Abbott.[1]

In the Law :—

Lord Eldon, Chief-Justice of Common Pleas, *is;* Sir Richard Arden to succeed.

---

[1] Mr. Abbott, afterwards Speaker, and created Lord Colchester.

Sir Richard Arden, Master of the Rolls, is; Sir William Grant to succeed.
Sir John Mitford,[1] Attorney-General, out; chosen Speaker; succeeded by Mr. Law.
Sir William Grant, Solicitor-General, out; succeeded by Mr. Percival.

Wednesday, Feb. 25th.—Mr. Pitt saw the Prince of Wales again this day; his Royal Highness having in the interval seen the Chancellor, the Duke of Portland, and Lord Spencer, &c., who took an opposite line from Mr. Pitt in the last regency; and it was explained that they would not now create any difficulty in passing the Bill with nearly similar provisions, if unhappily the necessity should arise.

The Bishop of Lincoln told me he had last night a long and interesting conversation with Mr. Pitt; in which he stated very fully and forcibly the public opinion respecting the mode of Mr. Addington's getting into office, imputing it broadly and plainly to intrigue,—rather more strongly than I have conceived it myself. The Bishop expressed an earnest hope that Mr. Pitt would not commit himself to any determination against not returning to office except on condition of support from the throne on the Catholic question; more especially to guard himself against being drawn into such a declaration by Mr. Fox in the House of Commons, either on Monday next, on the consideration of the state of the nation, or on any future day. Mr. Pitt made no promise to the Bishop on the subject; but appeared not to disapprove of the caution recommended.

[1] Afterwards Lord Redesdale, and Chancellor in Ireland.

The Lord Privy Seal (Lord Westmoreland) told me this morning that the King was somewhat deranged on Thursday last.

Lord Bruce,[1] last night at the opera, told Miss Jennings that Mr. Addington had for some time past had the most easy and constant access to the King at all hours, which gives additional sanction to the idea of his intriguing.

This brings to my recollection, that when the bishopric of St. David's was lately vacant, the King told Mr. Pitt that Dr. Huntingford (Warden of Winchester) would be the best man who could be thought of to fill the see, for learning and every other quality; which his Majesty could have heard from no one but Mr. Addington, who then possessed the King's mind with the impression to carry his point, lest he should fail with Mr. Pitt.

Thursday, February 26th.—The King's health, as reported by the physicians, the same as before, but the private accounts more favourable. A good deal of fever, which is thought fortunate, and other symptoms which are stated to have preceded recovery in the former case, in 1789.

Discussion with Mr. Pitt how long the Regency could be deferred, if unhappily his Majesty's recovery should not be speedy. Prepare for the consent to the Loan Bill, which will pass the House of Lords about Monday next. The Chancellor thinks his Majesty's hand may be obtained to it, as on the 24th to the

[1] The Marquis of Aylesbury's son.

Bread Bill. I suggested the importance and delicacy of such a measure, as it will be argued that if his Majesty's signature may be obtained to a Commission to assent to a bill which has passed both houses, it may equally be obtained to dissent to many which cannot be supported. The delicacy of this point increased by the Chancellor not seeing the King sign the instrument, which was given for his signature to Dr. Willis; the executive government therefore, *pro tanto*, in the hands of that gentleman. Great difficulty in this case; as no regency can be established without previous examination of physicians, &c. Difficulty also in communications with foreign Courts in the King's name on points of the highest national importance. No such correspondence during the last derangement,—no despatch of any consequence having been sent during the period of the King's illness. Difficulty also in the remaining Ministers resigning, and the new ones accepting, which Mr. Pitt admitted. He expressed a strong opinion that the Regent, if appointed, should call into his service Mr. Addington; that his Majesty, on his recovery, might find in his service the person he meant before his illness to place in it. Which opinion I combated earnestly, under a conviction of its being a mistaken one, and being impressed with the firm belief that Mr. Pitt's friends and the public would not bear such an arrangement. In the middle of this discussion we were interrupted, and Mr. Pitt went to Wimbledon to dinner.

Notice by Mr. Nicholl of a motion in the House of

Commons to-morrow respecting the present state of the country.

Friday, February 27th.—Sent Mr. Pitt a printed copy of the Regency Bill which passed the House of Commons, and was rejected in the House of Lords, in February 19th, 1789, on the King's recovery, with MS. alterations in the margin of the amendments made by the Lords, that he might have leisure to consider the points before his return to town. Not unlikely but Mr. Nicholl's notice has reference to the execution of the royal authority *in various respects* at this moment; despatches to foreign ministers, decisions on important national concerns and interests.

Sir Robert Peel told me he had been urged by many independent men to state in the House of Commons the necessity of Mr. Pitt remaining in a responsible situation, and not abandoning the country; referred plainly to the total want of confidence in Mr. Addington, and stated that to be general in and out of Parliament.

Was with Mr. Pitt some time before he went to the House. He had a firm persuasion that the Opposition would act with decorum, and would not create the smallest embarrassment till the situation of the King should be so decided as to render it evident whether a Regency will be necessary or not. He thought it not likely that they would adopt any measures plainly ruinous or seriously mischievous to the country, from a disinclination to destroy that Government which is the object of their ambition. On which

I observed that I thought *that* very likely to depend upon the probability they conceived there was of their obtaining their object. That if they should once completely despair of it, some of them were of a disposition (especially their leader) to do the utmost mischief they could. Mr. Pitt then said Mr. Fox had decided not to take his seat to-day, although he had before intended it, lest it should be attributed to his meaning to countenance Mr. Nicholl's motion. On going into the House of Commons with Mr. Pitt we found Mr. Sheridan on his legs, moving the adjournment of the House to Monday, to get rid of Mr. Nicholl's motion, stating the utter impropriety of any discussion of public matters in the present uncertain state of the King's health. Mr. Pitt gave him great credit for his conduct. Urged very strongly that no man with a heart, or who had the slightest feelings of humanity or of gratitude, duty, or affection for a beloved sovereign, would even allude to his situation at present, in the uncertain state he is in. He assured the House, at the same time, that before it became necessary to take any step of importance in public business, the state of his Majesty's health should be investigated, if unhappily, his Majesty should not be able to give the proper directions.

Mr. Addington was in the house for the first time since his re-election. Lord Hawkesbury declined taking his seat, from a doubt as to his eligibility, on account of the disqualifying clause respecting the third Secretary of State, or Secretary for the Colonies, in the Act of 1782, commonly called Burke's Act.

Mrs. Goodenough (sister to Mr. A.) told Miss Jennings that the King had an attack somewhat similar to the present in 1795, from which he recovered in about a week.

The Duke of Kent met Mr. Pitt coming in from Wimbledon, and told him the hopes of the King's recovery were more encouraging. His Majesty not yet so ill as to be put under any personal constraint.

Saturday, February 28th.—The public account of the King's health *somewhat* more encouraging than yesterday, and the private one very considerably so. An abatement of the fever and of the symptoms of derangement, with a reasonable degree of perspiration. On the whole, it seems probable that in the course of the ensuing week his Majesty's recovery may be sufficiently advanced for him at least to sign papers, and so avoid resorting to the painful and distressing measure of a regency, as on an attentive investigation of the state of the money it seems quite clear we can go on, provided the Loan Bill (which will be read a third time on Monday next in the House of Lords) shall receive the royal assent by the 10th March, or thereabouts.

Mr. Addington frequently with Mr. Pitt during the last three days.

I met Mr. Canning in the park, who expressed an anxious hope that if a necessity should arise for a regency, Mr. Pitt would not in that event think himself called upon to recommend (if it should depend on him) the Administration being placed in the hands of Mr. Addington.

Wrote in the morning to the Bishop of Lincoln, urging his coming to town, under an impression that practices would be attempted to induce Mr. Pitt to prevail with the Prince of Wales (in the event of a regency) to take Mr. Addington as his Minister. And believing that great advantage might be derived from one so intimately connected with Mr. Pitt being always near him; but in the afternoon I wrote again, saying that I did not think the necessity for the Bishop's coming so urgent, as the King's health happily promised so much better.

Sunday, March 1st.—The bulletins of the King's health very favourable, for the first time; and the private accounts extremely so.

Lord G——, in walking with me from early service at the Chapel Royal, told me he had been assured that Buonaparte, on hearing of the King's determination to make the change in the Administration, attributed it to derangement.

CHAPTER VI.

1801.

MR. ROSE'S DIARY FROM 1ST MARCH, TO 11TH JUNE, 1801.

Monday, March 2d.—The bulletins at the Queen's house much less favourable; stating an increase of the fever yesterday in the afternoon. The private account attributes that to the medicines given to his Majesty.

Mr. Grey[1] put off his motion for the state of the nation (on a suggestion from Mr. Ryder, in the absence of Mr. Pitt) to Wednesday, the 11th.

Letter from the Bishop of Lincoln that he had received the second I wrote on Saturday, but not the first. Wrote to the Secretary of the Post-office about it.

Mr. Fox took the oaths and his seat this day.

Tuesday, March 3d.—The public account of the King's health extremely favourable this morning; that his Majesty had had a good deal of rest. Less fever, and better in all respects.

Mr. Pitt desired to see me as soon as he came down-stairs, to tell me that the King had been so ill

[1] Afterwards Lord Grey.

in the early part of the afternoon of yesterday as to occasion the most serious alarms, that even his life was thought in danger from the violent turn the disorder was taking; that his person had undergone a visible change; and, on the whole, the physicians were in great despondency and alarm; but that about five o'clock in the afternoon the disorder was at a crisis, when his Majesty fell into a sleep, which was considered as the thing to lead to the best hope; that he continued in it for two hours, and after lying awake a short time, he fell asleep again, and did not stir till about four o'clock in the morning, when he awoke quite tranquil; asked what bed he was in (being sensible of its not being the one he usually slept in), and how long he had been ill. On being told eight days, he said he felt himself much better than he had been. At the crisis, his pulse was at 136; this morning at eight it was only 84. On the whole, the alteration for the better appeared to be most extraordinary. The King was thought so well, that the Queen and Princesses took an airing in their carriages. This account was brought to Mr. Pitt while in bed, before eight o'clock, by Mr. Addington.

Mr. Pitt then told me he had wished for an opportunity to explain to me more particularly what had passed between him and the Prince of Wales at those interviews he had had with his Royal Highness, which was, in substance, that he had expressed a willingness to submit his advice to his Royal Highness whenever

he should condescend to desire it; but that it must
be on the express condition, that if unhappily there
should be a necessity for a regency, that his Royal
Highness should acquiesce in the arrangement as
settled in 1789; that the Prince seemed to be struck
at that being put to him so distinctly, and perhaps a
little averse to the unqualified tones used (as if Mr.
Pitt was conscious of his manner of stating his determination having been severe), and that his Royal
Highness asked how some of those now acting with
Mr. Pitt would feel on the subject who had taken a
very different line on the former occasion, to which
Mr. Pitt replied he thought every one concerned in it,
without excepting his Royal Highness, could not
do better than accord with what was most evidently
the clear sense of the Legislature, expressed so as
not to be mistaken; the Prince then expressed uneasiness at some of the restrictions as likely to be
found extremely inconvenient. Nothing, however,
passed conclusive between them as to any arrangement of an administration. The interview ended with
the Prince saying that he must take time to consider
all that Mr. Pitt had said; his whole demeanour perfectly decorous and proper, as well with Mr. Pitt as at
the Queen's house, when he was there. Mr. Fox has
certainly not been with his Royal Highness, and Mr.
Pitt thinks he has not seen Mr. Sheridan.

Mr. Addington came to Mr. Pitt late in the day,
when I was with him, and said the accounts from the
Queen's house continued as favourable as possible.

The call of the House was deferred for a fortnight. Mr. Fox in the House.

Wednesday, March 4th.—Account of the King's health favourable—as improving.

Thursday, March 5th.—The same account of the King's health as yesterday—continued improvement.

On considering this day how long we could go on without the royal assent to any bill, it appeared that by the utmost management that could be used we might contrive to find money till the 24th. Of course, the Loan Bill must be passed on the 23d. In order, however, to secure that, we agreed that a Regency Bill must be ready before that day, even in the event of his Majesty going on in a progressive state of recovery, unless he should *be quite well* before the 12th, because that is the latest day to which an examination of the physicians can be deferred (whether by the Privy Council or by the House of Commons): in which case a bill could be brought in on the 14th, to pass by the 23d, as above mentioned; and that only on a supposition of the bill being allowed to go on without delay being created by opposition in any one of its stages; of course that it will not be safe to defer the inquiry of the physicians to the 12th, unless it can be ascertained that no delay will be created, in order to which Mr. Pitt agreed, the best mode would be to have an intercourse with Mr. Fox, either by letter or through some person who can communicate directly with him; first waiting upon the Prince of Wales again, to know whether his Royal Highness will acquiesce in the provisions of the last Regency Bill, with perhaps a modification in the restrictions as to peerages, confining that to one year, or till a certain period after the commencement of the next session of Parliament.

Friday, March 6th.—The public account of the King's health remarkably good. "Although the fever has not *entirely* subsided, his Majesty is considerably better;" but the private account still more encouraging. His Majesty this morning perfectly composed, and so well as to see the Queen for half an hour, during all which time perfectly rational; but once or twice a little hurried, of which he was sensible, and checked himself. He asked Dr. Willis the state of business in the House of Commons, and expressed himself perfectly satisfied with it, and the train matters were in; he desired the doctor would write to Mr. Addington to inform him how well he is, with directions to him to communicate the same to Mr. Pitt and Lord Eldon, which is a decisive proof of the accuracy of his Majesty's recollection of the state of the Administration when he was taken ill. The King was awake a considerable part of the night, but quite tranquil during the whole time, and this day ate his dinner with his usual appetite.

Lord Chatham told the Bishop of Lincoln he had not made up his mind decidedly on the Catholic question; but that the inclination of his opinion was against the question, and of course favourable to his Majesty's view of the subject.

Lord Moira, in the House of Lords, suggests the expediency of sitting *de die in diem*, to be ready to take any steps that the urgency of affairs might require, evidently pointing at a regency—while the King is rapidly recovering.

Mr. Pitt seems to admit more than he has at all heretofore done, during the last four weeks, the possibility of its being right that he should remain in, or rather return to, his situation; in which possible case it would become necessary to dispose honourably and advantageously of Mr. Addington.

Saturday, March 7th.—The physicians' note respecting the King's health still more encouraging than yesterday. Mr. Pitt told me the King was in his mind quite right, though a little fever remained; that his Majesty last night played at piquet with the Queen for half an hour, and saw the Dukes of Kent and Cumberland. The conduct of the Duke of Clarence, as stated by Lord Auckland, respecting the detention of the fleet, and by Mr. Harris respecting the head of the admiralty !

Sunday, March 8th.—The King's health continues improving.

Monday, March 9th.—The King stated by the physicians to be in the way of speedy recovery.

While I was in the porter's lodge at the Queen's house this morning, reading the bulletin, the Prince of Wales passed the door and went towards the apartments in the house, soon after which he was seen going into Mr. Addington's gateway, in New Palace Yard.

The King sent Dr. Thomas Willis this day to Mr. Pitt, to desire he would come to him, finding himself well enough to talk with him, and wishing to see him before any one else; but Mr. Pitt, conceiving Mr. Addington ought first to attend his Majesty, entreated that he might do so, and declined it himself.

Mr. Pitt told me the King saw the Duke of York last Friday, and is to see the Prince of Wales to-day.

About three o'clock, Admiral Payne called at the Treasury, and waited some time in my room, while I was at the Board; evidently with a desire to talk with me. He told me the Prince of Wales had not seen the King yet, which his Royal Highness felt painfully; that the Duke of Cumberland had last Monday sent to the Duke of York to apprize him of the King's situation, when his Majesty's life was thought to be in great danger, but that no intimation of it was conveyed to the Prince, about which he remonstrated with the Duke of Cumberland, who justified himself by saying he made the communication to the Duke of York, as he was in his Majesty's confidence, which the Prince thought an aggravation. The Admiral assured me the Prince had had nothing to do with any cabals which might have been going forward, and had seen nobody but Mr. Pitt and Mr. Addington; he added that the Duke of Cumberland's conduct had on the whole been most extraordinary; that he had complained loudly to the Prince of the Chancellor having obtained the King's signature to the commission, on the 24th of last month, to the Bread Bill, for which he said his Lordship deserved a rope and a hatchet.

In the House of Lords I saw the Chancellor

respecting the third reading of the Loan Bill, who told me the King was perfectly rational and well; that he had inquired very particularly about the state of public business, and about his Lordship's health; and, among other things, spoke of his having signed the commission for the passing of the Bread Bill, expressing at the same time some uneasiness lest he should not have written his name well.

Tuesday, March 10th.—The King approaching fast to recovery.

Question in the House of Commons respecting the examination of witnesses as to Mr. Horne Tooke being a priest. Mr. Pitt not in the House. Mr. Fox took part in the debate for the first time since his return to Parliament. Great irregularity and confusion. Specimen of what may be expected under the new Government. Mr. Pitt dined with me to meet Lord St. Vincent and Lord Eldon. Admiral Payne came early before dinner, and told me the Prince of Wales had still not seen the King, but expected to be admitted in the afternoon. The Duke of Cumberland had been with the Prince (accompanied by the Duke of Kent) yesterday, for the first time since the King's illness.

Wednesday, March 11th.—The King so entirely recovered as to want nothing but the recovery of his strength; and notice was given at the Queen's house that there would be no more bulletins after this day. On coming away from thence I met Doctor John Willis at the door of the porter's lodge, and exchanged only a few words with him; he just said he was almost worn out, he had gone through too much for any one man to stand.

The Chancellor and Mr. Addington saw the King to-day for the first time; the former had with him the commission for the royal assent to the Loan Bill which he was to give to his Majesty for his royal signature, if he should find him entirely well enough for business.

Thursday, March 12th.—Admiral Payne came from the Prince of Wales to tell me his Royal Highness had seen the King yesterday; but that he had not been with him more than a minute or two before Doctor Thomas Willis came into the room without having been sent for, and remained in it the whole time his Royal Highness was there, which of course prevented any confidential conversation, but that much passed of a general nature. Among other matters entered upon by his Majesty, he said he was glad to find the inquiries made about his health had been very general; the Prince answered, he believed everybody had been to the Queen's house who could either go there or be carried; to which the King replied, Mr. Fox had not been, but that Mr. Sheridan had, who he verily thought had a respect and regard for him; particularly dwelling on his conduct at Drury Lane Theatre, when the attempt was made on his Majesty's life by the madman who had been in the dragoons; which led his Majesty to ask whether the Prince was in the house at the time; who said he was not, but that he repaired there the moment he heard of the transaction. His Majesty then proceeded to tell what his own conduct on the occasion was: that he had spoken to the Queen in German to quiet her alarm: and then bursting into an agony for a few seconds, said with much agitation, there was a Providence or a good God above who had, and would protect him; in all other respects his Majesty was quite composed during the whole interview. His Majesty took up the conversation just as he had left it on Friday, the 20th of February, and said again he hoped Mr. Pitt would be comfortable; the Prince having before said he would be very poor, on which the King said "it would be his own fault," but did not explain himself. His Majesty's eyes were a good deal affected, was thinner, and had lost the ruddiness of his complexion. He complained of the looking-glass in his room as faulty in the reflection from it; it had been covered with green baize during his illness.

Admiral Payne expressed a wish that the warrant for the allowance for the Princess Charlotte might be made for the arrears from her birth.

The Admiral had hardly left me before the Chancellor came to me at the Treasury, and sat with me there for an hour and a half; his Lordship had also been with the King for about half an hour, when his Majesty signed the commission for the royal assent to the Loan Bill, on doing which he asked with some solicitude whether he had written his name well to the commission for the Brown-bread Bill, the signing which he perfectly recollected. His Majesty's whole manner perfectly collected, and possessing himself entirely. On the Chancellor giving him a true account

of the feelings of the people, and of their anxiety for
his Majesty's recovery, he appeared much affected,
and said he hoped it would please God to give some
continuance to his life, that he might prove to his
subjects how deeply sensible he is of their attachment
and love.

After stating some other particulars of what passed
at the Queen's house, his Lordship entered again very
much at large into all the circumstances which led to
the change of the Administration, particularly dwelling
on his being persuaded that some extraordinary influence must have acted on Mr. Pitt from Sunday the
1st to Tuesday the 3d of February, which induced
him to press the King so much on the point which
led to his resignation. Thought he had not been
treated with that degree of confidence previous to the
change which he might reasonably have expected;
which is the only thing like a complaint I have heard
from him. His Lordship then stated at some length
his opinion as to the probable consequences of the
new Government coming into office, and asked for
mine in such a way as to induce me to think I could
not withhold it; I therefore told him plainly, that
under the extreme contempt universally expressed for
them, and the conviction in the public mind on the
subject, it did not appear to me to be possible Mr.
Addington could carry on the government; his Lordship assented in that entirely, and added, he had been
extremely desirous of consulting with me whether it
is not still possible for Mr. Pitt to remain in office, or
to return to it immediately, which I did not hesitate

one minute to answer in the negative, under a clear conviction that Mr. Pitt cannot again be the King's minister till called upon by the country to come forward; his Lordship, however, urged me so forcibly to ask the question of Mr. Pitt that I did so, almost immediately, telling him at the same time the answer I had made, in which he concurred most heartily; and in consequence thereof I wrote so to the Chancellor, before I went to the House of Commons.

In the House, Lord Castlereagh proposed the bill for continuing martial law in Ireland, supported by a train of most respectable country gentlemen from thence, and Opposition were afraid to divide upon it.

Friday, March 13th.—Mr. Pitt expressed doubts to me whether he could send the Prince of Wales's warrants to the King for a loan to his Royal Highness from the Civil List, and an augmented allowance for the Princess Charlotte; but quite clear the latter was to have no retrospect beyond Lady-day 1800. If he does not send them, decides at least to leave them with Mr. Addington as a matter positively arranged.

Saturday, March 14th.—Mr. Pitt went to the King at three o'clock, and returned about half-past four, and I saw him at five for a few minutes, before he went on to Mr. Addington; he had resigned the Exchequer Seal to his Majesty; he said his Majesty possessed himself most perfectly, though naturally somewhat agitated on such an occasion; that his kindness was unbounded. Mr. Pitt said he was sure the King would be greatly relieved by the interview being over, and his resignation being accepted; adding, what I am sure was true, that his own mind was greatly relieved.

In the evening, between eight and nine, Doctor Thomas Willis came to me by his Majesty's command, to desire I would give what furtherance I could to two pension warrants, for 600*l.* a year to Lady Louisa Paget, about to be married to Colonel Erskine; which message he had received from the King while playing at cards with the Queen and Princesses; he mentioned other matters to me from his Majesty of little consequence, and he told me that although Mr. Pitt was an hour and a half at the Queen's house, he was not with his Majesty more than fifteen or twenty minutes.

Dr. Willis (on my expressing great satisfaction that his Majesty's illness had been of so short duration) reminded me that during his Majesty's former illness, in 1788 and 1789, he had told me that if his Majesty had then been under the care of his family from the beginning he would have been well much sooner.

Dr. Willis told me also the remark the King had made respecting Mr. Fox and Mr. Sheridan; in the same terms Admiral Payne did, and added further, that to that time Mr. Fox had not been to make an inquiry about him; which led Dr. Willis to look at the list, where he found Mr. Fox's name the very last upon it; he having been at the Queen's house on the 11th inst., between six and seven o'clock in the evening.

Sunday, March 15th.—Mr. Pitt explained to me much more at large what passed when he was with the King yesterday; repeated that his Majesty showed the utmost possible kindness to him both in words and manner; that his Majesty begun the conversation by saying, that although from this time Mr. Pitt ceased to be his minister, he hoped he would allow him to consider him as his friend, and that he would not hesitate to come to him whenever he might wish it, or when he should think he could do so with propriety; adding, that in any event he relied on his making him a visit at Weymouth, as he knew Mr. Pitt would go to his mother, in Somersetshire, in the summer.[1]

The King told Mr. Pitt he recollected that in 1780, he was sufficiently recovered to transact business on the 12th of March, and that he had therefore dated all the warrants (which were sent to him on Friday and Saturday, the 13th and 14th) on the 12th of this month.

Mr. Pitt sent to the King the two warrants for Lady Louisa Paget, and I wrote a note to Dr. Willis to apprize him of it, and to say that Mr. Pitt would not then trouble his Majesty with any other warrants.

Thursday, March 19th.—With Mr. Pitt alone the whole evening, when a conversation arose about his

---

[1] At the close of the last conversation Mr. Pitt had with the King before his illness, his Majesty expressed an earnest wish that Mr. Pitt would see him frequently as a friend; on which Mr. Pitt observed that his Majesty would, he was sure, on a little reflection, be aware that such visits might give rise to much observation and animadversion, and be attended with inconvenience.

own situation: on mentioning to him that an intention had been expressed by many friends of bringing forward a motion in the House of Commons respecting a grant to him, he assured me in the most solemn manner of his fixed determination on no consideration whatever to accept anything from the public; rather than do which he would struggle with any difficulties; that if he had had the good fortune to carry the country safe through all its dangers, and to have seen it in a state of prosperity, he should have had a pride in accepting such a grant; but that under all the present circumstances of the situation of the country, and of himself, it was utterly inconsistent with his feelings to receive anything. In all which (notwithstanding the severe pressure I am sure he has upon him) I could not do otherwise than entirely concur with him.

Friday, March 20th.—Mr. Steele told me the King had expressed a determined purpose to extricate Mr. Pitt from his pecuniary difficulties to the person from whom Mr. Steele had it, under a most solemn engagement not to mention the name of the person who told it to him; but that he could rely most firmly on the veracity of the said person; his Majesty told that person that he had talked with Lord Grenville about Mr. Pitt, who said to the King that he had good reason to believe Mr. Pitt was under no considerable pecuniary embarrassment, which surprised his Majesty a good deal; but he was convinced to the contrary by the said person above alluded to.

Saturday, March 21st.—My functions ceased as

Secretary to the Treasury, having been in that office exactly eighteen years, viz. nine months from July 1782 to April 1783, and from December 1783 to March 1801.

Monday, March 23d.—Signed a few papers at the Treasury, and took my leave of the five chief clerks there. In the evening met the Prince of Wales; strong assurances from his Royal Highness respecting myself and my son.

Tuesday, March 24th.—A council fixed for to-morrow, for the Great Seal to be given to Lord Eldon; but notice given to his Lordship this day, that the council will not be held till after Easter.

A drawing-room fixed for Thursday. Various reports respecting his Majesty's health during the last eight days of a doubtful and unpleasant nature.

Thursday, March 26th.—The Queen had a drawing-room. Mr. Fox and Mr. Sheridan there.

Saturday, March 28th.—The state of the King's health cannot be perfectly good; there are at least eight hundred warrants unsigned; and none are returned that were lately sent.

Saturday, April 4th.—The Chancellor told me he did not carry the commission to the King for the royal assent (which he intended to have done) in consequence of a message from Dr. Willis, saying his Majesty wished to walk early, and requesting therefore the commission might be sent to him. His Lordship had sent a list of the bills to which the royal assent was to be given, in a box on the preceding evening, which had not been usual. The signature to the commission very well written.

Met Mr. Addington in the street, who expressed an anxious wish to see me, although he had nothing particular to say to me, and requested I would call on him on Monday morning.

The account from Copenhagen (in Captain Hammond's letter) discouraging, as it appears the Danish fleet are in the basin, except three ships of the line, and a formidable defence to keep our ships out of bomb distance.

Sunday, April 5th.—Lord Eldon dined with me; only Mr. W.[1] with him, when we had much confidential conversation. The Duke of Cumberland told him that on the day when Lord Hobart and Lord Lewisham were appointed to their situations, it was intended the Great Seal should have been given to his Lordship, but that the present Chancellor, Lord Loughborough, told the King Lord Eldon was out of town, which prevented his attendance; his Lordship said he was in town, and had never had any intimation whatever that his attendance at the Queen's house was expected. Lord Eldon repeated what he had said to me on a former occasion, that no consideration should induce him to take the Seal till he was perfectly ascertained of the King being in a fit condition to give it to him, of which fitness he entertained great doubt at the present moment. His Lordship very seriously questioned the propriety of the Chancellor obtaining the King's

[1] Mr. White, Solicitor to the Treasury.

signature for the royal assent to the bills on Thursday last, as well as on the two former occasions. According to my own judgment, the obtaining the signature to the commission for the assent to the Brown-bread Act, on the 24th of February, was by much the most objectionable measure, as that was carried in by Dr. Willis when nobody was allowed to see the King; whereas at this time other acts are done by his Majesty, such as the papers laid before the House of Commons by his command on Wednesday last:

I found also, from Lord Eldon's conversation, he was persuaded Lord Thurlow would take the Great Seal if offered him, but without the speakership of the House of Lords.

Lord Kenyon told Lord Eldon that Lord Thurlow had been with him, and that his conversation about the King was perfectly shocking to his ears; that in short he was a beast, and that their conversation ended by his (Lord Kenyon) saying, I swear to God, my Lord, I believe he (the King) is more in his senses than your Lordship.

I learnt from Mr. White that Major Scott told him Lord Thurlow had been prevailed with by Mr. Fox to take the Great Seal, without the House of Lords, if they should be able to get into Government.

Monday, April 6th.—Saw Mr. Addington at his house at Downing Street according to his request expressed on Saturday last. My feelings on first entering the room he was in, in which I had been with Mr. Pitt daily, when in town, for more than seventeen years! Mr. Addington received me on his part with great seeming cordiality; at first spoke on general topics: said that Sir John Warren was blocking up Ganthaume, in Toulon, with the four sail of the line he carried with him into the Mediterranean, and two from Minorca, the French having seven; in speaking of the Danish business, he expressed himself sanguinely; I answered, I was sure that what could be done by man would be executed by the two admirals who commanded; he observed that Lord Nelson was the most likely to strike a great blow, though both were good, on which I reminded him of the distinguished courage, and still more remarkable presence of mind of Sir Hyde Parker, when he forced the passage of the North River, above New York, early in the American war, under circumstances as trying to an officer as ever happened in a hazardous enterprise. Mr. Addington said he was then almost thirty years younger; that he should prefer him to command the great fleet in the Channel, but that for such a service as that at Copenhagen he should prefer Lord Nelson; from whence I infer that Sir Hyde has stated to Ministers some greater difficulties in the way of destroying the Danish fleet than were expected.

On my rising to come away, Mr. Addington told me Mr. Pitt had mentioned to him his wish that I should be made a privy counsellor, and that he should very readily make that communication to the King, to show his good disposition towards me, and he hoped I should feel properly on the subject, and consider his doing so as a mark of kindness towards me. To which I answered that I had certainly suggested to Mr. Pitt, that if I could be made a privy counsellor, *through his interposition*, I should consider it as an honourable reward for my services to the public and my attachment to him; but that the value of it would be lost unless I felt that I owed the distinction to Mr. Pitt. Mr. Addington then said he hoped neither I nor my friends would disclaim any obligations to him; which induced me to observe that where no merit was claimed (conceiving that in the present instance he could take none to himself) there could be no ground for disclaiming. Mr. Addington then asked me what I should have done if Mr. Pitt had died? To which my answer was, that in that event my thoughts would not have been employed in considering whether I should be a privy counsellor or not; that I should, of course, have abandoned all thought about it. He then expressed a hope that I would admit his being the channel through which Mr. Pitt's wish should be expressed; and I replied instantly, perhaps a little quickly, that knowing Mr. Pitt's feelings, I was sure that out of office he could not think himself at liberty to communicate with the King, except through his Minister. Mr. Addington, before the words were well out of my mouth, said he hoped I believed him to be equally incapable of any improper communications with the King out of a responsible situation; which not appearing to me to call for any observation, I made none. It seemed to savour of a consciousness that my remark about Mr.

Pitt touched him somewhat. He concluded that part of the conversation (in the course of which he made repeated attempts to extort from me something like an acknowledgment of an obligation) by saying that he would take the earliest opportunity of submitting Mr. Pitt's request to the King, and he was certain there would be no hesitation in a compliance with it; adding, that he hoped I would allow him at least the satisfaction of assuring me he should have pleasure in being the channel of communication.

Sunday, April 12*th.*—The King much improved in his health. He saw Mr. Addington for a considerable time, and the Duke of York on military matters for two hours; then dined with the Queen, and had the Princesses with him in the evening.

Monday, April 13*th.*—The King not quite so well; which is attributed to his having exerted himself too much yesterday.

Tuesday, April 14*th.*—An account was received by a special messenger from St. Petersburgh of the death of the Emperor Paul, who died suddenly in the night of the 23d of last month; supposed really to have been in an apoplexy, he having had a fit of a dangerous kind some time ago.

The messenger brought to Count Woronzo (ill at Southampton, where he has been living ever since his functions ceased as ambassador from Russia) letters of credence to this Court, to be used as soon as a British messenger should be sent to St. Petersburgh, and a proclamation that the new Emperor meant to tread in the steps of his grandmother, the Empress

Catherine;—which probably will put an end to the Northern confederacy.

Wednesday, April 15*th.*—The authentic account from Sir Hyde Parker of the entire destruction of the Danish naval line of defence at Copenhagen, one of the most brilliant victories that ever did honour to the naval heroes of this country; and *in all its points* certainly exalting the national character of Great Britain infinitely higher than any occurrence that ever happened in any war we have carried on. Circumstances in the conduct of Lord Nelson marking his coolness, firmness, presence of mind, and resources in a situation of great difficulty, as superior, if possible, to his heroism in action. The conduct of Sir Hyde Parker, in *coolly looking on*, not intelligible to me; but his character for intrepidity and resource in a time of danger and difficulty is too well established to admit of a conjecture that his not engaging could arise from any improper motive.

Saturday, April 18*th.*—The conversation I had with Mr. Addington on the 6th, having impressed me strongly with a persuasion that he wished to take to himself the merit of making me a privy counsellor, to which the delay in the notification would give a sanction, I determined to decline it altogether. I accordingly wrote a letter to Mr. Addington to that effect, assigning as my reason that it would not now have the appearance to the public of flowing from Mr. Pitt's solicitation; determined at the same time not to allow the disappointment to influence my conduct in the remotest degree. Before sending the letter, however, I consulted Mr. Pitt on the subject, as there was a reference to his name and interposition in it, who entreated me so anxiously to delay sending it for a few days, that in his presence I threw it into my desk in my own room.

Monday, April 20th.—The King and royal family went to Kew. His Majesty rode there with the Prince of Wales, and after dinner rode again. The exercise, so much exceeding what his Majesty had lately taken, and his conversing with a great number of people, workmen and others, occasioned some degree of irritation and alarm.

Tuesday, April 21st.—Lord Eldon (Chancellor) was prevented dining with me this day, to meet Mr. Pitt, by having been sent for by the Prince of Wales. On his attending his Royal Highness, the Prince told his Lordship that it was the intention of his Majesty, declared yesterday, to devolve the government on him, the Prince; that he wished therefore the Chancellor would consider the proper mode of that being carried into effect; and *that it was the King's intention to retire to Hanover or to America.* The Prince had expressed in his letter, that the King was particularly desirous his Lordship should give to his Royal Highness a paper delivered into the hands of the Chancellor some days ago. He desired therefore that his Lordship would carry it with him to Carlton House, but in the conversation he did not ask for it. That the Queen and his brothers wished him to take measures for confining the King; that his Royal Highness very greatly disliked the Willis family being about the King, and he was therefore desirous of knowing if they were placed there by any authority, or how they might be got rid of. That his Royal Highness had seen Lord Thurlow, and wished the Chancellor to see him. To all which the Chancellor said very little; refused to see Lord Thurlow; the paper was not delivered; that Dr. Willis, &c. were not about the King by any positive authority, but on grounds of propriety and notorious necessity, justifying in the clearest point of view the measure. On many of the points no reply at all was made by his Lordship.

In the *Gazette*, a continuation of the title of St. Vincent to the children of the present Earl's sister, Mrs. Ricketts, with the dignity of a Viscount.

Wednesday, April 22d.—Breakfasted with Lord St. Vincent by appointment.

Agreed that Mr. Nelson (brother to the hero in the Baltic) should not be a Commissioner of the Navy, but that I would state to Mr. Addington Mr. Pitt's intention to place him on the Board of Customs or Excise.

His Lordship entered on the late glorious victory at Copenhagen, and told me the merit of the attack rested solely with Lord Nelson, as Sir Hyde Parker had been decidedly adverse to the attempt being made, and was overruled only by the perseverance and firmness of the former; and that in the middle of the action Sir Hyde had made the signal (No. 39) for discontinuing the engagement, which Lord Nelson said to the officer who communicated it to him, he was sure proceeded from some mistake. When it was mentioned to Admiral Graves, he asked if it was repeated by Lord Nelson; and on being answered in the negative, he said, " Then we have nothing to do with it." Lord St. Vincent then added, "For these and other causes," probably alluding to the armistice, " we have recalled Sir Hyde, and Lord Nelson is to remain with the command." His Lordship proceeded to say that this measure of necessity put the Administration under some difficulty as to rewards of honour to the officers who had distinguished themselves; and that he had thought it advisable to delay any distribution of medals or to recommend any stage in the peerage to Lord Nelson, conceiving that the whole might be done on the termination of the service with propriety, and without embarrassment respecting Sir Hyde Parker. My Lord told me that in the course of the action at Copenhagen two guns had burst in each of the three Admirals' ships, and one in another,—making seven in the whole; —by which accident a large proportion of the men were killed or wounded probably, who suffered in the battle.

After I had left his Lordship, it occurred to me that as no measures can be kept with Sir Hyde Parker, it might be desirable to confer the intended step in the peerage on Lord Nelson now, and the medals on the other officers; in which opinion Mr. Pitt concurring, I wrote to suggest that to his Lordship before twelve o'clock.

I sent his Lordship also a note of various suggestions for improvements in the naval service, a copy of which I think I gave to Lord Chatham when he was at the head of the admiralty in 1788 or 1789.

Sunday, April 25th.—Having seen in the *Gazette* of the 21st the grant of a new peerage to Lord St. Vincent, and knowing that Mr. Addington has had intercourse with his Majesty on other matters, I felt an increased reluctance to accept of being made a privy counsellor now; and I copied my letter to Mr. Addington, with necessary alterations, to send it to him to-day, and went up to Mr. Pitt to apprize him of my determination, to whom I stated, as strongly as I could, that the thing would (after such a lapse of time, and the King's pleasure having been taken on so many other matters) be absolutely hateful to me, instead of being at all pleasant. Mr. Pitt still, however, urged me so strongly not to send the letter that I again declined to do it. He assured me that Mr. Addington had not lately seen the King.

Tuesday, April 28th.—The Earl of Rosslyn (late Lord Loughborough) called upon me, and stated at much length what had lately passed between him and the King, and between him and the Prince of Wales. Of the former, the most interesting was, that when he attended his Majesty to deliver up the Great Seal, the King put into his hand a paper which he wrote in 1795, testifying his approbation of the recall of Lord Fitzwilliam, and the reasons for that; which paper, his Majesty said, would be a decisive proof that *he* had not changed his mind on the subject of the Irish Catholics; and he added, that he had a duplicate

of it, which he should soon put into the hands of
another person.

With respect to the conversation with the Prince
of Wales, it was very much the same as that with
the Prince and the Chancellor (Lord Eldon). Lord
Rosslyn had seen his Royal Highness twice, and heard
nearly the same things repeated, and had since received
a message, by Admiral Payne, on the subject of his
Royal Highness being Regent.

In the afternoon, after the House of Lords had
risen, when the Bill was read the third time for preventing seditious meetings, I sat more than an hour
with the Chancellor in his room, near the House, and
he told me he was under an engagement to his
Majesty to re-deliver to him the paper alluded to
above; but that Lord Rosslyn's copy was to be left in
his Lordship's hands. The Chancellor was under a
difficulty about the mode of obtaining his Majesty's
signature to the commission for the royal assent to the
Bills now ready for it; on which I suggested to him
that it appeared to me, *rebus sic stantibus*, to be more
desirable, upon the whole, so to manage the matter
as to have a letter from the King, transmitting the
commission signed by him; as that might perhaps be
more satisfactory than even his Lordship seeing the
King sign it, because he would then be in possession
of a written testimony of his Majesty's competency to
execute such an instrument. Whereas, in the other
mode, however his Lordship might be convinced of the
King being in a proper state to transact business, he
could hereafter have no means of *proving* it; in which

his Lordship concurred. He seemed to think it not necessary that his Majesty should be in an *uninterrupted* state of health and composure to justify his being called upon to discharge the ordinary duties of the Sovereign; but that it would be sufficient for his Lordship's justification if his Majesty should, at the time of his being called upon to perform any act of sovereignty, be in a proper situation to do such act.

Sunday, May 10th.—Mr. Braun[1] came to me with a message from the King, to desire I would ask Sir Henry Mildmay whether he would lend his house, in Winchester, for his Majesty's residence for a day or two, in his way to Weymouth. He came to my bedside, as I was extremely unwell at the time. I told him he might assure the King that he might depend on having the house, as Sir Henry authorized me to offer it two years ago for the use of the King, when it was supposed his Majesty was going to review the provincial troops in Hampshire, &c. In the course of conversation, however, Mr. Braun suggested that his Majesty had more than once dropped expressions of his persuasion that, if Cuffnells should be thought a fitter residence for him, he was sure I would let him have it. I was, therefore, induced to write on the 11th to Dr. Thomas Willis, to desire if he should ever hear a wish expressed about Cuffnells, that he would say, from me, I should be delighted if his Majesty would make use of it in any manner and for any time he might choose. I wrote, at the same time, to Sir Henry Mildmay, to request he would call on me.

[1] The King's page, an old confidential attendant.

Tuesday, May 12th.—Received an answer from Dr. Willis, telling me that the King would very thankfully accept of my house; with strong expressions of acknowledgment, as well for that as for my solicitude about him during his illness.

Mr. Braun and Mr. Bowman called in the course of a few days to settle about the apartments, and delivered messages to me from the King, that he expected I would remain at Cuffnells. After this, to request that at any rate that I would be so near it that I might be constantly with him during his residence there.

Sunday, May 16th.—Wrote to Mr. Addington to decline the honour of being made a privy counsellor, and to desire he would not propose it to his Majesty, as it could not now appear to be connected with, or to arise from, my services under Mr. Pitt's administration, or to be conferred on me at his instance; but that it would make no difference whatever in my conduct. To this letter no answer of any sort was returned!!

Monday, May 17th.—The Chancellor told me he had had a long conversation with the King, who was perfectly well. His Majesty told his Lordship that whatever he advised him to do *in writing*, he would implicitly comply with it.

Friday, May 21st.—The first public council for some time past was held at the Queen's house, at which Mr. Abbott and Mr. Wallace were sworn privy counsellors!

May 31st.—The King, at the instance of the Lord

Chancellor, agreed to defer his journey till the rising of Parliament; and at night I received a letter from Mr. Braun, written by his Majesty's command, to apprize me of it.

Tuesday, June 8th.—Mr. Pitt told me there was an intention of dissuading his Majesty from going to Weymouth, on account of the inconvenience likely to arise from the concourse of people there. Asked me about the house, late Lord Bute's, near Christchurch, which I told him was half taken down, and would not now do. Talked of Walmer Castle, as likely to afford accommodation for the King, and that Deal Castle would do for the attendants; to which I answered, that it was entirely for others to judge of the comparative risk stated, and also of that of disturbing the King's mind by turning him from a scheme he had an extreme fondness for.

Wednesday, June 9th.—The Chancellor dined with me alone, by his own desire. We had a long and interesting conversation on various points, public and private.

He told me the King had expressed much uneasiness at no notice having been taken by Parliament or his people of his recovery from his illness; that Mr. Addington had opposed any parliamentary proceeding in it, as no notice had been taken by the two Houses of his illness. This I stated as in my opinion a frivolous objection, because, if his Majesty had been afflicted with a fever of a common sort, or any other illness, the Houses would naturally have congratulated him on his recovery; and that the Privy Council having ordered public thanksgiving prayers in all churches throughout the kingdom, the matter was of sufficient notoriety for a congratulatory address; in which his Lordship seemed to concur. He mentioned the intention of making an attempt to prevent the Weymouth journey, accompanied with strong expressions of disapprobation. He told me that when at Kew with the King, some weeks ago, he found his Majesty in a house there, separated from his family, with the Willis's, &c. living with him; under which arrangement the King was extremely uneasy, and at length told the Chancellor he had taken a solemn determination, that unless he was that day allowed to go over to the house where the Queen and his family were, no earthly consideration should induce him to sign his name to any paper or to do any one act of government whatever. This resolution he affirmed, with the strongest declaration, that he would abide by, as a gentleman and as a king. Accordingly, the Chancellor consented to his Majesty going to the house where the Queen was.

Thursday, June 10th.—Doctor Thomas Willis came to me to express the King's wish again, that I would be so near him (as I declined remaining in the house) as to ensure my being with him the whole time he should remain at Cuffnells. He told me Mr. Addington had a positive determination to dissuade the King from going to Weymouth, which was seriously lamented by himself and brothers, and equally so by Dr. Gisborne and the other physicians, as likely to incur a serious risk of disturbing the King's mind. That the premises at Weymouth had within a few weeks been purchased from the Duke of Gloucester, alterations made, and hot and cold baths constructed there, under the directions of the physicians, and every preparation made for the journey; but that Mr. Addington was bent on effecting his purpose, and he believed he would make the report that day, much to his grief and uneasiness. He told me that unfortunately the King had taken a decided aversion to himself and the other medical people about him, and showed great impatience to get from under their restraint. That after his Majesty went to Kew, they had been under the necessity of removing him from the house where the Queen and Princesses were; but that *that* was not effected without a mark of violence from his Majesty towards him. He assured me, however, that his Majesty was now almost entirely well, and that there was every appearance he would remain so. He assured me also, that it was a subject of constant complaint and regret with the King that no notice had been taken by Parliament &c. of his recovery; contrasting that with the conduct of his people in Hanover, who had congratulated him on the occasion.

Friday, June 11th.—The Chancellor came to me before breakfast for half an hour. He complained of Mr. Pitt not having attended last night in the House of Commons, on the Indemnity Bill (respecting the commitments for treasonable practices), and said he should write to him, to desire he would urge the attendance of his friends in the House of Lords upon the discussion. He apprehended Lord Thurlow would oppose it strongly. His Lordship told me he would *strenuously resist* the King being diverted from going to Weymouth, under a clear conviction that the attempt even could not be made without great hazard. He again mentioned the address, and concurred with me in opinion about it, if it could be done so that his Majesty should receive it upon his throne, and not be pestered with others; to which I replied, that if it should be delayed till very near the end of the session, his Majesty would escape all others by his excursion to the sea-side. This his Lordship seemed to approve of.

Mr. Beresford, in talking of the extraordinary circumstances attending the debate on the Irish Martial Law Bill, on Wednesday evening, the 0th, told me that before that business came on, Mr. Addington said their intention was to propose the continuation of the bill to one month after the peace, which Mr. B. very much approved of; but that in less than ten minutes (and while Mr. Abbott was making that proposal), Mr. Addington returned to him and said, their friends would not support so long a continuance of the bill, to which Mr. B. replied, if so, there was no remedy but to take a shorter one; asking, however, who the friends were who alarmed him, to which it was answered Lord Folkestone and Mr. Calvert! Mr. Addington then said, he would send Mr. Vansittart to Mr. Ponsonby (who had risen to speak) to tell him he would propose the bill should be in force only one year, which Mr. Beresford dissuaded him from, as likely to make Mr. Ponsonby more bold in his objections; which effect was produced by the message. Mr. Addington then rose, and declared "HE HAD NEVER INTENDED TO PROPOSE THE BILL SHOULD HAVE CONTINUANCE FOR MORE THAN ONE YEAR, OR RATHER TO THE 25TH OF MARCH, 1802," and that in the hearing of Mr. Beresford, to whom he had half an hour before said it was settled to have the proposal made in the terms moved by Mr. Abbott! The latter was of course exposed to the most virulent attacks of the Opposition, of which they availed themselves to the utmost.

Mr. Tierney had appeared for some time past wavering—certainly holding back from the front ranks of opposition—and apparently making advances to Mr. Addington; but the conduct of that gentleman in the late debates made him relinquish all idea of connecting himself with such a head of a party.

Sir Charles Grey to be made a peer;—surely a reflection on Mr. Pitt,—his only merit could be his conduct in the West Indies; which, if *so* rewarded at all, should have been done in Mr. Pitt's administration.

I found myself unwell on the 28th May, the day I returned to London to dine as usual with some friends, at Mr. Dundas's, on Mr. Pitt's birthday (having been to Hampstead, at Whitsuntide, for the Friendly Societies); but went with Mr. Pitt to Deptford, Trinity Monday, June 1st. From the 2d I was confined to the house, with an inflammatory complaint in my lungs, till the 19th, when I went to Holly Grove.

CHAPTER VII.

1801.

CORRESPONDENCE ON MR. PITT'S RETIREMENT FROM OFFICE IN 1801, BETWEEN MR. ROSE, THE BISHOP OF LINCOLN, LORD AUCKLAND, MR. PITT, MR. ADDINGTON, AND LORD ELDON—MIS-STATEMENTS OF THE WHIG WRITERS ON MR. PITT'S ADMINISTRATION, AND THE CAUSES OF HIS LEAVING OFFICE.

[GREAT was the consternation with which the tidings of Mr. Pitt's resignation were received by his followers, who seemed to say, "Can these things be, and overcome us like a summer cloud, without our special wonder?" Either not knowing, or not appreciating at their real value, the motives by which he was actuated, they displayed their irrepressible dissatisfaction, and no small obliquity of judgment. The Bishop of Lincoln was much alarmed at the idea of the Roman Catholic Bill, and thought that by the promise of abandoning it all would be set straight again. In this he was quite mistaken, as well as in the corrections of Mr. Rose's letter to the King, which he suggested. The promise did not extend beyond the King's reign, and it was not true that it would hold good at all times and under all circumstances.—ED.]

Dr. Tomline, Bishop of Lincoln, to Mr. Rose.

[*Private.*]

" My dear Sir,

"I hear, and I think from good authority, that something very unpleasant is passing relative to a Roman Catholic Bill, which Government stands pledged to Ireland to introduce into the Imperial Parliament, and which is said to be disapproved by a great personage to such a degree that very unpleasant consequences indeed may follow. If what I hear concerning the intended measure be correct, I cannot but most earnestly deprecate it; and I am satisfied that it never can be carried through the House of Lords. I think that every bishop would be against it; it has already excited no small alarm amongst some of our bench. I am unwilling to write to Mr. Pitt about it, and you will judge whether it be expedient for you to mention to him what I have said. You and he both know that I am always ready to go up to town; but I could not well leave home till the 14th, as I have company coming hither out of Yorkshire and Suffolk the beginning of next week, and I have promised to preach in this church on the fast-day. Let me know what you think and wish; as I really am at present in a state of considerable anxiety and uneasiness.

"Adieu, my dear sir. Every good wish from this house to you and yours.

" Yours ever most truly,
" G. Lincoln.

" Buckden Palace, Feb. 6th, 1801."

LETTER FROM MR. ROSE TO THE KING.

"It affords me great satisfaction to be able to say to your Majesty that I am authorized by Mr. Pitt to assure your Majesty, that (in whatsoever situation, public or private, he may happen to be [1]) he will not bring forward the question respecting the Catholics of Ireland: and that if it should be agitated by others he will supply a proposition for deferring the consideration of it. And that I mention this with the less hesitation, from Mr. Pitt not having thought himself at liberty (for the reasons I stated last year at Cuffnells) to avail himself of your Majesty's very gracious and condescending kindness and liberality."

[Letters from Mr. George Rose, Lord Bolton, and Lady Chatham, may next be introduced, expressing their anxieties and regrets at the change.—ED.]

MR. GEORGE ROSE TO MR. ROSE.

"Holly Grove, Feb. 6th, 1801.

"MY DEAR FATHER,

"William is just come. The news so confounds and perplexes me (without, Heaven knows, the mixture of any but public feelings, except as to

[1] Instead of these words within parentheses, the Bishop of Lincoln suggested—"at no time, and under no circumstances." It is unnecessary to add, "during your Majesty's reign," as that must be fairly understood.—ED.

what relates to you) that, in the instant I have to write
in, I can but say the only single consolation I can feel
is the ease and retreat it holds out to you, and for
which my anxiety has been more than I can express.
We shall be but one family, please God; and no
trifling inconvenience can weigh for a moment against
the advantages of retirement to you after a life of such
unprecedented exertion and fatigue.

"The prospect of unhinging the Government to raise
a new one with so weak a head is too frightful. Is it
credible that I conversed very long to-day with a
gentleman [the King] hunting, who talked of all the
people most affected as if nothing had happened, or
was to happen, and who was in unusual spirits?

"May Heaven preserve you, my dearest Father,
"G. H. Rose."

LORD BOLTON TO MR. ROSE.

[*Private.*]

"Hackwood Park, 6th Feb. 1801.

"MY DEAR SIR,

"One hasty line to thank you truly for yours,
received this day. The confidential communication
of an event of real importance makes all our little
county arrangements seem still smaller. I am really
and truly sorry for this great change, although I by no
means wonder at Mr. Pitt's desire to withdraw for a
time from a weight which would have sunk most men
long ago. I would have had him at the helm till we
could have reached the port; but such strange and
contrary winds blow, that perhaps the superstition

of the crew must be awakened and yielded to, and a change of pilot for that cause alone must be made. Yet I wonder at the successor, not from doubt of his talents, but at his willingness to move from the other situation at such a time.

"I hardly venture to reckon upon all the good which may have been hoped. If the Speaker is placed there as a medium of attraction for conciliating parties, I can in some degree understand the object, although doubtful of success. If he is to be the minister upon the old ground, his House of Commons popularity with the other side will be soon gone. Some, indeed, have gone far in positive declarations against any peace to be made by Mr. Pitt, and may be a little freed by a new appointment; but this is the decided friend and confidant of Mr. Pitt.

"I will only add my best wishes for all possible satisfaction to Mr. Pitt, and success to his successor, if he does right, and I have no doubt about him. I am so out of the way of politics or political men that I am very ill qualified for judgment.

"You do not surprise me by your own resolution; for indeed you must be well tired of it all, and you are fairly now entitled to retreat. I could not have held out half so long, even if I had had health. I trust that happier days may come, when we may meet more comfortably in the country.

"How soon will this all take place? But it is unreasonable to ask a line from you, as you must be doubly hurried.

"I am half guessing a successor to you in this county. I think it would be agreeable to him; but all this confidential. Adieu.

"Ever most cordially yours,
"BOLTON."

MRS. STAPLETON[1] TO MR. ROSE.

"Burton Pynsent, 11th Feb. 1801.

"SIR,

"The rumours of the last ten or twelve days have kept Lady Chatham in a constant state of painful anxiety. Your silence upon the subject of Mr. Pitt's health,—of all things, next to his honour, nearest her heart,—satisfied her, from your former kind attention, that he was not seriously ill; and your most friendly, obliging letter of last night, relieves her from the very irksome, painful uncertainty of not knowing what to think *possible* or true of the various things, at best most cruelly unpleasant, which reached us in a desultory manner and style. A few lines, with yours, from Mr. Pitt, was the first information we received that could gain further faith than the fear that some severe storm was gathering. Pray God it prove not destructive. A change, with every favourable circumstance that the present appears to be attended with, it is impossible not to dread, must prove destructive at a period when unanimity and Mr. Pitt at the helm furnished sufficient difficulties to baffle with. His promised aid, with the will of the Almighty, may still

[1] Mrs. Stapleton was a friend of Lady Chatham, who lived with her, and latterly wrote letters for her.

support us; and, if things put on a less threatening aspect, his greater degree of relaxation from business will probably more firmly establish his health,— of such near consequence to almost the whole known world, whatever situation he may be in. His dearest mother and himself are so much one in mind and sentiment, that the rectitude of his conduct you now give to him, and ever his due, with his own account of perfect health, places her above any disappointment. To yourself she owes the knowledge of even the shadow of a new administration. Mr. Pitt simply mentioned the unfortunate event as unavoidable, with his feelings, and not a name. Lady Chatham entreats your acceptance of her best regards and sincerest thanks for your most friendly attention, which she shall ever retain the most grateful sense of; and ventures to flatter herself, as occasion offers, you will not withdraw the kindness of letting her hear any important event which she may otherwise lose, or not learn from equally good authority. God grant success to any right undertaking, and avert all fatal consequences from this most unlooked-for change. I don't think there is a better heart in human breast than Mr. Addington's, or a man that loves Mr. Pitt better; so far it is pleasant. I ought to have acknowledged the favour of your letter last night, but the post came in late, and went out by seven o'clock this morning.

"I am, Sir, your very much obliged,
"And obedient, humble servant,
"CATH. STAPLETON."

LORD AUCKLAND TO MR. ROSE.

[*Private.*]

"Palace Yard, February 8th, 1801.

"MY DEAR SIR,

"I have sent to Mr. Pitt the several documents respecting the proposed duties of postage, except, only, an explanatory paper, which you will find in the bundle of his minutes for the budget.

"As to the rest, stunned, grieved, and aggrieved, as I am, I shall now have ample leisure to think; and I have no particular desire to talk. I very cordially hope, however, that we shall meet, whenever it may not be disagreeable to you to spare a quarter of an hour.

"Believe me, most sincerely yours,

"AUCKLAND."

MR. ROSE TO LORD AUCKLAND.

"Sunday, February 8th, 1801.

"MY DEAR LORD,

"Mr. Pitt told me he had received the Post-office papers from you, which I dare say will justify our taking the sum you mentioned towards our taxes in the approaching budget.

"The allusion in the latter part of your note is to a subject as painful and distressing to me, in various points of view, as it can be to any individual in this country, the principals not excepted. Any discussion upon it with you for the present could answer no possible good end, and there are occasions on which conversation on *any* subject had better for a time be avoided between persons who have long been in the habit of talking confidentially on *all*."

[Mr. Rose, weighing the mediocrity of Mr. Addington against the superior talents of Mr. Pitt, not only rejected his solicitation to remain in office at the Treasury, but would not accept a favour from him; and the offer of being enrolled in the Privy Council was rejected, unless it was fully understood that it was the reward of his service under the ex-Minister, and that to him he was indebted for the honour. This is shown in the annexed correspondence.—Ed.]

Mr. Rose to Mr. Addington.

"Feb. 10th, 1801.

"I thought something fell from you this morning that implied a doubt whether, in my situation, you should have taken the same line I have. On points, exclusively of feeling, with which the judgment has not much to do, I can easily conceive two persons, whose habits of thinking are much alike, may differ. In this instance, I act on the impulse of my feelings; and I repeat to you, with the sincerest truth, that in any other situation whatever but that I at present hold, *I should have complied with the wish expressed by Mr. Pitt*, without the slightest hesitation; and that I am influenced by no motive but the one I expressed to you."

Mr. Rose to Mr. Pitt.

"*April 18th, 1801.*

" My dear Sir,

"I should not think myself justified in making any communication, where there is even a mention of your name, without apprizing you of it; but I have other and more interesting reasons for begging you to read the enclosed before I send it. I have been led to write it principally from what fell from Mr. Addington in the conversation I had with him twelve days ago. If you happen to recollect what I stated of that, I think you will not disapprove of this letter. If, however, you see anything objectionable in it, I will either alter it or put it in the fire.

"I am still lame; but I can get up to you in a carriage any time in the day, if you wish to see me."

Mr. Rose to Mr. Addington.

" My dear Sir,

"When you mentioned to me three weeks ago that Mr. Pitt had requested you to submit to his Majesty his wish that I might be made a privy counsellor, you told me you were persuaded there would be no hesitation on the part of his Majesty in a compliance therewith. In the course of that conversation I felt myself called upon to say, that, consistently with my feelings, I could owe the obligation only to Mr. Pitt, under an impression that the distinction being conferred on me early, would be considered as a proof that my services under him for more then seventeen years had rendered me worthy of the honour I sought; adding, however, that being aware (as circumstances had unavoidably prevented Mr. Pitt from submitting the request to his Majesty before he retired from office) it could now only be proposed by you, I was perfectly content *so* to receive what I had asked of Mr. Pitt. But as you have taken his Majesty's pleasure on various subjects in the interval since I saw you, and I have had no intimation from you respecting myself, the favour if granted could not have the appearance of flowing from Mr. Pitt's solicitation. I have, therefore, no longer any wish for the distinction at present, and desire to decline giving you any trouble about it. The reasons for the omission are to me quite unimportant.

"You know me, I trust, well enough to be quite sure that this determination does not arise from the remotest tendency to captiousness, or from any other cause than the one I have stated, and that the disappointment cannot produce any alteration whatever in my conduct.

"I am, my dear Sir,
"Your very obedient and faithful, humble servant,
"GEORGE ROSE.

"Old Palace Yard, April 25th, 1801."

MR. ROSE TO MR. ADDINGTON.

"May 17th, 1801.
"MY DEAR SIR,
"As my having the honour conferred upon me of being admitted to his Majesty's Privy Council

could not *now* be connected with my services under Mr. Pitt's administration, or appear to arise from his approbation of them, I could not consistently with my feelings receive it at present. I desire, therefore, to decline giving you any trouble about it.

"You know me, I trust, well enough to be very sure that this determination does not arise from any other cause than the one I have assigned, and that the disappointment cannot produce the slightest possible alteration in my conduct."

[It might be supposed that nothing could shake the determination here so strongly expressed by Mr. Rose, of resisting Mr. Addington's offer; especially since his eldest son entirely concurred in his view of the matter, and endeavoured to persuade him to adhere to it. But Mr. Pitt was so sincerely desirous to support his successor, so long as he committed no grave faults in his administration, which might compromise the interests of the country, that his friend could not stand out against his earnest and repeated entreaties that he would strengthen the government by accepting a seat in the Privy Council. The public would suspect the sincerity of his intentions, if his most intimate friend stood absolutely aloof from the Minister, and refused to accept the smallest obligation from him. Mr. Pitt seems to have requested Mr. Addington to name the subject to the King, and the latter not only complied with that request, but judiciously desired Mr. Pitt to make the communication to his friend. Mr. Rose having constrained himself to make this concession to the policy of Mr. Pitt, thought it a favourable opportunity to put forward the claims of his son for employment under the new Ministry; for though the ex-Minister's influence was crippled, it was not destroyed by loss of office, and he had a right to expect, that if he wished to obtain a situation for some competent and trustworthy person, his recommendation would not be disregarded. In this case there was no reason to hesitate. Mr. George Rose had already obtained distinction in the diplomatic line, and his previous character fully justified an application in his behalf.—

[After the short illness, occasioned by the change of administration in the beginning of the year, the King resolved to go to Weymouth, as a healthful and quiet place, but it was too far to get there in a day. Mr. Rose having learned that he did not like to sleep at Southampton, offered him the use of his house, called Cuffnells, on the borders of the New Forest, which pleased the King very much, and he employed his doctor, T. Willis, to convey to him the thanks, which are expressed in the first of the two following letters. The second is from Lord Eldon, who had been to visit the King at Weymouth, and, being obliged to return speedily to town, writes to Mr. Rose asking him to relieve him from a comical perplexity in administering justice between man and man. In the postscript there are some good remarks upon trafficking in Church patronage, and a revelation of the plague which the possession of that patronage entails upon the patron.—Ed.]

Dr. Willis to Mr. Rose.

"Kew House, May 12, 1801.

" Dear Sir,

" I am commanded by his Majesty to write to you, and say that he feels himself very much obliged to you for your offer of Cuffnells, which will be much more pleasing to him than being at Winchester. He has also desired me to write to his page, Mr. Bowman,—who has gone to Weymouth, and who was to call at Winchester on his way back, to make preparations for the King,—and say, that his Majesty now intends to stop at Cuffnells for three or four days, on his way to Weymouth; and that instead of his (Mr. Bowman's) going to Winchester, he desires he will now return by Cuffnells, and see into the accommodation there and in the neighbourhood.

" I cannot express to you how gratifying this offer of yours is to his Majesty. If anything should suggest itself that you might wish to say to Mr. Bowman, you would probably think it right to write to him to-night, at Gloucester Lodge, Weymouth. He will probably be at Cuffnells about Thursday. But it will be requisite that a letter should find him at Weymouth.

" Let me not forget to add, that his Majesty commanded me to say in this letter, that he had heard of your solicitude during his illness, and that he should ever remember it. Of this, also, he spoke to-day to Lord Eldon, who says he never knew the King to be at any time better.

"Should you wish to say anything further upon the subject of Cuffnells, I would advise that you called upon me (for I cannot come to you) at a house I have a few doors below the Rose and Crown, on Kew Green, somewhere about half after twelve to-morrow, if you can spare the time. This is of course not necessary; but I only state it, that if you wish it, you may know how you may see me. And I think his Majesty may be inquiring into particulars, which it might be satisfactory to him to know.

"I need not add that I have been obliged to write in a great hurry.

"I am, dear Sir, most truly,

"Yours very faithfully,

"THOS. WILLIS.

"I should imagine that the King will set off about the beginning of the second week in June. Her Majesty, the Queen, is delighted with the idea of stopping at Cuffnells."

LORD ELDON TO MR. ROSE.

"DEAR ROSE,

"I got to Weymouth on the morning of Monday, the 17th, and, according to what usually befalls me, I was compelled to leave it, and to return to town forthwith, setting out from thence on Wednesday evening. So that my expectations of making what may be called a stay there were utterly disappointed, and my golden hopes of being a night or two at Cuffnells fell to the ground. I could not help lamenting this for a great many reasons, principally, that I was unable to gratify my inclination to take you by the hand in my passage, and to assure myself by ocular proof that you are got quite well. I had some subordinate views undoubtedly; and principally one which relates to a subject that distresses me, because it puzzles me, and because it distresses poor Brodie, whilst it continues to puzzle me. The business in which he has been engaged I never heard of, whilst it has been pending in the House, except simply that I had been informed that there was some such business pending, and that Lord Rosslyn asked me if I would undertake to settle what should be done. Here it rested, without more being said to me till I received some of your letters, which were written certainly under a notion that I knew somewhat more of this matter than I really did know. In the next place, I was applied to by Mr. Adam and Mr. Brodie, to direct all papers to be removed from Evans's to Brodie's hands, and he joined in the proposition that 500*l*. should by me be ordered to be paid to each of them, and that Brodie should go on with the work.

"I was startled with this, for it was not till *after this* that the resolutions of the Lords were communicated to me. From these resolutions, as I understand them (pray tell me if I am right), the Lords, I conceive, have determined that Brodie is to go on with the work, but *in such manner as I shall direct*, and they are both to be paid in such manner for what is *past, as I also shall direct*. Now, in having taken the good-natured part of removing this business from that scene of squabble which I understand the committee-room exhibited, I have permitted myself to be placed in a situation of more difficulty than is at all comfortable. In the first place, with an absolute ignorance of all that has been doing, and responsible to the Lords for the propriety of my directions, ignorant both as to what Mr. Brodie has done, and as to what Mr. Evans has done, how can I, without complete information given me from some quarter, judge, in any sort, what I ought to direct to be paid to either of these gentlemen for the time past, so as to be able to account to the Lords why I ordered so much or so little, as it may happen, to be paid?

In the next place, as I understand the order, though Brodie is to proceed, he is to proceed as I shall direct. Now, I feel it prodigiously difficult,—in absolute ignorance of all that has been doing, and all that has been contended to have been rightly done, or injudiciously done, and with no more knowledge of the subject than your horse, or of the reasons why one plan has been thought good and another has been thought bad,— either to tell Mr. Brodie to proceed upon the plan he has hitherto been executing, or to tell him what better plan he can adopt and ought to pursue. And be pleased to note well, that by the Lords' order, the plan in future must be mine. Here I am without a soul to give me any information on the subject, and I cannot take my lesson from Brodie himself, whom I am to direct, and who into the bargain is a Scotchman :—a circumstance I feel, because I practically know, from my friend Loughborough's having got me into, and himself out of, this scrape, that I am not equal to gentlemen from that part of the island.

"In the meantime, Brodie gets nothing, and is starving. I am therefore mortified that the state of public matters robbed me of the opportunity of seeing you in my way from Weymouth; but it was impossible. But pray take up your pen, and tell me, if you'll be so good, to what extent, and how, these gentlemen should be paid for what is past, and *upon what grounds* they are to be paid now to any such proposed extent;—grounds which I can state and assign to the Lords when they look at the payment to that extent as my act. As to Brodie's going on in the manner he has hitherto proceeded, I really have not the power or the means of judging whether that be right; and, as I understand the resolutions of the committee, he is not to go on *so*, unless *I* think it right that he should. Now, I am so ignorant upon the subject, so little competent to judge whether it is right or wrong, that I do not even know what the quarrel has been, or on what grounds it has stood. Pray also tell me, as largely as your convenience will admit, what have been the different plans suggested, and what you think, and for what reasons, the best. I need not tell you that Brodie is hungry, and in a hurry, and therefore the sooner you can indulge me with a full answer the better. I am heartily sorry that I have got into this business at all. However, I must make the best of it I can.

"I found the King doing very well, but not I think in high spirits, which is perhaps so much the better. With my best regards to Mrs. Rose and all the family,

"Believe me, dear Sir, faithfully yours,

"ELDON.

"P.S.—I had forgot in the enclosed to say a word to you about Mr. B., who, you intimate, has a living to dispose of, and you suppose looks to a prebend. The thing is impossible for many reasons. In the first place, my serious opinion is, that though ecclesiastical men of the highest stations and best characters, 'multi et boni,' think nothing of these exchanges, there is an illegality about such transactions which makes it impossible for a man at the head of the law to have anything to do with them. I know this was the rule with my best predecessors, and I have positively refused already in many instances to take any part in them. In the next place, as matters now go on, that is, as nothing of any sort has in my time become vacant, or next to nothing, I look to a prebend rather with a wish to have some vacant than a hope; and I have two royal commands already for prebends. They happen also to suit my brothers-in-law, and some other people nearly connected with me, for none of whom I was ever able to get any provision in the church to which they belong, and I do hope anxiously, somehow or other, by some chance, not to fail in my last hopes on their behalf, though I am afraid I shall.

My friend, Lord Rosslyn, presented to nineteen livings in February. I have presented to two in four months; neither of them worth acceptance. A wish to oblige you, when I can, I ever shall anxiously have, and this I persuade myself you do me the justice to give me credit for. In these circumstances, to me it is provoking beyond endurance, that every day brings me as many letters for preferment, from men strangers to me, as if every parson in England were dead, though they seem to be all immortal."

[We have now come to the close of Mr. Pitt's first administration, the history of which has been greatly misunderstood, by friends and foes, and much undeserved obloquy has been cast upon him by both. Lord Malmesbury comes nearest to the truth, though even his account is mixed with considerable error. He says "This measure (the Catholic relief bill) is to be attributed in part to Pitt's carelessness, and in part to his want of real respect for the King; for had he been provident enough to prepare the King's mind gradually, and to prove to him that the test proposed was, as far as went to allegiance and supremacy, as binding as the present oath, no difficulty could have arisen. Instead of this, he reckons on his own power, never mentions the idea at St. James's, and gives time for Lord Loughborough directly, and for Lord Auckland indirectly, through the Archbishop of Canterbury and Bishop of London, to raise an alarm in the King's mind, and to indispose and exasperate him against the framers of the measure. This was very blameable in Pitt.[1] Afterwards, he fell still more under the influence of the backbiters who disseminate their malevolence in clubs and drawing-rooms, and accused him of playing a very selfish and criminal part:[2] of trying to be entreated by the King to keep the government in his own hands, or of letting his successors remain in office long enough to make peace, and then turn them out."[3]

If Lord Malmesbury had published his own Diaries, he would scarcely have allowed these unjust surmises to have held a place in them, since they are completely contradicted by the authentic facts which are afterwards detailed at great length.[4] If such was the treatment that Mr. Pitt received from his friends, it may be supposed that his opponents would not spare him. Lord Holland was not far wrong in saying that Mr. Pitt acquiesced in an expedient by which a ministry was formed for the express purpose of resisting a great national measure, which he had earnestly recommended; and it is true that he wished his friends who differed with him on that point to remain in office. But it is not true that he suggested that expedient; and it is not true that the ministry was formed chiefly of his own creatures and dependants. Still less is it true, that Lord Auckland and

[1] Diaries, &c. vol. iv. p. 3. [2] Ibid. page 3. [3] Ibid. page 40.
[4] Ibid. p. 75, et seq.

Lord Loughborough produced the breach between the King and Mr. Pitt.[1] Lord Brougham remarks upon Pitt's resignation: "Are the motives of it wholly free from suspicion? *Cui bono?* He was incalculably a gainer by it. Finding it impossible to continue any longer the ruinous expenditure of the war, he retired, placing in his office his puppet, with whom he quarrelled for refusing to retire when he was bidden; but the ostensible ground of his resignation was the King's bigoted refusal to emancipate the Irish Catholics."[2]

The bigotry which is here imputed to George III., calls forth, in another place, the wrath of the noble writer. Like the lion who is said to have a thorn in his tail, he lashes himself into ungovernable fury, and lavishes upon the unfortunate monarch the wealth of his invective, with a ferocity which shows that the most bitter animosity and the most unforgiving resentment, which he attributes to the King, had taken possession of his own breast. "*Ira furor brevis est:*" and certainly the inconsistency of his anger looks very much like a temporary mental alienation; for he says, "the habits of friendship, the ties of blood, the dictates of conscience, the rules of honesty, were alike forgotten; and the fury of the tyrant, with the resources of a cunning which mental alienation is supposed to

[1] Memoirs of the Whig Party, vol. i. p. 171.
[2] Historical Sketches of Statesmen in the time of George III., by Lord Brougham, vol. I, p. 201.

whet, were ready to circumvent or to destroy all who interposed an obstacle to the fierceness of unbridled desire."[1] And yet, in his calmer mood, the noble Lord does not forget the rules of honesty, but makes this candid acknowledgment: "That he (the King) only discharged the duty of his station by thinking for himself, acting according to his conscientious opinions, and using his influence for giving those opinions effect, cannot be denied."[2]

In remarking upon the intolerance of Percival and his party, Lord Brougham says, "They forget that those of opposite sentiments have exactly the same excuse for unyielding obstinacy that they have for rooted dislike towards adverse doctrines. They feel all the heat of intolerance, but make no kind of allowance for others feeling somewhat of the fire which burns so fiercely within themselves."[3] *Mutato nomine de te fabula narratur.* So easy is it to discern the mote in another's eye without perceiving the beam in our own. An additional instance of this "*furor brevis*" may be found in the charge brought against George III., of all men in the world, of forgetting the ties of blood. The sandy foundation on which this accusation rests, is stated thus: "The treatment of his eldest son, whom he hated with a hatred scarcely consistent with the supposition

---

[1] Historical Sketches of Statesmen in the time of George III., by Lord Brougham, vol. i. p. 201.
[2] *Ibid.* vol. i.   [3] *Ibid.* vol. i. p. 253.

of a sound mind, might seem to illustrate the shadier part of his personal disposition. He had *no better reason* for this implacable aversion, than the jealousy which men have of their successors, and the consciousness that the Prince, who must succeed him, was unlike him; and being disliked by him, must during their joint lives be thrown into the hands of the Whig party, the adversaries he most of all detested and feared."

No better reason for aversion! Now what was the character of the person thus disliked? After running a course of dissipation uninterrupted by any rational or worthy pursuit, prematurely exhausting the resources of indulgence both animal and mental, and becoming incapable of receiving further gratification, it was found that a life of what was called unbounded profusion, could not be passed without unlimited extravagance. He had become wholly selfish through unrestrained indulgence. He neither commanded respect, nor conciliated esteem. He had neither firmness nor truth in his character. "The Whig party, being the enemies of George III., found favour in the sight of his son and became his natural allies."[1] But perhaps this is an overcharged statement. It may be, but it is the statement of Lord Brougham himself. If the King therefore detested and feared the Whigs, it was not because they were Whigs. On the contrary, he declared to Lord

[1] Historical Sketches, vol ii. pp. 4, 5, 6

Malmesbury, that he himself was an old Whig. But there are better reasons for dislike than jealousy or whiggery, or even the despicable character of the man, which the historian of the statesmen of that reign can scarcely be permitted to ignore.

From his earliest youth, the Prince had been a source of pain and sorrow to his father. When he was fourteen years old the King was very ill. Lord Hertford said, "Think what he must feel at finding already that his son is so headstrong that he has not the least authority over him." His tutors too were driven away by his ungovernable temper. When he was eighteen, and became emancipated from the surveillance under which he had lived, he is described by Walpole as getting drunk, swearing, and intriguing with various women. This was the period too of the following complaint :—

"When we hunt together," said the King (in 1781), "neither my son nor my brother will speak to me; and lately when the chase ended at a little village, where there was but a single postchaise to be hired, my son and brother got into it, drove to London, and left me to get home in a cart, if I could find one. He complained, too, that the Prince, when invited to dine with him, came an hour too late, and all the servants saw the father waiting an hour for the son."[1] From the same authority we learn, that "the Prince of

[1] Memoirs and Correspondence of C. J. Fox, by Lord John Russell, vol. i. p. 270.

Wales had of late thrown himself into the arms of Charles Fox, and this in the most undisguised manner," who dictated his politics in his lodging; "and in this school did the heir of the crown attend his lessons, and imbibe them. Fox's followers, to whom he never enjoined Pythagorean silence, were strangely licentious in their conversations about the King. At Brookes's they proposed wagers on the duration of his reign, and if they moderated their irreverent jests in the presence of the Prince, it was not extraordinary that the orgies of Brookes's might be reported to have passed at Fox's levees, or that the King should suspect that the same disloyal topics should be handled in the morning, that he knew had been the themes of each preceding evening."[1] It was believed that he had demanded of the Lord Chancellor, and Lord Ashburton, "what redress he could have against a man who had alienated from him the affections of his son."

The true causes of the King's estrangement from his son are distinctly visible in the Diaries of Lord Malmesbury and Lord Eldon. In an interview with the Prince in 1785, Sir James Harris'[2] proposed to get Mr. Pitt to obtain from Parliament an income of 100,000*l.* a-year, on condition, that he would set aside 50,000*l.* to pay his debts and cease to be a party man. The Prince's answer was, "It will not do. I tell you the

[1] Memoirs, &c. vol. ii. p. 47.
[2] Afterwards Earl of Malmesbury.

King hates me. He would turn out Pitt for entertaining such an idea; besides I cannot abandon Charles (Fox), and my friends." How was it possible for the virtuous monarch to tolerate such a man, who shuffled from the path of duty by meanly pretending scruples about turning out Pitt, which was the very thing most desired by Charles and his friends; and who preferred association with profligacy to being an honest man and a good son? What a striking contrast to this undutiful conduct of the Prince is presented to us by his younger brother the Duke of Kent, who made this declaration of his feelings to Lord Eldon: "The King is my object; to stand by him at all times my first duty, and my inclination; and I think I cannot prove this more strongly, than by pledging myself always to support his servants. I have ever acted up to this profession, and I always will."[1]

But there is other evidence of the unworthy and unscrupulous behaviour which provoked the severity of the King, in their private correspondence. That private correspondence the Prince proposed to publish, because his requests, which were probably unreasonable, were refused, and his extravagance and dissipated manner of living reprobated. So callous and deadened was his conscience, that he said to Lord Malmesbury, who had seen the letters, "I cannot bring myself to say that I am in the wrong when I am in

[1] Lord Eldon's Life, by H. Twiss, vol. i. p. 455.

the right. The King has used me ill, and I wish the public knew what you now know, and had to pronounce between us." The sage counsel which he then received should have shown him the folly of his unfilial treachery; for Sir James Harris replied, "I should be very sorry indeed, Sir, if this was known beyond these walls; for I am much mistaken if the public would not pronounce a judgment widely different from what you think. It is not sufficient for the King to be wrong on one point, unless you are in the right in all; and as long as any part of your conduct is open to censure, the voice of the public will always go with the King."[1] Nevertheless, the Prince published the private correspondence. Who can wonder that this act of baseness rankled in the royal mind, and proved the only bar to a perfect reconciliation? When at a subsequent period, one solitary symptom of a better spirit touched the tenderness of a father's heart, the King said to Lord Eldon, "The Prince of Wales's making the offer of having the dear little Charlotte's education and principles attended to, is the best earnest he can give of returning to a sense of what he owes to his father, and indeed to his country, and may to a degree mollify the feelings of an injured parent; but it will require some reflection before the King can answer how soon he can bring himself to receive the publisher of his letters."[2]

[1] Lord Malmesbury's Diary, vol. ii. p. 129.
[2] Lord Eldon's Life, by H. Twiss, vol. i. p. 485.

There was another correspondence [1] published in 1803, but that contained only one short letter from the King, and cannot be accepted for the "letters" to which he alludes. But the manifest insincerity which the Prince's letters breathe throughout, the almost irony with which he beseeches an *affectionate* father to open his ears to the supplications of a *dutiful* son—supplications to which he knew full well the King could not, would not, and ought not to listen; and the prevaricating spirit of altercation with his brother the Duke of York, who steadfastly resolved to obey his father, show more desire to plague the King, and embarrass his government, than any serious wish to gain his confidence. The high military command to which he aspired had been repeatedly and resolutely refused, for obvious political reasons, which he does not attempt to controvert. From all this it is abundantly manifest, that the King had plenty of better reasons for disliking his eldest son, than the foolish jealousy which is imputed to him. Thirdly, Lord Brougham says, that the Whigs were "the adversaries whom he (the King) most detested and feared." How far this is true or otherwise, we shall have another opportunity of showing. At present it is sufficient to say, that it was not because they were Whigs; for, as we have seen, he said of himself that he was an old Whig, and the Whig administration of Queen Anne he con-

[1] Annual Register, 1803, p. 664.

sidered the most able we had ever had.¹ Lastly, the accuser asserts, that in all that related to his kingly office, he was the slave of deep-rooted selfishness; and yet he owns, that when he threatened to abdicate rather than do what he considered wrong, they who knew him were well aware that he did not threaten without a full resolution to act.² The Duke of Portland said, he was sure the King had rather suffer martyrdom than submit to the measure of Roman Catholic emancipation.³

It was no theological bigotry that actuated him in his pertinacious resistance to that measure, but a conscientious conviction that it was his duty. He probably knew little or nothing of the doctrinal differences between Protestants and Roman Catholics, but the oath which he had taken at his coronation bound him to support the established Church. In that sense he had taken the oath. In that sense he believed it was intended to be understood by those who framed it, and therefore he was resolved to abide by the obligation which the state had laid upon him, and to which he had vowed his unreserved adhesion. This is no mere surmise, or arbitrary assumption, but rests on the King's own declaration, and the uniform expression of his feelings on other occasions. To Mr. Pitt he wrote thus: "A sense of religious, as well as political duty,

¹ Lord Malmesbury's Diary, vol. iv. p. 44.
² Historical Sketches, p. 0.   ³ Ibid.

has made me, from the moment I mounted the throne, consider the oath, that the wisdom of our forefathers has enjoined the Kings of this realm to take at their coronation, and enforced by the obligation of instantly following it in the course of the ceremony with taking the sacrament, as a binding religious obligation on me to maintain the fundamental maxims on which our constitution is placed;—namely, that the Church of England is the established Church; that those who hold employments in the state must be members of it; and consequently obliged not only to take oaths against Popery, but to receive the Holy Communion agreeably to the rites of the Church of England." [1] Stronger still was his statement in a conversation with the Duke of Portland, in which he said, "that were he to agree to it, he should betray his trust, and forfeit his crown, and that it might bring the framers of the measure to the gibbet." [2]

In all this there was no symptom of antipathy to other creeds, or their professors; but a deep, ineradicable impression that he was bound by his oath to defend the Church to which he belonged from all encroachments. This was the uppermost idea in his mind during his illness; and when he came to himself, he said, after a silence of several hours, "I am better now; but I will remain true to the Church." [3] It was, in fact, the cause of his illness on that occa-

[1] Memoirs of Fox, vol. iii. p. 251.
[2] Lord Malmesbury, vol. iv. p. 44.   [3] Ibid. vol. iv. p. 19.

sion, which he thus signified to Mr. Pitt: "Tell him," said he to Dr. Willis, "I am now quite well; quite recovered from my illness; but what has not he to answer for, who is the cause of my being ill at all?"[1] No better proof can be desired of his warm affection for the minister who had served him faithfully for seventeen years, than the pain at parting from him which produced this derangement. He told General Bode that "this was the first and only difference of opinion between them; that the measure took him quite by surprise, and hurt him very much."[2] But that no "unforgiving resentment took possession of his breast," is proved by the conversation which he held with Lord Malmesbury a few months afterwards, in which "he spoke in friendly terms of Pitt,"[3] and by his desiring, through the Duke of York, to see him. If he had been a selfish man, he would have consulted his own ease, and undisturbed enjoyment of life, by yielding to the earnest entreaties of so great an authority. But he was cast in a nobler mould; and even those who most widely differ from the conclusion at which he arrived, must reverence the high sense of duty which prompted him to sever his strongest attachment, and sacrifice his peace of mind rather than do that which his conscience told him would be a great sin.

The state of the King's feelings on this subject,

[1] Lord Malmesbury, vol. iv. p. 32. [2] Ibid. vol. iv. p. 8.
[3] Ibid. vol. iv. p. 63.

after his recovery, is shown in the following extract from a letter of Sir George Rose, who at that time lived at Holly Grove, near Windsor, and frequently conversed with the King in his rides. He is writing to his father:—"Many points in the Bishop of Lincoln's letter are indeed highly satisfactory, and give a hope of termination to a state of affairs so abject, so galling, and so humiliating." (This refers to a scheme of Mr. Pitt's friends, unknown to him, to induce Mr. Addington to resign a post for which they considered him quite unfit.) "The obstinacy on the Catholic question is most mortifying. This country does not care a straw about it,—perhaps is against it; and with the enormous advantage of the Union, and the means of making various concessions, short of the grand one, we might safely have waited at least for experience to know whether it was indispensably necessary or not. In this neighbourhood it is distinctly understood, that Mr. Pitt put himself under the governance of Lord Castlereagh, who drove him to the question in the view to debase and pull down the established Church, to which he (his family being at the head of the Dissenters in Ireland) is peculiarly hostile. You will judge how this persuasion will render the resistance to Mr. Pitt's views acrimonious and insurmountable.

This leads me to a recent conversation, in which a firm belief was expressed (by the King), that Mr. Pitt, before the question had been agitated, or the violent hostility to it which drove him out was known, had pledged himself to some person (I suppose Lord Castlereagh was meant) to carry the question or to resign his office. I could not pretend to say that no such pledge existed; but, as I could not believe Mr. Pitt capable of giving it to that extent, upon a question in great measure speculative, and in the state of the country, and of a war which he had undertaken, I used every argument in my power, drawn from circumstances, the nature, principles, and high feelings of the man to eradicate this opinion. If what I said did not convince, I am sure it did not offend. I was told shortly before that, that Mr. Pitt had but one fault,—pride. I endeavoured, as far as I was able, to soften that opinion, and to put the amiable parts of his character in as strong a light as I could."

A similar charge has been preferred against Mr. Pitt by others of his friends besides the King; and where many voices concur in pronouncing the same sentence, it may usually be taken for granted that there is some truth in the allegation. But where better motives are sufficient to account for the phenomena of political conduct, it is the part of Christian charity not to attribute it to worse. Mr. Pitt's conduct has been much misunderstood, or rather it has not been understood at all. A recent writer in the *Edinburgh Review*, with all the assistance which the memoirs hitherto published can give, says, " His conduct at this crisis was as unintelligible to those of his contemporaries to whom it was known, as it is to us at present:" and again, "We confess ourselves at a loss to justify, and scarcely even to explain, the course which he pursued; why, if he was willing to remain in March, he was so resolved on resigning in February, or why, if he was so resolved on resigning in February, he was so willing to remain in in March, we are equally unable to determine."

Nevertheless, with the additional light reflected on this transaction by the Rose papers, the explanation is not difficult. Besides that self-respect, which, though invidiously denominated pride, is felt more or less by every great man, the two motives, which from first to last most swayed Mr. Pitt's political conduct, were attachment to his sovereign, and his duty to the country. For the long period of seventeen years, they had worked together in perfect harmony; but now a case had occurred in which they were at variance, and which impelled them in opposite directions. He knew the King's aversion to the measure he proposed, and yet he thought it his duty to propose it. But why (if Sir George Rose was right in saying, that at that time the country did not want it) did he voluntarily and suddenly bring forward a measure which he knew must make a breach between the King and himself? For it is well known that he was bound by no engagement to the Roman Catholics. He had given them no pledge or promise of relief, and his own declared opinion was, that it was a remote contingency depending upon their good conduct. But it is probable that the report then current was correct; and that Lord Castlereagh was the person who introduced the question into the Cabinet, not from any hostility to the Church of England, of which there is no ground whatever to suspect him, but because, having been employed to bring about the union, in his anxiety to accomplish the task assigned to him, he had overstepped the bounds of discretion, and encouraged hopes which he was not authorized to inspire.

The majority of the Cabinet, however, having decided in favour of the concession, Mr. Pitt was bound to report that decision to the King. Perhaps he was not without a hope, that the influence by which his Majesty had so long been governed, might overcome the resistance which he foresaw; but he also foresaw, that the only alternative would be his own resignation of office, unless the King should be satisfied with the assurance, that he not only would not introduce the measure himself during his Majesty's reign, but that he would do all in his power to prevent the discussion of it in Parliament. It was necessary, however, that such an assurance should be accompanied by one stipulation, for the sake of the country. It was impossible to administer its affairs with any tolerable chance of success if it should appear that the Minister did not enjoy the full confidence of the Sovereign; if the servants of the Crown were opposed by the Crown, and the Cabinet defeated by the King's own friends.

The condition, therefore, of his sacrificing his opinion, and retaining office, was, that the King should not use his personal influence to control the proceedings of Parliament. To this demand, however, the King refused to accede, and Mr. Pitt resigned. But when he found that to this desertion of him the King attributed the derangement of his mind, his inflexibility melted at such a proof of the monarch's personal attachment, and he felt that, according to his own expression, in proportion to the difficulty which a sovereign might have in accepting the resignation of a minister, who, for good reasons, sought permission to retire, so ought to be his love for such a sovereign[1]; and this moved him to write the contrite letter mentioned by Lord Malmesbury, retracting, it may be supposed, the condition on which he had insisted before.

It may be doubted, however, whether this letter was ever actually sent; at least, no notice is taken of it in Mr. Rose's Diary, amongst the confidential communications which he had with Mr. Pitt. Yet the feeling which would have dictated that letter, plainly existed; for we learn from the Diary, that at that period Mr. Pitt showed much more willingness to return to office than he had ever done since his resignation; which, of course, indicated an unconditional submission to the King's wishes. But it is not, therefore, to be assumed that he acted upon this impulse. His own deliberate feelings upon the whole subject are

[1] Gifford's Life of Pitt, vol. vi. p. 599.

recorded by Lord Malmesbury, as communicated to Mr. Canning. He said that "he went out, not on the Catholic question simply, as a measure on which he was opposed, but from the manner in which he had been opposed; and to which, if he had assented, he would, as a minister, have been on a footing totally different from what he had ever before been in the Cabinet."

This obliged him to resign; but as his sincere wish was, that his going out should distress neither the King nor the country, he had required no one to follow him. Those who did so, did it voluntarily, and against his desire. He had quitted office, leaving behind him means and preparations so likely to insure success, both in the expedition to Egypt then pending, and in the proposed attack on the Northern Powers,[1] as to free him, in his own breast, from any deserved reproach of deserting his post at an hour of distress, and of abandoning war measures when they were in an unprovided or inauspicious situation. It had been his anxious hope and endeavour to leave behind him such a ministry as would be most agreeable to his Majesty; and who, on all great national points, would act on the same principles that he had acted on. For this purpose he had pledged himself, but himself singly, to advise and support the present ministry. This pledge he considered as solemnly binding, nor ever to be cancelled, without the express consent of Mr. Addington.

[1] The fruit of this was the battle of Copenhagen.

Being asked whether, in case of war, it would not be his duty to resume office, he said, "I do not deny it; I will not affect a childish modesty; but recollect what I have just said; I stand pledged. I make no scruple of owning that I am ambitious; but my ambition is character, not office. I may have engaged myself inconsiderately, but I am irrecoverably engaged." When he was asked whether he would not seek to be released from his engagement, he answered, "I cannot bring myself to do it. It is impossible to prevent its wearing the aspect of caballing and intriguing for power."

This plain statement of facts entirely demolishes the unjust surmises of the Marquis of Buckingham, who seems to have gloated over every malevolent report, and viewed every action of Mr. Pitt through the distorting medium of a venomous ill-will. It shows that his retirement was not a sham; and that Addington was not his creature, his agent, or his representative, in any sense of preconcerted subordination, though the latter was weak enough *at first* to call himself his *locum tenens;* but, having tasted the sweets of office, he determined to hold it as long as he could, without consulting his friend, or attempting to secure his approbation of the measures by which the country was to be governed.

The hostility of the Grenvilles, after their long and intimate union with Mr. Pitt, is explained by an observation of Mr. Canning's. Lord Grenville, he said, cannot be persuaded but that Lord Buckingham would be a good and popular Prime Minister; and whenever his family come upon him with this idea, it bears down before it every other consideration. Such was his subserviency to his brother, who was infinitely inferior to himself in abilities and character, and who was described by Lord Mahon, on the evidence of his letters, as steeped in selfishness and pride, that though he had previously been ready to declare that the Catholic question was completely abandoned, and considered by him quite gone by and dead, and that the strongest assurances of this might be given to the King; yet afterwards, under the influence of his brother, he retracted, because he found that the question which he, on his part, had agreed to consider as given up, was by no means so readily to be put aside by others.[1] They were all piqued at finding that the Marquis was not held in the same consideration by Mr. Pitt, as in his own family, and vented their spleen in captious animadversions upon his conduct; yet that conduct, it is now perfectly clear, was dictated by principles which it is impossible not to admire.

The union with Ireland had brought the question of repealing the Roman Catholic disabilities into discussion in the Cabinet, the result of which was that Mr. Pitt concurred with the majority of his colleagues in judging that to grant the repeal

[1] Lord Malmesbury's Diary.

would be the wisest policy. Perhaps he foresaw that the time would come when it would be inevitable. But he felt no immediate necessity for forcing it forward; and he was unwilling to harass the mind of a Sovereign whose unvarying affection he had enjoyed for so long a time, and to embitter his life, which was not likely to have a long duration, by insisting upon a measure to which he was conscientiously opposed, and which the country not only did not demand, but probably viewed with apprehension and dislike. As the friend of the King, therefore, Mr. Pitt thought himself justified in engaging, as far as depended on him, to postpone the agitation of this question. But then, there were other duties to be taken into account. He was at the head of the Government, and maintained in that high position, not only by royal favour, but by the confidence of a large majority of the people of England; and it was his opinion, that he could not carry on that government with credit to himself, or advantage to the country, if he had to encounter a new sort of opposition,—the opposition of the King —or if any of the Opposition, or of his own colleagues, who did not concur in his views, and were not actuated by his motives, should bring forward the question, a case might arise in which it would be necessary for him either to suppress his conscientious convictions, or find himself at war with his sovereign, and perhaps defeated by the party called the King's friends. This he thought it necessary to guard against, by stipulating that no such party should be formed against him.

When, therefore, the King, conceiving that neutrality in such a cause would be treason to the Church, which his coronation oath bound him to defend, refused to abstain from exercising his influence to defeat the measure, nothing remained for Mr. Pitt but to resign his office. Still he was sincerely anxious that neither the King nor the country should suffer from his retirement, and therefore desired that his successor should be a personal friend of the King, and at the same time one who would continue to follow the same policy, which, in his judgment, was best for the country both at home and abroad: at home by the similarity of his financial arrangements, and abroad by strenuous warfare, or an honourable peace. He suggested no one; but when the King sent for Mr. Addington, who was on terms of intimacy with both, he thought his object was attained, and found out too late how much he was mistaken. The consequence was, that he not only promised Mr. Addington his support, but wished his friends to serve under him; for his own resignation was from motives entirely personal, and peculiar to his position; so much so, that he took no counsel, even of his closest intimates, till the die was cast and the act of his abdication signed.

But we must now go back to the spring of this year, when a cold interchange of letters took place between Mr. Rose and Lord Auckland, both bewailing the resignation of Mr. Pitt, but with a mutual reserve, which soon afterwards broke out into open hostility; for on the 21st of March, Lord Auckland, thinking himself aggrieved by it, because no provision had been made for him, attacked Mr. Pitt in the House of Lords, in a manner, which drew this remark from Lord Malmesbury:—" Lord Auckland has received from Mr. Pitt obligations that no minister but one possessing the power of Pitt could bestow, or any one less eager for office than Lord Auckland ask; yet scarcely has he left office, than Lord Auckland insinuates that he did it from some concealed motive, and that the ostensible one is insincere." For this speech Lord Auckland was much abused; and Mr. Rose, who was probably personally touched by the censure, resented it so much, that he declined all further intercourse with his ungrateful friend.

MR. ROSE TO LORD AUCKLAND.

"Saturday Evening, March 21st, 1801.

"The account I have had this day of what fell from your Lordship in the House of Lords last night, must interrupt the intercourse I have had with your Lordship during the last fourteen or fifteen years. Ever since I have mixed in public matters I have thought it possible that persons taking different lines in politics (separated very widely indeed on subjects of that sort) might mix pleasantly in private society, at least occasionally. But there are circumstances in the present case of so peculiar a nature as to render that impossible with respect to your Lordship and me. It would be as painful to me to enter upon these as I think it would be to you to have them even more directly alluded to. You will, of course, not take the trouble of calling on me for the papers we talked about this morning."

CHAPTER VIII.

1801.

CORRESPONDENCE AND NEGOTIATIONS RESPECTING THE PAYMENT OF MR. PITT'S DEBTS IN 1801, BETWEEN MR. ROSE, THE BISHOP OF LINCOLN, AND LORD CAMDEN—11,700*l*. SUBSCRIBED BY MR. PITT'S FRIENDS—THE KING'S OFFER DECLINED—MR. PITT'S FRIENDS URGE HIM TO WITHDRAW HIS SUPPORT FROM THE ADDINGTON ADMINISTRATION, ON A STRONG SUSPICION OF TREACHERY BEING INTENDED TOWARDS HIM.

MR. PITT's mind was so much devoted to public business, and engrossed by the affairs of the nation, that he entirely forgot his domestic concerns, and the duties of regulating his household. The consequence was, as might well be expected, that he became the prey of unprincipled men; his tradesmen and his servants plundered him at their discretion; for instance, in one year, the charge for his servants in London and at Hollwood—their wages, board wages, liveries, and bills, amounted to more than 2,900*l*. It may be supposed, that the large amounts entered against him for his stable and his housekeeping were neither controlled nor understood by him; but the heavy expense of his cellar, it is probable, was too well known and sanctioned. He was a great drinker of port wine, but he had no other extravagant taste. He was not a collector of costly curiosities or works

of art; he was not a speculator in schemes for
making money, or for spending it; he had no turn,
as his father had, for ostentatious extravagance; his
debts were not like those of Charles Fox, the effect of
gambling and profligacy. When in both cases the
partisans of the respective leaders offered to raise money
for their payment, Mr. Fox had no scruple in accepting their assistance, though a sense of honour induced
him from that time to abstain from gambling, which
was so much the more meritorious in him, because he
is recorded to have said, that the greatest pleasure in
life was to win a game of hazard, and the next was to
lose it. But Mr. Pitt was too proud to consent to be
treated like a pauper, living on charity, at the expense
of others; and when it was mentioned to him, he said
he would sooner return to his early profession, and
earn enough by practice at the bar to discharge his
debts. This, no doubt, he might have accomplished
without much difficulty, if he had remained out of
office; for who would not have been anxious to
employ his powers of oratory? George III. testified
his regard for so faithful a servant in the handsomest
way, by offering to pay 30,000*l.* out of the privy
purse, but, with the delicacy of true affection, desired
that it might not be known from what quarter the
payment came. No better proof than this can be
wanted of the truth of Wilberforce's statement, that
" the King and Pitt part on affectionate terms; the
King saying that 'it is a struggle between duty and

affection, in which duty carries it.'" But this most liberal offer was declined. Nevertheless, Mr. Pitt was reduced to the greatest extremities, and the trial was severe; for this great political financier not having been able to control his own finances, or to attend to the administration of his private revenues, his debts amounted to 45,864*l.*, and now that he was out of office, his creditors became clamorous. Executions were threatened, his houses were in danger of being stripped of their furniture, and his stables of their horses. In this emergency some of his most intimate friends came forward to his relief, by contributing a sum of money, which he was content to receive in the light of a loan, to avert the pressure of his most imminent embarrassments, and to save him from the mortifications and distresses which hung over his path. That sum was 11,700*l.* The proportions subscribed, as well as the general state of Mr. Pitt's debts at that time, will be given at the close of the following correspondence between the Bishop of Lincoln, Lord Camden, and Mr. Rose. Their letters show the timidity with which they approached the subject, and their great fear of offending Mr. Pitt, and meeting with a rebuff.—Ed.]

THE BISHOP OF LINCOLN TO MR. ROSE.

"MY DEAR SIR,

"You may rest assured that Mr. Pitt's assigned reason for not going to the Cambridge commemoration was considered unsatisfactory; but still, things remaining as they now are, I do not think that any opposition either to him or to Lord Euston would prevail. I have no expectation of seeing Mr. Pitt at Buckden, and indeed a visit to me without going to Cambridge, would only aggravate the offence. He cannot go to Cambridge before November with any propriety. It is exactly with me as it is with you;—the more I consider Mr. Pitt's debts, the more distressed and perplexed I am; but I think you consider relief as more practicable than I do. Lord Alvanley dined here on Tuesday, on his way to York, and came two hours before dinner, principally, I believe, to talk to me upon this subject. I found that Lord Camden had been talking to him, and that Lord C. had seen Joe Smith, and had likewise mentioned the subject to Lord Carrington. Lord Camden said that some of the creditors were growing very importunate, and that there was real danger of violent measures being soon taken against Mr. Pitt's horses, carriages, or furniture, at Hollwood or Walmer. Nothing had occurred to Lord C. and Lord A. but some subscription amongst Mr. Pitt's private friends; but then, of course, the difficulty of Mr. Pitt's consent, or acting without his knowledge, occurred; and also the difficulty of raising a sufficient sum. Lord Camden and Lord Carrington talked of 1,000*l.* each, but afterwards Lord Camden said they would go farther. Lord Alvanley said that he would give nothing which should diminish his principal;—he meant that he would advance only such a sum as could be spared

out of his income, but mentioned no specific sum.
I went so far with him as to say I had reason to
think that there was more difficulty in applying than
in raising the money; and that I believed the money
would be ready, if any mode could be devised for
paying the debts which should not be liable to
serious objections. He seemed to think that the
debts might be paid, and the receipts sent to Mr.
Pitt. But then, who is to pay the debts, and what is
he to say when questioned by Mr. Pitt? We parted
without being able to fix upon any plan. Indeed I
do not think our friend Lord A. a very good man for
such a business. The enclosed is a copy of a paper
which Lord Camden received from Joe Smith. If
Mr. Pitt would allow Hollwood to be sold by auction,
it would certainly sell for more than by any other mode;
and there might also be a contrivance for increasing
the sum. Would he consent to an auction? or does
he think of that mode of selling? To give more
than a common broker or purchaser would give, in
the common way, would be a very inadequate relief.
To offer *much more* than the real worth of the thing to
be disposed of, would immediately excite suspicion in
Mr. Pitt's mind, and wholly defeat the scheme. To
give a *little more* would answer no purpose. The
largeness of the debts is a great obstacle to any indirect
method of relief. I do not feel the confidence, I
must own, which you do, in the thing remaining a
secret if done by the King; and were it to be so
done, and ever known to Mr. Pitt, the mischief might
be very serious. Do not, however, suppose that I

fall short of you in reverence and admiration of the King's character. I entirely agree with you that Hollwood should not be kept. I am most decidedly of opinion that you may consult the Lord Chancellor, unless before you see him any practicable mode of effecting this great business shall have occurred—of which I despair.

"I am sorry that you have no faith in the conversation said to have passed between the King and Sir J. Banks. Is his Majesty satisfied that Mr. Pitt, during his Majesty's life, whether in office or out of office, would never bring forward the Catholic question? It seems to me very material that this should be strongly impressed upon his mind. I fear at Weymouth you will not have much opportunity for private conversation. Besides your objection to the scheme upon the score of disingenuity, it is a very important question, whether Mr. Pitt, upon discovering so peculiar an obligation to the King, would not refuse ever to take office again.

"Adieu, my dear sir. I shall be most anxious to hear from you.

"Believe me always most truly and
"cordially yours,
"G. LINCOLN.

"Buckden Palace, July 16th, 1801.

"Dundas has certainly a very fair claim to a peerage, and there ought to be no difficulty about it."

LORD CAMDEN TO MR. ROSE.

[*Most secret.*]

"DEAR ROSE,

"As I am confident there is no person more interested than you are in Mr. Pitt's public character and private convenience, I feel no difficulty in writing to you on a subject in a great degree connected with both those circumstances;—I mean the state of his affairs. In conversing with two or three of Mr. Pitt's friends most confidentially, I learn from the best authority, what I too well guessed before, that unless some arrangement takes place, and he is enabled to discharge a portion of his debts, he will suffer the greatest inconvenience.

"From communications I have had with Mr. Pitt himself upon this subject, I am convinced it will be more difficult to induce him to listen to any loan from his friends, than to induce them to offer it, and various expedients have suggested themselves to me in order to relieve him; but I am convinced, upon reflection, that he will discover any attempt to discharge his debts without his knowledge, and will be displeased at that sort of conduct in his friends. It has, therefore, been thought best that upon the review he cannot fail to be obliged to take of his affairs, it should be stated to him, which Long and Smith have undertaken to do, that it is impossible to discharge the bills that are owing, unless a sum of money is raised; that they know such a sum can be raised, if he chooses, without any interest being paid; but as we are sure from what he has said that he will not allow of that sort of loan, the payment of, or at least the undertaking on his part to pay, the interest, must be submitted to. Long and Smith have also undertaken to tell Mr. Pitt that they can procure the money, but that he must not know the source. This secrecy is absolutely requisite, and without it I certainly can have no share in it. With it I have been desirous of taking as active a part in the transaction as I can: 18,000*l.* or 20,000*l.* is the least sum which, together with the sale of Hollwood, upon which Long writes me word he has determined, will relieve him. There are those who are ready and desirous to give or to lend some part of this sum, and they are Mr. Pitt's most intimate and confidential friends; beyond these I think we ought not to apply, and there would indeed be little chance, if we did, of retaining the secret. Those who can afford it have agreed to lend 1,000*l.*,—or more, if they please;— those to whom such a sum is inconvenient will give 500*l.*, below which sum it is thought not proper to go.

"I have thus given you a sketch of this plan; if it were in my power to give you more details, I would do it; but I trust I have said enough to enlist you as our assistant in this undertaking, which I am aware there is no one so fit to direct. Pray let me hear from you, with an account of your opinion upon this business, and the sum you will be willing to lend upon it. Lord Carrington, Lord Bathurst, myself, Smith, Long, the Bishop of Lincoln, Lord Alvanley, and some others, are eager upon the subject. I do not mean to mention it to any of the present Administration.

"You had better direct to me in Arlington Street.

"Most sincerely yours,
"CAMDEN.

"Bayham Abbey, July 23rd, 1801."

THE BISHOP OF LINCOLN TO MR. ROSE.

"MY DEAR SIR,

"I thank you for your short note and long letter. I believe the 5,800*l.* to be a separate debt of Mr. Pitt's, originally charged upon Burton, for which Lady Chatham ought to pay interest, but does not. The security was transferred to Coutts when he advanced the money. *I cannot bear the idea* of Mr. Pitt accepting any office in the gift of Mr. Addington. I cannot think that Hollwood would sell for 10,000*l.*, except it were by auction. I am very anxious you should have such a conversation as you propose with Mr. Pitt, when you see him at Cuffnells. You may, perhaps, gain from thence some new light. It cannot leave us in a more perplexed state than we are in at present, and I am confident he will not be offended at it. I have told Mr. Pitt that I should be at the Deanery next Friday noon, and that I should be glad to see him on that day, or any of the two or three following ones, if he be still in the neighbourhood of London. I have also written to Joe Smith. If I hear anything of importance, or anything passes between Mr. Pitt and me, you may depend upon my communicating it to you instantly.

"I really think that even if others were to bring forward the Catholic question, Mr. Pitt would find means of not acting contrary to the King's sentiments. *I am confident* he thinks so, and it seems to me highly important that the King should know it. Perhaps you may also ascertain this point when Mr. Pitt is at Cuffnells. I agree with you entirely about the private subscription amongst *friends;* the sum is far too large.

"I own I do not see any great objection to Mr. Pitt having a second sinecure place, provided it comes directly from the King, and it was understood that he owed it to him only. *The Pitts* are most perfectly out of the question in my judgment.

"Kindest compliments and wishes from Mrs. T. and myself.

"Yours, ever most truly and affectionately,

"G. LINCOLN.

"Buckden Palace, July 24th, 1801.

"Surely facts have proved to demonstration that Mr. Pitt was deceived with respect to the state of the Irish Catholics; and this may justify a change of sentiment, as upon the Reform Question.

"Pray remember the Prebendal Papers."

MR. ROSE TO LORD CAMDEN.

"MY DEAR LORD,

"You do me but justice in supposing that I feel great anxiety respecting Mr. Pitt's situation. I can say with the sincerest truth, that it disturbs me incessantly by night and by day. I had a long conversation with Mr. Pitt on the subject, before I left London, which I became less satisfied with in proportion as I reflected on his statements, unquestionably sanguine ones. This led me into a correspondence with the Bishop of Lincoln, full and explicit on all points of the case, and on the possible ways of extricating Mr. Pitt, as any *probable* ones, I own I cannot devise; for he has most unequivocally declared to me that no consideration shall induce him to accept of relief from Parliament (if he could even be sure of an unanimous vote), or from the King, who, if we may judge from former circumstances, has it not to give; or from individuals. He will not, I think, easily be brought to submit to promise not to ask who *lends* the money, because he knows that in his situation a loan is a positive gift. I am not sure whether I ever told you, that in the spring of 1789 the merchants of London agreed to raise 100,000*l.*, and to present it to him as a token of their gratitude for his services to the country, and of their warm approbation of his public conduct. One body of them raised their proportion of 20,000*l.* instantly. The remainder would have been completed in a few days, of which I had intimation, with assurances that not a name of a subscriber would ever be known to Mr. Pitt; and not choosing he should be taken by surprise, I mentioned it to him, when he desired me to express to the party from whom I had my information, his positive and unalterable determination never to receive a shilling in that mode. The subscription now proposed would certainly be a cheaper one, but in my own mind, there are objections to it stronger than to the other, unless it can be confined to an extremely small number of most intimate and confidential friends. Would it be fair to subject him to obligations to persons, who, however liberally and disinterestedly they may feel, he would not like to be obliged to? For myself, tho smallness of my means will hardly be believed, but I am willing to take from those who can ill spare it (I mean Mrs. Rose and my daughters), to contribute to make up the sum wanted. I cannot, consistently with my feelings, avoid saying this; and yet it might, to some, savour of ostentation, with the impression on my mind, that Mr. Pitt will not avail himself of a subscription. I think 25,000*l.* must be found to put him at ease; to raise which more than thirty persons must of course contribute, if the subscription is to be made up of sums of 1,000*l.* and 500*l.* Are there half of that number you would choose to call upon?

"In my last letter to the Bishop of Lincoln, a few days ago, I told him my determination to state distinctly to Mr. Pitt the absolute necessity of his availing himself of *some mode* of assistance to avoid the consequences you allude to, which would certainly be injurious to him as a public man, and, of necessity, to the country, the interests of which are inseparable from his conduct and character; and would be not less painful to the feelings of himself and his friends. I expect to see him soon on his way to Weymouth and to his mother; and I have a plan to propose to him, easy and certain in execution if he will acquiesce in it, that I have not

thought myself at liberty to allude to in the remotest
possible way to any human being except the Bishop
of Lincoln, which I *think infinitely less exceptionable*
than a subscription of twenty or thirty persons, and
which would leave him in possession of a very large
part of his income. If he refuses that, the other mode
may be resorted to on his return to London, and I
should hope Smith might, by seeing the most urgent
of the creditors, prevent any disagreeable measures
being taken during that interval. If, however, your
Lordship is clearly of opinion that a subscription
should be entered into immediately, tell me so, and
I will explain to you with the utmost fairness my
pecuniary situation, and what I will contribute. You
will have the goodness to consider the *particulars* I
have here entered into as strictly confidential and to
be confined to yourself. I feel myself on most delicate
ground, and surrounded with difficulties. You will, I
hope, be able to devise means of deferring the measure
thought of for two or three months without referring
to me, if you shall concur in thinking it advisable to
do so. I agree with you most entirely in the propriety of not communicating on the subject, in any
event, with persons in the present Administration;
but I am persuaded your Lordship would not include
Steele in that number, nor Ryder, if he was in a state
to be spoken to. I am grieved to the heart at the
accounts I hear of the latter. He can very ill be spared.
You know as well as I do, the correctness of the judgment of both, and their cordial attachment to Mr. Pitt.

If the subscription shall be decided on, I know no man living I should more wish to be consulted than Steele.

"I am, my dear Lord,
"Very truly yours,
"GEORGE ROSE.

"College, Christchurch, July 26th.

"The objections to the subscription plan (to me insurmountable) are of a nature which prevents my committing them to paper in a hurry, even to your Lordship. I will cheerfully go as far as Farnham, under the colour of a visit to the Bishop of Winchester, more than sixty miles from hence, to meet you, that we may talk these matters over, if you shall wish it; or even to London if it shall be thought essential; though in the present state of my health, I had rather avoid the latter, for I am still forced to observe strict rules. I write this by return of post. If anything further occurs to me, you shall hear from me again."

THE BISHOP OF LINCOLN TO MR. ROSE.

"MY DEAR SIR,
"Yesterday's post brought me your letter, enclosing Smith's; and it also brought me a letter from Lord Camden. I believe I mentioned to you that I had a long conversation, at the Deanery, with Lord C. just before I left town, about Mr. Pitt's affairs. This letter is to inform me, that Mr. Pitt had consented to a sum of money being raised, by way of loan, amongst his friends, but he does not know whether it be pro-

posed that interest should be paid; that is, this point seems not to be settled. That it is intended to apply to *intimate* friends only; that Mr. Pitt is not to know from whom the money comes; that 18,000*l.* or 20,000*l.* are to be raised; that those who can afford it, are to advance 1000*l.*, or more if they please, and none less than 500*l.*; and that a progress is made to the amount of 7000*l.* or 8000*l.* Lord C. seems himself to have had no conversation with Mr. Pitt, but only with Long, Smith, and Lord Alvanley; and Mr. Pitt's consent seems to have been communicated by Long. I was rather at a loss to know what answer to give; but I have just written to him, that it is to no purpose to discuss whether this be the best plan that could be devised. That being the only one to which Mr. Pitt would consent, it must be adopted by his real friends, and acted upon with zeal and discretion. That the two principal points to be attended to were, secrecy and care not to apply to any person to whom Mr. Pitt ought not to owe such a favour. That I despaired of secrecy, as so many must be privy to it. That with a view to give it as little resemblance as possible to the subscription for Fox, the money should be advanced as a loan, not as a gift (Lord C. in his letter had mentioned gift); and also upon interest, without the slightest idea or wish in the contributors that either principal or interest should ever be paid. That at the end of the year, Mr. Pitt's affairs should be looked over, and if there should be any surplus, which there certainly would not be, it should go as interest; and that Mr. Pitt's friends would not suffer any debt incurred in the year to remain undischarged at the end of it. Have I said anything wrong or improper? I have not mentioned your name, or alluded to our correspondence, or the subject of it. Shall I say anything about you, or will you write to Lord Camden, or Long, or Smith? I forgot to say that I had declared myself ready to contribute 1000*l.*, and that I would mention the subject to the Bishop of London and another friend; and that I considered 20,000*l.* at least as necessary. The precise sum of course depends upon the price that Hollwood and the reversion of the pension sell for. Will they together produce 20,000*l.*? I think they would, if Hollwood were sold by auction, to which I shall press Mr. Pitt, if I see him. Could the King be informed of this plan, and if so could he be permitted to contribute? This seems to me a very nice and delicate point. Let me hear from you, if possible, by return of post, and in that case direct your letter hither. If you do not write till Wednesday, direct to the Deanery, where I shall be on Friday noon. I entirely agree with you in your distinction of *true* and *fair* value, and I am also satisfied that all Mr. Pitt's property of all sorts, if sold in the ordinary way, would not clear him. My mind is a little relieved at the prospect of something being done to which he will not object. I feel very anxious that his feelings should be consulted, though I am fully aware of his thoughtlessness, blameable thoughtlessness, in this respect. I cannot bear the idea of his having less than his Cinque Ports to live upon, or at least

2,500*l.* a year. He cannot live upon less with any degree of comfort. I shall be impatient to hear from you. If I see Mr. Pitt in town, may I state to him the King's proposal to you, that Mr. P. may be in possession of all circumstances before any step is taken, or shall I mention it to Lord Camden, if I see him? He wrote to me from Bayham Abbey, but he seems not stationary there, as he desired me to direct my answer to town. I have told him that I shall be in London on Friday, for two or three days, and perhaps he may wish to have some conversation with me. Adieu; kindest compliments and wishes.

"Yours, ever most truly, and affectionately,

"G. LINCOLN.

"Buckden Palace, July 26th, 1801."

LORD CAMDEN TO MR. ROSE.

[*Most secret.*]

"Bayham Abbey, July 28th, 1801.

"DEAR ROSE,

"I agree in many of the suggestions in your letter, and in the wisdom of many of your observations. I have been induced to interest myself in this business from the persuasion that communication and correspondence will bring matters into some train, although it may not be precisely that which is the subject of the first proposal. I am by no means wedded to the particular plan I have mentioned, which has been proposed to me by Long and Smith, and is not calculated to raise so large a sum as 25,000*l.*: but I hope that a smaller sum than that will answer a very good purpose. As Mr. Pitt's particular friends are now dispersed, it is not probable that any great progress will be made in the transaction upon which we have corresponded; and you will therefore, I doubt not, have ample time to speak to Mr. Pitt upon the proposition you have to submit to him. Another mode in which Mr. Pitt might be induced to accept the assistance of his friends, would perhaps be, that they should enter into joint bonds with him, and that then they (his friends) should raise the money, and pay it to the nominal person who advances it upon that security. This would prevent the *danger* of *joint bonds*, to which I am extremely averse; but then the secrecy cannot be preserved. All my anxiety is to preserve Mr. Pitt's mind from the embarrassment, and his character from the imputation, which executions and actions for debt always cast upon a man; and whether by subscription, loan, or gift, or by any trouble I can take, I can relieve him, I shall conceive my time and my money well employed. I am therefore ready to listen to and adopt any suggestion calculated to the object; but as Mr. Pitt has so many friends interested for his ease and credit, do not let us suffer him to lose the benefit of such a connexion. You will, therefore, let me hear from you when you think yourself at liberty to communicate any further. I certainly did not mean to exclude Steele and Ryder, to both of whom I feel in the same manner as you do. Bathurst and Long have communicated with the former. I imagined the latter too ill to be addressed on such a subject. I do not think it will

be of essential use that we should meet at present, and
I also, who have not been well, should find a journey
to Farnham not advantageous to my health; and at
present I really think it unnecessary. If anything
occurs, you shall hear from me; and I hope to hear
from you, when you have anything to tell me.

"Most truly, sincerely yours,
"CAMDEN."

THE BISHOP OF LINCOLN TO MR. ROSE.

"MY DEAR SIR,

"The letter which I wrote to you on Sunday
makes any detailed observations upon the letters
which I received from you this morning unnecessary.
I return them, and at the same time I send you Lord
Camden's letter to me. I have no copy of mine to
him, but I mentioned to you the substance of it. I
now rather doubt whether I was right in concluding
that Mr. Pitt had said he would consent to the loan,
&c. I inferred it from these words, "to which he
will consent," in Lord C.'s letter to me, page 2.
I shall write to Lord C. to ask an explanation
upon that point by to-day's post. The more I consider this most distressing business, the more I am
convinced of the importance of laying immediately
before Mr. Pitt the King's proposal. I cannot bear
the idea of anything being done from that quarter
without Mr. Pitt's knowledge, and Mr. Pitt ought to
be apprised of every circumstance before he decides.
I really think that a delay of two or three months
should not be risked, at least, not without con-

sulting Smith, who is better acquainted than you or
I with the disposition of the creditors. I fear some
of them are very clamorous. I received a letter from
Mr. Pitt this morning, in which he says, that I shall
find a note from him at the Deanery on Friday
morning, fixing either Friday or Saturday for me to
dine with him in Park Place. I am engaged to dine
with the Bishop of London, at Fulham, on Friday;
but I shall, of course, put off that engagement and
dine with Mr. Pitt, if he should fix Friday. I will
make a point of having a full conversation with him
about his affairs, and the modes of relief, with or
without mentioning to him his Majesty's proposal, as
you shall direct in the letter which I expect to receive
from you here on Thursday, or to find at the Deanery
on Friday. If I by any accident shall not hear from
you, I shall, of course, say not a syllable about his
Majesty's proposal. The great point seems to be to
make Mr. Pitt consent to something effectual, which
will leave him a comfortable income and not embarrass
him in any respect in future.

"Lord Camden's idea that Mr. Pitt is not to know
who subscribe, seems to me a very good one. I think
you see this subscription in a stronger point of view
than I do. Indeed, I think it very objectionable, and
that it cannot be kept secret; but considering it as
the only plan to which Mr. Pitt would consent, I am
disposed to try it. Something must be done, and without assistance Mr. Pitt would, as you first observed,
be left literally without a shilling. Adieu. Kindest
remembrance to all your ladies. I scarcely know

whether to direct this letter to Cuffnells or the College.

"Yours, always most truly and affectionately,

"G. LINCOLN.

"Buckden Palace, July 28th, 1801.

"Pray return Lord Camden's letter, and remember my Prebendal Papers."

THE BISHOP OF LINCOLN TO MR. ROSE.

"MY DEAR SIR,

"I have had a pretty full conversation with Mr. Pitt about his affairs, and upon the whole am inclined to think that he would agree to a subscription; but, I am decidedly of opinion that he ought to have laid before him every plan and idea which is in contemplation before he determines upon any one. I also think that something must be done, as speedily as may be. No one can state to him so properly, and with so fair a hope of success as yourself, the King's proposal; consequently, I think that it would be right, and may be useful, that you should come to town as soon as possible; and as some preparation, I have just now told him that you have *something* of a very delicate and important nature, relative to his private affairs, to communicate to him, and that you are not unwilling to come to town on Tuesday for the purpose of stating it to him. He said that he would see you at any time on Wednesday morning you would fix. I thought, that if I did not mention the business thus far to him, he might be out of town, and you might wait several days without seeing him. As a further strong reason for your coming, I am persuaded that Mr. Pitt will not go into the west for some weeks, and he already thinks that it may be best for him to go straight for Burton; and then afterwards, if he has time, make his other visits. Therefore there is some doubt whether you will see him at all at Cuffnells, and certainly not for six or eight weeks, and I think much longer.— All these things put together, I think it pretty clear that you will set out from Southampton on Tuesday morning, and arrive in town either that evening or Wednesday morning; and I have determined to stay in town to see you, though I really must a second time put off my father and mother from coming to Buckden, which will give me a good deal of pain:— but I am very anxious to see you and to talk with you, and I do not like to leave London without some plan being settled, or at least some better prospect of a decision than there is at present. I think it may be right for Long to come to town too when you are here, but I see no use in Steele or Lord Camden being here; but if you are of a different opinion you will write or send to them. I say nothing more, as I really have not time to enter upon the particular subjects of your letter written yesterday, and as I hope to see you so soon. Mr. Pitt is very well. I write in Park Place. Adieu.

"Yours, most truly and affectionately,

"G. LINCOLN.

"I will meet you in Palace Yard any hour you may fix.

"Saturday, August 1st."

THE BISHOP OF LINCOLN TO MR. ROSE.

"MY DEAR SIR,

"The conversation with Mr. Pitt yesterday was very short. We first examined the statement which was placed before us in Hill Street, and Mr. Pitt made some deductions and some additions, in consequence of money which had been paid and debts incurred since that paper was made out. The result was more favourable by about 2,000*l.* as I thought: he thought by about 3,000*l.* I then told him that some of the creditors were extremely importunate and put to serious inconveniences by the want of the money, and that it was very much to be wished that the debts of all the common tradesmen, at least, which were to a large amount, should be immediately discharged; and all other plans being rejected there remained only the one which I had mentioned to him the day before,— namely, the assistance of private friends.—To this he expressed his readiness to accede. I then asked him whether he persisted in his determination to know the names of those friends from whom he was to receive this assistance: he answered, most certainly. I then told him that the matter had been considered, and that six of his friends, namely, Lord Camden, Steele, Rose, Long, Smith, and myself, were ready to stand forward and put his affairs into such a situation immediately, that he might assure himself that he would suffer no inconvenience or embarrassment from his creditors. He signified his consent without a moment's hesitation, and added, there were no persons to whom he had rather owe a kindness or accommodation than those whom I had mentioned. I instantly said, 'Then I believe, sir, we need not trouble you any further; you and J. Smith can engage for the thing being done.' Thus ended the conversation. I went and told Lord Camden, who seemed perfectly satisfied with what had passed. I then returned and sat with Mr. Pitt alone at least half an hour. He said nothing about this particular plan, but mentioned an idea of insuring his life, and assigning the policy as a security for the money he borrows. I am inclined to think that this would be a better scheme than selling a part of his Cinque Ports, and ought perhaps to be adopted in preference to any other, if he resolves to do something. I am confident he *means* to pay interest, and I think he will not be easy unless he provides some security for the principal. He thinks he shall want, after the sale of Hollwood and his reversion, about 12,000*l.*; the interest and insurance of which sum would be about 1000*l.* a year. But that point, when I have leisure, I can ascertain accurately. I wish him to do nothing, and I do not despair of the thing working on as it is. You will observe that neither the whole sum to be advanced by these six persons, nor the proportion of each, was mentioned. I thought it a great point to get the business left to us in this general manner, and shall be happy to hear that you approve what passed.

"The above is a copy of what I wrote to Long, and having the same story to tell you, and very little time, I troubled Mrs. T. to copy it. When you go to Weymouth, do not forget the Catholic question. Remember my Prebendal Papers. All well here. Kindest compliments.

"Yours, ever most truly,
"G. LINCOLN.

"Buckden Palace, August 7th, 1801."

THE BISHOP OF LINCOLN TO MR. ROSE.

"MY DEAR SIR,

"I am very glad that you think of going to Weymouth, and I am impatient that you should have the conversation with the King. Recollect that when the King was recovering from his illness, Mr. Pitt saw Dr. J. Willis at Mr. Addington's; and before Mr. Addington, authorized Dr. Willis to tell his Majesty that during his reign he would *never* agitate the Catholic question; that is, whether *in* office or *out* of office. Mr. Pitt left Dr. Willis and Mr. Addington together. I saw Dr. Willis's letter to Mr. Pitt, and I suspect that the message was not properly and fully delivered. All this is of course private history, but I think it very important. Joe Smith has sent for Bullock from town, and as soon as there are *means* the bills will begin to be discharged. Soane's office has offered only 19,000*l.* for the pension of 2,000*l.* a year for the three lives of Lady Chatham, Lord Chatham, and Mr. Pitt, which is a *Jewish* offer. I have desired Smith to apply to other offices. *Pray* send my Prebendal Papers, as the Prebend is near lapsing. Mrs. T. thanks Miss Rose for her letter. Kindest compliments, and every possible good wish to you all. Adieu.

"Yours, always most cordially,
"G. LINCOLN.

"Buckden Palace, August 14th, 1801.

"Our wheat is all carried, and I hear from every quarter excellent accounts of the harvest."

THE BISHOP OF LINCOLN TO MR. ROSE.

"MY DEAR SIR,

"I am confident that Mr. Pitt's message and the determination of his own mind were not confined to his bringing forward the question himself. Mrs. Pretyman now recollects the account which I gave her of this business at the time, and she is certain that the words I used were, that the 'Catholic question should never again give his Majesty any trouble during his reign.'

"It was expected, as you know, that the Opposition would bring forward the question last session; and Mr. Pitt's intention was to have resisted it upon this ground,—that such a proposition ought to be brought forward only by his Majesty's ministers, and that he should oppose it now, and at all future times, whenever it should be brought forward from any other quarter.

"This is a general principle, and would apply to all times and cases, even, indeed, if another King were on the throne. It is true that Mr. Pitt cannot prevent the discussion, but he may always find means to get rid of the question. What those precise means may be, will depend upon circumstances at the time, but I am positive you may answer for this; that Mr. Pitt will never bring forward the Catholic question himself, and that he will resist it if brought forward by another, during the King's reign: and this, whether Mr. Pitt be in office or not. Surely he was as much pledged upon the question of reform, as upon the Catholic question. The former he had actually moved; the latter he has not. The enclosed is perfectly correct and proper. I prefer the words in the parenthesis, and it does not appear to me necessary to add, ' during your Majesty's reign:' that is understood.

"I thought the paper alluded to by you a most imprudent and unfortunate one, but I was not aware that Mr. Pitt adopted it in any degree that would fetter him hereafter. I have no copy of it. I perfectly agree with you in what you say of such pledges.

"I have only time to add our kindest wishes to all our good friends at Cuffnells.

"Yours, most truly and affectionately, &c.

"G. LINCOLN.

" Buckden Palace, August 18th, 1801."

ESTIMATE OF MR. PITT'S DEBTS IN 1801.

To Coutts, advanced upon security of Burton Pynsent	£5,000
Ditto. on Bond	6,000
Ditto. overdrawn	1,750
Mortgage, Hollwood	11,000
State of Debts, 1st of February	7,408
Old Debts, Hollwood	2,190
Mr. Soane	2,098
Bills unpaid	9,618
	£45,064

CONTRIBUTORS TO THE SUM OF £11,700 ADVANCED IN 1801.

Lord Camden		£1,000
Lord Bathurst		1,000
Bishop of Lincoln		1,000
Lord Carrington		1,000
Mr. Steele		1,000
Mr. Rose		1,000
From Scotland, supposed to be—		
Lord Melville	£1,000	
Duke of Buccleugh	1,000	
Duke of Gordon	1,000	
Chief Baron	1,000	
		4,000
Mr. Wilberforce		500
Mr. Long		500
Mr. Joseph Smith		500
Uncertain, probably from Lord Alvanley		200
		£11,700

[On the 1st of October, 1801, Mr. Pitt showed how much he was in the confidence of the Government at that time, by sending to his correspondent the first intimation of the preliminaries of peace being signed, before the fact was publicly known.—ED.]

MR. PITT TO MR. ROSE.

"Park Place, Oct. 1st, 1801, 6 P.M.

"DEAR ROSE,

"Though I have but a moment to save the post, I must send you one hasty line, to tell you that the die is at length cast, and the preliminaries are actually signed. I am not at liberty to-day to mention particulars, but I think I can venture to promise you that the terms, though perhaps not in every point exactly what one should wish, are, on the whole, advantageous, and certainly very creditable to the country. I hope to be able to send you a fuller account tomorrow or next day. The signature has but just taken place, and will not be made public till tomorrow morning.

"Ever sincerely yours,

"W. Pitt."

Mr. Pitt to Mr. Rose.

"Park Place, Oct. 3d, 1801.

"Dear Rose,

"On coming to town this morning for a few hours, I have just found your two letters. I will, with the greatest pleasure, take an early opportunity of mentioning your son to Lord Hawkesbury, who will, I flatter myself, be very favourably inclined to consider his pretensions; but I think it would be clearly desirable that he should also himself state his wish to be considered as a candidate for any proper situation in the foreign line, and that you should, at the same time, write to Lord Hawkesbury.

"I hope the particulars which you will have received by this morning's post, from Hiley, will have answered your expectation.

"Ever sincerely yours,

"W. Pitt."

Mr. Pitt to Mr. Rose.

"Park Place, Monday, Oct. 26th, 1801.

"Dear Rose,

"I received your letter yesterday morning, just as I was setting out from Walmer. All the sentiments it states are precisely those which I feel, and in which, I think, all moderate and dispassionate men will concur; but I fear there are some of our friends who will not be found to be of that number. I am very glad that you have determined to come up, and, if it will really be no inconvenience to you to be in town on Wednesday, I shall be much obliged to you, as there are many points connected with finance on which I wish much to converse with you, and on which I have some large projects in my mind.

"Ever sincerely yours,

"W. Pitt."

[About the end of this year there seems to have been a suspicion amongst the friends of Mr. Pitt, that some acts of treachery towards him had been practised by certain members of the Government, in order to lower him in public estimation, and withdraw from him the affection of the King. Evil rumours were circulated about him, and royal messages were withheld. It is not likely that Mr. Addington would have wished to injure him; but injury may sometimes be inflicted by forgetfulness and reckless language. Certain, however, it is, that from this time Mr. Pitt's friends began to besiege him with importunities to withdraw his support, and let the Administration die of a political atrophy; in which, after a long struggle, they succeeded. The Bishop of Lincoln and Mr. Rose led the way.—ED.]

THE BISHOP OF LINCOLN TO MR. ROSE.

"You will easily believe, my dear Sir, that your letter was as little satisfactory to me, as your conversation with Mr. Pitt was to you. I will not, however, trouble you with my lamentations, as you know precisely how I feel upon this most truly mortifying subject. There is, however, one point upon which I must express my anxiety, and that is, that you will *yourself* contradict, to the King, the account which he received of Mr. Pitt's determination to resign last *October*; and also that you will state to his Majesty, that his message to Mr. Pitt to keep his engagement of visiting him at Weymouth, was never delivered. These subjects the King has already mentioned to you, and surely there can be no impropriety in your recurring to them. A little breach of etiquette may be risked in matters of such importance. Be assured that Lord C. is not a fit person to trust such an explanation to; and, indeed, no one is so well suited to it as yourself. I entreat that you will not leave the neighbourhood of Windsor without accomplishing this object; and I hope that in every conversation you may have with his Majesty, you will be upon the watch for any opportunity which may offer of opening his eyes.

With respect to Mr. Pitt, the point to urge to him seems to be, that the conduct he is now pursuing is the very one most calculated to lower his influence and consequence in the country; and that others are taking great pains to bring about the same thing, and are aiming, in all their measures, to be able to do without him. The only 'ray of hope' your letter conveys is, where you say that Mr. Pitt owns he feels uncomfortably. If he will but cease to have such complete confidence in Mr. A., and see that he does not deserve his active support and assistance in the degree he has hitherto given it, circumstances will soon point out some line of conduct different from his present, and perfectly consistent with his honour; which, after all, is the first thing to be considered. If Mr. Pitt withholds his advice and direction, the face of things will soon be changed. Insufficiency and profligacy will soon appear, and the public will be convinced that Mr. Pitt has just ground for altering his conduct.

"You seem to think of going soon to Cuffnells. If we do not see each other before you set out, pray let me know by letter whether I be at liberty to state to Mr. Pitt any of the circumstances and facts you have mentioned to me, and to comment upon them. I am fully aware that nothing must be done or said to revolt Mr. Pitt.

"I have written to Mr. Carthew, as you suggested, and directed my letter to him at No. 12, Queen Anne Street West; concluding that he had not changed his habitation. If he has, pray send after the letter, and in any case I should be glad you would inquire whether he has received it, as I should be sorry if it fell into other hands.[1]

"If this should find you at Holly Grove, pray distribute our kindest compliments to all your party. Mrs. Pretyman desires to be kindly remembered to you.

"I am, my dear Sir,
"Always most truly and cordially yours,
"G. LINCOLN.

"Buckden Palace, Nov. 19th, 1801.

"I think you might urge to Mr. Pitt the effect— —the revolting effect—which the continuing his present line of conduct will have upon his real friends, and the most respectable men in the country firmly attached to the constitution; now that A. has taken Tierney and formed a coalition with Opposition: and the real magnanimity of his conduct is not understood, but his motives misrepresented."

THE BISHOP OF LINCOLN TO MR. ROSE.

"MY DEAR SIR,

"The King is, in my judgment, perfectly clear. The design most certainly is to kick away the ladder; and this makes me exceedingly anxious that no further assistance should be given upon the subject of finance, or indeed upon any other point. Surely Mr. Pitt's eyes must be soon opened. Pray watch the debate on the 25th, and see whether new light cannot be collected

[1] Allusions to letters intercepted at the Post-Office, as stated with regard to Mr. Pitt.

from the speeches of certain persons; and if anything appears, do not fail to state it strongly to Mr. Pitt.

"It seems to me very desirable that you should have some conversation with Steele, not only on his own account, but as some criterion to judge how Mr. Pitt's other friends feel concerning what is now going on.

"I see no objection to the receiving 1,000*l.* from Lord Rolle; but I think the thing should first be mentioned to Lord Camden. Above all, do not fail to show the last paragraph in the enclosed *Times* to Mr. Pitt, and to tell him of the communication between Hiley Addington and Mr. Waller. I hope you will keep the enclosed paper, or send it again to me, that we may keep it with other things of a similar nature. The spirit of Jacobinism is surely visible in the above paragraph. In great haste.

"Yours, ever most truly and affectionately,

"G. LINCOLN.

"Buckden Palace, Nov. 20th, 1801.

"Pray let me hear again from you."

MR. ROSE TO MR. PITT.

"Holly Grove, Nov. 22d, 1801.

"MY DEAR SIR,

"The opportunities I have had of talking with you on confidential matters lately have been so interrupted, that I fear nothing but the strongest attachment to you, and the most sincere and unaltered regard for the public interest, could have induced me so often lately to press on your attention, points which appear to me as important for the latter as they are to yourself. My want of discretion may be blamed, but you cannot mistake my motive. To the hour of your announcing to me that Mr. Addington was to succeed you, I considered him as one of your most attached and devoted friends, and was in the habit of going to him in preference to any other person on the most confidential matters. The very day on which I was informed by you of that event, I had appointed to see him in order to have a conversation of the sort. I can therefore have no prejudice against him, nor can I have been led to express to you the opinion I entertain of what is going forward at present by any interested motive. I shall not have the remotest wish to see you in office again so long as you continue to feel that you cannot return to it with credit and comfort. But, having a firm impression on my mind that there is a systematic plan, originating I know not where, to lessen you as well in the opinion of the public as of the King, I do feel most anxiously desirous that that should be counteracted; conceiving it to be for the interest of both, as well as from considerations of a nature personal to yourself, that it should be done as effectually as possible. At the same time I cannot help deeply lamenting that you see the difficulties in the way of your returning to the public service so forcibly as you do; and I feel convinced that the best aid you can give in a private station is very far short of what you could do if you had the direction of matters, of which recent experience can leave no doubt. I may be mistaken as to a negotiation having been attempted with any other person in opposition besides Mr. Tierney; but I believe his reception by Mr. A. affords a ray of hope to Mr. Fox and every other enlightened Jacobin in the country, as well as to the gentleman himself. They will naturally speculate on the possibility, at least, of that opening the way to more of their friends, perhaps finally to the exclusion of Mr. A.; and to an adoption of some of their measures, when it may not be in your power to prevent it. It will be a great satisfaction to me to have a quiet hour or two with you before I go into Hampshire. I wish indeed to have your opinion as to the best mode of combining the matter in my two pamphlets, so as to connect all that is material respecting finance in your administration. I hope, therefore, you will have the goodness to come here with me the end of this week—though you must be in town on Sunday."

Mr. Rose to Mr. Pitt.

"Holly Grove, Dec. 7th, 1801.

"My dear Sir,

"My son, with the same opinion as my own on the subject of the wish you expressed to me on Friday, and repeated with increased anxiety the day following, has not diverted the strong inclination I have felt, since our last conversation, to comply with your desire; and it is a great relief to me that I can thus give another proof of my strong attachmment to you.

"You will, I am sure, permit me to say to the *very*

few to whom I shall think it necessary to say anything, that I did not ask the seat in the Privy Council from Mr. A. but that I receive it at your instance, because I shall receive it under circumstances of a very different nature from those that existed when I sought it as *a distinction*. I had been Secretary of the Treasury under you longer than any person had held the situation who was appointed in the whole of the last century. I had not been entirely idle when the exertions were making which opened the way for the Administration to come in, at the head of which you rendered such important, and, I may say, unexampled services to your country; and in the early part of it especially I had laboured indefatigably. I had acquired some influence in the county in which I settled, and brought forward usefully to Government the infinitely greater weight of others,—at the same time that I secured to myself and my family, honestly and fairly, a permanent paliamentary interest; and I was at the time of your retiring from office the only person who remained in the same political employment so filled on your entrance into the public service. If I had been selected for an honour then, it would naturally have been considered as a reward for the sort of claim I thought I had when I asked for it; and I should have had an honest pride in receiving it: it must come to me very differently now. I assure you, that, seriously, I do not state this with an intention either of making a merit in acquiescing in your wish, or of suggesting anything in the shape of a grievance;

both are utterly repugnant to me. I have not the slightest ground of complaint, and my attachment is more strongly riveted to you than when you were in power. I wish you only to be apprised distinctly why I was solicitous for the object before, and hesitated to comply at once with your wish when I saw you were earnest about it. Having taken my determination, I shall drive from my mind every reflection that can be painful about it; and you shall never see or hear of a symptom respecting it that is unpleasant.

"It was not my intention to have said anything more to you about the object my son has at heart; but I found here the *Times* of Saturday, in which persons are mentioned for all the missions open, I believe, except Madrid, without any notice taken of him. I imagine Mr. Drummond is at Naples. If the information had been in another paper, I should not have much regarded it; but I happen to know that Lord Hawkesbury particularly favours that one, though I have no imagination that he can influence it. One of the gentlemen named (Sir James Crawford) came into the line long after my son, as Mr. Frere and Mr. Drummond did. I am perfectly sure that there is not an individual in it whose education was likely to qualify him better for it. At the head of Winchester School a year or two earlier than usual, he had an opportunity of spending eighteen months in Geneva, under the care of one of the ablest and most respectable men there, in attaining modern languages, acquiring the principles of the law of nations, &c., and then went to Cambridge at eighteen. As soon as he had taken his Bachelor's degree, he was placed under Lord Auckland at the Hague, with the privilege of seeing the whole correspondence of Europe, then passing through there, where he remained for more than a year, working at least ten hours a day, till Lord Grenville sent him to Berlin, with the charge of the King's affairs, on the ground of the character he heard of him, without any application from me; and I had the satisfaction of being told repeatedly, by his Lordship, that he was most entirely satisfied with him. I know, too, that Lord Malmesbury (an impartial judge at least) has several times spoken of him in extremely flattering terms, from the observations he had opportunities of making while he was with him at Berlin. It was not in the smallest degree my son's fault that he has not been employed for some years.

"You will not, I trust, understand me as conveying a wish that you should do anything on the subject in the remotest degree unpleasant to you. I flattered myself that *your* support of reasonably fair pretensions with Lord Hawkesbury would have been decisive. If it shall prove otherwise, it will not make the slightest alteration in my mind or conduct. If it is meant to open Naples, I think my son would be perfectly satisfied and happy with it."

MR. ADDINGTON TO MR. PITT.

"Downing Street, Dec. 19th, 1801.

"MY DEAR SIR,

"I expressed to his Majesty, on Wednesday, your wish and my own that Rose and Long should become members of the Privy Council. He acceded to it most graciously, and I have told Long what has passed. The communication to Rose should, I think, proceed from yourself, and I hope this will be in time to enable you to make it by this evening's post.

"I will take my chance of finding you at home at three to-morrow.

"Yours, affectionately,

"H. ADDINGTON."

THE BISHOP OF LINCOLN TO MR. ROSE.

"Deanery, St. Paul's, Dec. 23rd, 1801.

"MY DEAR SIR,

"I remained in town till the 14th, and then went with Mr. Pitt to Cambridge. On the 16th, after dining at a great feast in Trinity College Hall, we went to Buckden, and he left us on the 19th. I did not receive your very interesting letter till I reached Buckden; and the short time I was there I was so occupied by company and business (having an Ordination on the 20th) that I really had not leisure to write to you. I set out from Buckden yesterday, and came hither this morning. I saw very little of Mr. Pitt while I was in town. He was a day or two at Lord Hawkesbury's, and then he went to Hollwood. When he was in town he was engaged every day to dinner. I scarcely know why, but I could not bring myself to enter upon any of these important subjects on which I knew I should differ from him as we went along in the carriage, and I felt almost an equal reluctance when he was at Buckden.

However, in the last walk we took on the Friday, we fell insensibly into politics, and he talked with his usual openness and good temper. I expressed very decidedly my opinion concerning the insufficiency of the present Administration, especially upon subjects of finance, and reprobated the dangerous tendency of that spirit of candour and conciliation which had hitherto marked his conduct to Mr. A. I endeavoured to prove to him that he would materially injure his own character, if he continued upon his present intimate footing with Mr. A., and if he abstained from declaring his opinion upon the measures which he really disapproved. I told him that such a line of conduct appeared to me a betrayal of the interests of his country. I mentioned the pains which had been taken, and which were still continued, to lower him in the estimation of the public, and I ventured to say that his present conduct was precisely what his enemies wished and his friends could not approve.

"I am willing to think that I made some impression upon him. He owned that the opening of the distilleries was 'perfectly absurd.' He said that if the peace establishment should not be settled as he wished, or that one or two certain measures of finance should not be adopted, he would certainly declare his opinion in Parliament. He seemed to think it not impossible but this opportunity might be afforded him.

"Upon the Catholic question our conversation was less satisfactory. He certainly looks forward to the time when he may carry that point, and I fear he does not wish to take office again unless he could be permitted to bring it forward, and to be properly supported. I endeavoured to convince him that he had been deceived by those on whom he relied on this question, as far as Ireland itself was concerned, and that the measure would be very unpopular in England. I did not seem to make much impression upon this point, but I had not time to say all I wished and could have said. I thought it better not to touch upon the treacherous part of a certain person's character and conduct. That point had been fully urged by you, and I had no new matter to state. It appeared to me wiser to argue upon public grounds, and upon regard and concern for his own character.

" When he was leaving Buckden, I told him I hoped I should see him in town this week, as I did not think of being in London again till the first of April. He received that information in a manner which struck Mrs. Pretyman and me exceedingly; and immediately said that he would make a point of coming to town for a day on purpose to meet me. In the course of the conversation I have alluded to, I said there were other matters upon which I wished to talk to him, but which I could not then enter upon, and I am inclined to think he is desirous of talking to me again.

" He was certainly not in so good spirits after this conversation, and he remained some time in his room doing nothing immediately after it, although he knew that a large party from Cambridge was waiting for him in the drawing-room. I am confident that he is not perfectly easy in his own mind about public matters, and I am satisfied that his uneasiness will increase.

"What may be the termination of this strange, uncomfortable state of things at home, even without any fresh convulsion in Paris (which seems expected), it is impossible to conjecture.

"I have been interrupted several times, and have now only time left to say that Mr. Pitt told me of your acceptance, &c. with great satisfaction, and he said he should write to you as soon as he got to town. I was delighted that you had so full a conversation at Windsor. I hope you will tell Mr. Pitt about the offer to Grey. Depend upon it, such incompetency and such knavery cannot long go on and prosper.

"I shall stay in town till Monday, perhaps Tuesday. I left Mrs. Pretyman not quite well; she has fever hanging about her, which disturbs her sleep, &c.

"Kindest compliments to your party at Cuffnells.

"Yours, most cordially and affectionately,
"G. LINCOLN."

MR. SMITH TO MR. ROSE.

"Hereford Street, Dec. 24th, 1801.

"MY DEAR SIR,

"Messrs. Biddulph and Cocks have informed me that you have paid in to my account one thousand pounds, which I will take care to apply to the discharge of certain debts.

"I am, dear Sir, yours very faithfully,
"JOS. SMITH."

CHAPTER IX.

1802.

CORRESPONDENCE BETWEEN MR. PITT, MR. ROSE, THE BISHOP OF LINCOLN, AND MR. CANNING, RELATIVE TO THE ADDINGTON ADMINISTRATION.

[THE debate alluded to in the following letter seems to be that in which the question arose, whether the debts of the Civil List should be paid by Parliament; and whether the King should, or could, be bound to keep his expenditure within the sum allowed him at his accession to the throne. Another question then raised was, whether the Prince of Wales was not entitled to be reimbursed for all the sums, minus the expenses of his education, which were paid to the Crown out of the Duchy of Cornwall, during his minority. — ED.]

MR. PITT TO MR. ROSE.

"Park Place, Friday, Feb. 19th, 1802.

"DEAR ROSE,

"I knew nothing of the precise day on which the Civil List was to be brought on till I returned to town accidentally on Tuesday, after a week's absence at Walmer. The Committee is now sitting from day to day, and, I imagine, will probably make a report in the course of the next week, though I have not happened to hear anything particular as to their progress. It is certainly very material that nothing should be omitted which can place the subject in a clear and just point of view; and though I think the leading parts of the case will be so clear on the face of the accounts that they will hardly escape notice, the materials which you have in your possession may be of considerable use. If, therefore, it is really no inconvenience to you to come for a few days next week, I shall be very glad of it; and, indeed, there are some things connected with the debate of last week which I should be glad to talk with you about. Awkward as that debate was in some of its circumstances at the moment, I am persuaded, in its consequences, it has done, and will do good.

"I shall be in town all next week, unless, perhaps, for a single day either on Wednesday or Friday.

"Ever sincerely yours,

"W. PITT."

[In the next letter, the modest simplicity of Mr. Pitt's character is remarkably exemplified in the slight notice which he takes of a high compliment which had just been paid him by a numerous body of his supporters, on which most men would have delighted to dwell without any undue self-complacency. Nearly nine hundred persons, the most eminent in rank, character, and talent, assembled in Merchant Taylors' Hall, on the 28th of May, to celebrate Mr. Pitt's birthday.—ED.]

Mr. Pitt to Mr. Rose.

"Walmer Castle, June 7th, 1802.

"Dear Rose,

"I felt, as you will believe, truly obliged to you for your very satisfactory account of the 28th, and for all the trouble you have had since in prolonging my furlough here. Immediately on receiving your letter, I returned to Mr. Darke the copy of the paper in question, with a certificate, which, as I have heard nothing since, I suppose fully answered the purpose.

"This air, and the quiet and retirement which I have been enjoying, have been of great use to me. I mean to remain here till quite the end of the week, and am not without hopes of stealing another eight or ten days afterwards before the dissolution, which, I imagine, we may expect somewhere about the 24th or 25th; at least, if it be true, as I am told, that all the business will be out of the House of Commons on the 28th.

"Ever sincerely yours,
"W. Pitt."

[In the following notice of the general election, in 1802, it will be observed that Mr. Pitt identifies himself with the ministerial party, in opposition to the Foxites, whom he calls Jacobins: a name which the leaders of that party had earned for it, by their sympathy with the French Revolution; but it is remarkable also for his characteristic forbearance in avoiding personalities. He alludes to them in general terms; but there is no attack upon any one individual. The rest of the letter is an overflowing of kindness towards his correspondent and friend.—ED.]

MR. PITT TO MR. ROSE.

"Bromley Hill, Saturday, July 10th, 1802.

"DEAR ROSE,

"I was sincerely glad to find that the election at Southampton passed in a manner which must have been so satisfactory to yourself and your son. You will have seen that ours at Cambridge was perfectly quiet; and it was not only quiet, but attended with every mark of zeal and cordiality. I wish we had as good accounts of three or four other places, where (as it has turned out) the Jacobins have triumphed, and, in some instances, unaccountably; but, upon the whole, I do not see anything likely materially to change the relative strength of parties or the general complexion of the House.

"I am likely to be detained by different engagements near town for a week or ten days, and shall then return to Walmer Castle, where I shall be most happy to see you whenever you find it most convenient, and have a fair wind. I shall probably not go to Somersetshire till late in the autumn; but I hope to find an opportunity of making a coasting voyage, and returning your visit in the course of the summer. If your sons are with you when you embark, I shall be very glad, if it suits them, to be of your party. I am going on extremely well, and expect to pass muster as a stout and able-bodied seaman by the time I see you.

"Ever yours,
"W. PITT."

[The determined hostility with which the Bishop of Lincoln continued to assail the Addington Administration is displayed in these three following letters, and also the perseverance with which he endeavoured to shake the "*immobile saxum*" of Mr. Pitt's mind.—ED.]

THE BISHOP OF LINCOLN TO MR. ROSE.

"MY DEAR SIR,

"I have this morning received a long letter from Mr. Pitt, and you will like to know the contents of it, if you have not heard from him yourself. He says that the Bath waters agree with him, and he seems to have a very confident hope that they will be of material service to his health. He is going to Burton this week, for a day or two. Not thinking it right to be absent from the meeting of Parliament, in the present state of the country, he means to be in town about the 19th, to stay for five or six days; then go to Walmer for ten days, pass through town in his way to Bath, where he hopes to arrive about the 10th of next month, and to stay there till Parliament meets after the Christmas holidays. All this is, of course, subject to what may arise to require attendance upon the House of Commons. In speaking of political matters, he says the state of things is full of difficulty; that during the summer he knew nothing of what was going on, except from the newspapers; that in passing through London, on his way to Bath, he was glad to learn that the line taken by our Government was such as he approved; and that their future intentions seemed to be right. He thinks that war with France cannot long be avoided. This is the substance of what he writes; and I own that the political part of his letter has not given me much satisfaction or comfort. I am aware that he has a very difficult part to act; but I think he will injure his own character if he expresses, which I fear he will, an unqualified approbation of the conduct of our present ministry.

"All things taken together, the situation of the country seems to me truly alarming. I write in great haste, and have only time to add our kindest respects to Mrs. Rose.

"Ever most affectionately and truly,

"G. LINCOLN.
"Buckden Palace, Nov. 7th, 1802."

THE BISHOP OF LINCOLN TO MR. ROSE.

"MY DEAR SIR,

"I thank you for your letter which I received this morning, and rejoice most heartily that Mr. Pitt has desired to see you at Bath. I really think that your meeting may be very useful. I am most decidedly of opinion that what you propose to state in the House of Commons is exceedingly right in itself, and of the highest importance. It ought surely to be said as early as may be on the first day, before people have committed themselves. I have no doubt there are many members whose minds are in suspense, and who would be determined by such a speech as you describe. Remember to state your approbation of the preliminaries, and to mark strongly the conduct of ministers since they were signed; and that the only chance of preserving the peace and sparing the country is by having a firm, able, and respected ministry. If, however, you mean to wait for Mr. Pitt's full and cheerful consent, I fear your speech will never be made. Consider whether you need mention your intention to him, provided he be not in the House, and you have reason to think that what you will say will not be opposite to his real opinion.

"I wish to apprize you that I wrote a very strong letter to Mr. Pitt, last Monday, entreating that he would not, in the House of Commons, express an unqualified approbation of the late measures of Government; reminding him that he had not been consulted during the summer, and that now his assistance was likely to be wanted, they were paying court to him; that they used 'every effort and every art' to obtain his support when necessary. I told him how much ministers were despised in the country, and begged that he would not identify himself with such men. And, lastly, I begged that he would stay at Bath, for which his health afforded a sufficient reason, and wait to see what turn things will take. I told him also, which I am sure is true, that by giving his unqualified support to the present Ministers, he would lose the confidence of the country.

"Remember that you cannot do your country a greater service than by making the speech you meditate. I write in great haste, and have only time to say that I shall expect with great impatience your next letter. Adieu.

"Yours, most affectionately and truly,

"G. LINCOLN.

"Buckden Palace, Nov. 11th, 1802."

THE BISHOP OF LINCOLN TO MR. ROSE.

"MY DEAR SIR,

"Your compromise is, upon the whole, as good a mode of settling the business as could be expected. I was confident that Mr. Pitt would not consent to your making your intended speech; and I agree with you in thinking it a great point that Mr. Pitt should not attend at the opening of the session under the present impression of his mind. I almost shudder at the idea of Mr. Pitt's expressing his approbation of the late measures of Government.

"I am persuaded that Lord Grenville will take a directly opposite line, and I greatly fear that Mr. Pitt will soon be driven to make his choice between the present ministers and Lord Grenville, with those who will act with him. I fear it, because I am convinced that Mr. Pitt will support Government.

"I am very glad that you are remaining at Bath; and, if anything occurs, I trust that I shall hear from you. You say nothing of Mr. Pitt's health.

" Adieu. Mrs. Pretyman desires her kindest compliments.

" Ever, my dear Sir, most truly yours,
" G. LINCOLN.
" Buckden Palace, Nov. 17th, 1802."

[The correspondence which closes this year consists of letters from Mr. Canning to Mr. Rose, with answers to some of them. They contain evidence of the high veneration with which Mr. Pitt was regarded not only by men of ordinary stamp, but by the brilliant talents of Mr. Canning; they show Mr. C.'s anxiety not to cross that great man's path, or throw any obstacle in the way of his purposes, whatever they might be; and the perseverance with which he endeavoured to worm out from his friend Rose his secret feelings and opinions, in order to regulate his own course in accordance with them, proves his conviction, that no one else enjoyed so large a share of Mr. Pitt's confidence, or was admitted to see so much of the interior of his mind; but they also show how much machinery was at work to influence those feelings and opinions against Mr. Addington, and to undermine the Administration.—ED.]

MR. CANNING TO MR. ROSE.

" Dogmersfield, Thursday, Nov. 11th, 1802.
" MY DEAR SIR,
" It has been a great disappointment to me that the invitation of our friend Sir H. Mildmay did not

happen to find you disengaged this week. Independently of the pleasure of meeting you here, I was very particularly desirous of an opportunity of some communication with you before the opening of the session, upon subjects, not very fit to be discussed by letter, upon which I am confident you would feel as I, and other persons whom you would have found here feel upon them:—and to the measures relating to which you could, and I am persuaded would, have contributed the most efficacious and valuable assistance.

"I should be very glad to know if you are likely to be in town before the meeting—and how soon?

"I return to town from hence on Saturday; and for that, and the few first days of the ensuing week, a letter would find me at Lothian's Hotel. On Thursday or Friday, I have promised to meet Mr. Pitt at Dropmore, on his road from Bath; and shall return to town either with him, or the day after him. If, with this knowledge of my motions, you could contrive to give me notice of yours, so that we might fall in with each other the first time that we are within each other's reach, I shall be very desirous of profiting by the opportunity.

"Believe me, my dear Sir,
"Very sincerely yours,
"Geo. Canning.

"P. S. I understand that you intend taking this place on your way to town. If that should be the case, and if you would let me know beforehand the time of your coming, I would endeavour to meet you."

[Towards the end of the year Mr. Pitt went to Bath to recruit his failing health; and being now out of the trammels of office, the next letter shows more of the affectionate kindness which he felt for Mr. Rose, than when his head was full of matters of business. It shows also that he was still determined to support the Government on material points, though he seems to apprehend, that something might be introduced into the speech from the Throne, which might make him desirous to be absent from the address. It brought Mr. Rose into that immediate contact with him which induced Mr. Canning to write the following letters.—Ed.]

MR. PITT TO MR. ROSE.

"Bath, Nov. 7th, 1802.

"DEAR ROSE,

"Your letter of yesterday reached me this morning. I am very sorry you should have given yourself a moment's trouble about my mislaid letter, as its contents were not such as to make the accident of any consequence. I had been meaning to write to you to tell you, what I know you will be glad to hear, that I am much the better for my visit hither; and I meant also to say to you, that if you have really no engagement to make it inconvenient to you, you would make me very happy if you can let me have the satisfaction of seeing you while I am here. There are many points too long for a letter which I shall be very glad, if we meet, to talk over with you. I mean to go on Thursday to my mother's, but shall return here in time for my afternoon's draught of the waters on Saturday; and from thence shall continue here till the business of the session calls me to town. It is possible things may take a turn that may make me wish to be present the day of the Speech, which will, I understand, be on Monday the 22d; but it is quite as likely that I may not see occasion to go till either the vote for the army or navy, or some material motion, is brought forward.

"Perhaps even the circumstances may be such as to make me doubt about going at all before Christmas; but of this I shall know more in a short time. If it suits you to be here on Saturday by dinner, I shall be happy to see you then; if not, the first day afterwards that you find in your power.

"Ever sincerely yours,
"W. P."

MR. CANNING TO MR. ROSE.

"Lothian's Hotel, Saturday, Nov. 20th, 1808.
" MY DEAR SIR,

Though I have but a moment to save the post, I will not put off till Monday giving you the pleasure, which I am sure you will derive, from hearing that Lord G. (whom I have seen to-day) appears to enter cordially into all the considerations of delicacy towards Mr. P., which you thought it of so much importance that he should entertain; and that the line of argument which he has laid down to himself, is one which will carry him *safely* past all the embarrassing and uncomfortable points of difference between them. There is no intention of moving any amendment.

"In return for this intelligence, I shall be glad to hear from you that Mr. P. continues satisfied with his wise and saving determination to remain where he is; and that he has done himself the justice to avoid (and to say that he *must* avoid) mixing himself by *advice* in the councils for which he ought to be in no degree responsible.

"Yours, dear Sir, very sincerely,

"G. C."

MR. CANNING TO MR. ROSE.

"37, Conduit Street,
"Monday, Nov. 29th, 1802.

"MY DEAR SIR,

"The last letter with which I troubled you produced me so comfortable an answer, that I cannot forbear to give myself the chance of another such return for the very little that I have to tell you.

"The navy estimates come on on Wednesday: they mean to vote 50,000 seamen—as it is understood, only for three months. I should like very much to know (but without in the smallest degree intending to make any use of my knowledge) Mr. P.'s opinion of the sufficiency or insufficiency of such a vote. I do not write to him to ask—first, because I wish not to trouble him with letters just at present more than is absolutely necessary (he is much better left to his own reflections); and secondly, because I do not think it fair to put such a question to him at a moment when, if put from other quarters, I trust he would decline to answer it. But if you should happen to collect what he thinks upon the subject, and should see no impropriety in letting me know it, it would be some satisfaction to my mind. I certainly have my own opinion: but I should be desirous to avoid stating one opposite to *his*—at least I would not do so knowingly. However, the debate will be in a great measure independent of this particular question.

"Above all things, I anxiously hope to hear from you that he remains firm in his resolution to abstain from attendance, or interference.

"The voting the establishments *for three months* appears to me to relieve him from the only awkwardness which he could possibly have felt—that of not being present at the settlement of the permanent peace establishment. This measure is confessedly temporary, adapted to *their* view of the circumstances of THE moment, to which he is no party, and liable to revision hereafter; when it will (I trust) be his business to revise it.

"Peel is not in town. I stated *your* Swiss argument for you—and it was not answered—as indeed it could not well be.

"Ever, my dear Sir,
"Most sincerely yours,
"G. C."

Mr. Canning to Mr. Rose.

"Conduit Street, Tuesday, Nov. 30th, 1802.

"My dear Sir,

"As I mentioned to you yesterday that the estimates were to be voted only for three months—which was then true—I think it right to let you know that the Doctor¹ has just announced the intention of voting them for the year. This, I am persuaded, is Ryder's doing, and it is done wisely. I do trust that it will make no alteration in Mr. Pitt's intentions of staying where he is.. But it makes it still more desirable, to know if possible, what are his ideas of the force that ought to be kept up. The Navy comes on to-morrow, 50,000 seamen, as I before told you. The proposed amount of the Army I have not heard. It (the army) does not come on till Wednesday. Fox, it is now confidently said, will not attend *either*, certainly not the navy. God knows he has done mischief enough already, and may well rest contented for a while with the tone to which he has brought the Government down. Perhaps, indeed, he is so well contented that he thinks it dangerous to risk any apparent diminution of his influence with them by attending debates on which he thinks they may receive a lesson from other quarters; and it is obviously his policy not to be obliged at the present moment to express a difference of opinion with Addington.

"You shall hear from me again as anything occurs.

"Yours very sincerely,

"G. C."

¹ The sobriquet by which Addington was familiarly designated.

MR. ROSE TO MR. CANNING.

"Bath, Nov. 30th, 1802.

"MY DEAR SIR,

"I conceive it to be quite impossible for Mr. Pitt to form an opinion of the sufficiency or insufficiency of the 50,000 seamen for three months, without any information whatever of what has been going forward lately, or of the actual situation we are in with France,—I mean as to the probability or improbability of a war with her. There are passages in Lord Hawkesbury's speech, either on the first or second day, which looked like his having no intention to lay papers before Parliament relative to the late discussion with the First Consul. That they should not do so now, is intelligible, and perhaps proper; but calling for a vote, evidently for a larger force than they can possibly mean for a peace establishment, can only be justified by the persuasion ministers have of the necessity for such a force on account of a conduct on the part of France which creates a just alarm in their minds. I can conceive discussions, even of importance, with a foreign country, passing even without papers laid, when Parliament is not called upon to act in consequence of them; *but when it is,* information at some period or other is surely demandable. Ministers may surely be driven to say why 50,000 men are desired for three months; they need not tell the specific cause, but they must admit that something extraordinary leads to it. Mr. Pitt went out for his ride before I got your letter, and I have no chance of an opportunity of talking to him on the above subject before dinner, but I am quite sure he could say nothing upon it at all satisfactory. His health improves evidently, and he holds his resolution now to a certainty not to go to London, about which, however, he was a good deal shaken at the end of last week."

MR. ROSE TO MR. CANNING.

"Bath, Dec. 1st, 1802.

" MY DEAR SIR,

"I thought it right, under so considerable a change in the vote for the seamen, as you mention, to show the letter I have just received from you, to Mr. Pitt, who desires me to say to you nearly what I did from myself yesterday;—that at this distance, and utterly uninformed as he is of everything that could enable him to form a judgment on the subject, he can express no opinion whatever upon it. It appears manifestly to be better to vote the strength for a year than for a short period, as showing a better countenance to *the enemy*. The number may be increased in the course of the session, if it be found necessary, and if so large a force should not be wanted, the surplus money may be otherwise disposed of. The period of the naval vote being extended strengthens my remark of yesterday respecting information of some sort being communicated to Parliament. In 1793, the vote was for 45,000 seamen; for 10,000 in 1792. I am not sure whether papers were then laid, but the ground for that augmentation, I am sure, was stated and debated. I trust Mr. Pitt will not be induced by anything that one can foresee as likely to happen to change his opinion respecting his remaining here."

MR. CANNING TO MR. ROSE.

"Conduit Street,
"Thursday, Dec. 2d, 1802.

"MY DEAR SIR,

"Many thanks to you for your letter of yesterday, which I have just received. You will have seen with no small indignation how quietly the navy estimates went off yesterday. As far as *I* am implicated in the guilt of that remissness, I will honestly own to you that my excuse is this—that I wished to hear from you again before I opened my lips upon the subject. The change from three months to a year, though laudable in itself, appeared to me (as I now see it does to you) only to aggravate the folly and inconsistency of the conduct of Government, and to make their want of fair explanation with Parliament still more reprehensible. But I did not feel sure how it might have been represented at Bath; and though I am very far (as I hope you will understand me throughout) from either presuming to ask, or still less taking for granted that I have heard, anything of Mr. P.'s opinions, yet I thought that if he had been fully informed and fully satisfied upon the subject, he would have said so, and that would, with *me*, have been decisive against saying a word. As it is, you will be better satisfied with to-day than yesterday. And the loss of one day does us no harm. It has shown how little disposition the Government has to communicate information; and the indignation which everybody, whom I have seen or heard of, feels at such a vote *so* passed, will be a great help to us to-day, and will take off any imputation of a vexatious seeking of opportunities to oppose. You shall hear from me again, and I hope you will send me from time to time any hint that may occur to you.

"Yours most sincerely,
"G. C."

MR. ROSE TO MR. CANNING.

"MY DEAR SIR,

"I have no hesitation in saying that I believe such a vote as was adopted by the House of Commons on Wednesday, is, I believe, unexampled in the history of Parliament; I mean without a syllable said on the subject by the ministers. My observation was purely my own, and not meant to implicate Mr. Pitt in the remotest degree. It is impossible at the present instant to be too cautious, not only of using his name, but of saying anything that can lead to conjecture as to what his opinion is.

"I shall return to Cuffnells early in the next week, and I think Mr. Pitt will probably go to Long Leat about the middle of it.

"I am, my dear Sir,
"Yours, &c.
"G. R.

"Bath, Dec. 3d, 1802."

MR. CANNING TO MR. ROSE.

"Conduit Street, Friday, Dec. 3d, 1802.

"MY DEAR SIR,

"I hope the debate of yesterday will satisfy you and will not *dis*-satisfy Mr. P., as I am confident, if fairly represented to him (and if a mischievous paragraph in the *Morning Chronicle* does not deceive, and alarm him), there is no reason why it should. The disavowal which was obtained from Hawkesbury of Fox's doctrine of small establishments, I hope he will consider as an essential point gained, and (though I do not see that any paper, except the True Briton, states that part of what I said at all sufficiently) I am sure he will think *I* did right in hailing as cordially as I did this symptom of returning good sense and consistency. Hawkesbury's language was the more important; and it was the more important that it should be strongly remarked upon, as Addington had shirked in the meanest and most pitiful manner the whole of the questions which T. Grenville addressed to him; and indeed his (A.'s) whole exhibition was as contemptible as even I could wish. His own troops were heartily ashamed of him, and there is but one voice amongst all who heard his waverings and shufflings, that this man cannot govern the country; that we are not safe in his hands. Will he be the last man in the country to perceive this? We shall see on Wednesday how A. will face Fox if he comes down. *Then* (since he has not done it sooner) he must be called upon to adopt Hawkesbury's disavowal. But, depend upon it, Mr. P.'s presence would do us no good as yet. For God's sake let him remain quietly where he is, unpledged, unmixed with anything that is going forward. Assure him (what is strictly true) that his name was not once brought into question in last night's debate; nor shall be, unforced, by any of *us*.

The Grenvilles we cannot answer for, nor are they at all considered as answering for him. We keep ourselves quite distinct from them.

"You will be glad to hear, and so will Mr. P., that Sturges distinguished himself in last night's debate most eminently. His speech was unquestionably the best of the night; and as a proof of its impression, old Pulteney came across the House to thank him for it, and to subscribe to every sentiment that it contained.

"Ever sincerely yours,
"G. C."

Mr. Canning to Mr. Rose.

"Conduit Street, Saturday, Dec. 4th.

"My Dear Sir,

"Do not be alarmed lest I should have misunderstood *you*, or misquoted Mr. P., or quoted him at all. Be assured I have done no such thing. What I said to you of my readiness to say nothing if he had thought fit to say to me through you, 'Hold your tongue,' is purely between ourselves. I never quote him. I do not pretend to hear from him. Others do, but I hope I am not to believe them. I trust to hearing from you again on Tuesday.

"Ever sincerely yours,
"G. C.

"The effect of Thursday's debate is excellent. The marked difference of the language of Addington and Hawkesbury, in respect to Fox's doctrines, strikes people as one could wish. With Hawkesbury it is,

I am persuaded, Ryder's doing; but I am heartily glad that *he* has profited by Ryder's advice. A., I trust and believe, is doubly armed in vanity and folly against any such impression."

MR. CANNING TO MR. ROSE.

"Conduit Street, Monday, Dec. 6th, 1802.

"MY DEAR SIR,

"I have this moment received your letter of yesterday, and as you talk of leaving Bath on Wednesday, lose not a moment in answering it.

"I am not sorry that you are *not* so satisfied with the result of Thursday, since your dissatisfaction is so entirely on the right side. I am quite aware that we did not do half of what we might have done; but recollect the *fetters* in which *we* act from the dread of misrepresentation to Mr. P.; from the apprehension of being mixed up too much in public opinion with the Grenville opposition of last year (which would do us a disservice just at the present moment that you cannot well calculate without being on the spot); and above all, under the uncertainty which some of the letters of last week from Bath had created, and which a thousand lying reports, circulated with incredible industry on Wednesday or Thursday, had contributed to aggravate, respecting the possibility of Mr. Pitt's coming up; an event which, whatever had been the real motive, they (the Addingtons) would not have failed to ascribe to the opposition to *them*; on which interpretation, our going one step or shade beyond what Mr. P.'s opinion, when he arrived, might turn out to be, would have appeared to countenance them. The 'others,' to whom I alluded as quoting letters supposed to be received from Bath, are people hanging on to Addington and Hawkesbury, who have told those, that related it to me again (and I believe for the purpose of its being so related to me), that Mr. P. had written to A. last week, offering to come up if he was wanted; that he had written to Hawkesbury, dictating the answer to be made to Fox, in consequence of which H. made that declaration on Thursday; which *therefore*, perhaps, as well as on other accounts (I mean because it was understood to proceed from Mr. P., and because I believed it to proceed not indeed *directly* from *him*, but from Ryder speaking his sense), I thought it right to hail *for a great deal more than it was really worth.*

"In what sense he did write to Ryder, I would give much to know. Ryder's wish to see Mr. P. where he ought to be, and where he must be again, it is impossible to doubt; but his tenderness for A. is so great, that he supplies him beforehand with all the means he can of meeting the strong points to be brought against him; and thereby, I think, throws difficulties in the way of Mr. P.'s return, in exact proportion as the faults which it is to remedy are rendered less observable. I cannot help being of opinion that in his precise situation he might properly *abstain* as much as Mr. P. himself does.

"Of what has been written to Long, if one is to judge from the effect, I cannot but judge well, as he has not been in the House (I believe) since the first day—certainly has not stayed out any debate.

"After all, the essential point is that of which your letter of to-day brings the continued assurance,—Mr. P.'s not coming up. This will give us on Wednesday an opportunity of more free debate, and more clear *speaking out* than we have yet ventured. The two last debates, and especially the Attorney-General's speech (which was a very good one of its kind), were full of taunting invitations to us to say distinctly what we meant,—whether we agreed with the Grenvilles in thinking Ministers unfit, &c. &c. And our *discretion—over*-discretion, I should think it, if there were not room to repair it on Wednesday—has had the effect of emboldening the Doctor's friends to assert, and of inclining stupid and shabby people to believe, that all that we have been doing is *purely out of pique to Addington*, and not in the smallest degree from devotion to Mr. P. It is impossible to acquiesce in this imputation; but I am not sorry that we have borne it in silence thus long, and I hope that even on Wednesday that silence will not be broken without fresh and instant provocation:—but *that* we shall assuredly have, and as assuredly we must not suffer ourselves to be misconstrued and misrepresented to so mischievous a purpose any longer.

"Wednesday will afford opportunity for most of the observations in your letter;—many of which, however, were pressed out lightly last week, but remaining perfectly unanswered by Ministers, make the less figure in report.

"I entreat you to let me have your last words from Bath. I cannot but be concerned that you are leaving him.

"Ever, my dear Sir,
"Most sincerely yours,
"G. C.

"Have you time to state your Exchequer Bills' observations?"

CHAPTER X.

1802.

MR. ROSE'S DIARY, FROM THE 11TH OF NOVEMBER TO THE 27TH OF DECEMBER, 1802.

[Mr. Rose's Diary of this year (1802) occupies only the two last months. The commencement of it is the substance of an attack which he would have made in the House of Commons upon the Addington administration, if he had not been prevented by Mr. Pitt. The rest consists of frequent conversations between them at Bath and at Cuffnells, in which the one is always using the spur and the other the rein; the one eager for the fray, the other checking his ardent desire to turn out the Government. It was not that Mr. Rose thirsted for place. He might have retained his office, and was vehemently pressed to do so by Mr. Pitt, at the time of his resignation; but he had been accustomed to see the reins of government held by a firm and unfaltering hand, and could not bear the feebleness and vacillations to which they were now consigned. Notwithstanding all the difficulties that stood in the way, and all the objections which were but too apparent, his devoted attachment to his friend led him to conclude that nothing could save the country, which was then hovering between peace and war, but his return to power. But Mr. Pitt's attachment to the King weighed down the scale on the other side. He had promised his support and assistance; and the strictness of his principles bound him to keep that engagement, even under great provocation to think himself released from it; for Mr. Addington forgot that the obligations in such a contract are reciprocal: that if he wanted assistance, he must ask for it; that he could not expect to find in Mr. Pitt an obsequious follower, ready to support every measure, whether good or bad, and to sanction every plan, however objectionable, and proposed without his previous concurrence; that, in fact, the relation in which his predecessor stood to him was that of a guide, to be consulted on all occasions, to whose experience and authority he ought, for the most part, to defer. But that was not the light in which Mr. Addington chose to view it. He prided himself on being independent; and it was only at rare intervals, and under circumstances of great perplexity, that he resorted to Mr. Pitt for advice. It argues, therefore, a great amount of self-complacency in him, when his biographer declares that, "to the close of his life, he considered that he had been unkindly and unfairly treated by Mr. Pitt. He promised him his assistance and advice whenever he might request it, and nevertheless removed to a distance where it would be impossible to consult him;

he would neither be the adviser of the Administration nor its head: nothing would satisfy him but its dissolution."[1]

Could it really be expected that Mr. Pitt would put himself at the head of a Government falling to pieces from its weakness, without infusing some new blood into it? With this proviso, Mr. Addington was willing to accept his advice, but his Cabinet rejected it. His advice was never asked at any other time, except on two or three isolated points, of which no judgment could be formed separate from the context of his policy. It has been proved that he went to Bath for his health, though he sometimes stayed there to avoid being mixed up with the passing of measures about which he had not been consulted, and of which he disapproved. But Bath and Walmer were not situated in America or Australia. His friends found it not impossible to consult him at either of those places, and a letter would have reached him in two days. He who expected a servile assistance from him, as Aladdin did from the charm-bound Genius, deserved to be disappointed. It is true that when Lord Hawkesbury wrote to him, as related in these notes, in order to obtain from him an *ex-post facto* sanction to a course of policy about which he had never been consulted before, he evaded the compromising effects of that manœuvre by the plea that they were too far asunder; but it is quite obvious that this was not his real

[1] Pellew's Life of Lord Sidmouth.

opinion; that it was only a specimen of diplomatic
insincerity, a retort courteous for the disingenuous
treatment which he felt that he had received. In one
of his conversations he had stated that the plea of
ignorance upon the subject would have drawn down
upon him additional papers, which would only have
added to his embarrassment: for he was too friendly
to the Government to censure when it could do no
good, and he was too honest to applaud what he was
unable to approve. The whole object of his answer was
to prevent his hearing anything more about the matter.
It was not impossible that it was too late.—ED.]

Mr. Rose's Diary resumed.

Cuffnells, Thursday, November 11.—On reflecting
on the present appearance of public affairs, uninformed
as I am of what has been doing by Government
during the last two or three months, I think it right
before I see Mr. Pitt, to embody in a few notes what
occurs to me from the conjectures I can form.

If Ministers have held a language to France that
their proceedings in Switzerland (violent, atrocious, and
unjustifiable as they have been) shall be considered as
a just ground of war,—or if they have used anything
like a serious threat that this country will resent them,
especially if that has been done without a certainty
that Austria will be a principal in the quarrel,—it will
be difficult to find terms strong enough to express a
censure of their conduct; especially as at the time

the correspondence began, the remotest hope could
not be entertained of the co-operation of Russia,
because the change of the Minister of that country
by the appointment of Count Woronzow, brother to
the Great Chancellor, (who is unfortunately suspected
to be corrupt, and not to have so decided an influence
as was at first supposed,) had not then taken place.
This opinion is formed not under a doubt of the
infinite importance that ought to be attached to the
independence of Switzerland, nor from a want of a
warm feeling for the cruel and lamentable situation that
that brave and virtuous people are in; but from a
clear and strong conviction that our interposition can
produce no possible good to the sufferers. It is quite
certain that we can send them no force, and that even
with the aid of our purse, they cannot collect a sufficient strength to resist the power of France suddenly
poured in upon them, as well from that country as
from Italy. Can any man in his senses hope that the
First Consul will attend to the threats[1] of our Ministers (conveyed in the strongest expressions they could
devise) to save Switzerland, important as it is to all
his views of aggrandizement and security, when they
tamely and quietly suffered the most direct and
unequivocal insults and injuries to be inflicted upon
us since the signing the preliminaries, without, as it
is believed, a representation on the subject? It will
be sufficient to state a few of these occurrences.

[1] Demosthenes, in the Second Olynthiac, observes, "Words, in
general, if not supported by deeds, appear frivolous and vain; and
in proportion as we use them with greater promptitude and alacrity,
so do all mankind more assuredly disbelieve them."

First.—France prevailed with Spain, or rather ordered her, to cede the province of Louisiana; the importance of which does not appear to me to be sufficiently felt. The French have everything now within their grasp except the precious metals. In this province they may assemble with ease an army sufficient for the conquest of Mexico, on which it borders. The soil and climate are equal to any in the world; and if it shall be found difficult to march an army to take possession of the Spanish wealth, on account of not being able to find provisions, &c. in an unsettled country, the voyage across the Gulf must be short (favoured by the trade wind), and not easily interrupted. This will not appear romantic, or improbable, when the spirit of enterprise of French troops is considered, especially under a certainty of acquiring great wealth and other luxuries; and the invincible indolence and want of discipline of the Spaniards, as well as the utter dislike the natives have to them. The acquisition gives the French also an immense influence with the American States, by completely bringing under their subjection the State of Kentucky, already a very flourishing county, and likely to become infinitely more so, from the healthiness of the climate and the fertility of the soil, in which respects it has at least equal advantages with Louisiana, and is better inhabited. The exports from Kentucky already amount to about .1,500,000*l*., though it has not been settled five-and-twenty years. The communication between it and the other States of America, for the conveyance of goods by land, is impracticable, being divided from them by the Alleghany mountains. The only outlet it has, therefore, is by the Ohio, which falls into the Mississippi; which latter is navigable much higher than where it receives the former, without either a fall or a rapid. The situation of New Orleans, about thirty or forty leagues up the river, must give the French the command of the navigation most completely. Must not the representatives of this State be under the direct influence of France in the Congress? And will not the mischief of stopping the trade between this and other parts of the continent of America, produce a considerable effect in the other States? It will evidently, too, shut us out of all trade with the county of Kentucky, fruitful in flour, hemp, and naval stores.

Secondly.—France was permitted to consolidate with itself the Italian Republic, deeply affecting thereby not only the balance of power in Europe, *but some of the most important commercial interests of this country.*—Compare this alone with Switzerland!

Thirdly.—She was allowed to make such terms in the definitive treaty respecting Malta, as insured to her the possession of that island whenever she should please to have it; the insufficiency of a Neapolitan garrison is notorious. But if the bravest troops in the world had been stipulated for, and adequate in number to the defence of the place, the French would have nothing to do but to direct the King of Naples to order his troops to march out and allow their's to possess themselves of the island; and he must instantly obey, or they would without hesitation dispossess him of his kingdom. If the French should not avail themselves of the interval while the Neapolitans are in Malta to get possession of it, how is it afterwards to be preserved in a state of independency? There is no way in which an income can be found to maintain a sufficient garrison and support the whole establishments. The revenue of the island is trifling; the estates of the Knights are almost all gone; those in Germany are distributed amongst the indemnities; in Spain they are confiscated; in France they are of course passed into other hands;—in short, none of any consequence are left. The provisions therefore under the definitive treaty were a mockery upon us, and not capable of being carried into effect.

Nothing surely can be worse than loose stipulations in a treaty of peace, or such as are difficult to execute. They are sure to occasion strife and ill-blood, and when a proper time occurs bloody and expensive wars. It were better infinitely at once to know what we are to depend upon,—the best or the worst we have to expect. In making peace, it is of the last importance to avoid, as far as honour and foresight will enable us, the occasion of future wars.

Fourthly.—The Island of Elba, (which in our hands had proved impregnable,) ceded by the definitive treaty to Tuscany, was immediately taken from the King of Etruria, a monarch of French creation, and annexed to the dominions of France; which country thereby acquired another important port in that part of the Mediterranean, for the protection of their commerce and the annoyance of ours. Tuscany too was taken into their hands, including the important port of Leghorn; and in the East Indies the still infinitely more important port of Cochin. No notice is taken of the advantages acquired to France on the side of Brazil, by the boundaries as settled by the definitive treaty. I do not understand that part of the subject sufficiently to remark upon it with accuracy.

It is quite clear that the four points before enumerated, relate distinctly and plainly to the immediate interests of this country; and to these may be added France retaining possession of the port of Flushing (and of course of the whole Island of Walcheren in which is the port of Middleburg, the principal mart for the East India trade), a most important one for their own commerce, and in a future war for the annoyance of ours; giving the French too a *direct* power in the affairs of Holland, deeply affecting our commerce and navigation, as well as greatly adding to the before gigantic strength of France. All these occurrences happened after the signing of the preliminary articles of peace. These were borne, as far as the public are aware, with patience; they were certainly borne with submission;—for not a single remonstrance was known to have been made,—not an observation upon them in the papers favourable to Government. So matters stood, when the French, in the month of September, interfered in a most atrocious manner with the affairs of Switzerland, and in October proceeded to acts of positive violence. Here the Ministers interfered, to what extent I know not,— but they *certainly* made the conduct of France a subject of loud complaint and remonstrance, if not of threat.¹ Much pains were taken to rouse the feelings, and spirit of the country, by the papers connected with Government, and with considerable success. Having so roused them, the Ministers appeared to feel strong, and to decide on hostility if France should not recede. Thus in the spirit of chivalry and romance, embarking in the cause of Switzerland (without any aid or support whatever); after having allowed the French to injure and to insult us in the manner already alluded to under the four different heads,—deeply affecting our navigation and commercial interest.²

It is essential next to consider the state this country was in when we patiently submitted to these injuries.

Firstly.—We had then the greatest navy, beyond all comparison, that this country ever had, with 135,000 seamen.

Secondly.—We had a large army well disciplined and inured to service.

¹ On this part of the subject it is curious to refer to the address on the peace, as proposed by Mr. Windham, and as amended by the Ministers :—"And above all, that his Majesty will uniformly determine and prepare to defend against every encroachment the great sources of the wealth, commerce, and naval power of the empire." On these points can there be any comparison between the annexing all Italy, Louisiana, probably Malta, Flushing, &c. &c. to France; and her establishing her power more firmly in Switzerland ?

² "A spirited behaviour in almost any circumstance of strength, is the most politic as well as the most honourable course. We preserve a respect at least by it, and with that we generally preserve everything; but when we lose respect, everything is lost. We invite rather than suffer insults, and the first is the only one we can resist with prudence."—*Account of the European Settlements in America.* (Supposed to have been written by Burke).

We had a disciplined militia that had been embodied nine years.

We had about 30,000 volunteers, in general tolerably well trained, and in most places well instructed how to act and what to do in the event of an invasion.

We had a great number of armed vessels hired, and ships fitted, for the defence of the coast.

There were in the whole 101 sail of pendants, under the command of Lord Nelson, between Beachy Head (Hastings) and Harwich, for the protection of the coasts of Sussex, Kent, and part of Essex, to prevent the approach of the enemy to the capital.

Thirdly.—We had almost all the colonies of France and Holland, and some of those of Spain.

Fourthly.—We had upwards of 25,000 French seamen, and more than 10,000 Dutch and Spanish, in our prisons.

Fifthly.—The commerce and navigation of France were utterly annihilated; those of Holland and Spain most materially crippled; and the manufactures of the former in a state of the utmost depression.

And lastly.—Exclusively of all these advantages, while the definitive treaty was depending, an account came of Toussaint resisting the force sent by the First Consul against Saint Domingo, which put completely at our mercy twenty-nine sail of the line, with frigates, armed transports, &c., and 35,000 troops. If we had interposed hostility, we should not only have secured the greatest part of these, but have enabled Toussaint to resist successfully the attempts of France, and deprived her for a long time at least, perhaps for ever, of that invaluable island, the trade to which, when the island was in full cultivation, was considerably more than one-third of the whole commerce of France. By an account in my possession the value of the exports from Saint Domingo to France alone, was to the amount of 10.000,000*l.* sterling; and to America they were immense.

After losing such an opportunity as this, and suffering the injuries before enumerated under the four heads, when we were armed at all points,—we are now threatening to go to war for the protection of Switzerland! And in what condition are we for war as compared with our situation in the five preceding instances?

The following table shows the *average* number of seamen in each year, not the greatest number in each; and to these are to be added the men in the hired armed ships, cutters, armed transports and storeships;—in the whole 7 or 6000 men at the least:—

	VOTED.	ACTUALLY MUSTERED.
1793	45,000	69,000.
1794	85,000	83,700.
1795	100,000	101,700.
1796	110,000	112,800.
1797	120,000	120,000.
1798	120,000	119,900.
1799	120,000	122,500.
1800	120,000	128,700.
1801	135,000	132,800.

This would afford an encouraging prospect for the remanning our navy two or three or more years hence with an increased trade; but it is perfectly certain for the reasons stated, that *that* could not be expected *now*.

In the first place,—our navy at present is reduced almost to the peace establishment; not more than 44,000 men left, without a hope of getting as many more in the course of two or three years. No exertions will man a frigate; nor can it be expected that after a service of six, seven, eight, or nine years, men will immediately enter as they did in the former war, though in a year or two they would probably not be reluctant. We should not in the first year get men enough to complete the crews of the ships wanted for the protection of the capital, on the scale of the last war, and all the rest of the coast left destitute, as well as our foreign possessions.

Secondly.—Our army is greatly reduced, with a difficulty of recruiting it as in the case of the navy. Ministers say we have a stronger army and navy now than we ever had before in peace. But the comparison with a view to the present question is to be made with what they were in the war;—more especially considering the means of strength and offence we have given to the French.

The militia are disembodied,—and when reassembled the men will be raw and undisciplined; many of the officers too have quitted, and few will be found to supply their places.

The volunteer corps are disembodied, and in most instances will not be found again.

The armed vessels are discharged and the gunboats sold.

Thirdly.—All the colonies of France and Holland are restored, not only affording those countries the means of commerce and navigation, but of reviving their manufactures; and, worst of all, of getting possession of our colonies in the West Indies, and of greatly annoying us in the East Indies.[1]

Fourthly.—The French have the whole number of from 25,000 to 95,000 seamen to man their fleet at once, as under their government they will be able to lay their hands on them directly.

Fifthly.—The commerce and navigation of France is already or in part restored, and will progressively go on, having the whole Mediterranean to herself, and advantageous treaties with Spain and Turkey; Italy her own; and the East Indies opened to her.

Lastly.—Saint Domingo is now quietly in the possession of France.

When the whole of this plain statement is considered, is it possible to account for the conduct of Ministers but by imputing it to the weakest imbecility? They suffer the grossest injuries from France, affecting directly our commerce, navigation,[2] &c. &c. when they had in their hands the means of repelling them; and as soon as they have greatly reduced the force of the country, they threaten to go to war for an object interesting enough, God knows, but one not *immediately* connected with the welfare of Great Britain, or affecting our commercial interests, &c.

[1] Cochin given up to France by the Dutch; which can only be for the purpose of annoying us, as there is no commerce to that place.
[2] See again the Address on the Peace.

What has been said of the Ministers putting up with the injuries before enumerated, applies only to them personally. In reasoning on the expediency of war or peace at present, that conduct, I am aware, should not be mixed with the question. The gross inconsistency of their proceedings is sufficient to decide as to their utter incapacity for their situations; but when that is admitted, and taking the question of Switzerland by itself, no rational man will suppose we ought, in the actual state of the country and of its resources in various respects, to threaten France with war. It is ridiculous to suppose she will mind our bullying when we cannot strike. We must thus recede, and add one more degradation to the list before given, and so confirm more strongly to France that she may treat us as she pleases with impunity. Is not this, as I have already said, rather provoking insults than merely bearing them? It was truly observed that the first is the only one that can safely be resisted.

These are the reflections which occur to me,[1] and which I have thus hastily stated before I leave Cuffnells, in consequence of a letter from Mr. Pitt, at Bath, requesting me to go to him there.

Bath, November 13th, 1802.—Arrived at Bath, and found Lord Camden and Lord Carrington with Mr. Pitt. In the evening I was quite alone with the latter.

[1] I had determined to state these in my place in the House of Commons, under a persuasion that such a statement would open the eyes of many independent and respectable men to the utter incapacity and unfitness of the present Ministers; but I was so strongly dissuaded from it by Mr. Pitt, as to induce me to give it up.

I learnt from him that he had known nothing during the latter part of the summer of what had been going forward respecting foreign politics but what he collected from newspapers, except that in passing through London, on his way from Walmer here, he had some conversation with Lord Castlereagh, Lord Hawkesbury, and Mr. Addington. That even then he saw no papers, and could therefore have only an imperfect knowledge of the steps they had taken respecting the business of Switzerland, or of the grounds on which they had proceeded; but that from all he knew he thought Ministers had done right in interposing about Switzerland, even without having previously ascertained whether we could have a co-operation of the German Emperor; that as the Swiss had applied to us, with offers on their part to resist the tyranny and injustice of France, if they could have our support, our refusing them *that* until we could hear from Vienna, might occasion the loss of a favourable opportunity of preventing a further dangerous aggrandizement of the power of France.

I found, in the course of the conversation, that Mr. Pitt had been led to express the foregoing opinion to the Ministers he talked with (Lord Castlereagh is in the Cabinet); and knowing the generosity of his nature, with the high point of honour on which he invariably acts, it occurred to me strongly and irresistibly, that the proceeding on the part of Mr. A. and Lord H. was unfair in the highest degree. I mean by making no previous communication, nor consulting Mr. Pitt at all, in the course of the correspondence with France, and then endeavouring to entrap him into a sanction of measures which they now find will either make them superlatively ridiculous or involve the country in war, for an object *already absolutely lost*, by the unequivocal submission of Switzerland; but which, if still open for contention, would be beyond all possible comparison of less importance to the country than those already mentioned, which they shamefully bore with tameness and pusillanimity. I found too that Mr. Pitt meant to attend Parliament on the 23d, (the debate on the King's speech), and from all that passed I had a firm and clear conviction that in that case he would, on the principle on which he has acted invariably since his resignation, commit himself to an approbation of the measures taken by Government with respect to Switzerland. Under the impression stated in a preceding page, deeply fixed in my mind, and persuaded that it was of the last importance to the public good and to his own unsullied character, that he should not lose the weight and consideration which he now justly has in the country,[1] by supporting measures, which I am most confidently persuaded he would not himself have adopted if he had been in administration, I used all the means in my power to dissuade him from attending the House of Commons

[1] It is hardly possible to imagine anything so extraordinary respecting the public mind, as the warm and universal esteem in which he is at this moment held by all descriptions of persons, when it is considered that the grounds on which he went out of office are yet unexplained, which is incalculably to his disadvantage; and that every newspaper, except the *True Briton*, is eternally abusing him; and even that is much louder in commendation of Mr. Addington than of him.

on the day of the opening of the Session. He discussed the matter with me temperately, and with his usual kindness, but came to no determination. He told me Lord Bathurst, who was here a few days ago, had expressed the same wish, without saying why, or entering into any reasons for it.

Sunday, November 14th.—A good deal of general conversation in the course of the day, chiefly respecting the opinions Mr. Pitt had entertained and expressed to some of the Ministers, about the interposition in favour of Switzerland; in the course of which he relaxed a good deal as to the propriety of it.

Monday, November 15th.—The conversation was renewed respecting Mr. Pitt's attending Parliament on the opening, and with regard to my intentions already referred to. Mr. Pitt said, if I made such a statement as that, it would be impossible to avoid people suspecting that I was acting in concert with him, more especially as it would be known that I had been with him here; that if he absented himself as I wished, and I went up, it would not be to be wondered at if it should be said and believed that the part I took was connected with him. I felt the justice of this observation, but renewed my urgency respecting the importance of his not committing himself, so as to be implicated in the blunders and disgrace of the Ministers. And the discussion ended in a positive assurance from Mr. Pitt that he would not go to London, and on my promising to remain here with him, with which he declared himself to *be perfectly satisfied.*

Mr. Pitt, however, said he could not avoid going to

London for the votes for the army and navy, if there should be the least difficulty about a large peace establishment.

In the course of the discussion this day I found Mr. Pitt much less reluctant about taking office. He at first urged to me the improbability of his being able, if he came in, to do anything of essential service to the country; to which I replied, I thought he might in the finances, and settling the peace establishment; but above all, that a strong Government, in which the country would have confidence, and that would be respected abroad, would prevent a repetition of insults and injuries, which would otherwise be heaped upon us till we should be compelled to go to war; and that if it should not be able to avert that evil, it would be prompt in making the utmost exertions the country should be found capable of, at the first moment they could be made,—which is evidently of the last importance.

Mr. Canning having written earnestly desiring to see me in my way to London, if possible, and if not, as soon as possible after my arrival there, I this day wrote to him, to say that Mr. Pitt had decided to stay here, which I was perfectly sure was right, and that I should remain with him. I expressed a wish also that Lord Grenville might not go such lengths in the House of Lords, as might make it extremely difficult for Mr. Pitt and him to act together; which I did in the hope that it would be conveyed to his Lordship, and take the chance (however desperate) of its producing some effect.

Tuesday, November 16th.—Nothing material occurred in the course of this day; but I took different opportunities of quietly suggesting what occurred to me, as carrying conviction, that our interposition (especially considering the manner of it), in favour of Switzerland, could have no other end than humbling the country by one more degradation, and so provoking further aggression; which seemed to me to produce considerable impression on Mr. Pitt, and made him *entirely satisfied* with his determination not to leave Bath.

Wednesday, November 17th.—This morning, Mr. Canning arrived about nine, in consequence of my letter, having travelled all night. Finding that Mr. Pitt would not go up, he wished to discuss some points with him.

I had much conversation with Mr. Canning, in which I did not disguise from him at all my general view of matters, nor the advice I had given to Mr. Pitt.

In the evening, I was alone with Mr. Pitt, and he told me he had received in the forenoon a packet from Lord Hawkesbury, with papers respecting matters now depending with France, accompanied by a wish to know his opinion on the whole subject; and that he felt very considerably embarrassed by it. This led to a further retrospect of all that we had before discussed, and especially as to the opinion he expressed in his way hither from Walmer; on which subject I said all I could to strengthen his mind, on the ground of his being surprised in a manner not at all justifiable. He admitted that the papers now sent were by no means sufficient to enable him to judge of all that has passed; but said, if he should state that as the reason for giving no opinion, they would, of course, furnish him with more papers. After much consideration, he agreed to write to Lord Hawkesbury "that he felt the absolute impossibility of making up his mind on proceedings of such a nature as he had consulted him upon, by any information that could be communicated at the distance they were from each other." So I trust he stands clear of any responsibility, and cannot be identified with the blunderers, which appears to be equally important to his own character and the public good.

Thursday, November 18th.—Mr. Canning communicated to me a plan in agitation (amongst persons who are strongly of opinion that the weakness and imbecility of the present Government must plunge the country deeper and deeper in disgrace and mischief) to induce Mr. Addington to relinquish the government, by convincing him of the dangerous situation in which he stands, and the want of confidence of the country in him; the hope of accomplishing which rests on some very respectable men, entirely unconnected with Mr. Pitt, making such a statement as shall shake Mr. Addington, and prevail with him to make overtures to Mr. Pitt; a persuasion being entertained that if Mr. Addington refuses that, a separation from Mr. Pitt must necessarily follow.

This plan struck me instantly as very unlikely to succeed, as well as highly objectionable, and to be attended with considerable hazard :—not likely to succeed, because unless there should be a decided falling off of support in Parliament, or a plain manifestation of the public mind in some unequivocal way, Mr. Addington's vanity will never allow him to believe the country entertains any belief of his insufficiency, or that it wishes for a change; he might also find difficulties with his colleagues: hazardous, because, if there should be the remotest trace of any concert with Mr. Pitt in the plan, or any plausible ground afforded for imputing that to him, it would be likely to affect his character deeply. In this Lord Camden concurs, to whom Mr. Canning mentioned the plan, as well as to me. I am strengthened in my opinion, too, by learning from Mr. Canning that the person proposed to take the lead in the business is Mr. Cartwright, member for Northamptonshire; who, although as respectable and independent a man as lives, is known to be an enthusiastic admirer of Mr. Pitt, and was the person who seconded the motion of thanks to him in the last Parliament.

Mr. Canning assured me that Lord Grenville had a most anxious desire to continue well with Mr. Pitt, and that he would do nothing to produce a separation from him; that he would not take the line in the House of Lords of endeavouring to force the country into a war, in any event, as its only resource against the spirit of ambition and aggrandizement of France; and that his Lordship had given him the most unequivocal assurance that he would be entirely satisfied if he could see Mr. Pitt again in the Administration, without a desire of coming into office himself. On the whole, I derive great comfort at the account Mr. Canning gave me of the state of Lord Grenville's mind, and of his intentions.

In the evening, Mr. Canning set off for London.

Friday, November 19th.—Lord Camden left us to go to Lord Bathurst's and to London; and Lord Mulgrave arrived. In the evening, more conversation with Mr. Pitt about his coming into office. He admitted to me that he now found his health quite equal to the duties of it; and that he should have no reluctance to enter on them again, if his coming in could be brought about in a manner perfectly satisfactory to himself.

I thought it right, in this conversation, to mention to Mr. Pitt the plan respecting which Mr. Canning had talked to Lord Camden and to me, that I might not, in discouraging it, act upon my own judgment; and he concurred entirely with Lord Camden and me on the subject.

Thinking over what passed last night, I talked to Mr. Pitt about difficulties that might occur in arrangements, even if the way to his taking office should be opened in a manner that might satisfy him; and I suggested, in particular, a serious doubt whether he could be safe in taking his former situation, with Mr. A. in the Cabinet, considering the personal influence the latter had acquired with the King, and the degree of weight he would have with him. To which Mr. Pitt answered he should have no apprehension of *that;* that he was persuaded the King must have seen there is no firmness of character in Mr. A., and that his Majesty must also be convinced before now of his deficiency in other respects. I own, however, I am not at ease on the point. His Majesty may be aware of what is obvious enough in Mr. A.; and yet the latter may have so ingratiated himself, as to have it in his power to make impressions on the King's mind very unfavourable to any one he may wish to injure. I know the use that has been made of partial or inaccurate information of what has passed in the Cabinet in the last Administration, as well as on other occasions.

Mr. Pitt thought he could not make any arrangement that should exclude Lord Hawkesbury or Lord Castlereagh, both of whom he pressed to take office with the present Government.

The conversation was renewed about the mode in which he should decline to give any opinion on the present state of foreign affairs, and what has been done on the subject; and Mr. Pitt promised he would write to Lord H., as was agreed on Wednesday; and that he would also write to Mr. Addington, thinking it better to speak out to him at once. He agreed with me, on reflection, that it is hardly possible it can be necessary he should fulfil his intention of going to the House for the army and navy votes, as alluded to on Monday last, there not being the remotest probability of large ones being objected to. In the event of his not going up, he said he would stay here till about the 18th of December; then go to Cuffnells with me for two or three days, and proceed by the coast to Walmer.

Sunday, November 21st.—Received a letter this morning from Mr. Canning, in which he says, " Lord Grenville (whom I have seen to-day) appears to enter cordially into all the considerations of delicacy towards Mr. Pitt which you thought it of so much importance that he should entertain; and that the line of argument which he has laid down to himself is one which will carry him *safely* past all the embarrassing and uncomfortable points of difference between them. There is no intention of moving an amendment." This gives me great comfort, and is, indeed, all that could be expected or wished from Lord Grenville; as it affords the best possible chance of Mr. Pitt and him acting together, if an occasion shall offer. Mr. Pitt has written to-day, as he agreed to do yesterday, to Lord Hawkesbury, not only declining to give an opinion as to what has been done, but in a manner that must prevent their attempting to draw him in to mix himself by advice in councils, for which he ought in no degree to be responsible.

No copy of the speech sent to Mr. Pitt, in which he expressed great satisfaction, as relieving him from any embarrassment on the subject.

Monday, November 22d.—I found, from the conversation at breakfast this morning, that Mr. Pitt did not write to Mr. Addington yesterday, thinking it would be too formal; but that he stated to Lord Hawkesbury that the sort of approbation he had conveyed of measures, when he was passing through London, must not be considered as at all conclusive, as it arose from partial information; and that, on the subject of the despatch which he returned to him, he could make no observation at all. That he would on no account attend the House of Commons; that he imagined, indeed, there was little chance of that being of any importance; but that, in any event, he knew too little of the grounds on which they had proceeded to be of any use; and that it was essential to his health to persevere in drinking the waters. Lord H. had written, pressing urgently Mr. Pitt's attendance in the House of Commons.

Tuesday, November 23d.—Mr. Pitt is decidedly of opinion that Ministers will recede from their complaints of the conduct of France, which must necessarily be a submission to the First Consul;[1] and as necessarily an encouragement to him to offer injuries or insults of a more direct nature to us than overrunning Switzerland; and that no occasion is less likely to interest Austria than the late business. If Buonaparte should now take measures without disguise, for securing Malta, or wait till he gets the Cape, all the difficulties of our situation, suggested before, will open upon us as forcibly as they do now. We must expect *that*, because we have provoked it. Is the island of Malta, in the present moment, an object to go to war for? Where will the encroachments and aggrandizement of France end? She will next unite Holland with herself; will again get possession of Egypt, of which we shall not be able a second time to dispossess her. In neither of which

[1] This of course arises out of the despatch of Lord Hawkesbury, which he returned to his Lordship on Sunday.

cases will Austria move a finger, as Switzerland was
an object infinitely nearer to her than these.

Wednesday, November 24th.—Mr. Pitt received a
letter from Lord Camden, who had seen Lord Spencer
and Lord Grenville, both concurring that his returning
to office is the only thing that can save the country;
confirming what Mr. Canning wrote, that they would
not move an amendment to the address, but that,
consistently with the line they had firmly taken,
they must of necessity expose the conduct of the
Administration in their late proceedings (which I
cannot regret), and point out to the public the
absurdity of them; not intending, however, to go on
making motions in the House of Lords, or to take
any measures merely to harass Government. That
Lord Lowther had been applied to to move the
address, which he had declined. Lord Nelson was to
second. Mover not settled, but hopes of the Duke of
Rutland. That it appeared to him (Lord Camden)
that Lord Lowther had been consulted on the suggestion of a statement to Mr. Addington of the necessity
of Mr. Pitt's coming in, and of the propriety of its
being proposed by Mr. Addington himself.

Mr. Long told Lord Camden that the opinions
of influential persons in the City appeared to be
that Government had been too brisk in holding a
threatening language, and too ready to recede. That
D. Jenncus had seen General Anderossi, who said
to him the clouds were gathering, and would soon
burst; an indication probably of the intentions of
Buonaparte.

Lord Camden had a conversation with Lord Castlereagh, who particularly regretted Mr. Pitt's absence, but would not blame it, on Lord Camden stating the ground of want of information, &c. The latter endeavoured to impress on persons in general whom he saw, that Mr. Pitt's absence was owing only to the state of his health.[1]

Lord Bathurst thinks Mr. Pitt should go up for the vote of the army and navy, to take an opportunity of giving a support to Government relative to the country being put in a state of respectable defence, and of showing to the public that he is not desirous of abandoning it altogether in a time of great difficulty. I am not averse to that. My anxiety from the first has been, that Mr. Pitt should be kept quite clear of all participation in the blunders and mischief of the late proceedings of the Cabinet respecting Switzerland.

Thursday, November 25th.—Received a letter from Lord Camden, expressing a wish to know whether I had learnt Mr. Pitt's sentiments respecting the plan alluded to above, as his Lordship suspects Mr. Canning has not been discreet in his language; and rather speaks as he wishes, than as he is authorized to do. To which I answered, that I had thought it safer and better to talk with Mr. Pitt on that plan,

---

[1] [In the King's speech this sentence occurred:—

"To maintain the true principles of the constitution in CHURCH and State, are the great and leading duties which you are called upon to discharge."

Upon which Mr. Rose remarks:—

"The CHURCH could only be introduced into the speech to revive what led to Mr. Pitt going out of office, and to create fresh difficulty to his returning to it; and so it strikes him."—ED.]

than to act at all on my own judgment about it; though I was nearly certain he could not approve of any measure being taken by his friends to attain the end proposed. I therefore had a full conversation with Mr. Pitt about Mr. Canning's suggestion the day his Lordship left us, and found him entirely concurring with us in the matter; that Canning had indeed promised he would not stir in it; and that I hoped his zeal (however well intended) would not lead him to take any step which might in the remotest possible degree implicate Mr. Pitt.

[A long account of the speeches in Parliament upon the address is here omitted, with the criticisms upon them; such details having now lost their interest, and affecting very little the character of the speakers.— ED.]

Friday, November 20th.—Lord FitzHarris wrote to his father that Canning's speech was not as much cheered as he could have wished;—that there appeared in the House much apathy, and on the part of individual members a considerable degree of neutrality, as if waiting for something to lead their opinion, and to direct their judgment. And that in the House of Lords *that* opinion was still stronger;—that Lord Pelham told him, when they met in the House at half-past three, no Peer had been found who could be prevailed on, by any entreaties, to move the address; and that at last they were reduced to the necessity of resorting to Lord Arden.¹ Lord FitzHarris described

¹ Recently made a Peer by Mr. Addington.

Lord Grenville's speech as remarkably able, and the defence very weak.

This state of doubt and of uncertainty in the minds of the members of both Houses, the truth of which I have no doubt of, rather confirms the inclination of my mind as to the expediency and propriety of Mr. Pitt going to London to attend the House on the vote for the army, in order, by the line he may then take, to show (without reflecting in the smallest degree on the conduct of Ministers) that he has had no communication with them on the late proceedings respecting continental politics; but at the same time taking the opportunity to hold an encouraging language to the country, and to give a *right* tone to the public opinion, which may otherwise take a *wrong* one.

Mr. Pitt showed me letters from Lord Grenville, Mr. Ryder, and Mr. Canning.

Lord Grenville, in substance, expressed a hope that if Mr. Pitt should not agree with him in the whole extent of his speech of Tuesday, yet he trusted there was nothing in it different from the ideas he had before stated to him. 'That what he said of the only mode by which the country could be saved,' he spoke from the sincerity of his heart, without the remotest idea to his own interest or ambition;—with no wish beyond the enjoyment, peaceably and securely, of the station in the country in which Mr. Pitt's friendship not unseconded by his own exertions) had placed

---

[1] Mr. Pitt coming into office.

him. He doubted, however, whether both security and independence are not out of our reach. His sense of the absolute impossibility of safety but in Mr. Pitt's hands, has increased greatly since the meeting of Parliament; taking the language of Ministers in the House of Commons (for in the House of Lords they are incapable even of answering an attack) that the general impression they wish to give, is of a resolution to execute the peace to the very last iota in despite of everything which has occurred, or may occur, on the part of France. That the countenance Ministers give to Fox's declaration against war *in any case*, and the degree to which they court and receive his protection, sheltering themselves under his wing from attacks, and answering them only by criminations of all that passed before their accession to office, have *lowered materially the tone and spirit of the public*. That Ministers have, to a certain extent, succeeded in impressing the public with a belief that Mr. Pitt's return to office must tend to a renewal of the war; whereas his (Lord G.'s) sincere opinion, which he stated, is, that Mr. Pitt's return is precisely the only possible mode by which peace can be preserved. That the only thing which gives the Ministers support is the persuasion that they will not go to war. Lord Grenville added that he learns, from a quarter of indisputable authority, that Cochin is ceded to France by Holland; and that the Vienna news is, that the First Consul has laid hands on Tuscany.

Mr. Canning states the protection afforded to

Government by Mr. Fox, and the complacency with which it was received; dwells a good deal on the attacks made on the old Government, particularly respecting the proceedings at the treaty of Lisle; justifying those at Amiens, particularly by Lord Hawkesbury and Mr. Addington,—the former in a violent authoritative declamation; and the latter, in a style of crimination of his predecessors entirely uncalled for by anything that had passed. Thinks if Mr. Pitt is not Minister, Mr. Fox will be. Is persuaded that no out-of-doors' measure (such as had been thought of) will attain the end. (I am heartily glad he now sees this.) Says the Ministers are determined to hold out. Thinks the impression against them must work and spread; and that it is doing so already.

Mr. RYDER thinks that what fell from Mr. Addington did not justify the manner in which Canning took it up. He thinks Mr. A. alluded only to the old comparison between the *Projet* of Lisle and the *Treaty* of Amiens, for the purpose of arguing that Lord Temple (still less Lord Grenville) could not fairly state that there was not so much difference in the terms of the two as to make such a material difference in the danger of our situation. That Lord Hawkesbury dwelt more upon the distinction between a first *projet* and a treaty: and contended that, considering the difference of the circumstances, as much attention was shown to our allies in one case as in the other. To the unfairness of that comparison some objections were made by Lord Morpeth. Canning stated the *projet* as an *ultimatum*;[1] and commented on the generosity of the present Ministers in justifying themselves at the expense of their predecessors. Bragge remarked, that the observations respecting the two treaties had been made before; and that Canning's present conduct would not answer the end proposed. On the whole, Mr. Ryder saw nothing in the speeches of Lord H. or Mr. A. that called for Mr. Canning's attack; and thinks they had no such intention as imputed to them, as the argument had been repeatedly used last year. Regrets much Mr. Pitt's absence, at a time when the knowledge of his opinions, and the tone he would give, is much wanted. Mr. Ryder does not go into the extremes of the violent alarmists, yet is far from being satisfied with the tone taken by Government. There is too much apparent acquiescence (in spite of words thrown in now and then to the contrary) in the opinion of Fox and Wilberforce; or at least too little disposition to state distinctly the points in which they differ from them. Thinks the times must soon call Mr. Pitt forth; but

[1] This was not correct. It is true as to Lord Grenville only, who would certainly have gone out of office rather than have receded from it. But it is equally certain that when Lord Malmesbury's instructions were delivered to him, Mr. Pitt stated to him distinctly, that if he found the French plenipotentiary would not accede to the terms of the *projet*, he should be allowed to resort to the Cabinet for further instructions; and Mr. Pitt further told Lord M. (in full confidence that his Lordship would exert his utmost energy to obtain all that was proposed in the *projet*) that if he failed in that, he should be authorized to give up the Cape of Good Hope. Mr. Pitt said this however, under a fixed persuasion that in that event Lord Grenville would resign. Mr. Canning probably knew nothing of this: but it was unfair of him to make any assertion on the subject.

wishes to see him march in through open doors, and not through a breach.

Saturday, November 27th.—Mr. Pitt continues to express the utmost willingness to take office himself if a fair occasion shall offer; but thinks it quite impossible for Lord Grenville to come in with him, if such an occasion soon presents itself, on account of the language he has invariably held respecting the present Ministers. About that, however, no difficulty can arise, if his Lordship is sincere in the expressions in his letter, the substance of which I stated yesterday. Of this, however, there is no reason to doubt.

On reading the debate of Wednesday, as given in all the papers, it is curious to observe Mr. Fox's language respecting the folly of quarrelling with France on commercial points, compared with the language he held in the debate on the commercial treaty with France in 1786-7. He *now* thinks all commercial jealousies foolish and contemptible. He *then* thought an easy commercial intercourse with France highly objectionable, as likely to abate that spirit of hostility which should always exist in the minds of the people of this country against France.

Sunday, November 28th.—Mr. Pitt, this morning, expressed to me that he should feel considerable embarrassment on going to London, from what he conceived to be an impossibility of avoiding to see some of the Ministers previous to his being in the House of Commons, particularly his brother; that he could, indeed, as little avoid seeing Lord Castlereagh (who had lately taken office at his particular entreaty) and Lord Hawkesbury, nor, if it should be desired, Mr. Addington himself; and that in the interviews with them his explaining himself on all such points as should be put to him would be a necessary consequence. That he would be then placed in a situation of doing so without full and complete information of all circumstances before him, and be drawn into a responsibility, in the public opinion, for all that had passed, because his general line in the House would certainly be that of support to the Government. I had hoped that he might go to London only the evening before the vote for the army (which is to be on the 6th of next month), state his sentiments in the House that day, as before agreed on, and return here the next morning. But agreeing with him, upon reflection, that when in London he could not avoid having communication with the Ministers, and so unavoidably implicating himself with them, I entirely concur, upon the whole, that it is most desirable he should remain quietly here; being, however, still aware that some inconvenience and risk may be incurred by this alteration of his intentions, adhering to the opinion before stated as to the advantages that might arise from his going up. But thinking the *danger* of mischief greater than the prospect of good *hopeful*, I strongly incline to Mr. Pitt's remaining here.

Lord Bathurst came in after the conversation I had with Mr. Pitt; and, finding me alone, asked me what Mr. Pitt's determination was. On my mentioning to him what had passed between Mr. Pitt and me, he said

that he adhered to the opinions he expressed to me a
few days ago; admitted that the embarrassment Mr.
Pitt alluded to would be a distressing one, but thought
he would have to encounter that whenever he should
go up; and that if by hanging aloof he showed evident
signs of hostility to Mr. Addington, he would throw
him into the hands of Mr. Fox, whose support he had
already thankfully received. Not blind, however, to
that, nor to the other circumstances already referred
to, I still think it of the utmost importance Mr. Pitt
should not commit himself with the Ministers respecting the late measures, which he would most certainly
do, in the public persuasion, if he were to go up now.
It is by his character and his talents that he must
save the country, if these can be made available to
the object; both of which would suffer deeply in
the estimation of every reflecting mind if he should
identify himself with these men and their measures.
I told Mr. Pitt, when he came in from riding, what
had passed between Lord Bathurst and me; after
which they had a separate conversation when I went
up to dress for dinner.

Monday, November 29th.—In the evening Mr. Pitt
told me Lord Bathurst had urged to him all he did to
me; but that he continued to think with me, it was
better he should not attend Parliament before the
holidays. Mr. Pitt renewed the conversation about
his attending Parliament, which led to a more particular discussion than has hitherto taken place respecting
his actual situation with Ministers and the conduct it
may be right for him to hold with them and towards

them. This conversation was long and temperate, every part of the subject was fully considered, and the consequences of each line that might be taken carefully adverted to. The result was a fixed determination expressed by Mr. Pitt not to advise Ministers how to act on any point in future. This he feels the necessity of, on various grounds. The advice he has hitherto given has either not been adopted, or has been followed in a manner entirely different from his intention, and so as not to produce the effect proposed by him. He also feels the impossibility of being able to form correct judgments on matters respecting which he has not full information and seen the whole correspondence, &c. &c. He will give his general support to Government whenever he can. That, to be sure, will be of little use.

Observations in the *Courier* very pointed on the conduct of Mr. Fox.

Tuesday, November 30th.—Received a letter from Mr. Canning, in which he begs I will tell him whether Mr. Pitt is satisfied that the intended vote of 30,000 men is sufficient for the navy for three months. To which I answered, that I was perfectly sure Mr. Pitt could not form an opinion of the sufficiency or insufficiency of the vote without any information whatever of what has been going forward lately, or of the actual situation we are in with respect to France; I mean as to the probability or improbability of a war with her. I observed to Mr. C. that there is a passage in Lord Hawkesbury's speech, which looks like his not intendding to lay any papers before the Houses respecting the late negotiation—suggesting to him also the propriety of Ministers being called upon to assign some *general* reason, at least, why 50,000 seamen are now desired, a number certainly beyond any peace establishment that can be intended, and must be founded on some conduct on the part of France; the correspondence about which must unavoidably become subject of parliamentary inquiry hereafter, if on perusal of the papers that measure shall be thought proper. It cannot be doubted that when the interposition of Parliament is called for it has a right to information.

Wednesday, December 1st.—Received a letter from Mr. Canning, in which he says Mr. Addington had just given notice that he should vote the increased number of seamen for the year,—which he thinks was on the suggestion of Mr. Ryder;—trusts it will make no alteration in Mr. Pitt's intention of remaining here; but considers it as rendering it still more desirable he should know, if possible, what Mr. Pitt's ideas are of the force that ought to be kept up. Mr. Fox not expected to attend either debate; certainly not that on the navy.

Under so direct an application for Mr. Pitt's sentiments on the matter, I thought it right to show the letter to him; and by his desire I told Mr. Canning nearly what I did yesterday from myself, "that at this distance, and utterly uninformed as he is of everything that could enable him to form a judgment on the subject, he can express no opinion whatever."

Lord Malmesbury told me he heard Sheridan was

to go down to-day,[1] to abuse Mr. Pitt and his friends;
to lessen them, if he could, in the public opinion. His
Lordship also told me that a friend of his heard Mr.
Fox say lately that he did not think it at all likely he
should ever be Minister himself, but that he was determined, if possible, to prevent Mr. Pitt ever again being
so. In the course of a long conversation with Lord M.,
he talked a good deal about Mr. Fox, said he had known
him from very early years, and all his habits and ways
of thinking; that he was sure his earliest principles of
strong Toryism were still rooted in his mind; and that
if he ever should attain the government in a situation
in which he could act according to his own opinions, he
would be a high prerogative minister; but that he did
not think the country would endure him. His Lordship
then went on to say, that in a tour he had made
through Gloucestershire and Herefordshire, and a considerable extent of the central part of England, the
enthusiasm for Mr. Pitt was as strong as amongst his
most particular friends, even with the quietest and
most retired people he saw.

He told me, too (what the Count himself had said,
in substance, to me and my eldest son before he left
England), that Woronzow, on his return to this country
where he is daily expected, would co-operate most
heartily with Mr. Pitt or Lord Grenville, in uniting

[1] He did not do this till the 8th, when he made a most brilliant speech
with much quizzing on Mr. A., but replete with invective on Mr.
Pitt; artful towards the King, and deprecating Mr Pitt being forced
on his Majesty after what had passed on the Catholic question! He
had forgot his justification of Mr. Fox being forced on the King in
1782, in a manner unprecedently offensive.

this Court with that of Petersburgh; but that if he should find the same people in office as he left, he would get himself superseded in the embassy, and return to Southampton, despairing of being able to do any good in this mission.

Thursday, December 2d.—Nothing occurred of any importance to-day. Mr. Pitt received a letter from the father of the man who now keeps Bull's library, expressing great satisfaction that he had lived to see the son in 1802 subscribe to the library which the father had been a constant subscriber to from 1750 to 1757; in which interval he (the late Earl of Chatham) used to have a young man from the library to read to him at hours when that was shut up; and that the book he principally read to him at one period was Josephus's History of the Wars of the Jews.

Friday, December 3d.—In the *Times* of yesterday is a most virulent and elaborate attack on Mr. Pitt and his friends, and a most fulsome panegyric on the present Ministers; but written with ability. The editor of this paper is in habits of constant intercourse with the Minister's brother. This essay is detestable in all its parts; but more particularly so for the language in which Mr. Pitt is grossly censured for his skulking from office in a disgraceful manner in the hour of danger, and abandoning his sovereign.

Saturday, December 5th.—The debate on the report of the vote for the seamen, is one of the most extraordinary I ever read. The tone taken by Ministers in refusing all explanation on such a measure is certainly unexampled; there *never* occurred an instance of a large increase being proposed in the naval or military establishment without either explanation given, or papers laid. Ministers were pressed for the former, but were allowed at last to triumph, with saying to the Opposition, You are for a large vote as well as us, there is no difference of opinion; what is all this discussion about? To which the answer was obvious, You may intend this armament for one purpose, we may think it requisite for another: we have a clear and distinct right to know generally what your reason for it is.—Do you mean it is a regular peace establishment? If you do, we may agree with you or we may not. Do you mean it to give effect to any pending negotiation with France? Is it on account of additional strength recently acquired by France, that makes her more likely soon to go to war with us? Is it on account of Malta, respecting which fresh difficulties have arisen? In short, is it all or any of these reasons that induce you to continue armed? Some answer might have been extorted. Those who differ from Ministers certainly gave them great advantage, in allowing the vote for the seamen to pass in the committee without comment; but that did not deprive them of the right to insist upon information in another stage of the business. It is worth while to refer to what was done in the instances of the Spanish, Dutch, and Russian armaments in 1787, 1789, and 1790.

Something was gained in the debate by fixing Lord Hawkesbury to a declaration for a large peace establishment, from which Mr. Addington however shrank. What can Mr. Fox say to the number of seamen voted? He has positively and recently declared for a very small peace establishment; he has also in the strongest terms expressed his conviction that we have nothing to fear from France. What then is this armament for? and where are all his strong assertions against blind confidence? But there *is no possible ground* on which he can avoid resisting the measure of a large navy.

On talking to Mr. Pitt this evening about the long article of abuse against him and the late Ministers in the *Times*, he grew to feel the utmost resentment and indignation at it; and said, if not apologized for in the same paper, or commented upon in the *True Briton* in the next paper, he should consider it as countenanced by the Administration; and that he would write to Mr. Steele to desire he would say to Mr. Addington, that unless it was disavowed in some shape in the same manner the calumny was published, he must consider it as sanctioned by him.

We were led insensibly again to discuss at great length the situation he would find himself in if he should return to the Administration by himself, or nearly alone; and be in the end agreed with me, that he could not take office with any degree of safety to himself, or hope of doing good to the public, without Lord Grenville and Lord Spencer doing the same.

Sunday, December 6th.—In the evening Mr. Pitt said he would certainly write on the morrow to Mr. Steele, as he had said yesterday; but it struck me that his doing so would, almost to a certainty, lead to some embarrassing and equivocal explanations:—that

Mr. A. was very sorry for the attack, but that Mr. Pitt must know how unmanageable the editors of newspapers were, and most of all Mr. Walters of the *Times;* adding just as much as he should think might suffice to prevent Mr. Pitt acting on the resentment he must naturally feel at the mixture of insult and injury, but in no degree sufficient to remove the impression made by the libel. It seemed probable, too, that the opening an intercourse of any sort at this moment with Mr. Addington might be productive of much inconvenience, as he might avail himself of it to introduce other subjects. After that was considered, Mr. Pitt gave up his determination to write to Mr. Steele, or to have any communication with Ministers on the subject.

Monday, December 7th.—I mentioned to Mr. Pitt this morning what had occurred to me yesterday on reading the newspaper, as to the proceedings in the House on the exchequer bills; in all which he agreed with me entirely; and said, he was the more surprised at Mr. Addington's intention, because he had repeatedly stated to him the indispensable necessity of providing at once for any extraordinary expenses which might occur in years of peace. Thus Mr. Addington had always admitted the principle, and had given him the strongest assurances that he would on no occasion, nor in any emergency, depart from it. That so late as the last summer he discussed the importance of it with him and Lord Hawkesbury; both eagerly embracing the measure, the latter most warmly: after which he dined with Lord Hawkesbury, to meet Mr. A. and Mr. Vansittart. Mr. A. did not come, but Mr. V. agreed to the whole extent of what was urged by Mr. Pitt, and undertook to prepare materials for consideration; Lord Hawkesbury continuing anxious that there should not be the least relaxation from the plan.——Mr. Pitt, after that, returning through London on his way here, saw Mr. Addington, not more than seven weeks ago, when the point was again discussed, and the *strongest possible assurances given* by Mr. Addington, that nothing should induce him to depart from what had been so strongly enforced by Mr. Pitt, and admitted by him.

Tuesday, December 8th.—Mr. Pitt this morning revived the conversation about Mr. Addington's departure from the system of raising the money wanted for extraordinary services within the year, and told me that on reflection it appeared to him the more astonishing, as the last deliberation at Mr. Addington's was a full one, and that Mr. Vansittart was present with a plan (such as it was) for raising the money :—founded on the mischievous basis, completely reprobated and abandoned by us, of a £5 per cent. impost on the customs and excise.

Wednesday, December 9th.—I left Bath and returned to Cuffnells.

In the newspapers of the 11th of December I noticed Mr. Addington's statement of the supplies and ways and means for the ensuing year, on which the following observations occur :—

" He states the necessity of raising £5,000,000 for the service of the year, by exchequer bills, which he says he shall either fund at the end of the session or

borrow money to pay off;—evidently, therefore, not
entertaining a thought of raising any part of the money
within the year; thus departing from his solemn engagement to Mr. Pitt, and from the principles on
which the stability of public credit most essentially
rests. There will therefore be a debt incurred in this
second year of peace equal to the capital redeemed
by the commissioners:—where is the system of the
sinking fund which was to be inviolable?"

Friday, December 24th, 1802.—Mr. Pitt came to
Cuffnells. He told me that nothing had occurred after
I left Bath till three or four days ago, when Lord Castlereagh arrived there, who, from a variety of circumstances,
certainly was there on purpose to sound Mr. Pitt on
the present state of affairs; although in the whole
of the conversations between them Mr. Addington's
name was never mentioned, except in a direct message
delivered from him to Mr. Pitt, "requesting to know
his opinion, whether he thought it would be right to
make a compromise with the Prince of Wales, by
setting his income clear on condition of his Royal
Highness waving his claims to the arrears of the
Duchy of Cornwall, previous to his coming of age;"
which can only be done by the public paying off the
debentures at present payable out of the Prince's
revenues. The inclination of Mr. Pitt's opinion was
against a *compromise* in such a case; thinking the
arrears should be paid if due; if not, that the question of setting the Prince's income free should be
considered separately. Mr. Pitt, however, found it
impossible to avoid the conversation turning on public

affairs in general. His Lordship told him that great
difficulties had arisen respecting an arrangement about
Malta; and that the present inclination of the Cabinet,
in order to obviate these, was to leave the nomination
of a Grand Master to the Knights, who were to
assemble *somewhere*, perhaps in Russia, for the purpose of choosing three of their number, out of whom
the Pope should select one; and Mr. Pitt understood
him, that if that should be found impracticable, then,
in that case, the Pope to name one of the Knights.
To which suggestion Mr. Pitt told me he did not
hesitate to express his decided disapprobation. At
the same time he told Lord Castlereagh he was sure,
from the statements he had seen of Mr. Addington's
budget, that he had made great mistakes which would
prove highly inconvenient. This conversation, or a
part of it, his Lordship unquestionably communicated
to Mr. Addington.

Saturday, December 25th.—On this day Mr. Pitt
received a letter from Mr. Addington directed to him
here, requesting to see him as early as he should
arrive in town or in the neighbourhood of it. I
conceive it to be clear that the communication was
made by Lord Castlereagh to Mr. Addington, because
the latter could not know Mr. Pitt was here except
from his Lordship; and because, during all the negotiations with Switzerland and France, Mr. Addington
never held any correspondence whatever with Mr. Pitt,
except a single conversation he had with him on
passing through London; nor had he any intercourse
with him about his budget. The eagerness to see

him now, therefore, could arise only from the panic occasioned by the observations Mr. Pitt made to Lord Castlereagh at Bath. Mr. Pitt feels it quite impossible to avoid the interview with Mr. Addington, under so decisive a request, and I can say nothing against it. Feeling, however, very considerable apprehensions that at the meeting, the low cunning and artful management of the one, opposed to the candid and generous nature of the other, may lead the latter to a disclosure, not only of all his opinions, and a detail of the gross blunders committed by the former in France; but also to give him his advice on every point of importance,—I thought it my duty to say everything I could to put Mr. Pitt on his guard; which I did with the utmost earnestness, and supported by every argument that occurred to me; under a strong conviction that if Mr. Addington's ignorance and incapacity is not detected and made manifest now, he will acquire such a character with the King and the public, as may be likely to fix him in his situation for such a period as will ensure the destruction of the country, by the tame and pusillanimous conduct of the present Government. The concessions they have already made, must impress the French with a persuasion that there is nothing they will not bear; and of course the First Consul will go on from one aggravation to another, till the country will be so goaded, as to drive the Government into a war, whether they are willing or not.

Sunday, December 20th.—Mr. Pitt told me, on

Mr. Dundas's peerage being mentioned, that he was beyond measure surprised at it; that he had not heard one syllable from him on the subject since they parted early in the summer; that he had indeed had no letter from him for some months; but what was most extraordinary, that when he last saw him, Mr. Dundas stated to him a variety of reasons why it was *impossible* for him to accept a peerage.

I renewed the conversation, while we were riding, about the interview with Mr. Addington; and Mr. Pitt gave me fresh assurances that he would be as much upon his guard during it as possible.

Monday, December 27th.—I again revived the subject of Mr. Pitt's interview with Mr. Addington, and he repeated to me his assurances of being on his guard, and promised he would write to me (of course in a guarded manner as it could only be by the post), after the meeting between them shall be over, to tell me what has passed. On talking over matters at breakfast by ourselves, he expressed great doubts whether in the event of a possibility of a way being opened for him to come into government, he could form an Administration with which he might act usefully to the public; about which, on the sudden, I could offer no distinct opinion; entertaining, indeed, considerable doubt on the subject, on the slight consideration I could give it. During the three days Mr. Pitt was here, we went carefully over all the papers on finance, necessary to a full and most attentive consideration of Mr. Addington's statements on the opening his budget; and he agreed with me entirely in all my conclusions, going away perfectly persuaded that the whole of those statements were founded on *gross errors* arising from the most childish *ignorance;* thinking too that it would be impossible for him to avoid delivering his thoughts on the subject in the House of Commons.

Mr. Pitt brought with him and showed me the *Times* of the 14th, in which there was a libel on him, and the late Government, more gross and offensive than the former one, which he felt so strongly.

END OF VOL. I.